FRENCH CONNECTIONS

FRENCH CONNECTIONS

Cultural Mobility in North America and the Atlantic World, 1600–1875

EDITED BY
Robert Englebert & Andrew N. Wegmann

LOUISIANA STATE UNIVERSITY PRESS   BATON ROUGE

Published by Louisiana State University Press
lsupress.org

Copyright © 2020 by Louisiana State University Press
"A Deliverance from Demons: Possession and Healing at the Seignurie of Beauport" copyright © 2020 by Mairi Cowan
All rights reserved. Except in the case of brief quotations used in articles or reviews, no part of this publication may be reproduced or transmitted in any format or by any means without written permission of Louisiana State University Press.

Louisiana Paperback Edition, 2022

Designer: Barbara Neely Bourgoyne
Typeface: Garamond Premier Pro

Cover image: *Carte particulière de l'Amérique septentrionale, 1741*, by Henry Popple. Courtesy Library of Congress.

Library of Congress Cataloging-in-Publication Data
Names: Englebert, Robert, editor. | Wegmann, Andrew N., editor.
Title: French connections : cultural mobility in North America and the Atlantic world, 1600–1875 / edited by Robert Englebert and Andrew N. Wegmann.
Other titles: Cultural mobility in North America and the Atlantic world, 600–1875
Description: Baton Rouge : Louisiana State University Press, [2020] | Includes bibliographical references and index.
Identifiers: LCCN 2020017746 (print) | LCCN 2020017747 (ebook) | ISBN 978-0-8071-6970-4 (cloth) | ISBN 978-0-8071-7456-2 (pdf) | ISBN 978-0-8071-7457-9 (epub) | ISBN 978-0-8071-7818-8 (paperback)
Subjects: LCSH: North America—Civilization—French influences. | French—North America—History. | French—Colonization. | France—Colonies—America—Social life and customs. | France—Colonies—America—History. | North America—History—Colonial period, ca. 1600–1775. | North America—History—19th century. | Canada—History—To 1763 (New France) | Canada—History—1763–1867.
Classification: LCC E29.F8 F745 2020 (print) | LCC E29.F8 (ebook) | DDC 970.04—dc23
LC record available at https://lccn.loc.gov/2020017746
LC ebook record available at https://lccn.loc.gov/2020017747

CONTENTS

vii   Acknowledgments

1   Introduction: Patchwork and Pathways in French Colonial History
ROBERT ENGLEBERT AND ANDREW N. WEGMANN

11   A Deliverance from Demons: Possession and Healing at the Seigneurie of Beauport
MAIRI COWAN

35   Mask of the Colonizer: French Men, Native Passions, and the Culture of Diplomacy in New France
WILLIAM BROWN

73   The Ancien Régime Culture of Labor Mobility and Migration to New France
LESLIE CHOQUETTE

97   A French Huguenot's Career as a British Colonial Administrator in Acadie/Nova Scotia/Mi'gma'ki, 1710–1750
GREGORY KENNEDY AND VINCENT AUFFREY

124   The Trials of Brother Chrétien: A Case of Ruin and Redemption in the French Atlantic
CHRISTOPHER HODSON

146   Family Formation, Race, and Honor in Colonial Haiti's Free Communities, 1670–1789
ROBERT D. TABER

Contents

170 From Voyageurs to Emigrants: Leaving the St. Lawrence Valley for the Detroit River Borderland, 1796–1846
GUILLAUME TEASDALE AND KAREN L. MARRERO

193 Making Indians in the American Backcountry: *Récits de voyage,* Cultural Mobility, and Imagining Empire in the Age of Revolutions
ROBERT ENGLEBERT

221 Chasing *La Chasse-Galerie:* Honoré Beaugrand and the Life of a Journalistic Voyageur
JAY GITLIN AND RYAN ANDRÉ BRASSEAUX

244 Epilogue: "Next Stop, Honoré Beaugrand": Connections, Dislocations, and Redirections
BRETT RUSHFORTH

253 Contributors
257 Index

ACKNOWLEDGMENTS

I am starting to write this on a plane traveling north to south, a fitting direction in the grand scheme of things. When I think back to the days this project first took form—the conversation with Robert after our panel at SHEAR in New Haven in 2016, the drinks later that evening, the phone calls, the conversations with Leslie and Jay and Ryan over dinner, again in New Haven, with the Québécois, Cajuns, and New Orleanians at Mory's—I realize exactly how long, indeed how many plane rides, this book has taken. Perhaps that is because it came about rather randomly, an idea after a panel in a new city with almost entirely new people. In fact, I had never met Robert before that panel on French North America in New Haven. But as a result of it, we both noticed that our historical minds worked similarly and that our ideas, however geographically distant, fit within the same story and context. The product of that realization is, at last, this book; and I have him to thank for first broaching the idea of putting it together. As far as coauthors and coeditors are concerned, I could not have asked for a better one. We read every word of this volume together, made every edit in consult with each other, wrote volumes of emails back and forth, and spent hours on the phone over international lines. He has become a close friend, and I look forward to what crazy ideas we can think up next.

I could not live with myself if I did not give this next person an entire paragraph of his own for reasons that stretch far beyond the bounds of this volume. Since I first met him in St. Louis a number of years back, where we both first realized who each other was, Jay Gitlin has been a mentor, a guide, a dear friend, and a member of the family. He has introduced me to worlds and ideas I never knew and would never have known existed. From an afternoon of stories wandering through the former Calhoun College's guestbook at Yale to dinner with the New Orleans family at Antoine's after giving talks on Jackson and New Orleans at the Historic New Orleans Collection, Jay has lent me his constant support, enthusiasm, and *joie de*

Acknowledgments

l'histoire each time I have had the pleasure of sharing the stage, the table, and even the same room with him. He is a special person, a true friend, and a magnificent historian. We are lucky to have his and Ryan Brasseaux's essay grace the pages of this volume, and I am lucky to have found him as a friend, mentor, and "cousin."

It is somewhat awkward writing the acknowledgments to a volume made possible so much by the work of others. Although their names appear more prominently elsewhere, I want to thank each of the contributors to this volume for putting in the time, thought, effort, and patience required to produce such outrageously good work and to handle the madness of the volume's editors. Many of the contributors here outrank me in both genius and experience, but at each step of the way, even after repeated, likely very annoying, emails and prods, they all showed a willingness and dedication to making both their essays and the volume as a whole the best possible product. As a collective, they did not *need* to have time for this. But they made it, and for that neither I nor Robert could ever thank them enough. So I will keep it at this: Thank you for entrusting us with your work, for donating your words to our cause, and for being part of this years-long project. If I could hug you with words, I would. This is my attempt at doing so.

Other wonderful, even magical, people whose names do not necessarily appear prominently in these pages deserve recognition and thanks. Bertrand Van Ruymbeke was one of the first people we asked to contribute to this volume, but his work on his opus, *Histoire des États-Unis,* could not grant him the time. In spite of that, though, he became a very close friend and a mentor of the highest caliber. Alors, merci Bertrand. Merci pour tout. On that side of the Atlantic, I would also like to thank Gilles Havard, Allan Potofsky, Elodie Peyrol, Emma Hart, Trevor Burnard, Céline Ugolini, Iris de Rode, Nicholas Guyatt, and Elsa Grassy, all of whom have lent their support to this volume either through friendship, conversations, or both.

Closer to home, Randy Sparks, Andy Burstein, Nancy Isenberg, Aaron Sheehan-Dean, Sue Marchand, Marianna Dantas, Lou Roper, Laurent DuBois, Julia Gaffield, Chris Willoughby, Urmi Engineer-Willoughby, Spencer McBride, Siddhartha Mitter, Ben Wright, Whitney Stewart, Emily Conroy-Krutz, Adam Pratt, Claire Cage, Tom Ward, Walter Biggins, and Dana Rasch have been constant friends, colleagues, and conversationalists, entertaining new ideas and making life a better, more interesting place.

At Delta State, my colleagues in the history program—Brian Becker, Tom Laub, and Chuck Westmoreland—have embraced me, my work, and my insanity from day one. They gave me a chance not only with a rare job but with an autonomy of

Acknowledgments

thought and sense of belonging I frankly did not think was real in academia. Beyond colleagues, they are friends, and I appreciate them beyond the humble expression of words. Chuck in particular, as my fellow Americanist, has done more for me than he will ever know. I hope one day, somehow, I can repay that continued favor. Also at Delta State, then or now, I must thank Dave Breaux, Garry Jennings, Jamie Dahman, Leslie Green-Pimentel, and Carrie Freshour for their friendship, support, and ideas. At Louisiana State University Press, Rand Dotson, who reached down to the mire of common people to lift up this volume, has been the ultimate editorial guide, leading this project from start to finish with clarity, confidence, and encouragement. He deserves folkloric songs in his name.

At risk of going on too long, as the music starts to play, Maia, Padraig, Sophie, Jeanne d'Arc, this and everything I have ever done is for you and always will be.

—A. W.

I am unlikely to be able to add much to Andrew's effusive remarks. I feel very fortunate to have had the pleasure to work with such a talented and dedicated coeditor. We began by approaching this project from our own distinct areas of scholarship, and through a series of intellectually enriching conversations found common ground, a clear vision, and a single voice. As Andrew mentioned, this was a true collaboration. I cannot thank him enough for his time, dedication, and friendship. I often liken editing collections to the challenge of herding cats, but perhaps I need to revisit this, because the contributors exceeded all expectations, from the quality of the essays to meeting deadlines. I am indebted to them for trusting us with their excellent scholarship and it is truly an honor to have had a hand in bringing their work to a broader public. Our sincerest thanks to the anonymous reviewer, whose comments helped make this collection stronger, and to Louisiana State University Press and Rand Dotson for their support of the project.

This collection would not exist without the encouragement of the indefatigable Jay Gitlin, a mentor and friend. I first met Jay when I was a somewhat zealous junior scholar who had the unenviable task of critiquing his book at a conference. He was both kind and gracious in response to my brash assertions. We should all aspire to such collegiality. Many scholars have acted as sounding boards and offered general counsel over the last few years, including Nicole St-Onge, Catherine Desbarats, Allan Greer, Jean-François Lozier, Helen Dewar, Gilles Havard,

Acknowledgments

Dale Miquelon, Chris Parsons, Joseph Gagné, Zoazig Villerbu, Céline Carayon, Andrew Sturtevant, Alexandre Dubé, Bob Morrissey, Scott Berthelette, Jennifer Palmer, and Maxime Dagenais, to name only a few. You have been instrumental in shaping my understanding of French colonial history in North America and the Atlantic. I hope that I have done those conversations justice. My sincerest thanks to the Social Science and Humanities Research Council of Canada (SSHRC), and especially to Yves Frenette, for including me in the partnership grant Trois siècles de migrations francophones en Amérique du Nord. Putting one's work out into the world is a humbling experience. As I frequently remind my students, no book is perfect, and this collection is no exception. I accept responsibility for any and all shortfalls, look forward to the debates the book will hopefully generate, and am grateful for the help of many colleagues and friends along the way. Finally, this collection would not have been possible without the support of some very special people. To Heather, Audrey, and Ben. For the love and joy you bring me, the endless patience you have shown me, and to all the adventures that await us.

—R. E.

FRENCH CONNECTIONS

Introduction

Patchwork and Pathways in French Colonial History

ROBERT ENGLEBERT AND ANDREW N. WEGMANN

In 1978, long before the subject of French Atlantic history rode in on the coattails of its more celebrated (and critiqued) English and Iberian siblings, Dale Miquelon recounted the story of the Dugard family of Rouen, whose business ventures exposed networks of a complex French maritime commercial empire.[1] This detailed business history, with an analysis of trade partnerships, regulations, insurance rates, profits, and losses, linked the French metropole to both Canada and the Caribbean. Although the imperial state looms large throughout Miquelon's work, it nonetheless promulgates an eighteenth-century French Atlantic where individuals like Dugard and his family "helped shape [the world] in its continual process of becoming."[2] Similar stories produced by such individual initiative were a far cry from the bold imperial vision of a massive transatlantic triangular trade and the movement of colonial commodities, Metropolitan finished goods, and enslaved Africans across vast oceans that Louis XIV's chief minister, Jean-Baptiste Colbert, had espoused during the seventeenth century.[3] As more recent scholarship has shown, Colbert's fanciful notion of a closed imperial commercial system, where colonies and merchants were obliged to adhere to the strictures of mercantilist policy, turned out to be pure reverie, complicated by the imperial state's relative impotence with regard to imposing absolutist control across the sea.[4] What resulted was a far more fluid and haphazard colonial patchwork. Roguish colonists, sovereign Indigenous peoples, and both enslaved and free people of color regularly frustrated imperial plans of grand design and exposed the limits of power and control in distant lands. Much like the Dugard family of Rouen, the characters that made up this patchwork were instrumental in shaping a broad, diverse francophone world in a perpetual state of becoming. But what drove this constant state of change? What was this "Greater France," this distant colonial world, and how do we understand its ever-shifting contours? Perhaps the answer lies less in the categories of empire or Atlantic history and more in the great variability of French cultural mobility.

Mobility is critical, for it was the organizing principle around which French cultures in North America and the Atlantic coalesced.[5] In places as geographically detached and culturally disparate as Canada, the *pays d'en haut*, the *pays des Illinois*, Louisiana, Acadia, West Africa, Saint-Domingue, Guadeloupe, and the broader French Caribbean, the movement of people, goods, and ideas informed an expansive reconceptualization of "Frenchness" from the seventeenth century well into the nineteenth century. This cultural mobility was more than just the transference of a metropolitan conception of what it meant to be French from one locale to another. It was a process by which culture was transformed and reinvented through the inherent tensions borne of social, cultural, and physical displacement.[6] Throughout the French Atlantic realm, then, from permanent coastal spaces to more itinerant communities hundreds of miles inland, mobility itself became one of the active ingredients of localized identity formation.[7]

Scholars, including some of those who appear in the following pages, have produced a groundswell of remarkable studies on communities culturally defined by movement *away* from their prescribed "homelands."[8] Christopher Parsons, for example, persuasively suggests that despite ecological similarities between "old" and "new" worlds, which prompted vigorous imperial debate and extensive efforts to cultivate a New France, colonial society emerged out of adaptations to the particularities of the local North American *terroir*.[9] People and places like New Orleans and French and Spanish Louisiana; Massachusetts and the Puritans in the anglophone realms; the Acadians first from France, then New France, then the Gulf Coast; and, of course, Africans forced into the Atlantic Slave Trade by the millions buttress a robust and extremely valuable body of scholarship that has expanded the modern student's understanding of the Atlantic World and its complex cultural and social networks. Indeed, some of the most valuable recent studies have come from this renewed effort to investigate the nuances of individual identities and experiences against a vast Atlantic cultural and geographic backdrop.[10] As Jennifer Palmer so eloquently reminds us, it was the quotidian interactions—the "intimate bonds"—which connected peoples, places, and spaces across and around the Atlantic, with profound consequences for French colonial and metropolitan cultural axioms, particularly with regard to race and gender.[11]

Introduction

This same effort has produced a significant body of scholarship in recent years focused on Louisiana, the Gulf Coast, and the French colonial expansion out of the Caribbean and onto the southern coast of continental North America. Louisiana, along with its largest, most important city, New Orleans, has become a harbinger of new approaches that crack the veneer of imperial French unity and paint scenes of cultural independence, imperial failures, and social and racial complexity. Though tending in prior decades to fall into a sense of regionalism, restricting Louisiana and the Gulf Coast, perhaps unjustly, to an isolated circum-Caribbean framework, more recent scholarship on French Louisiana's place in the broader Atlantic realm has provided valuable models not only for viewing Louisiana in a larger context but also for investigating the cultural nuances and singularities further afield in the French Atlantic.[12] Indeed, most recently, Cécile Vidal has spearheaded a profoundly important and robust effort to bridge the historiographical and cultural gaps between Louisiana and other, similar locations and communities across the French Atlantic World. From her work and that of her contributors and others like her, Louisiana has become a beacon of multidimensional scholarship, a guide to following pathways of cultural mobility and identity formation beyond the limits of the Gulf Coast. Combined with the work of Rebecca Scott and Jean Hébrard, who have literally traced the transatlantic lives of nineteenth-century Creoles, Frenchmen, and Louisianans, the body of scholarship led by Vidal and supported by other emerging thinkers has brought Louisiana into the French Atlantic and yet still has maintained its singular path of cultural movement and growth.[13] *French Connections* follows this lead. And as the episodic and multidimensional essays in this volume show, without actually focusing on Louisiana directly, analyses of French North American culture and mobility can benefit from embracing and engaging those same provocative, multidirectional approaches that have made Louisiana's historiography so attractive, important, and previously isolated from that of the rest of the North American mainland.[14]

The current volume draws from and builds on all of this. Taken together, the essays here usher the reader from place to place, people to people, process of change to process of change. As Brett Rushforth describes in the epilogue, they serve as stops along a historical subway line, each with its own unique character and context and yet also connected to the broader phenomenon of cultural mobility—a *fil conducteur*—that occurred across the vast spaces of North America and the Atlantic World.[15] Many of the men and women discussed in this volume were, by most measurements, French; but they were also more than that, more fluid, less rooted in physical space, something between the colonized and the colonizing, the physical and the imaginary.[16] By showing this complex and often isolated process within a series of episodes—or stops along a single line—the collection establishes that French colonial identities did not take a single form or emanate from a single centralized source. Instead, they formed around and as a direct result of the movement of people, goods, and ideas across the complex patchwork of imperial, colonial, and Indigenous spaces in North America and the Atlantic World.[17] Each of the essays, having concentrated on a separate space, community, or path of movement, contributes to the framing of this francophone world as diverse, disjointed, and complex, and yet in many ways tied together by cultural mobility.

Placed within a chronological framework, the first three essays in *French Connections* concentrate largely on performative aspects of French cultural mobility. In the opening essay, Mairi Cowan explores the processes by which ideas of spiritual balance—good versus evil, God versus the Devil—survived the transatlantic voyage to 1660s Québec and became transmuted in specific ways to fit a colonial context. As Cowan argues, the realities of the French colonial frontier shaped both the language of demonic possession and the actions one could take to end it, all of which stretched and redefined gendered notions of priestly authority and female power in the young French settlement. Moving beyond the pale of settlement at Québec, William Brown posits in the second essay that French imperial understandings of diplomacy as performative rhetorical exchange were deeply rooted in metropolitan political and educational culture. Constructing a backdrop of the "North American stage," Brown demonstrates how the French performance of "Indianness" became central to Franco-Indigenous relations throughout the seventeenth and early eighteenth centuries. In the third essay, Leslie Choquette addresses the cultural and economic foundations of migration to New France. Drawing on a well-established history of labor mobility in ancien régime France, she asserts that old patterns of labor migration directly informed developing transatlantic networks of culture and movement within New France and ultimately contributed to the emergence of French colonial identities in a broad and fluid North American world.

The middle three essays delve more concretely into distinct cases of cultural mobility and identity formation throughout the wider French Atlantic. Gregory Kennedy and Vincent Auffrey focus on the strange career of Paul Mascarene. A Huguenot refugee in the service of the English Crown in the late seventeenth century, Mascarene moved from Europe to New England to Mi'gma'ki/Acadie/

Nova Scotia in pursuit of professional advancement, navigating the cultural and economic interests of several vastly different political spheres. By following Mascarene's winding path, Kennedy and Auffrey explore the intricacies of professional identity politics in an age of imperial rivalry. Constrained by a Frenchness that defied easy definition, the case of Mascarene forces us to rethink the use of basic ethnic labels in a complex Atlantic imperial context. Christopher Hodson's essay explores the life and legacy of one Louis Turc de Castelveyre, better known simply as Brother Chrétien. In a fascinating and breathless study that jumps from France to New France, Saint-Domingue, the Spanish side of the island, and ultimately a courtroom, Hodson considers how a conman's familiarity and experience with the French colonial realm exposes the fragmented nature of imperial authority while at the same time serving to highlight interconnected pathways of the French Atlantic. Robert D. Taber follows with an examination of how religious cultural norms in the French Caribbean could be stretched and employed in creative and unexpected ways. He argues specifically that free people of color in "colonial Haiti" used sacramental records as multidirectional tools for "racialization, social acceptance, and accessing the power of the state." It was in these records that free people of color, usually placed outside, if not actively beneath, society throughout the diasporic world, came face-to-face, sometimes literally, with the nomenclature of acceptance, subjecthood, and political existence in the island colony.

The final three essays all deal with French cultural mobility in a period when the French Empire was either unraveling or had officially come to an end in North America. Guillaume Teasdale and Karen Marrero investigate the survival and continuity of French culture at Detroit through a period of Anglicization/Americanization. The "constant migrations of French families *and* single men from the St. Lawrence Valley" to Detroit, as late as the 1840s, show that the town may have become an English and American political space, but that beneath this new imperial veneer, it very much remained a French cultural space. Robert Englebert examines the *récits de voyage* of French émigrés during the late eighteenth and early nineteenth centuries. He contends that men like Georges-Henri-Victor Collot and his famed colleague the comte de Volney both identified a preexisting culture of French mobility in the historic Illinois Country and "performed their own act of intellectual mobility" in their ethnographic descriptions of French creole *others*. This was a profound act of imperial imagining, meant to frame seemingly forgotten French peoples in relation to the possibility of a renewed French Empire in North America at the end of the eighteenth and early nineteenth century. Fittingly, the final essay connects many of the places discussed in preceding pages. Jay Gitlin and Ryan André Brasseaux paint a broad portrait of the French cultural world through the life of Honoré Beaugrand, a transnational *Canadien* who worked and published in New Orleans, France, Algeria, Montréal, and even Maximilian's Mexico during the latter half of the nineteenth century. Beaugrand spent much of his adult life on the move, and the narratives he crafted about his travels established what Gitlin and Brasseaux describe as a "pan-Franco identity," the product of a "journalistic voyageur" dedicated to challenging the limits of transnational identities in an age of national consolidation and colonial reconquest.

The essays in this collection depict a world in motion tied together through the ubiquity of cultural mobility in North America and the Atlantic World. It is not all-inclusive. Few approaches ever are. But here, if anything, we start a conversation, ask for further study, and provide salient examples of cultural mobility across a wider, diverse French cultural space. We are, of course, not the first to posit the value of such far-reaching interconnectivity and multidimensional approaches, antecedents of which can be found in the Braudelian spatial model, the emergence of Atlantic and World history as stand-alone topics, and the recent body of scholarship focused on Louisiana, the Gulf South, and the northern edges of the circum-Caribbean.[18] We are reticent, moreover, to trumpet this collection as part of a paradigm shift, aware that historiographical turns sometimes promise far more than they deliver.[19] By focusing, however, on the processes by which these communities, peoples, cities, and towns remained both culturally French and geographically localized, products of both the North American *terroir* as well as imagined cultural and political antecedents across the Atlantic, we believe that *French Connections*, as well as similar volumes, can serve as part of a vanguard for a more coherent and nuanced history dedicated not to borders and boundaries but to paths carved and threads followed.

NOTES

1. Christopher Hodson and Brett Rushforth, "Absolutely Atlantic: Colonialism and the Early Modern French State in Recent Historiography," *History Compass* 8, no. 1 (2010): 102. Hodson and Rushforth appropriately note the critical role of French historians in developing Atlantic history in the 1940s and 1950s, but also identify the retreat from French Atlantic history in the 1960s, 1970s, and 1980s. Dale Miquelon's work came out at the very time that scholars eschewed the French Atlantic.

2. Dale Miquelon, *Dugard of Rouen: French Trade to Canada and the West Indies, 1729–1770* (Montréal: McGill-Queen's University Press, 1978), 166.

Introduction

3. W. J. Eccles, *The Canadian Frontier, 1534–1760* (Albuquerque: University of New Mexico Press, 1983), 62; and Christopher L. Miller, *The French Atlantic Triangle: Literature and Culture of the Slave Trade* (Durham, NC: Duke University Press, 2008).

4. Several works regarding the relative weakness of the French imperial state include James Pritchard, *In Search of Empire: The French in the Americas, 1670–1730* (New York: Cambridge University Press, 2004); Eric Hinderaker, *Elusive Empire: Constructing Colonialism in the Ohio Valley, 1673–1800* (New York: Cambridge University Press, 1997); Kenneth J. Banks, *Chasing Empire across the Sea: Communications and the State in the French Atlantic, 1713–1763* (Montréal: McGill-Queen's University Press, 2002); and Bertrand Van Ruymbeke, *From New Babylon to Eden: The Huguenots and Their Migration to Colonial South Carolina* (Columbia: University of South Carolina Press, 2006). A wave of new imperial history has shown that the relationship between the imperial state, colonies, and colonists was somewhat more nuanced and complicated than previously assumed. See Hodson and Rushforth, "Absolutely Atlantic"; Alexandre Dubé, "Making a Career out of the Atlantic: Louisiana's Plume," in Cécile Vidal, ed., *Louisiana: Crossroads of the Atlantic World* (Philadelphia: University of Pennsylvania Press, 2014), 44–67; Guillaume Aubert, "'To Establish One Law and Definite Rules': Race, Religion, and the Transatlantic Origins of the Louisiana Code Noir," in Cécile Vidal, ed., *Louisiana*, 21–43; Owen Stanwood, "Between Eden and Empire: Huguenot Refugees and the Promise of New Worlds," *American Historical Review* 118, no. 5 (2013): 1319–1344.

5. In his 2004 work, Stephen Greenblatt suggested that scholars consider mobility as "the constitutive condition of culture." Six years later, in "A Mobility Studies Manifesto," he expanded upon this initial observation by laying out five key aspects for studying mobility: foundational expressions of literal movement; the importance of analyzing hidden and conspicuous movement (both literally and metaphorically); the centrality of contact zones in cultural exchange; the tensions between "individual agency and structural constraint"; and the relationship of mobility to the notion of rootedness. See Stephen J. Greenblatt, *Cultural Mobility* [PDF] (2004 [cited Feb. 13, 2019, www.fas.harvard.edu /curriculum-review/essays_pdf/Stephen_J_Greenblatt.pdf]), and "A Mobility Studies Manifesto," in *Cultural Mobility: A Manifesto* (New York: Cambridge University Press, 2010), 250–53.

6. Cécile Vidal, "Introduction: « Nos ancêtres les Gaulois » ou la francité dans la laboratoire colonial (XVIe-XIXe siècle)," in *Français? La nation en débat entre colonies et métropole, XVIe-XIXe siècle*, ed. Cécile Vidal (Paris: EHESS, 2014), 14–16. Also see: Dean R. Louder and Eric Waddell, *French America: Mobility, Identity, and Minority Experience across the Continent*, trans. Franklin Philip (Baton Rouge: Louisiana State University Press, 1993).

7. Several works have used mobility as an analytical structure, placing identity formation of more localized communities within the distance they experienced, and indeed created, between themselves and the metropole. See Shannon Lee Dawdy, *Building the Devil's Empire: French Colonial New Orleans* (Chicago: University of Chicago Press, 2008), 4–20, 230–46; Brenda MacDougall, Carolyn Podruchny, and Nicole St-Onge, "Introduction: Cultural Mobility and the Contours of Difference," in Nicole St-Onge, Carolyn Podruchny, and Brenda MacDougall, eds., *Contours of a People: Metis Family, Mobility, and History* (Norman: University of Oklahoma Press, 2014), 7–11; Michael A. Gomez, *Exchanging Our Country Marks: The Transformation of African Identities in the Colonial and Antebellum South* (Chapel Hill: University of North Carolina Press, 1998), 4–18, chap. 7; and Caree A. Banton, *More Auspicious Shores: Barbadian Migration to Liberia, Blackness, and the Making of an African Republic* (New York:

Cambridge University Press, 2019), 3–14, 103–17. For a more modern approach, dealing largely with these same structures within the African diaspora of the postcolonial age, see Michael A. Gomez, *Reversing Sail: A History of the African Diaspora* (New York: Cambridge University Press, 2005), chap. 8.

8. Christopher Hodson, *The Acadian Diaspora: An Eighteenth-Century History* (New York: Oxford University Press, 2012); Gregory M. W. Kennedy, *Something of a Peasant Paradise? Comparing Rural Societies in Acadie and the Loudunais, 1604–1755* (Montréal: McGill-Queen's Press, 2014); Leslie Choquette, *Frenchmen into Peasants: Modernity and Tradition in the Peopling of French Canada* (Cambridge, MA: Harvard University Press, 1997); Carl A. Brasseaux, *The Founding of New Acadia: The Beginnings of Acadian Life in Louisiana, 1765–1803* (Baton Rouge: Louisiana State University Press, 1987); Colin M. Coates, *The Metamorphosis of Landscape and Community in Early Quebec* (Montréal: McGill-Queen's University Press, 2000); Carl J. Ekberg, *French Roots in the Illinois Country: The Mississippi Frontier in Colonial Times* (Urbana: University of Illinois Press, 1998); Francois Furstenberg, *When the United States Spoke French: Five Refugees Who Shaped a Nation* (New York: Penguin, 2014); Allan Greer, *Peasant, Lord, and Merchant: Rural Society in Three Quebec Parishes, 1740–1840* (Toronto: University of Toronto Press, 1985); Thomas Wien, Cécile Vidal, and Yves Frenette, eds., *De Québec à l'Amérique française, Histoire et mémoire: Textes choisis du deuxième colloque de la Commission franco-québécoise sur les lieux de mémoire communs* (Québec City: Les Presses de l'Université Laval, 2006).

9. Christopher M. Parsons, *A Not-So-New World: Empire and Environment in French Colonial North America* (Philadelphia: University of Pennsylvania Press, 2018).

10. See, for example, Cécile Vidal, ed., *Louisiana: Crossroads of the Atlantic World* (Philadelphia: University of Pennsylvania Press, 2014); Gwendolyn Midlo Hall's two masterful works, *Africans in Colonial Louisiana: The Development of Afro-Creole Culture in the Eighteenth Century* (Baton Rouge: Louisiana State University Press, 1992), and *Slavery and African Ethnicities in the Americas: Restoring the Links* (Chapel Hill: University of North Carolina Press, 2005); John Wood Sweet, *Bodies Politic: Negotiating Race in the American North, 1730–1830* (Philadelphia: University of Pennsylvania Press, 2003); Karen Ordahl Kupperman, *Indians & English: Facing Off in Early America* (Ithaca, NY: Cornell University Press, 2000); Gilles Havard, *Empire et métissages: Indiens et Français dans le Pays d'en Haut, 1660–1715* (Paris: Presses de l'Université Paris–Sorbonne, 2003); Natalie Dessens, *From Saint-Domingue to New Orleans: Migration and Influences* (Gainesville: University Press of Florida, 2010); Emily Clark, *The Strange History of the American Quadroon: Free Women of Color in the Revolutionary Atlantic World* (Chapel Hill: University of North Carolina Press, 2013); Jorge Cañizares-Esguerra, Matt D. Childs, and James Sidbury, eds., *The Black Urban Atlantic in the Age of the Slave Trade* (Philadelphia: University of Pennsylvania Press, 2013); Randy J. Sparks, *Where the Negroes Are Masters: An African Port in the Era of the Slave Trade* (Cambridge, MA: Harvard University Press, 2014); Julia Gaffield, *Haitian Connections: Recognition after Revolution in the Atlantic World* (Chapel Hill: University of North Carolina Press, 2015); Laurent Dubois, *A Colony of Citizens: Revolution and Slave Emancipation in the French Caribbean, 1787–1804* (Chapel Hill: University of North Carolina Press, 2004); Sophie White, *Voices of the Enslaved: Love, Labor, and Longing in French Louisiana* (Chapel Hill: University of North Carolina Press, 2019); Trevor Burnard, *Planters, Merchants, and Slaves: Plantation Societies in British America, 1650–1820* (Chicago: University of Chicago Press, 2015); and, among many others, Sara Fanning, *Caribbean Crossing: African Americans and the Haitian Emigration Movement* (New York: New York University Press, 2015).

Introduction

11. Jennifer L. Palmer, *Intimate Bonds: Family and Slavery in the French Atlantic* (Philadelphia: University of Pennsylvania Press, 2016), 11–17.

12. Daniel H. Usner, "Rescuing Early America from Nationalist Narratives: An Intra-Imperial Approach to Colonial Canada and Louisiana," *Historical Reflections* 40, no. 3 (2014): 4–5. Also see Peter H. Wood, "From Atlantic History to a Continental Approach," in Jack P. Greene and Philip D. Morgan, eds., *Atlantic History: A Critical Appraisal* (New York: Oxford University Press, 2009): 279–98; Burnard, *Planters, Merchants, and Slaves*; and François Furstenberg, "The Significance of the Trans-Appalachian Frontier in Atlantic History," *American Historical Review* 113, no. 3 (2008): 647–77.

13. The historiography of Louisiana in the Atlantic World is robust. For some of the most notable studies of Louisiana's place in the wider Atlantic, see Vidal, ed., *Louisiana: Crossroads of the Atlantic World*; Rebecca J. Scott and Jean M. Hébrard, *Freedom Papers: An Atlantic Odyssey in the Age of Emancipation* (Cambridge, MA: Harvard University Press, 2012); Hall, *Africans in Colonial Louisiana*, and *Slavery* and *African Ethnicities in the Americas*; Havard, *Empire et métissages*; Dessens, *From Saint-Domingue to New Orleans*; Clark, *The Strange History of the American Quadroon*; White, *Intimate Voices of the African Diaspora*; Fanning, *Caribbean Crossing*; Bradley G. Bond, ed., *French Colonial Louisiana and the Atlantic World* (Baton Rouge: Louisiana State University Press, 2005); Arnold R. Hirsch and Joseph Logsdon, eds., *Creole New Orleans: Race and Americanization* (Baton Rouge: Louisiana State University Press, 1992); Gilbert C. Din, *Spaniards, Planters, and Slaves: The Spanish Regulation of Slavery in Louisiana, 1763–1803* (College Station: Texas A&M University Press, 1999); Rebecca J. Scott, *Degrees of Freedom: Louisiana and Cuba after Slavery* (Cambridge, MA: Harvard University Press, 2005); Peter J. Kastor and François Weil, eds., *Empires of the Imagination: Transatlantic Histories of the Louisiana Purchase* (Charlottesville: University of Virginia Press, 2009); Dawdy, *Building the Devil's Empire*; Erin M. Greenwald, *Marc-Antoine Caillot and the Company of the Indies in Louisiana: Trade in the French Atlantic World* (Baton Rouge: Louisiana State University Press, 2016); Lawrence N. Powell, *The Accidental City: Improvising New Orleans* (Cambridge, MA: Harvard University Press, 2012); Andrew N. Wegmann, "The Vitriolic Blood of a Negro: The Development of Racial Identity and Creole Elitism in New Spain and Spanish Louisiana, 1763–1803," *Journal of Transatlantic Studies* 13, no. 2 (Spring 2015): 204–25; and, among many others, Cécile Vidal, *Caribbean New Orleans: Empire, Race, and the Making of a Slave Society* (Chapel Hill: University of North Carolina Press, 2019).

14. Of particular note, a number of recent works have made valuable and welcomed attempts to bridge the academic gap between Louisiana's robust historiography and the rest of French North America and even areas outside the French colonial purview. In this way, the fascinating and provocative approaches used to study Louisiana and New Orleans, particularly in the realm of race and cultural development, have begun to inform new studies of other parts of the Atlantic World. This has resulted in an important new discursive relationship between a previously largely isolated Louisiana historiography and much less focused, more sweeping French North American historiography. At the center of this effort is Cécile Vidal, whose two recent books, *Louisiana: Crossroads of the Atlantic World*, of which she served as editor, and *Caribbean New Orleans*, have done a marvelous job at introducing French North American historiographies to the multidimensional approaches that have made Louisiana so well studied but isolated from the rest of its continental world. For other studies that to varying degrees apply Louisiana history to other places in the Atlantic World, see Mark F. Fernandez, *From Chaos to Continuity: The Evolution of Louisiana's Judicial System, 1712–1862* (Baton Rouge: Louisiana State Uni-

versity Press, 2001); Thomas Jessen Adams and Matt Sakakeeny, eds., *Remaking New Orleans: Beyond Exceptionalism and Authenticity* (Durham, NC: Duke University Press, 2019); Andrew N. Wegmann, *Skin Color and Social Practice: The Problem of Race and Class in the Atlantic South, 1718–1862* (Athens: University of Georgia Press, 2021); and, among others, Jennifer M. Spear, *Race, Sex, and Social Order in Early New Orleans* (Baltimore: Johns Hopkins University Press, 2009).

15. Within the context of Louisiana, see, most notably, Vidal, ed., *Louisiana: Crossroads of the Atlantic World*, 7. For the subway metaphor, see Brett Rushforth's epilogue to this volume.

16. For a selection of nuanced interpretations regarding the fluidity, construction, and imposition of identity in French colonial North America and the Atlantic world, see Andrew N. Wegmann, "To Fashion Ourselves Citizens: Colonization, Belonging, and the Problem of Nationhood in the Atlantic South, 1829–1859," in Whitney Nell Stewart and John Garrison Marks, eds., *Race and Nation in the Age of Emancipations* (Athens: University of Georgia Press, 2018), 42–43; Caree A. Banton, "Who Is Black in a Black Republic? Labor in the Remaking of Black Citizenship in Liberia," in Stewart and Marks, eds., *Race and Nation in the Age of Emancipations*, 131–36; Robert Englebert, "Colonial Encounters and the Changing Contours of Ethnicity: Pierre-Louis de Lorimier and Métissage at the Edges of Empire," *Ohio Valley History* 18, no. 1 (2018): 45–69; Vidal, "Introduction: « Nos ancêtres les Gaulois » ou la francité dans la laboratoire colonial (XVIe-XIXe siècle)," 14–16; Gilles Havard, "'Protection' and 'Unequal Alliance': The French Conception of Sovereignty over Indians in New France," in *French and Indians in the Heart of North America, 1630–1815*, ed. Robert Englebert (East Lansing: Michigan State University Press, 2013), 114–17; Denys Delâge, "Poursuivre la décolonisation de notre histoire," in *Représentation, métissage et pouvoir: La dynamique coloniale des échanges entre Autochtones, Européens et Canadiens (XVIe-XXe siècle)*, ed. Alain Beaulieu and Stéphanie Chaffray (Québec City: Presses de l'Université Laval, 2012), 45–47; Spear, *Race, Sex, and Social Order in Early New Orleans*, 2–4; Sue Peabody, "'A Nation Born to Slavery': Missionaries and Racial Discourse in Seventeenth-Century French Antilles," *Journal of Social History* 38, no. 1 (2004): 113–15; Jennifer Morgan, *Laboring Women: Reproduction and Gender in New World Slavery* (Philadelphia: University of Pennsylvania Press, 2004), 49–52; Guillaume Aubert, "'The Blood of France': Race and Purity of Blood in the French Atlantic World," *William and Mary Quarterly* 61, no. 3 (2004): 439–78.

17. Catherine Desbarats and Allan Greer, "North America from the Top Down: Visions from New France, 2015," *Journal of Early American History* 5, no. 2 (2015): 109–36; Catherine Desbarats and Allan Greer, "Où est la Nouvelle-France?" *Revue d'histoire de l'Amérique française* 64, no. 3–4 (2011): 31–62.

18. For some of the challenges to these approaches, see Bruce Mazlish, "Comparing Global History to World History," *Journal of Interdisciplinary History* 28, no. 3 (1998): 386–88; Alison Games, "Atlantic History: Definitions, Challenges, and Opportunities," *American Historical Review* 111, no. 3 (2006): 741–43; Nicolas Canny, "Atlantic History and Global History," in Jack P. Greene and Philip D. Morgan, eds., *Atlantic History: A Critical Appraisal* (New York: Oxford University Press, 2009), 319.

19. Allan Greer, "National, Transnational, and Hypernational Historiographies: New France Meets Early American History," *Canadian Historical Review* 91, no. 4 (2010): 695–724.

A Deliverance from Demons
Possession and Healing at the Seigneurie of Beauport

MAIRI COWAN

Not long after the ships left Québec to return across the Atlantic in the autumn of 1660, residents of the small French settlement on the banks of the St. Lawrence River began to worry about a case of demonic possession in their midst. The apparent victim was Barbe Hallay, an adolescent who had traveled from France to Canada with her family the previous year. Shortly after her arrival, she began working as a domestic servant in the nearby seigneurie of Beauport. Here, according to the Ursuline nun Marie de l'Incarnation, phantoms were seen, a drum and flute were heard, and stones detached themselves from walls. The suspected instigator of this demonic infestation was Daniel Vuil, a Huguenot miller who had come to Canada on the same ship as Hallay.[1] François de Laval, the vicar apostolic, sent priests to the seigneurie, and he even went himself to chase away the demons, but to no avail. The infestation continued. When the priests grew tired from traveling between Québec and Beauport, Hallay and Vuil were brought into Québec. She was placed in the Hôtel-Dieu hospital by the order of Laval, who (the hospital's *Chroniques* says) judged this necessary for the good of the girl, afflicted as she was by some kind of "malefice."[2] At the Hôtel-Dieu, the Augustinian nun Catherine de Saint-Augustin battled against the demons by night, while Hallay helped care for the patients by day.[3] Vuil, meanwhile, was put in prison, investigated for signs of witchcraft, and finally executed.[4]

Even after the ministrations of the hospital sister and the death of the suspected witch, Hallay was still reporting infernal visitations. And they were getting worse. When she returned to Beauport, Marie Regnouard, wife of the seigneur, took matters into her own hands to liberate her servant from the demons.[5] For an account of what happened, we can read a report signed by Regnouard herself. In it, we are told that a demon came to torment Hallay as she lay sleeping on about October 15, 1662. Regnouard went to help, as she had done before, but this time she placed a rib bone of Jean de Brébeuf against the side of Hallay. In the words of Regnouard's account, "the demon made [Hallay] make several contortions of her arms and her legs and generally all her body and said to me several times 'remove this, woman, remove this from me, because I burn, I burn.'" Worth noting here is that the movements of Hallay's body and the words coming from her mouth were interpreted as being controlled by the demon, not the demoniac. Regnouard's spoken instructions were therefore directed to the demon, not to Hallay. Regnouard conjured the demon in the name of the living God and by the merits of the very holy Virgin Mary and demanded that he tell her the name of the person whose relics he was insisting she remove. They argued for a time, until Regnouard commanded the demon, by the merits of the saint whose relics she was using, to depart. Then she saw something "like a breath" leave from the mouth of the girl, and Hallay "began immediately to speak and to say 'Jesus, Mary, Joseph' and to make the sign of the cross on her forehead, on her mouth, and on her heart." This return to speech and gesture in conformity with Catholic religious practice was a sign for Regnouard that Hallay was freed from the possession—at least for the moment. The account continues with Hallay saying that the demon had left, but that two witches who had been accompanying the demon were now at the foot of the bed. The witches were apparently visible only to Hallay, but Regnouard dealt with them too. She conjured them in the name of God to leave the demon that they served. They said several words to Regnouard, but she could not hear anything except a low buzzing or hum. Hallay relayed the witches' speech: they had come to bring her to the Sabbath but—as the copy of the report at the Hôtel-Dieu concludes rather abruptly—since that day, the girl had neither seen nor heard either demon or witch, and she was of a freer mind than she had been for the two and a half years of her agitation by demons. This episode was now over, but a coda came later. The copies of the report kept at the Archive of the Jesuits contain an additional section saying that four and a half months after this deliverance, Hallay met a certain man suspected of witchcraft. He tried to put her onto a cart that he was driving, and he said some impertinent things to her. She resisted, then was tormented by demons again for eleven days. The demons made a very large noise in the room of Hallay and threw a stone from the chimney with such force that Seigneur Giffard rose from his bed thinking that the chimney had fallen; it has been verified, the report adds, that this chimney, which had smoked before, smoked no longer. Regnouard made devotions once more to Jean de Brébeuf to obtain a second healing for the poor girl, and since that time Hallay remained entirely delivered.[6]

When the possession of Barbe Hallay has been discussed by historians, it usually forms just a small part in a larger study of folklore or religion. Whether characterized dismissively as a miller's susceptibility to feminine charms and an appearance of will-o-the-wisps,[7] enumerated among the relatively infrequent witchcraft accusations in Québec,[8] given as an example of female religious authority,[9] used to show the early modern association between madness and demonic possession,[10] or, most recently, included in an evaluation of how European fears made their way across the Atlantic in attenuated form to New France,[11] analysis of the alleged possession tends to miss a crucial part of the story: the role played by Marie Regnouard.[12]

This essay considers Regnouard's actions as a way to assess the continuity of expectations from Old to New France.[13] Basic beliefs in demons and theories about how to confront them moved across the Atlantic in completely recognizable form, but people changed their behaviors when trying to heal the demoniac. In some ways, Regnouard behaved in conformity with how someone of her gender and class in France was expected to behave. As a noblewoman, Regnouard would have had duties that included caring for members of her household who, like Hallay, required physical care. And this she did. But Regnouard's care extended far beyond what women in Europe at the time were encouraged to provide, reaching even into a spiritual domain usually forbidden to them. In this respect, Regnouard departed from French convention. To understand how and why Regnouard, a lay woman, was able to perform a ritual that was normally restricted to clerical men, requires a consideration of how socio-religious aspects of French culture shifted as they moved from France to New France in the mid-seventeenth century. The demographics of settlement, the porous boundary between spiritual and medical healing, and the reputation of a local martyr all shaped people's perceptions of the possession and allowed Regnouard to exercise a degree of spiritual authority far beyond what would likely have been accepted in France. Regnouard's deliverance of Hallay from demonic forces shows that she, and those in Canada who supported her, brought familiar forms of Catholicism with them and then modified these transatlantic ideas according to local circumstances.[14]

Discernment, the Demoniac, and the Demographics of New France

Before analyzing Marie Regnouard's deliverance of Barbe Hallay, it is worth tracing some of the earlier developments in the suspected possession to establish what was known about the case and how people's attempts to discern its true nature were connected both to what they knew in France and to unique demographic challenges in the colony. Many of its features resembled trends in cases of possession from early modern Europe, which helps to explain why it was quickly and widely interpreted as being some form of demonic attack, but several elements distinguished the possession of Hallay from the European pattern and influenced how it was finally resolved. These elements arose in a colonial North American context where there was a shortage of young French women for the male French settlers to marry, a political emphasis on maintaining a Catholic identity for the colony, and a pronounced anxiety about being under threat from forces beyond the borders of New France.

By the time Regnouard was delivering her servant from demonic tormentors, stories of Hallay's assault by demons had become quite widespread in Québec. The variety of words used to describe the phenomenon indicates the same difficulty with discernment that writers were struggling with in France. Vicar Apostolic François de Laval wrote that Hallay was afflicted by "malefice,"[15] the Jesuit Paul Ragueneau that she was "possessed,"[16] and the Ursuline nun Marie de l'Incarnation that she was "possessed" or "obsessed."[17] An inventory in the Archives du Séminaire de Québec lists a series of anonymous items from the spring of 1661 about a certain girl "infested" with demons, including one about "the diabolical infestation that has followed Barbe Hallay, and of Daniel Vuil accused of magical spells"; another about by what marks the diabolical infestation was known; a monition against Vuil and other witches; an attestation about the innocence of Hallay; and proofs against Vuil, accused of witchcraft.[18]

To use an explanation favored by Brian Levack in interpreting stories of demonic possession, the people implicated in this case were "playing roles and following scripts that were encoded in their respective religious cultures."[19] This particular cultural performance was in the tradition of France, but the theater of New France changed the plot somewhat. Pronouncements about demonic agency were not foregone conclusions, and uncertainty about the exact form of the demons' interference—whether possession, obsession, or infestation—was common in early modern Europe. Intellectuals who wrote about demonology advised caution in discernment, since signs that indicated possession looked much like signs of illness or even fraud.[20] In Hallay's case, a number of things would have suggested to observers that they were facing a genuinely demonic presence. As an adolescent female, Hallay fit the profile of a typical early modern European demoniac in terms of age and gender. Effects on Hallay's body were what Europeans had come to expect in cases of possession, including physical pain, convulsions, and vomiting. Her claim that witches were involved was consistent with demonological theories that possession could be initiated through the actions of a witch, and the person accused of using witchcraft to cause the possession, Daniel Vuil, fit the profile of a witch in several respects. One was his gender, since men outnumbered women among those suspected of witchcraft in parts of France.[21] His occupation of miller might have added further suspicion, casting onto him the negative reputation carried by both literary and real millers as a group that was often associated with seigneurial exploitation and dishonest work in late medieval and early modern Europe.[22]

According to Marie de l'Incarnation, the immediate cause of the possession was a broken promise of marriage: Vuil "wished to marry a girl who had come across with her father and mother on the same vessel, saying that she had been promised to him: but because this was a man of bad customs, he was never listened to. After this refusal, he wished to arrive at his ends by means of the tricks of his diabolical art."[23] This tactic of using witchcraft to win over a young woman would probably not have surprised Marie or other French settlers, since the use of love magic by a male suitor on a female was thought to be a significant cause of possession in early modern Europe.[24] It resonated with the settlers in New France too, but in a very different demographic situation. New France had a lot more French men for every marriageable French woman than Old France did, and this imbalance contributed to differences between how marriages were formed in the two places, despite their sharing the same basic laws.

Hallay's precise age at her arrival in Canada is difficult to establish, but when she disembarked at Québec, she was probably between thirteen and sixteen years old. This was at the low end but within the range of when most women first married in seventeenth-century New France.[25] She had reached the age of consent and was therefore able to choose her spouse. In law, she was also perfectly within her rights to withdraw from an agreement to marry if she chose. Marriage was based on the free exchange of vows, as it had been in the medieval period, but by the seventeenth century its formation had also taken on additional requirements in both canon and civil law. The Tridentine decree *Tametsi* in 1563 stated that to be valid, a marriage needed to take place before witnesses, including a parish priest. French royal edicts from 1556, 1579, and 1639 added further conditions by insisting upon consent by parents, the proclamation of banns, and the presence of four witnesses at the wedding. Punishment for minors who married in secret or against their parents' wishes could be severe, in theory even capital. In this socio-legal context, although no marriage could take place without the consent of Barbe Hallay and her parents, custom would have weighed on Hallay to follow through with any agreement she had made.[26] Indeed, because of the sex imbalance in the colony, she would have felt intense social pressure to marry once she reached New France, and she therefore might have felt uncomfortable withdrawing from any agreement to marry.[27] With six or seven marriageable men for every marriageable woman among French settlers, the pattern of marriage differed between the sexes. Men generally had to establish themselves before they were able to find a spouse, while unmarried women tended to marry quickly after arrival, and usually within a year.[28]

Hallay may not have felt ready to marry anyone yet, or she may not have wanted to marry Vuil in particular. He had not established himself in the colony, and reactions to him in Canada strongly suggest that he would not have been considered suitable for the companionship that early modern French people generally expected from marriage. The word "*amitié*" was used to describe a desirable bond between spouses, and it implied an expectation of mutual respect and intent to care for one another even while assuming that the husband would have authority over the wife.[29] Vuil probably did not look promising as a companion in "*amitié*." Marie de l'Incarnation alluded to his "bad customs" in her first account of the demonic torments, and in 1668, she added that Hallay had refused Vuil's offer of marriage because he was suspected of "*maléfices*."[30] His few appearances in the records from Québec all point to a disruptive and even criminal figure. Paul Ragueneau's *La vie de la mère Catherine de Saint-Augustin*, published in 1671 but drawing upon earlier sources, states that Vuil was hanged for pronouncing blasphemies and profaning the sacraments.[31] The *Journal des Jésuites* for February 1661 reports that Vuil was imprisoned as a relapsed heretic, blasphemer, and profaner of the sacraments, and the entry from October 1661 recording Vuil's execution might be interpreted as saying that his capital crime was illegal trade in liquor with Indigenous people.[32] Historians have disagreed on whether Vuil was executed for illegal trade in alcohol[33] or for religious crimes,[34] but whatever the reason, this reputation for antisocial behavior reflects poorly on Vuil as a potential spouse.[35] Regardless of the suitor's reputation, Hallay was not alone in backing away from a promise of marriage. Some women changed their minds about whom to marry, and sometimes quite suddenly. In fact, at least 10 percent of female immigrants signed a marriage contract with a man they would never wed, and they often did the signing shortly before marrying someone else.³⁶ Unlike most women who broke a contract, however, Hallay did not enter into another engagement soon after.³⁷ Women had quite a lot of latitude in deciding whom to marry, but aside from those who took religious vows, young women in New France were not really given the choice of simply not marrying at all. If the avoidance of marriage altogether was Hallay's desire, there was no easy way for her to maintain a celibate state; her status as demoniac, whether consciously adopted as a strategic response to pressures on young women or not, shielded her from unwanted nuptials.

The repeated emphasis in the sources on Daniel Vuil's Huguenot background points to another force shaping the reactions to Hallay's possession: geopolitical religious uncertainty both in France, a kingdom still religiously divided, and in New France, a colony facing imperial competition from Protestant New England. Catholicism was a central part of the identity of New France, but it was insecure in practice. The official exclusion of non-Catholic colonists had been launched in 1627 with the foundation of the Compagnie des Cent-Associés, whose charter called for the peopling of the colony with French Catholics and declared that descendants of the French living in New France along with Indigenous people who professed the Catholic faith would be counted and reputed *"naturels François."*³⁸ Protestants were present in New France too, in spite of official exclusion. Although there was no church of any Protestant confession established nor, other than briefly when a Lutheran minister served during the time of the Kirke brothers in Québec, any clear leaders of a Protestant community, some individual Protestant merchants from Europe made annual visits to New France, and they occasionally crossed the Atlantic in slightly larger groups.³⁹ Marguerite Bourgeoys, founder of the Congrégation de Notre-Dame de Montréal, wrote with some exasperation of her experiences on board a ship returning to France in 1659, saying that the ship was "almost entirely Huguenot." Only seven or eight of the passengers were Catholic, and these hardly left their chambers. The Protestants, by contrast, had a much more public presence on the ship. They sang their prayers "evening, morning, and other times," and it took the determination of Montréal's formidable nurse Jeanne Mance asking them not to sing for them to stop.⁴⁰ Protestant migrants were supposed to be instructed in the Catholic faith and then publicly renounce their heresy at arrival, although many might actually have abjured without formal instruction, undertaking instead the simple process of signing an act of abjuration in a parish church or chapel.[41] These abjurations did not assuage the worries of the colony's religious elite, who could not be certain that they were made in full sincerity. By 1670, Laval wrote of his concern that Protestants were a danger both to France and to Canada because of their disloyalty to the king and because they could revolt and seek help from the English in New England.[42]

It was at about this same time that representatives of Church and Crown in the colony were also growing increasingly concerned about another group of converts, the Indigenous Christians in New France. With a shift in their policy of *francisation* (Frenchification) during the 1660s, they began to insist on a more complete assimilation into colonial society.[43] This insistence did not succeed. The French missionaries were supposed to be bringing Indigenous peoples to the "True Faith" of Catholicism, but the conversions were much lower in number than hoped, the missionaries were making concessions to those who wished to maintain ties to traditional practices that were deemed unacceptable by leaders in church and state, and these missionaries were sometimes even being accused—not without reason— of bringing deception, discord, and death into the Indigenous communities who hosted them.[44] The earlier ideal of creating a New France that would exceed the Old to become regenerated and improved, a Jerusalem composed of citizens destined for heaven, was proving unattainable.[45] As cracks were appearing in the religious foundation of New France's geopolitical identity, the colonists became concerned about a Huguenot witch causing a demonic infestation.

The colonists living in Québec during the years of Hallay's possession wrote in a still more anxious tone about the Five Nations of the Haudenosaunee, called the Iroquois by the French. The French and the Iroquois had been at peace since 1653, until the eruption of warfare again in 1660 rekindled the settlers' fear of attack.[46] A rumor reached Québec in the spring of that year about a group of Iroquois preparing for an invasion. The scribe of the *Chronique de L'Hôtel-Dieu de Québec* reported that when the Augustinian nuns heard news of an Iroquois army threatening Québec, they deliberated about what they should do. They were advised that they could not safely stay in their monastery after dark, nor the Ursulines in theirs, since neither had defenses sufficient against a sudden attack. So, except for a few nuns who stayed behind to care for the sick, the Augustinians went every day before sunset to the College of the Jesuits to spend the night there.[47] The scribe of the *Annales des Ursulines de Québec* recorded similar worries about an imminent Iroquois attack. Laval came to their convent and, finding it not strong enough, obliged the nuns to leave and stay with the Jesuits. They too slept in the Jesuit College each night, while during the day they stayed in their own convent, guarded by soldiers.[48] Marie de l'Incarnation's letters describe their state of exhaustion and fear. The bishop had the Holy Sacrament removed from the Ursuline church, and the governor ordered two corps of guards placed at the convent. Redoubts were built, windows were fitted with shutters, and narrow slits were put into walls through which missiles could be fired. "In a word," as Marie put it, "our monastery was converted into a fort guarded by twenty-four very resolute men."[49] The Ursulines took still more precautions by making provision of gunpowder and lead, and by borrowing weapons that were always ready in case of alarm. All this took a toll on the nuns. Marie wrote that they had not rested day or night over the course of five weeks, and that she was "extremely tired" from attending to twenty-four men and providing them with what they required for war and food. Even when in the dormitory, fear of an alarm kept her listening all night so that she would be ready to give the soldiers their munitions in case of attack.[50] In a letter to her son the following year, she admitted a feeling of vulnerability that must have been shared by many French colonists: with the freezing of the St. Lawrence River from late fall until spring, they were stuck in North America for half the year, and if they were attacked when no ship was in port, they could not save themselves.[51] Taking a broader view, Jérôme Lalemant wrote to the superior-general of the Society of Jesus in Rome about "trepidation" in the whole colony.[52] Historians have calculated that the number of French killed or taken captive in the early years of the Iroquois wars was probably quite low, and that the Five Nations of the Iroquois Confederacy had many international concerns beyond the small French settlements.[53] No matter the precise number of fatalities and the real designs of the Haudenosaunee warriors, however, the French settlers were clearly living in a nervous state of apprehension as the drama of Hallay's possession unfolded.

A young female demoniac who showed the expected symptoms, suspicion that a witch had instigated the assault, a general environment of religious uncertainty and perceived threat from outsiders: these features of the possession of Barbe Hallay are consistent with a general pattern of demonic possession in early modern Europe. The colonists who wrote about the case presumed that the demons and witches they believed they knew in France could also be found in New France, and this continuity makes sense in a context where the settlers presumed Christianity to have a universal truth.[54] But certain details of the colonial context in which the case played out were markedly different from what people had known in Europe. A gender imbalance that had French settler men outnumbering French settler women, a religious geopolitical theory of an ideal Catholic colony running up against a reality where many of the inhabitants were not ideally Catholic, and an anxiety among settlers about an imminent and existential threat of attack by the Iroquois all contributed to the most unexpected thing about this case: the identity of the person who relieved Barbe Hallay of her torments.

The Seigneurial Healer

The accounts of Marie Regnouard's actions on the night of October 15, 1662, describe them as a deliverance (*"delivrance"*), a relief (*"soulagement"*), and a healing (*"guerison"*). Looking beyond these words to the procedure being described, one might be struck by a conspicuous resemblance to something else: an exorcism. Regnouard ritually invoked a possessing demon using adjuration (calling the demon), interrogation (asking the demon whose relics she was using, to which the demon responded with a correct answer), prayer (in the names of God and the Virgin Mary), and sacred objects (a relic).[55] She did not employ the full rite as laid out in the *Rituale Romanum*,[56] but the essential elements were there. Even the invocation of a local holy person was typical of exorcisms of the time, which often presented variations and improvisations on the Roman Rite.[57] Regnouard described herself as speaking with the demon, not with Hallay, and her performance had the expected effects of exorcism in agitating the demon and causing the demoniac increased suffering during the procedure itself before finally casting out the possessing demon.[58]

So, if Regnouard's actions constituted an exorcism, and a successful one at that, why would none of the copies of this account describe them as such?[59] A simple answer is that the practitioner's gender and lay status ought to have rendered her categorically unsuitable to perform that ritual. In a slightly earlier period, most people seeking an exorcist showed little preference for either a man or a woman, clerical or lay; they cared more for personal reputation and geographical proximity. But starting in the late sixteenth century, ecclesiastical authorities tried increasingly to prevent lay people from practicing exorcism, and women who claimed to be able to discern a supernatural cause for an illness became more vulnerable to accusations of witchcraft.[60] By the early seventeenth century, the exclusion had been made more complete, and the 1614 *Rituale Romanum*'s section on exorcism insists that only a priest or another lawfully appointed officer of the Church can exorcise.⁶¹

Such attitudes may explain why Regnouard's actions were not called an exorcism, but they raise perhaps a still more interesting question: why did she perform these actions at all, if they constituted some form of exorcism in all but name? It was certainly not something she undertook in secret. Three copies of her account survive, and she was indirectly assisted by the Jesuit priest Paul Ragueneau, who had given her the rib bone of Jean de Brébeuf that she used. Ragueneau had also supplied Catherine de Saint-Augustin, the nun caring for Hallay at the Hôtel-Dieu hospital, with her relic of Brébeuf. Jesuits were leaders in the European campaign to exorcise growing numbers of possessed, and they were also enforcers of a clerical monopoly on exorcism, so it seems especially noteworthy that the two women who attempted to rid Hallay of demons used the relics of a martyred Jesuit given to them by another Jesuit.⁶² It is even more striking when considering that Canada was hardly suffering from a shortage of priests at this time. Several had already tried to exorcise the infested seigneurie at Beauport, but they all had failed. Catherine de Saint-Augustin described herself as "nailed to the cross of Canada,"⁶³ and she gained a reputation as someone capable of fighting demons with what one historian has called "heroic charity," so her efforts to remove the possession from Hallay are not totally out of place.⁶⁴ Regnouard's assistance is more surprising. Her social position in the colonial society of New France, as well as her connection with medicine in Québec, both help to explain it.

Marie Regnouard was born in the region of Perche, northwestern France, in 1599 to a family of some standing. Her father was the "sergent royal" in the city of Mortagne, her godparents were nobles, and her brother was a prior. At the time of Marie's marriage in 1628, her recently widowed mother, Jacqueline Michel, promised and obliged herself to feed and lodge the couple for two years, and to maintain the future bride as befitted "her quality."⁶⁵ Marie's husband, Robert Giffard, was also of high status, with nobility on both his mother's and his father's side holding the title of *seigneur*.⁶⁶ Before leaving France, Giffard successfully petitioned the Compagnie des Cent-Associés for a seigneurie in Canada. He was granted, in perpetuity, land along the St. Lawrence River that was one league in length and one and a half leagues deep.⁶⁷ When the family came to Québec in 1634, Regnouard was thirty-five years old and able to sign her own name. She had borne two children already and was heavily pregnant with her third. She gave birth in Fort Saint-Louis eight days after coming ashore.[68] The child's godparents were Guillemette Hébert, member of one of the most important land-holding families in the colony, and Samuel de Champlain, commander of New France.[69] In 1635, Champlain put in his will that Marie Regnouard was to receive a tableau of Our Lady that was in his room.[70] With such notables among her friends and supporters, Regnouard was obviously well connected to those leading the colony as it was being relaunched following a brief occupation by the English.

By the time she was delivering her servant from demons, Regnouard was over sixty years old and well established in New France. Her high social status and good connections did not mean that she led a life of ease and abundance—indeed, she used black cloth from old soutanes given to her by the Jesuits to line sleeves.[71] But as the female head of a seigneurie, she was expected to care for all who lived under her authority.[72] Regnouard was assertive in this capacity. At one point during the reported argument with the demon she responded to the demon's claim that Hallay belonged to him with the forceful statement: "you have lied, damned spirit ... she is mine ... God, and her father and her mother gave her to me." Clearly, Regnouard felt responsible for the well-being of Hallay, and she knew that her role as caregiver was widely accepted.

Regnouard likely had some medical expertise as well. Her immediate family included at least two medical practitioners.[73] Her husband, Robert Giffard, had first come to Canada as ship's surgeon in about 1620.[74] Back in France following the surrender of Québec to the English in 1629, he was listed as a master surgeon and as an apothecary.[75] Upon his return to Canada, he was the surgeon at the Hôtel-Dieu in Québec, and between 1634 and 1668 he was sometimes also described as a physician and as an apothecary.[76] Whatever the exact nature of his position, Giffard was a practitioner and not just a theoretician. For example, in 1640 he assisted an Algonquin woman with a difficult birth, in which both mother and child survived, and he tended to a nun at the Hôtel-Dieu who was suffering from several illnesses.[77] The second member of Regnouard's family with medical experience was Françoise, the daughter born just days after Regnouard's arrival at Québec. Françoise became a pensioner at the Hôtel-Dieu at the age of seven, and the first Canadian-born postulant five years later. As a nun of the choir, she took the name Françoise Marie de Saint Ignace, then made her profession and went into perpetual claustration in 1650. She died in 1657 following a long and painful illness. Looking back on earlier years in her life, her obituary characterized her decision to care for the sick as having been a godly one undertaken with the courage of a martyr. The devil had tried to persuade her that she would lead a holier life in the world rather than remaining celibate, but she persevered, and decided to employ herself "to the service of the poor sick all the days of her life."[78] The relationship between a sick person's body and spirit was close in New France, so that it was not just the physician, surgeon, and apothecary who had the power to heal, but nuns like Françoise as well.[79]

Regnouard was not an "authorized healer" like her husband and daughter, but even in the absence of occupational markers she was a healer nonetheless.[80] The category of bodywork as used by Mary Fissell as a way to think about attending to the human body goes some way to explaining Regnouard's care for Hallay. Fissell argues that "using bodywork as a category enables us to start at the bedside of the sufferer, attending to the physical labor entailed in the cure of the sick."[81] However, Fissell does not say much about exorcism except in the context of men doing bodywork. She gives the example of "pastors exorcising the demons that tortured a person physically as well as spiritually" and adds that this example of healing done primarily by men was a second-order effect of gender roles: "It is not the healing as such that is gendered, but the social roles through which that healing is accomplished."[82] If Regnouard was taking on social roles normally gendered masculine in early modern Europe, her bodywork fits with arguments that gender did not function quite the same way among French people on both sides of the Atlantic. She was able to extend her agency into the sphere of religion, where in Europe leaders of both church and state were trying to push women further out of public life. The model for French colonists in Canada was still fundamentally patriarchal, but Regnouard, benefitting from the broader trend in which new restrictive gender ideologies from France were delayed taking hold along the shores of the St. Lawrence, was able to establish for herself a divergence from patriarchal limitations.[83]

A Martyr's Intercessory Assistance

Not everyone in New France agreed on the scope and effects of demonic activity,[84] but contemporary observers who wrote about the possession of Hallay did agree on this: it was the relics of Jean de Brébeuf, Jesuit priest and martyr, that brought about the departure of the demons. Marie de l'Incarnation wrote that when Hallay was at the Hôtel-Dieu, the demons and the magicians finally took themselves away by the intercession of Brébeuf.[85] The reports signed by Regnouard are careful to credit the success of her efforts to Brébeuf as well, noting that the previous attempts with other saints' relics had not worked. In her argument with the demon, when she demanded that he tell her whose relic she was using, the demon answered that "it's a relic of a saint who had been martyred among the Huron by the Iroquois." Charles de Lauson de Charny, the signatory of the second part of the report, added that the return of the demons was reasonably to be attributed to the intention of God, to show the glory of his servant. Brébeuf had chased the demons away the first time, and only after more devotions were made to Brébeuf did Hallay become and remain entirely delivered.[86]

Clearly, it was Jean de Brébeuf who was supposed to be the real hero of this tale. Described by Marie de l'Incarnation as "a holy man who spilled his blood for the sustenance of faith in this country,"[87] he was a strong link between European Catholicism and North American evangelism. As news of Brébeuf's grisly martyrdom spread among the French in North America and Europe, the story of his life and death came to fit neatly into the established hagiographic pattern of the Christian martyr, and his physical remains came to be treated as relics.[88] Catherine de Saint-Augustin fed a dying Protestant sailor some water into which a bone had been either dipped (according to Ragueneau's *Vie*) or added in the form of ground-up powder (according to Le Mercier in the *Relation*). The relic-infused drink led the sailor both to the recovery of physical health and to conversion to Catholicism.[89] In 1674, Thierry Beschefer wrote that he and other Jesuits helped end the "phrénésie" of a fellow Jesuit, François Boniface, with the help of Brébeuf. They had tried opium to calm the frenetic priest, but it was a series of prayers to Brébeuf and the touching of the head with Brébeuf's bone that finally brought Boniface back to his senses.[90] The most prominent champion of Brébeuf was Paul Ragueneau, once Brébeuf's superior, later a caretaker for the martyr's relics and reputation. It was he who ordered that the remains of Brébeuf be disinterred and boiled in lye so that they could be recovered, and he who most compellingly imbued Brébeuf's death and the larger story of the end of the Huronia mission with meaning through messages of courage and hope.[91] It was also Ragueneau who gave precious relics of Brébeuf to Catherine de Saint-Augustin and Marie Regnouard. He was Catherine's confessor, and he maintained a very close relationship with her. Ragueneau's connection with Regnouard is less clearly documented, but her family maintained good relations with the Jesuits, giving and receiving gifts on several occasions.[92] The bones of Brébeuf had migrated in a living body from France to New France, and then as a relic from the contact zone of Wendake / Huronia to Québec. When a piece arrived at Beauport, it was used by a lay woman in a ritual of deliverance, relief, and healing that succeeded where earlier attempts by nuns and priests had failed.

Delivered from demons, Hallay went on to live a remarkably unremarkable life. In 1666, she was working as a domestic servant in a house in the town of Québec. In 1670, she married Jean Carrier, whom she may have met at the Hôtel-Dieu, where he worked as a domestic. By 1671, she was back at the Hôtel-Dieu herself, but now as a wage-earning worker rather than as a patient. She and Carrier moved across the river, and with their children became a successful *habitant* family.[93] No trace of Hallay's earlier possession appears to have left a mark, at least not in the documentary record. Perhaps the colonists no longer worried much about demonic interference. Behaviors that could have appeared typically demonic were being interpreted otherwise. In one instance, a Jesuit became violent and insensible, screaming almost continually, biting and hitting those who tried to help with such aggression that he had to be bound; he was diagnosed not as a demoniac, but as frenetic.[94] In another, three women from Beaupré suffered from fainting, convulsions, and the loss of speech, hearing, and understanding; they did not suspect that demons were responsible, and consulted physicians before making vows to St. Anne and visiting her shrine at Beaupré. Their symptoms might not even have been all that unusual, if the scribe recording their healing at the shrine is to be believed: he wrote that these women were being very troubled by an evil that ran quite ordinarily in Canada.[95] Cures were still sought at holy places and through the intercessory power of saints, but the maladies were not interpreted as demonic in origin. Even though civic and religious leaders took an interest in Hallay's case for a few years in the early 1660s, no waves of panic or persecution followed. The demonic infestation had been contained.

Those who observed the possession of Barbe Hallay expected that some things were transmitted across the Atlantic fully intact. This was especially true with Catholic religious claims: demons existed, they would behave in the same ways as they did in Europe, and they could be fought using a holy relic. For all the continuity of ideals, however, the experience of colonization forced the French to admit the need for flexibility in practice, and these same observers in seventeenth-century New France also accepted that some things would change in the voyage to North America. Women would have more choice in potential spouses, Indigenous nations could help or harm French settlements, and the most effective living human agent in the battle against a demon was not a priest in a church or a nun in a hospital, but a lay woman in her manor wielding the bones of a migrated martyr.

NOTES

1. Marie de l'Incarnation, *Correspondance*, ed. Dom Guy Oury (Solesmes: Abbaye Saint-Pierre, 1971), 667–68.

2. Archives des Augustines du Monastère de l'Hôtel-Dieu de Québec, *Chroniques de l'Hôtel-Dieu de Québec*, vol. 2, 1639–1958, 153.

3. Marie de l'Incarnation, *Correspondance*, 813–15. It is surprising that the demoniac was not considered dangerous. The order's constitution of 1631 specifies that if someone has a "mal dangereux" or a "frenesie naturelle," they cannot be admitted. Rénald Lessard, *Au temps de la Petite Vérole: La médecine au Canada aux XVIIe et XVIIIe siècles* (Québec: Septentrion, 2012), 210.

4. Marie de l'Incarnation, *Correspondance*, 667–68; Lucien Campeau, S.I., ed., *Monumenta Novae Franciae (MNF)* IX (Montréal: Éditions Bellarmin, 2003), 630, 638.

5. Regnouard's actions are vividly presented in three unpublished documents. One, conserved in the Archives des Augustines du Monastère de l'Hôtel-Dieu de Québec (A.M.H.D.Q.), was signed by Marie Regnouard at Beauport on 25 February 1663, and the other two, conserved in the Archives des Jésuites au Canada (A.S.J.C.F.), were signed by Regnouard at Beauport on 8 March 1663. All three are nearly identical on most points (although with some different spellings and a few different words), and each is written from the first-person perspective of Regnouard. The Jesuit Archive versions also contain additional material in a second section appended on 9 April 1663. A.M.H.D.Q., "Recit du Soulagement d'une possedée par l'Entremise des Reliques du R. P. Jean de Breboeuf dheureuse et saincte memoire"; A.S.J.C.F. Q-0001, 251.Il, "Recit de la Deliurance D'une possedée par l'entremise des reliques du deffunct R. P. Jean de Breboeu[f] d'heureuse et sainte memoire."

6. A.M.H.D.Q., "Recit du Soulagement d'une possedée par l'Entremise des Reliques du R. P. Jean de Breboeuf dheureuse et saincte memoire"; A.S.J.C.F. Q-0001, 251.Il, "Recit de la Deliurance D'une possedée par l'entremise des reliques du deffunct R. P. Jean de Breboeu[f] d'heureuse et sainte memoire."

7. Robert-Lionel Séguin, *La Sorcellerie au Québec du XVIIe au XIXe siècle* (Ottawa: Leméac, 1978), 25–30.

8. Jonathan L. Pearl, "Witchcraft in New France in the Seventeenth Century: The Social Aspect," *Historical Reflections/Réflexions Historiques* 4, no. 2 (1977): 41–55; Marie-Aimée Cliche, *Les pratiques de dévotion en Nouvelle-France: Comportements populaires et encadrement ecclésial dans le gouvernement de Québec* (Québec: Les Presses de l'Université Laval, 1988), 69–72.

9. Timothy G. Pearson, "'I Willingly Speak to You about Her Virtues': Catherine de Saint-Augustin and the Public Role of Female Holiness in Early New France," *Church History* 79, no. 2 (June 2010): 305–33.

10. André Cellard, *Histoire de la folie au Québec de 1600 à 1850* (Montréal: Boréal, 1991), 24, 49–50.

11. Leslie Choquette, "From Sea Monsters and Savages to Sorcerers and Satan: A History of Fear in New France," in *Fear and the Shaping of Early American Societies*, ed. Lauric Henneton and L. H. Roper (Leiden: Brill, 2016), 53–59.

12. Exceptions include an editorial note for the "Journal des Jésuites 1660" in the *Momumenta Novae Franciae*, which says that "Un récit de Marie Renouard, dame de Beauport, éclairera cette affaire." See *MNF* IX, 526 n. 47. Julia Boss writes that "Marie Regnouard of Beauport was able to exorcise a demon from her servant Barbe Hallay" using a rib bone of Jean de Brébeuf, "Writing a Relic: The Uses of

A Deliverance from Demons

Hagiography in New France," in *Colonial Saints: Discovering the Holy in the Americas, 1500-1800*, ed. Allan Greer and Jodi Bilinkoff (New York: Routledge, 2003), 225; and Timothy G. Pearson's *Becoming Holy in Early Canada* (Montréal: McGill-Queen's University Press, 2014), 235, which in an endnote mentions the copy at the Jesuit archives that "suggests that Barbe Hallay was exorcised by a laywoman." None of these publications mentions the copy at the Hôtel-Dieu.

13. For a sample of how scholars have traced continuities and changes in beliefs about witches and the devil as they moved across the Atlantic in British and Spanish colonies, see Jon Butler, *Awash in a Sea of Faith: Christianizing the American People* (Cambridge, MA: Harvard University Press, 1990); Elaine Braslaw, *Tituba, Reluctant Witch of Salem: Devilish Indians and Puritan Fantasies* (New York: New York University Press, 1996); Mary Beth Norton, *In the Devil's Snare: The Salem Witchcraft Crisis of 1692* (New York: Vintage Books, 2003); Fernando Cervantes, *The Devil in the New World: The Impact of Diabolism in New Spain* (New Haven, CT: Yale University Press, 1994); Laura A. Lewis, *Hall of Mirrors: Power, Witchcraft, and Caste in Colonial Mexico* (Durham, NC: Duke University Press, 2003).

14. There is not much evidence of the transoceanic administration that Kenneth J. Banks sees as essential to the slightly later creation of a "French Atlantic." Banks highlights not only a desire on the part of the metropolis to reshape the colony, but also the efficient gathering and transporting of information, and even the metropolitan understanding that local people in the colonies had to be heard when providing the necessary information. *Chasing Empire across the Sea: Communications and the State in the French Atlantic, 1713-1763* (Montréal: McGill-Queen's University Press, 2002).

15. A.M.H.D.Q., *Chroniques de l'Hôtel-Dieu de Québec, vol. 2, 1639-1958*, 153.

16. Paul Ragueneau, *La vie de la mère Catherine de Saint-Augustin: Religieuse hospitalière de la misericorde de la Québec en la Nouvelle-France* (Paris: Chez Florentin Lambert, 1671), 163.

17. Marie de l'Incarnation, *Correspondance*, 886-87. Possession was generally seen as a demon's seizure of a person's body from within, whereas obsession was a form of demonic attack from outside. Sarah Ferber, *Demonic Possession and Exorcism in Early Modern France* (London: Routledge, 2004), 25; Brian P. Levack, *The Devil Within: Possession and Exorcism in the Christian West* (New Haven, CT: Yale University Press, 2013), 16-17. In his biography of Catherine de Saint-Augustin, Ragueneau explained the distinction by saying that with possession, the devil becomes the master of a person, taking away their thought and their freedom, speaking through the mouth of the possessed, and that with obsession, the person knows that their afflictions are caused by demons. Ragueneau, *Vie*, 172, discussed in Pearson, "'I Willingly Speak to You about Her Virtues,'" 317.

18. Disappointingly, the inventory does not supply the identity of the person receiving the items, nor the items' destination. It is undated, but it mentions episodes from 12 February to 15 March 1661, and therefore was likely compiled at about the time when Vuil was imprisoned. Archives du Séminaire de Québec (ASQ), Polygraphie 2, no 33, "Inventaires de toutes les pieces mentionées qui ont esté envoyées touchant les affaires qu'on a eu avec Mr. d'Argenson," transcribed in Marcel Trudel, *Histoire de la Nouvelle-France III: La seigneurie des Cent-Associés 1627-1663, Tome 1: Les événements* (Montréal: Fides, 1979), 317-18.

19. Levack, *The Devil Within*, quotation on p. 29. See also viii-ix, 6-15, 29-30, 139-68.

20. Sharon T. Strocchia, "Women on the Edge: Madness, Possession, and Suicide in Early Modern Convents," *Journal of Medieval and Early Modern Studies* 45, no. 1 (2015): 53-77; Levack, *The Devil Within*, 23-26; and Ferber, *Demonic Possession and Exorcism in Early Modern France*, 10-11, 17.

21. Levack, *The Devil Within*, 170–84, 191–93; Ferber, *Demonic Possession and Exorcism in Early Modern France*, 26, 115–17.

22. William Monter, "Witchcraft Trials in France," in *The Oxford Handbook of Witchcraft in Early Modern Europe and Colonial America*, ed. Brian P. Levack (Oxford: Oxford University Press, 2013), 218–31; Paul Freedman, "The Miller," in *Historians on Chaucer: The "General Prologue" to the Canterbury Tales* (Oxford: Oxford University Press, 2014), 373–74.

23. Marie de l'Incarnation, *Correspondance*, 667–68.

24. Sarah Ferber "Demonic Possession, Exorcism, and Witchcraft," in *The Oxford Handbook of Witchcraft in Early Modern Europe and Colonial America*, 575–92.

25. In both the 1666 and 1667 censuses her age is given as twenty, and in the 1681 census it is given as thirty-six. See "Recensement du Canada," 1666, 13, mf. roll F-765, Library and Archives of Canada (LAC), Ottawa, Canada; "Recensement du Canada," 1667, 61, mf. roll F-765, LAC. Paul Ragueneau, in his biography of Catherine de Saint-Augustin, said Hallay was sixteen: *Vie*, 164. According to these documents, she would have been born between 1645 and 1647, making her between twelve and fifteen years old at the time of her arrival. Marcel Trudel places her age at twelve in *Catalogue des immigrants 1632–1662* (Montréal: Hurtubise, 1983), 403. Women's age at first marriage was younger than in Europe at the time, with most marrying between the ages of fourteen and twenty-three. For women, the median age at first marriage was twenty and for men it was twenty-eight. Males married particularly between twenty-two and thirty-two. Hubert Charbonneau, Bertrand Desjardins, André Guillemette, Yves Landry, Jacques Légaré, and François Nault, *The First French Canadians: Pioneers in the St. Lawrence Valley* (Newark: University of Delaware Press, 1993), 97–100.

26. Notwithstanding changes to the law, some couples still celebrated their weddings privately, or began their sexual relationship after the marriage contract was signed or a verbal agreement was made but before the wedding itself. Merry Wiesner-Hanks, *Christianity and Sexuality in the Early Modern World: Regulating Desire, Reforming Practice* (London: Routledge, 2010), 134–35, 151–54; Suzanne Desan, "Making and Breaking Marriage: An Overview of Old Regime Marriage as a Social Practice," in *Family, Gender, and Law in Early Modern France* (University Park: Pennsylvania State University Press, 2009), 1–3; François Lebrun, "Amour et mariage," in *Histoire de la population française*, vol. 2, *De la Renaissance à 1789*, ed. Jacques Dupâquier (Paris: Presses Universitaires de France, 1988), 294–317.

27. Hallay and her family arrived toward the end of a period of rising migration from France, but the French population in the colony had still reached only perhaps 1,700. Leaders of the colony hoped for a rise in population and put in place policies and incentives to bring this about both through immigration and through natural increase, but New France remained a notoriously unattractive destination for French migrants. By 1663, the French population of New France had risen to a little over three thousand, with almost two hundred in the region of Québec. Leslie Choquette, *Frenchmen into Peasants: Modernity and Tradition in the Peopling of French Canada* (Cambridge, MA: Harvard University Press, 1997), 165; Marcel Trudel, *Beginnings of New France, 1524–1663* (Toronto: McClelland & Stewart, 1973), 256–57; Charbonneau et al., *The First French Canadians*, 34–36; Raymond Roy and Hubert Charbonneau, "La nuptualité en situation de déséquilibre des Sexes: Le Canada du XVIIe siècle," *Annales de démographie historique* (1978): 285. On the difficulties of attracting migrants and keeping them in Canada, see Peter N. Moogk, "Reluctant Exiles: Emigrants from France in Canada before 1760," *William and Mary Quarterly* 46, no. 3 (1989): 463–505; Marie-Ève Ouellet, "Un pouvoir

de remplacement: Les enjeux féminins de la migration de retour au Canada sous le Régime Français," in *Femmes, cultures et pouvoir: Relectures de l'histoire au féminin, XVe-XXe siècles*, ed. Catherine Ferland and Benoît Grenier (Québec: Les Presses de l'Université Laval, 2010), 145–68.

28. Charbonneau et al., *The First French Canadians*, 65, 79–83, 187.

29. Desan, "Making and Breaking Marriage," 9, 11.

30. Marie de l'Incarnation, *Correspondance*, 813.

31. Ragueneau, *Vie*, 163–64.

32. The phrasing makes it unclear whether trading in liquor was the reason for the execution of only another prisoner named la Violette, or for the execution of both him and Vuil. In the margin next to this entry, it says "Executions pour la traite," but this annotation is written in a different hand and with a different ink than the main body of the text, which says "Le .7. Daniel Vvil pendu ou plustost arquebusé; & le .11. vn autre nommé la violette; & vn f8eté le Lundy. 10. p^r auoir traité aux sauuages de l'eau de vie." A semicolon seems to appear after "arquebusé" in the original manuscript but is not included in either the 1871 edition or the *MNF*. Archives du Séminaire de Québec, MS-48, Journal des Jésuites 154, 158; *Journal des Jésuites* (Québec: Léger Brousseau), 1871, 303; *MNF IX*: 630, 638.

33. The entry on Vuil by André Vachon in the *Dictionnaire Biographique du Canada* says that Vuil was possibly imprisoned for trading alcohol, and that "it was unquestionably 'for trafficking in spirits with the Indians'" that Vuil was executed. André Vachon, "Vuil, Daniel," in *Dictionaire Biographique du Canada*, vol. 1 (Toronto: University of Toronto Press, 1986), 165. Gustave Lanctôt thought that Vuil was arrested for relapsing into heresy, that he left prison, and was subsequently re-arrested for trade in alcohol. Gustave Lanctôt, "Une accusation contre Mgr de Laval," *Rapport* 1944–45, 11–25. Raymond Boyer wrote that Vuil was imprisoned under an accusation of magic, witchcraft, and profaning of the sacraments, but that he was shot for having violated the ordinance against trading alcohol with Indigenous people. Raymond Boyer, *Les Crimes et les Châtiments au Canada français du XVIIe au XXe siècle* (Montréal : Le Cercle du Livre de France, 1966), 297.

34. Trudel, *Histoire de la Nouvelle-France*, vol. 3, tome 1, 316–19; Vincent Grégoire, "Le meunier, la domestique, et l'hospitalière: entre magie, 'possession,' et 'obsession' en Nouvelle-France au 17ième siècle," *Cahiers* XIII, no. 1 (2010): 72–76; Peter Moogk finds that the execution was by hanging, and that the crimes were blasphemy, profaning of holy objects, and providing liquor to Indigenous people. Peter Moogk, "The Crime of Lèse-Majesté in New France: Defence of the Secular and Religious Order," in *Canadian State Trials Volume I: Law, Politics, and Security Measures, 1608–1837*, ed. F. Murray Greenwood and Barry Wright (Toronto: University of Toronto Press for the Osgoode Society for Canadian Legal History, 1996), 67. The editor of the *Monumenta Novae Franciae* concluded that the means of Vuil's execution—that is, shot by arquebus—was because he had been a soldier, and that the reason for his execution was not for trading eau-de-vie, which would have been too severe a punishment for the crime, but perhaps was Vuil's relapse into heresy. Leslie Choquette determines that he was shot, the only person in New France to have been executed for sorcery. Choquette, *Frenchmen into Peasants*, 131; Choquette, "From Sea Monsters and Savages to Sorcerers and Satan," 55–56.

35. Trade in liquor was the subject of an ongoing dispute between religious and civil authorities at high levels. The governor tolerated it, but the bishop opposed the practice and wrote that it not only led to public scandal, but also put all Christianity in danger of total ruin. *Mandements, lettres pastorales et circulaires des évêques de Québec*, publiés par H. Têtu et C. O. Gagnon, volume premier (Québec:

Imprimerie Générale, 1887), 14–15, 30–32, 40, 41–42, 43–44; Trudel, *Histoire de la Nouvelle-France*, 308–16, 323–30.

36. Charbonneau et al., *The First French Canadians*, 90.

37. Hallay did eventually marry, but not until 1671. She took as her spouse Jean Carrier, a worker at the Hôtel-Dieu, and they established a successful habitant farm—an improved parcel of land, usually in the St. Lawrence River Valley, on which a single *habitant* family grew both subsistence and commercial crops—on a seigneurie across the river from Québec.

38. *Édits, ordonnances royaux, déclarations et arrêts du Conseil d'État du roi, concernant le Canada* (Québec: Imprimés par P. E. Desbarats, 1803), I: 1, 7; Marc-André Bédard, *Les Protestants en Nouvelle-France* (Québec: La société historique de Québec, 1978), 20.

39. Bédard, *Les Protestants en Nouvelle-France*, 25–30; Choquette, *Frenchmen into Peasants*, 149. In his investigation into the successes and failures of tradesmen, J. F. Bosher has found only a few cases of "religious discrimination directly damaging a merchant's business," although he suspects that such discrimination may have been quite fundamental in determining merchants' success and failure. "Success and Failure in Trade to New France, 1660–1760," *French Historical Studies* 15, no. 3 (1988): 457–58.

40. *Marguerite Bourgeoys, Textes choisis et présentés par Hélène Bernier* (Montréal: Fides, 1958), 35–36.

41. The oath is recorded in the Archives de l'Archidiocèse de Québec, "Registre des abjurations d'heresie depuis 1662 jusqu'à 1757"; and Bédard, *Les Protestants en Nouvelle-France*, 65–68.

42. Bédard, *Les Protestants en Nouvelle-France*, 28–29, 81.

43. Mairi Cowan, "Education, *Francisation*, and Shifting Colonial Priorities at the Ursuline Convent in Seventeenth-Century Québec," *Canadian Historical Review* 99, no. 1 (2018): 1–29; Saliha Belmessous, "Être français en Nouvelle-France: Identité française et identité coloniale aux dix-septième et dix-huitième siècles," *French Historical Studies* 27, no. 3 (2004): 510–515, 539; Gilles Havard, "'Les forcer à devenir Cytoyens': État, sauvages et citoyenneté en Nouvelle-France (XVIIe–XVIIIe siècle)," *Annales Histoire, Sciences Sociales* 64, no. 5 (2009): 989–1000; and Saliha Belmessous, *Assimilation and Empire: Uniformity in French and British Colonies, 1541–1954* (Oxford: Oxford University Press, 2013), 28–30.

44. Mairi Cowan, "Jesuit Missionaries and the Accommodationist Demons of New France," in *Knowing Demons, Knowing Spirits in the Early Modern Period (c. 1400–1750)*, ed. Michelle D. Brock, Richard Raiswell, and David R. Winter (Basingstoke: Palgrave Macmillan, 2018), 211–38.

45. *MNF* III, 51–52; Gilles Havard et Cécile Vidal, *Histoire de l'Amérique française* (Paris: Flammarion, 2014), 173–74; Brigitte Caulier, "'Bâtir la Jérusalem des Terres froides': Réflexion sur le catholicisme français en Nouvelle-France," in *Mémoires de Nouvelle-France: De France en Nouvelle-France*, ed. Philippe Joutard and Thomas Wien (Rennes: Presses universitaires de Rennes, 2005), 235–49.

46. Havard and Vidal, *Histoire de l'Amérique française*, 97; Gilles Havard, *The Great Peace of Montreal of 1701: French-Native Diplomacy in the Seventeenth Century* (Montréal: McGill-Queen's University Press, 2001), 47–50.

47. AMHDQ, *Chroniques de L'Hôtel-Dieu de Québec 1639–1958, Registre no. 2 Première Partie: 1639–1698*, 3–4, 8.

48. Archives des Ursulines de Québec, *Annales des Ursulines de Québec 1639–1822* 1/E, 1, 3, 2.0001, 12 v.

49. Marie de l'Incarnation, *Correspondance*, 619–21, 625. The *Journal des Jésuites* for May 1660 mentions the Ursulines and Hospitalières coming to the Jesuit College to sleep: *MNF* IX, 519.

50. Marie de l'Incarnation, *Correspondance*, 633–34.

51. Marie de l'Incarnation, *Correspondance*, 672.

52. *MNF IX*, 420–21.

53. Trudel, *Histoire de la Nouvelle-France*, 260; Daniel K. Richter, *The Ordeal of the Longhouse: The Peoples of the Iroquois League in the Era of European Expansion* (Chapel Hill: University of North Carolina Press, 1992), esp. 64–65; Yann Lignereux, "Une mission périlleuse ou le péril colonial jésuite dans la France de Louis XIV: Sainte-Marie des Iroquois (1649–1665)," *Revue d'histoire de l'Amérique française* 69, no. 4 (2016): 5–26. For discussions and estimates, see John A. Dickinson, "La guerre iroquoise et la mortalité en Nouvelle-France, 1608–1666," *Revue d'histoire de l'Amérique française* 36, no. 1 (1982): 31–54.

54. Luke Clossey, *Salvation and Globalization in the Early Jesuit Missions* (New York: Cambridge University Press, 2011), 130–31.

55. Ferber, *Demonic Possession and Exorcism in Early Modern France*, 3; Levack, *The Devil Within*, 100–105.

56. *Rituale Romanum, Editio Princeps (1614)* (Vatican: Libreria Editrice Vaticana, 2004), 206–27; Moshe Sluhovsky, *Believe Not Every Spirit: Possession, Mysticism, and Discernment in Early Modern Catholicism* (Chicago: University of Chicago Press, 2007), 91. In the 1658 edition of the Rituale Romanum held at the seminary archive, the section on exorcism does not show any obvious marks of use, unlike the section on baptism, which has drops of candle wax and damp-looking markings at the bottom crease where the book would have been held. It also contains on the inside of the front cover a list of some baptisms performed in the 1680s. Archives du Séminaire de Québec, *Rituale Romanum*, Venice 1658.

57. Sluhovsky, *Believe Not Every Spirit*, 91.

58. Levack, *The Devil Within*, 81.

59. Vincent Grégoire points out that Catherine de Saint-Augustin's actions are never described as an exorcism either. He makes no mention of the unpublished accounts in the Jesuit and Hôtel-Dieu archives, but his observation about terminology extends to these sources as well: "Le meunier, la domestique, et l'hospitalière," 82–84.

60. Sluhovsky, *Believe Not Every Spirit*, 37–38; Levack, *The Devil Within*, 94–97; Susan Broomhall, *Women's Medical Work in Early Modern France* (Manchester: Manchester University Press, 2004), 113; and Ferber, "Demonic Possession, Exorcism, and Witchcraft," 575–92.

61. *Rituale Romanum*, 206–27; Levack, *The Devil Within*, 63, 88–91.

62. Levack, *The Devil Within*, 97.

63. Pearson, *Becoming Holy in Early Canada*, 97.

64. Pearson, "'I Willingly Speak to You about Her Virtues,'" 311. See also Dominique Deslandres, "In the Shadow of the Cloister: Representations of Female Holiness in New France," in *Colonial Saints*, 131–33.

65. Joseph Besnard, "Les diverses professions de Robert Giffard," *Nova Francia* 4 (1929): 323; *Bulletin des recherches historiques*, 1903, vol. 1, 267–70; Françoise Montagne, "Du nouveau sur Robert Giffard, promoteur de l'émigration percheronne," *Cahiers percherons* 25 (1967): 29–30.

66. Montagne, "Du nouveau sur Robert Giffard," 27–28; Joseph Besnard, "Les préliminaires de l'Émigration percheronne," *Nova Francia* 5 (1930): 66–75.

67. He contracted with a master mason and master carpenter that they and their families would clear and cultivate the lands in return for travel expenses and all their necessities for at least three years, plus he would have houses built for their families. Besnard, "Les diverses professions de Robert Giffard," 327, and "Les préliminaires de l'Émigration percheronne," 68–70; and Michel Langlois, *Dictionnaire Biographique des Ancêtres Québécois (1608–1700), Tome II* (Sillery: La Maison des Ancêtres, 1999), 347–49.

68. Trudel, *Catalogue des immigrants 1632–1662*, 36.

69. Montagne, "Du nouveau sur Robert Giffard," 32, 34.

70. *MNF* III, 31; Benoît Grenier, *Seigneurs campagnards de la Nouvelle France: Présence seigneuriale et sociabilité rurale dans la vallée du Saint-Laurent à l'époque préindustrielle* (Rennes: Presses Universitaires de Rennes, 2007), 280.

71. "on donna à madame Giffar de l'estoffe noire de vieille sotanne pour doubler des manches" *MNF* VI, 424.

72. Jan Noel, *Along a River: The First French Canadian Women* (Toronto: University of Toronto Press, 2013), 34; For women's medical practice as household skill in New England, see Rebecca J. Tannenbaum, *The Healer's Calling: Women and Medicine in Early New England* (Ithaca, NY: Cornell University Press, 2002), 19–22, 31.

73. "Medical practitioners" is being used here as it was by Margaret Pelling and Charles Webster in their study of London and Norwich in the sixteenth century, where they defined "medical practitioner" as "any individual whose occupation is basically concerned with the care of the sick." *Health, Medicine and Mortality in the Sixteenth Century*, ed. Charles Webster (Cambridge: Cambridge University Press, 1979), 166. See also Monica Green, "Women's Medical Practice and Health Care in Medieval Europe," *Signs* 14, no. 2 (1989): 444–46. Thank you to Catherine Pimentel for this reference.

74. Montagne, "Du nouveau sur Robert Giffard," 29.

75. Besnard, "Les préliminaires de l'Émigration percheronne," 74, and "Les diverses professions de Robert Giffard," 322–29; and Montagne, "Du nouveau sur Robert Giffard," 29–31.

76. *MNF* V, 388; *MNF* VII, 225; Lessard, *Au temps de la Petite Vérole*, 203; Trudel, *Catalogue des immigrants 1632–1662*, 35–36; Alfred Cambray, *Robert Giffard: Premier seigneur de Beauport et les origines de la Nouvelle-France* (Cap de la Madelaine, 1932), 187–88; Pierre-Georges Roy, *A travers l'histoire de l'Hôtel-Dieu de Québec* (Lévis, 1939), 29; Thomas-Edmond Giroux, *Robert Giffard Seigneur colonisateur au Tribunal de l'histoire, ou La raison de fêter le troisième centenaire de Beauport 1634–1934* (Québec: L'action Sociale, 1934); Montagne, "Du nouveau sur Robert Giffard," 33. François Rousseau says Giffard was a surgeon in *La Croix et le scalpel: Histoire des Augustines et de l'Hôtel-Dieu de Québec I: 1639–1892* (Sillery: Septentrion, 1989), 100. The *Dictionary of Canadian Biography* says that in 1640 he became the first doctor in the Hôtel-Dieu, an apothecary, and held the honorary title of "doctor in ordinary" to the king. Honorius Provost, "Giffard de Moncel, Robert," in *Dictionary of Canadian Biography*, vol. 1. Lessard says that Giffard was both surgeon and physician, but not one with a degree from a faculty of medicine and was rather a surgeon by training: *Au temps de la Petite Vérole*, 203–4, 224–25.

77. *MNF* V, 81, 108.

78. AMHDQ, *Chroniques de L'Hôtel-Dieu de Québec 1639–1958, Registre no. 2 Première Partie: 1639–1698*, 1, 17, 32, 90–91, 151. Terrence Crowley has argued that a religious life in New France offered protection, service to others, and an ordered existence with self-direction in daily life. Terrence Crowley,

"Women, Religion and Freedom in New France," in *Race and Gender in the Northern Colonies*, ed. Jan Noel (Toronto: Canadian Scholars' Press, 2000), 101–18.

79. Lessard, *Au temps de la Petite Vérole*, 20.

80. Montserrat Cabré, "Women or Healers? Household Practices and the Categories of Health Care in Late Medieval Iberia," *Bulletin of the History of Medicine* 82, no. 1 (2008): 18–51; and Gianna Pomata, "Practicing between Earth and Heaven: Women Healers in Seventeenth-Century Bologna," *Dynamis* 19 (1999): 119–43.

81. Mary E. Fissell, "Women, Health, and Healing in Early Modern Europe," *Bulletin of the History of Medicine* 82, no. 1 (Spring 2008): 10–11.

82. Fissell, "Women, Health, and Healing in Early Modern Europe," 1–17.

83. Allan Greer, "Women of New France," in *Race and Gender in the Northern Colonies*, 88–90; Noel, *Along a River*; and Leslie Choquette, "'Ces Amazones du Grand Dieu': Women and Mission in Seventeenth-Century Canada," *French Historical Studies* 17 (Spring 1992): 632, 654. See also Pearson, "'I Willingly Speak to You about Her Virtues,'" 305–33; Deslandres, "In the Shadow of the Cloister," 135–37; Choquette, "From Sea Monsters and Savages to Sorcerers and Satan," 57–58; and Natalie Zemon Davis, *Women on the Margins: Three Seventeenth-Century Lives* (Cambridge, MA: Harvard University Press, 1995), 63–139.

84. For a variety of views on whether Jesuits in New France believed that demons were present in Indigenous societies, for example, see Peter Goddard, "The Devil in New France: Jesuit Demonology, 1611–1650," *Canadian Historical Review* 78, no.1 (March 1997): 40–62; Luke Clossey, *Salvation and Globalization in the Early Jesuit Missions* (New York: Cambridge University Press, 2011), 130–31; Dominique Deslandres, *Croire et faire croire: Les missions françaises au XVIIe siècle* (Paris: Fayard, 2003), 437–45; Cowan, "Jesuit Missionaries and the Accommodationist Demons of New France."

85. Marie de l'Incarnation, *Correspondance*, 813–15.

86. ASJCF Q-0001, 251.Il, "Recit de la Deliurance D'une possedée par l'entremise des reliques du deffunct R. P. Jean de Breboeu[f] d'heureuse et sainte memoire."

87. "ce saint homme qui a répandu son sang pour le soutien de la foy en ce païs." See Emma Anderson, *The Death and Afterlife of the North American Martyrs* (Cambridge, MA: Harvard University Press, 2013), 21–53, and James Taylor Carson, "Brébeuf Was Never Martyred: Reimagining the Life and Death of Canada's First Saint," *Canadian Historical Review* 97, no. 2 (2016): 222–43, for discussions of Brébeuf's martyrdom as a model death both for European Catholics and for the Wendat.

88. Allan Greer, "Colonial Saints: Gender, Race, and Hagiography in New France," *William and Mary Quarterly* 57, no. 2 (2000): 33–35.

89. Ragueneau, *Vie*, 362; and Reuben Gold Thwaites, ed., *The Jesuit Relations and Allied Documents*, volume 50 (Cleveland, OH: Burrows Brothers, 1899), 87–89.

90. AJC-GLC, Q0001, D320, discussed in Nicholas Overgaard and Mairi Cowan, "A 'Very Particular Assistance' from Jean de Brébeuf: Opium, Relics, and a Cure for Phrénésie in Seventeenth-Century New France," *Findings/Trouvailles* (June 2017).

91. Anderson, *The Death and Afterlife*, 55–57, 63–65, 70–72.

92. On the eve of Epiphany, 1646, Giffard gave them a bottle of spiced wine. *MNF* VI, 695. See also *MNF* VIII 158 for when he gave a gift of capons, and *MNF* VIII 157 for when he and Marie Regnouard received a gift from the Jesuits.

93. "Recensement du Canada," 1666, "Recensement du Canada," 1667, "Recensement du Canada," 1681, LAC; A.M.H.D.Q., "Recettes et Depenses de l'Hôtel-Dieu de Québec 1665 à 1725," 72.

94. AJC-GLC, Q0001, D320; Overgaard and Cowan, "A 'Very Particular Assistance' from Jean de Brébeuf."

95. "plusieurs femmes fort incommodées d'un mal qui course ordinairement en Canada": ASQ Paroisses Diverses No. 84, XIV; Mary Corley Dunn, "The Miracles at Sainte-Anne-du-Petit-Cap and the Making of a Seventeenth-Century Colonial Community," *Canadian Historical Review* 91, no. 4 (2010): 611–35.

Mask of the Colonizer
French Men, Native Passions, and the Culture of Diplomacy in New France

WILLIAM BROWN

In August of 1690, Louis de Buade de Frontenac, governor-general of New France, addressed an urgent council of more than five hundred Native emissaries at Montréal. The French were at war with the joint forces of colonial New England and the Five Nations of the Iroquois Confederacy—the Oneida, Mohawk, Onondaga, Cayuga, and Seneca—and he hoped to persuade his Odawa, Wabanaki, Wendat (Huron), Nipissing, and Mission Iroquois allies to launch a surprise attack on the Confederacy's homelands in western New York.[1] As Onontio, or "Great Mountain," the governor embodied the dynamic ritual persona through which French officials and Native communities had negotiated relations with each other for nearly half a century. In the Aboriginal language of kinship that underpinned their diplomacy, he held the fictive status of "father" to his Indigenous "children"—a role that entitled him not to command obedience in the manner typical of fathers in France, but rather to invite his allies to hear him speak, to provide them with gifts and protection, and, if they were so inclined, to mobilize them for battle.[2] Yet Frontenac already knew his listeners were dubious. In recent years the French had failed repeatedly to shield their allies and even their own settlements from Iroquois raids, and now some headmen openly wondered: did Onontio truly want war, or would he abandon them for a separate peace at the first opportunity?[3]

As the governor concluded his speech with an impassioned call to arms—"I now put the war hatchet [*casse-tête*] back in your hands... & I have no doubt that you will know what to do with it!"—he sensed that words and gifts alone would not dispel their doubts. Offering the *casse-tête* with great fanfare in the midst of the council represented a familiar symbolic request to make war against a common enemy, but as Frontenac knew, the decision to accept or reject it rested entirely with his allies, who might well decide that peace better served their interests if he did not convince them otherwise.[4] "They asked me to explain myself clearly," he reported afterward, "which I did ... by taking up the tomahawk myself and singing the war song, in order to accommodate their way of doing things."[5] The colonial official and chronicler Claude-Charles Le Roy de La Potherie later described the scene:

> Monsieur de Frontenac, Hatchet in hand, began the War song; the principal French Leaders, with similar weapons, joined him, [and] all sang it together. The [Mission] Iroquois ... the Hurons & the Nippissings also joined the sway. One would have said ... that these Actors were possessed by the gestures & the contortions that they were making. The *Sassagouez*, or cries & howls, that Monsieur de Frontenac was obliged to make in order to conform to their ways, added still further to the Dionysian fury. Then they held the war Feast, which was more of a pillage than a meal.[6]

In La Potherie's telling, the French used what they knew of the *casse-tête* and other Indigenous customs to produce "gestures & contortions ... cries & howls" convincing enough not just to incite the Natives to war, but even to persuade a European observer that the "Actors" themselves were "possessed" by a "Dionysian fury" of their own making. To stir their allies' passions, he claimed, Frontenac and his officers were "obliged" to "conform to their ways."

This essay examines how the embodiment of Onontio drew together two branches of learning: the administrative ethnography of Indigenous peoples and the performance of Native passions. To French officials, Natives became both objects of study whose customs could be defined and routine interlocutors whose feelings must be "managed" in face-to-face settings. Securing their compliance seemed to require not only a working knowledge of their traditions and values but also a diplomatic persona whose deportment would inspire their respect and affection. In their efforts to understand and influence Indigenous peoples, aristocratic officers fused habits of performance nurtured in metropolitan schoolrooms and in public life with the expertise of missionaries and non-elite go-betweens who had lived among Natives and knew—or claimed to know—how to accommodate them. The unfamiliar demands of Indigenous diplomacy encouraged them to observe Natives closely, to record their customs, and to construct an essential idea of their character that might be used to better convert, convince, or control them. In short, by embracing the indigenized persona assigned to them by their allies, the French made both "knowing" Indians and performing "Indianness" central to the governance of their North American empire.

Performances such as Frontenac's counter familiar narratives about the fluidity, hybridity, and creolization of French identity in colonial spaces.[7] In recent decades, the "Frenchness" of historical writing about New France has waxed and waned and waxed again.[8] Scholars of late have sought to reincorporate Old World practices and preconceptions into the history of encounters, balancing metropolitan and imperial perspectives with local and ethnohistorical approaches to produce more dynamic, unfolding, and interrelated accounts of French-Indigenous relations.[9] Yet too much emphasis on the ways in which cultural mobility promoted mutual borrowing or *métissage* risks obscuring the meaningful circumstances where it did not.[10] In certain cases, such as those of Marie de l'Incarnation and Georges-Henri-Victor Collot explored elsewhere in this volume, the experience of empire served to reinforce emerging notions of Frenchness that defined non-Europeans as colonized Others.[11] How do we account for such a disparate range of individual and collective responses?[12] In this context, historians would do better to "[reconstruct] individual cultural adaptations" on their own terms, "without any forced recourse to identity."[13]

In the case of those French who, like Frontenac, accommodated Indigenous customs strategically and selectively, *persona* (literally: "mask") offers a more useful analytical concept than identity. As shorthand for an alter ego temporarily assumed to achieve a social or political end—as opposed to a more or less cohesive and abiding interior sense of self—persona aptly captures the tendency of seventeenth-century Europeans to define themselves by the scrutiny of others.[14] Leading royal administrators quite consciously adjusted their speech and behavior to appeal to Indigenous audiences, but their conformity to Native norms did not amount to lasting identification or even acceptance; rather, it was instrumental and often begrudging.[15] To exercise some measure of influence over their powerful but alien allies, the king's men learned to imitate them. In doing so, they extended an aristocratic habit of performance rooted in Old World practices of rhetoric, drama, dance, diplomacy, and courtly dissimulation to the New World. Their performances show how the incoherence of individual "selves" split between French and Amerindian personae could act as a force of cultural and imperial cohesion.[16]

The strategic adoption of Native customs was vital because no other European empire depended more heavily upon Indigenous allies than France. The French were never able or willing to establish a large settler colony in the New World, nor did they ever subjugate or assimilate more than a handful of Native people. By maintaining a delicate suite of alliances with the Iroquoian- and Algonquian-speaking peoples of the Great Lakes and the St. Lawrence Valley, however, officials in New France were able, for a time, to project an imperial presence that stretched from Biloxi to Hudson's Bay and from Acadia to the Mississippi Basin—challenging the more populous British colonies along the Atlantic coast for access to the peoples, furs, and territories of the North American interior.[17] If negotiators exercised some agency in determining the nature and extent of their accommodations, their alliances were nonetheless forged according to diplomatic protocols that were fundamentally Indigenous.[18] As a result, their survival rested in large part upon the ability of French officers to perform the ritual roles given to them by their allies.[19]

Strategic imitation did not mean successful manipulation. Successive wars with the Haudenosaunee (Iroquois) and Mesquakie (Fox) were too multifaceted, and the French too weak or inflexible or underinformed, for even the most competent diplomacy to realize once and for all the Crown's vaunting ambitions to defeat the Five Nations, dominate the fur trade, and isolate the English along the Atlantic seaboard. French strategy mattered, but its aims could be achieved only with a combination of good fortune and Indigenous collaboration—and even then only briefly. French negotiators, moreover, could not always reconcile royal policy or their own self-interest with the competing agendas of their allies (which, however difficult to extract from French sources, were plainly just as various and changing). In examining diplomatic performances in this period, the following pages will explain not how France's diplomacy succeeded or failed, but how officials constructed, deployed, and disseminated an administrative ethnography they believed necessary to accommodate the Native "way of doing things" in their encounters.[20]

The New World Is a Stage

Well before they arrived on American shores, French administrators were extensively trained in the play of personae. Indeed, personation and identification were fixtures of life in the aristocratic social circles from which most royal officers came.[21] In the Jesuit *collèges* and seminaries that many of them attended, they learned to debate both sides of any question, and they were enjoined, following Cicero, to move their listeners by first feeling themselves what they would have others feel.[22] Schooling in rhetoric "[transported] them to other countries and other times," where an orator's gestures and expression were as important as his words, since "gestures are understood by all nations."[23] The animating principle behind classical oratory was that a good speaker crafts every phrase and every movement to the visceral needs and passions of his listeners. In imitating the style of ancient orators, *collégiens* practiced persuasion "much less by the truth of the facts ... than by a sort of charismatic momentum, one would almost say drunkenness."[24] Like the "Dionysian fury" incited by Frontenac and his men, this "charismatic momentum" was calculated to win the hearts of those who could not be swayed by words alone. The same principles applied to lessons in drama, where pupils learned to experience vicariously the inner lives of characters both ancient and modern, to convey their emotions believably, and to see their positive and negative qualities as models for action.[25] Jesuit pedagogues considered such performative skills essential to young men who would one day be leaders: "Whereas an ordinary peasant is nearly invisible to society," the thinking went, "to be a leader is to be looked up to and therefore to be looked *at*, to be scrutinized, by those one leads."[26]

The studied play of affect and persuasion in the *collèges* thus aimed to prepare young noblemen for the everyday demands of public life. The social and political legitimacy of aristocratic power turned upon the possession of honor, and honor was something claimed and contested in a variety of "scripted" performances ranging from duels and almsgiving to deathbed confessions.[27] In an increasingly stratified society where status was measured by ritualized courtesies exchanged or withheld in face-to-face encounters, hiding one's true feelings behind a polite façade became a practiced art. The noble culture of performance may have reached its apogee at Louis XIV's court, where increasingly baroque codes of courtesy were enforced under pain of social exclusion and political isolation.[28] But masters of etiquette insisted that flexibly adapting one's deportment was a skill that applied everywhere.[29] Like dance—another realm of social discourse drilled into young noblemen from an early age—courtesy was an embodied art that at once cultivated and displayed all of the classical virtues of serenity, *grandeur*, and self-possession associated with good breeding, and elite men were expected to exercise it before all manner of people wherever their duties might take them.[30]

It made perfect sense to think of public life as a stage because contemporaries considered the "real" world to be a mere sideshow to the more profound reality of an existence governed by God. To elites who understood this life to be transient and illusory, theatrical metaphors captured the deceptive shallowness of temporal affairs. The very elements of Baroque drama that so appealed to aristocratic audiences—masks and costumes, metamorphoses, mistaken identities, deceit, clothing switches, trompe l'oeil, double entendre, and plays-within-the-play—at once reflected and reinforced a widespread belief that the things of this world obscured the underlying "truth" of the next. According to churchmen and moralists, the knowledge that everything around him was simply appearance liberated the Christian from attachment to this life and helped him to move more effectively through it, just as the consciousness of the actor that he was acting allowed him to perform his role all the more convincingly.[31]

The same theatrical worldview underpinned conventional ideas about politics and diplomacy. François de Callières—Louis XIV's private secretary, a seasoned diplomat, and brother of Frontenac's successor as governor, Louis-Hector de Callières (1698–1703)—described the ideal ambassador as one who "resembles in a way the Actor, exposed upon the stage before the eyes of the Public to play great roles." Diplomatic ceremonies were "plays," he continued, in which ambassadors represented "the *personnage* of the king."[32] According to Callières, "a negotiator ... must know how to accommodate himself to [the humors and fancies] of others; may he be like Proteus ... always ready to assume all sorts of figures according to the needs of the moment."[33] The notion that diplomatic success hinged on the protean flair of ambassadors was shared by the rhetorician and royal historiographer Jean de Lartigue, whose *La politique des conquérants* numbered among the books Frontenac kept in his library. If the governor read it, he would have learned that France's destiny as a universal empire depended upon men like himself, who could "assume different faces and represent diverse personae" in the course of their negotiations: "[The diplomat] will consider the nature of the people & the Nation with whom he negotiates. ... He will study their humor to accommodate himself to their inclinations."[34]

The leading officers who served in North America were hardly untouched by these cultural currents. Many of them had received training in classical oratory, either directly from the *collèges* or the seminary at Québec, or indirectly through their close collaborations with Jesuit missionaries (more on the missionary influence below). Most of them were veterans of the court, knew its protocols, and had participated in its festivities. They generally obtained their appointments after long careers of administrative, diplomatic, or military service in Europe.[35] In North

America, where they and other observers frequently compared Native song and dance to balls, ballets, and opera, the appropriation of Indigenous rhythms of movement as political spectacle would have seemed only natural.[36] The *récits de voyage,* missionary epistles, and other printed exotica that comprised much of their reading often represented the New World as a stage, to the point that one leading specialist has dubbed these works a "theater" whose literary conventions hewed closely to those of Baroque drama.[37]

From the earliest years of colonization, moreover, New France itself was both a site and a subject of theater. In 1606 the lawyer and poet Marc Lescarbot celebrated the safe return of Samuel de Champlain and Governor Jean de Poutrincourt to Port Royal, Acadia, by staging a nautical masque, in which four costumed "*sauvages,*" mimicking the pageantry of royal entry ceremonies, recognized the sovereignty of the French over their people.[38] Three decades later Governor Charles Huault de Montmagny brought the stage to Québec, where his secretary played the starring role in a "Tragi-comedy" whose demon characters spoke Algonquin (the better to "strike [the Natives'] eyes and their ears").[39] When Governor Pierre de Voyer d'Argenson arrived to assume his post in 1658, he visited the Jesuit seminary where a schoolboy, the future magistrate René-Louis Chartier de Lotbinière, improvised a play in the role of "the spirit of the forests, the interpreter for the foreigners."[40] Governor Jacques-René de Brisay de Denonville later joked that a box of "Eskimo clothing" he sent to the navy minister was "fit for a masquerade."[41] The syncretic thrust of these performances (and imagined performances) is a reminder that one of the chief aims of early modern theater was to translate seemingly universal human experiences across lines of cultural difference. By representing Europe to itself through a "savage mirror," colonial officers, like contemporary dramatists, questioned what it meant to be civilized, made the foreign familiar, and staked political claims to overseas spaces.[42]

It was in a world accustomed to thinking about performance and public life in these ways that French approaches to Native diplomacy made sense. Although most seventeenth-century observers had come to see nobility as a social order defined by birth rather than as a mere "profession" exercised by the virtuous, the honor and authority that came with it were often achieved rhetorically, through the manipulation of signs that persuaded others of one's status and power.[43] If the self-conscious play of appearances was fundamental to the aristocratic experience in Europe, naturally, it was no less so in America. Masks of authority, diplomatic pretense, rhetorical training, dramatic arts, and the everyday histrionics of high society all formed part of a theatrical sensibility that permeated elite culture on both sides of the Atlantic. The conventional wisdom that life represented a series of "stages" on which noblemen displayed their virtues conditioned the way they moved through the world wherever they went (and often, by extension, conditioned displays of deference and emulation among their social inferiors).[44] By temporarily adapting their verbal and physical deportment in ways that took them far from what was socially normative in France, the leading officers in New France embodied an indigenized persona that their successors would inherit and adjust to meet the shifting demands of Native diplomacy.

Sauvages and Politicians

The etiquette that governed Indigenous politics was as complex and subtle as any code of courtesy in Europe, and observing it demanded a similar degree of mental and physical discipline, but from the 1660s onward some officials claimed with mounting conviction that Native diplomacy was about more than following protocol: it was above all a matter of passion. According to La Potherie, who based his history of the Iroquois Wars on firsthand experience as well as on reports supplied to him by longtime negotiators, diplomatic ceremonies were a "Stage," and those who spoke, sang, and danced in their midst were "actors." He described Native councils and war feasts as moments of extraordinary emotional intensity during which orators' spirited words and contorted faces were "accompanied by very violent gestures and movements."[45] In a rhetorical environment inhabited by "wild" peoples who lived beyond the civilizing influence of law, faith, and learning (the definition of *sauvages*), the French had to match their allies' emotional pitch with fulsome displays of their own: "One must have great political skill to manage these peoples," he observed, adding that they could be won over only through a face-to-face "eloquence" whose "great charms ... touches the ears ... animates the passions ... fortifies the mind ... excites the affections of the soul ... [and] has a gift of persuasion when it insinuates itself pleasantly."[46] La Potherie stated his case with exceptional literary gusto, but his chosen metaphors and arguments permeated French administrative reportage and printed relations in the decades after 1663. By casting Native diplomacy as a stage, he and other officials not only glorified French negotiators as superior performers to whom the eyes of the world should be drawn, but also made their actions intelligible to European readers as a rhetorical exercise with real political stakes.⁴⁷ In the New World, as in the Old, eloquence achieved emotional power, and emotional power was political power.

Visual artifacts of councils held during this period capture the French view of Native diplomacy as a stage for the interplay of words, gestures, and feeling. The thematic link between eloquence, movement, and emotion pervades the scenes of Indigenous politics published by the Baron de Lahontan in 1703, for instance. In one essentialized image, headmen engage in animated speeches, dances, and other ceremonies of war and peace. The emphasis on abstract Indigenous bodies and bodily rituals reinforces Lahontan's argument that Natives channel their passions into collective political action in a way that is closer to nature, more sincere, and hence more virtuous than their European counterparts.⁴⁸ Another drawing depicts talks held between Governor Joseph-Antoine Lefebvre de La Barre and the Onondaga headman Outreouti in September 1684. The governor, seated regally in a chair and flanked by two interpreters, faces Outreouti, who declaims proudly while holding a pipe. The members of their entourages are shown standing or sitting in stylized poses—their arms outstretched or akimbo, their hands pointing or supinated, their heads turned this way and that. Even in this still image, perpetual motion is encoded in their bodies, whose dramatic gestures would have implied both lively discussion and intense feeling: lively discussion because educated Frenchmen understood gesture to be fundamentally aligned with speech, and intense feeling because words and gestures together formed the art of rhetorical delivery (a conception shared by many of their Indigenous counterparts).⁴⁹ La Barre's stillness in the midst of the action only heightens the sense that movement and passion were necessary in such encounters. Although the governor seems to project the serenity befitting a man who represents the royal dignity, the text made clear that his feeble message and aloof manner were a diplomatic flop, so much so that he listened with benign incomprehension as the defiant Outreouti dismissed him with a litany of eloquent barbs.⁵⁰

To the French, emotional manipulation by a well-deployed Native persona seemed like the surest means to control peoples governed by a curious mix of reason and impulse. On one hand, Natives appeared more than capable of reflective, complex, and strategic political behavior.⁵¹ On the other hand, they seemed prone to flights of feeling or fancy that overpowered their customary self-possession. According to the experienced negotiator and former commandant of Baie de Puants Nicolas Perrot, they would "believe anything" when their imaginations were "heated up" by dreams or drink or rumor, and their minds were "dominated imperiously" by sentiments of ambition, vengeance, and vainglory that "possess their hearts entirely."⁵² In other words, Natives seemed to lack the refinement necessary to impose reasonable restraint upon their emotions as fully as Europeans could do. The key to negotiating with them, Perrot argued, was to exercise the same emotional volatility in a strategic way, alternately bribing, flattering, chiding, and intimidating them in order to exploit the vicissitudes of their passions.⁵³

To be sure, such reductive notions about Native hearts and minds reflected long-standing assumptions about the impetuousness of "savage" peoples, but they also drew upon preconceived ideas about the emotional vulnerability of any public audience, even a European one. In a 1689 handbook for lawyers and preachers, the rhetorician Étienne Dubois de Bretteville voiced the wholly conventional belief that humans are governed by feeling, not intellect: "The mind has long been the dupe of the heart . . . to win over a man's reason, it is necessary first to win over his passion." The problem for Bretteville and other observers was that the heart of man seemed like "an abyss whose shadows we have never penetrated . . . a new world yet to be discovered."⁵⁴ Nonetheless, they were confident that close and sustained scrutiny of anyone's outward appearances would reveal his true feelings in the end. Although contemporaries debated the precise workings of the heart and its passions, most believed that emotions operated according to regular patterns that could be identified by physical and verbal clues.⁵⁵ Natives seemed to be no exception to this rule, and the ambition of the French to discover the "new world" of their hearts was entirely consistent with a Baroque political culture that privileged passion as the animating force in public life.

Unlike persuading parishioners or *parlementaires* in France, however, manipulating the Natives of North America meant learning to detect passions from an unfamiliar set of cues displayed by seemingly inscrutable peoples.⁵⁶ La Potherie noted that one could easily mistake Natives' "brutal" manners for anger, while at other times they deliberately hid their "violent feelings" behind a stoic façade.⁵⁷ Intendant Antoine-Denis Raudot (1706–10) agreed that they often put a deceptively placid face on the rolling boil of their emotions.⁵⁸ Summing up decades of frustration among missionaries and royal officers, La Potherie lamented that "the Savage mind is difficult to know; he says one thing & thinks another."⁵⁹ Close observation was the only way to discover the Natives' true feelings, he concluded, and the charged atmosphere of diplomatic councils and war feasts provided some of the few occasions when their customary poise was absent: "The Savage is naturally phlegmatic, something is needed to excite him; only the hope of making war somewhere reveals at the same time the sentiments of his heart."[60]

As they adapted metropolitan preconceptions about persuasion and the passions to an unfamiliar audience of Native headmen, royal officials drew inspiration from the examples bequeathed by their predecessors. The founding governor of New France, Samuel de Champlain (1608–35), served as a touchstone model of strategic imitation and accommodation. Champlain's *Voyages*—a text owned by Frontenac—described how he had forged alliances with his Native "brothers" by immersing himself in their ceremonies.[61] Montmagny (1636–48) continued the pattern. It was he, after all, who forged a rare peace with the Mohawks in 1645 that earned him the Iroquoian sobriquet Onontio, or "Great Mountain"—a title derived literally from his name (*mont* meaning "mountain," and *magny*, like *magnus*, meaning "great"). Not only did Montmagny bequeath a role that would outlive him for more than a century; he also showed his successors how to play up aspects of their own material, religious, and political culture that appealed to Native beliefs in the spiritual power of certain gestures and objects, combining fireworks shows and other displays of mastery over "the fire" with feasts and gift-giving.[62] His example taught the French how to make Onontio legible to his allies as a powerful warrior, a liberal host, and master of a seemingly endless supply of miraculous and useful goods.[63]

Royal officials worked within patterns established by their predecessors, but they learned how to embody a compelling indigenized persona primarily from those who actually lived on Native ground—namely, Jesuit missionaries. After establishing a permanent foothold in the colony in 1632, the "black robes" became renowned as the colony's foremost experts in Native customs.[64] After observing that Native orators obtained influence through their "tongue's end" and that they succeeded "not less by gesticulation than by language," the missionaries imitated their movements and inflections. "There is nowhere in the world where Rhetoric is more powerful than in Canada," claimed Father Paul Le Jeune.[65] The same principles of persuasion taught by Jesuit rhetoricians in France underpinned their missionary campaign in North America, since they believed that Natives could be moved like any other audience: by imitating their manner of speech, appealing to their prejudices, and inciting them to action through a "charismatic momentum" of carefully calibrated words and gestures.[66] By dint of their ministry, the Jesuits became the first Europeans to develop stable and studied Native personae. They trained their tongues, faces, and bodies to conform to Indigenous norms, deploying "holy artifice" in order to heed Christ's call to "be all things to all men in order to win all."[67]

Embodying Onontio

In a diplomatic arena where performance was paramount, royal officials studied what missionaries and governors had done, but they did not—indeed could not—follow past precedent to the letter. In the years immediately following the Crown's takeover of the colony, the needs of the French and their allies changed rapidly, as shifting political and demographic circumstances redefined the terms, relationships, and geography of their alliance. Between 1663 and 1673, the French population of New France ballooned nearly fourfold, from around 2,500 to over 8,000, just as epidemic disease and the continuing pressure of the Beaver Wars (1629–1701) were devastating their Native allies and driving them westward.[68] Demobilized French soldiers and officers, meanwhile, began to establish trading posts along the Great Lakes and down the Mississippi River. As Peter Cook has shown, the fraternal metaphor that had structured diplomacy since the time of Champlain was replaced at this time by a paternal one. All parties adopted a ritual vocabulary that reflected the new balance of power between them. The French, who understood fathers to hold coercive authority over their sons much as a king commands his subjects, eagerly embraced a patriarchal role that seemed to promise a similar dominion over their willful Native allies; their allies, for whom fatherhood implied protection and generosity but not political mastery, hoped to receive greater relief as French "children" than as "brothers"; Iroquois headmen, momentarily war-weary, accepted that Onontio was the father of his allies in order to make better terms with him, or even became his "children" themselves, knowing that it obliged far less deference, in their own terms, than if they were his "nephews."[69]

The term "father" represented a flexible metaphor through which the French and their Indigenous allies could rebuild relations as warfare, disease, and dislocation transformed the political landscape around them; broad acceptance of it allowed French administrators to invest the role of Onontio with new meaning. It is no accident that this moment coincided with Frontenac's lengthy tenures as governor (1672–82, 1689–98). From his earliest days in the colony, Frontenac represented himself as a father to his enemies as well as to his allies.[70] Over the course of his career his speeches, paperwork, and letters to court consistently portrayed Onontio as the patriarch of France's Native alliance, just as many Indigenous headmen professed to be his "children," and together they established a firm new precedent for all concerned.

In rightfully tearing down the long-standing image of Frontenac as a Great White Man who "mastered the savages," scholars have sometimes diminished or pathologized his embrace of the Onontio persona, but in doing so they risk overlooking how his performances—and the reductive, self-serving reports they generated—both reflected and reinforced emerging administrative ideas about the governance of Native passions.[71] After all, it seems clear that the governor himself took his role quite seriously. When he received orders to "Frenchify" the Wendat in 1673, he promised to spend his first winter in Canada learning Iroquoian. While there is no evidence to suggest that he followed through on his pledge, he recognized that a command of the language would enable him to acquire the sort of rhetorical prestige held by the Jesuits.[72] In the absence of Native language skills of his own, he managed his interpreters closely, insisting that they translate his speeches word for word as he had written them down, and even in his original French their contents obeyed the conventions of Native oratory (I will have more to say about these speeches later).[73] He further immersed himself in Indigenous culture by "adopting" eight Iroquois children given to him as peace hostages.[74] The gesture amounted to a serious sacrifice for the Five Nations, who risked precious kin in what was likely a bid to secure French military support.[75] But it also represented an accommodation for the governor, who, although clearly relishing the opportunity to Frenchify the children (and hence outdo the Jesuits), agreed to raise two of them in his own household at a time when adoption was viewed with deep suspicion and rarely practiced by the nobility in France.[76]

Frontenac played up the magnificence and condescension of Onontio in ways that would have been utterly familiar to any European courtier. In order to make a lasting impression upon Native delegations, he engaged in extravagant feasting, gift-giving, and firearms displays. At a time when the Crown was increasingly unwilling to fund such largesse, he also doled out small pensions, medals, and other strategic tokens of regard and affection to individual headmen whose own rhetorical prowess, he believed, would amplify Onontio's voice among their people.[77] Fusing the manner of an absolute monarch and an alliance chief, he demonstrated favor through an economy of access to his person, permitting some Natives to weep at his knees or eat at his table while banishing others from his presence or ignoring them with a studied coldness.[78] He shifted quickly and consciously between emotional registers. When the Onondaga requested a truce with him to mourn the dead killed by a joint French-Odawa war party in 1697, he haughtily threw the belt back in the face of their emissary, promising that "since the Iroquois were weeping over so trifling a blow, he would soon give them another reason for crying, and would again make them feel the weight of his Tomahawk." He then turned to several Odawa onlookers, gently pointing out to them that he could have made peace but, as their "faithful father," he would never do so without including them.[79]

To the French, spectacular displays, elaborate ceremonies, and histrionic modes of oratory and gift-giving all represented conventional modes of persuasion, yet the pressures of continuous warfare encouraged them to adopt more transgressive ways of winning Native hearts, as well. Slavery was illegal in metropolitan France, but French governors did not scruple to strengthen their alliance by doling out Iroquois prisoners as slaves, sacrifices, or adoptive children; in the course of ritually "covering" their allies' dead, they eventually made Onontio the region's largest distributor of Indigenous captives.[80] Scalping and torture, too, became important tools of French diplomacy.[81] While Champlain and Montmagny had condemned torture and adamantly refused to be present when their allies carried it out, Frontenac and his successors showed no such qualms.[82]

Vengeful, ritualized, and elaborate public torture was hardly unknown in early modern Europe, but its Native American counterpart struck Europeans as un-Christian and barbaric, and it was not until the intensification of the Beaver Wars in the final quarter of the seventeenth century that French officials embraced it as an integral part of Onontio's persona. Frontenac, who could be rather lenient toward both European lawbreakers and Native prisoners when it suited him, willingly rendered enemy captives to his allies when he thought doing so would shore up his influence. He sometimes ordered that Iroquois prisoners be burned by his own men.[83] These executions gave force to his threats to "roast" or "commit to the kettle" those children who disobeyed him.[84] It was in light of such gruesome accommodation that the English—no strangers to brutal intercultural violence themselves—accused the governor of "not acting according to the manners of Europeans," which, in a sense, is precisely what he intended to do.[85]

Royal officials justified their adoption of Indigenous forms of violence not by claiming that Natives were any less deserving of Christian mercy than Europeans, but rather by identifying torture and slavery as indispensable elements of Onontio's image. How could he fail to reciprocate ways of killing and "eating" that clearly held enormous significance for Natives? If administrators felt obliged to mimic the "very violent gestures and movements" they witnessed in council, they felt no less strongly that ritual torture was a necessary and persuasive diplomatic language.[86] La Potherie insisted that "the French character is the enemy of inhumanity," yet he also believed that officers in Canada "cannot dispense with making a public example" of their captives in the ways expected of an alliance chief.[87] To pass for great warriors in America, he explained, the French must take a relative view toward the rules of engagement: "What would be barbarity among us, may pass for virtue in an Iroquois."[88]

To aristocratic observers, the notion that French preeminence derived from a culturally ingrained ability to manipulate Native passions could be substantiated by the careers not only of elites like Frontenac, but also of backwoods diplomats such as Perrot. In recommending Perrot to his superiors, Frontenac praised him as someone who "has acquired much credit among the Western nations, by the long practice and knowledge he has of their humor, manners, and languages."[89] Others touted him as a model of how to "manage the minds" of France's allies.[90] La Potherie, who based his history primarily on reports supplied to him by the Jesuits and Perrot himself, reverently described how Perrot, known as Metaminens, had engaged in all "the rodomontades that one must affect with [the Natives]": defeating their shamans in spiritual combat, fabricating dreams that prophesied their deliverance or destruction, and convincing them that he controlled fire and the weather.[91] Perrot was no aristocrat, but in deploying his Native persona to build and maintain alliances far from the centers of French settlement, he nonetheless seemed to embody precisely the sort of labile "tact" and "intelligence" that his aristocratic patrons believed crucial to their diplomacy.[92]

Perrot was a former Jesuit *donné,* and like the missionaries who had trained him, he shed European standards of dignity, comfort, and behavior in order to manufacture charisma on Indigenous terms. He claimed to suffer with good humor the ritual welcome of the Iowas, who smeared his head and shoulders with their tears and saliva and snot, served him raw and bloody bison tongue, and hugged him from behind in the midst of their dances, "making him move along with them in [their] manner." When the Mesquakie seemingly mixed metaphors by asking him, as their "father," to let them "drink . . . milk suckled from [his bosom]," he cleverly thrust forward his tobacco pipe, "telling them that it was his breast that he had always offered in order to feed them." And he repeatedly persuaded Native emissaries to make the long and dangerous trek to Montréal and Québec, where governors invoked him in their speeches, knowing that their authority along the Great Lakes depended in part upon a close identification with his own. In narrating his exploits, Perrot and his contemporaries depicted him not only as a protean ambassador, but even as something of an alliance chief in his own right—an Onontio of the west who wielded authority by mediating conflicts, distributing gifts, fighting bravely, commanding the elements, and delivering a series of improvised speeches that showcased his "Native" virtues.[93]

Perrot's perceived successes invited the French to see the strategic performance of Indianness as an expression of their *grandeur*. Like Frontenac, he seemed to showcase the political fruits that a well-deployed Native persona could bear. From both men's careers, observers drew a lesson: since Perrot and Frontenac could enact Indianness without risking their essential civility, they could teach the French how to know and govern an Indigenous empire. "No man will ever know better than [Frontenac] the mind [*ésprit*] of the savages who fear and love him," declared the governor's commandant at Michilimackinac, Antoine de Lamothe Cadillac, in 1694.[94] Frontenac and Perrot became the twin heroes of La Potherie's narrative primarily because each of them demonstrated "the secret of making himself commendable among these Peoples."[95] It was for this reason that the well-connected priest and champion of colonization Jean Bobé recommended La Potherie's history as a guide to the "measures necessary" to preserve New France. By reading La Potherie's account, he suggested, future officers could learn to pattern themselves after those whose indigenized personae had insinuated a familiar brand of order into Native politics.[96]

This political lesson was reinforced most dramatically by incidents where the French represented different Native communities to each other as actual Natives looked on. When three Seneca headmen initiated peace talks with Frontenac in 1695, for instance, they selected a French officer and former captive, Louis-Thomas Chabert de Joncaire, to speak for them. "We have adopted your Son, Joncaire, whom we have named *Sonnonchiez*," he explained to Frontenac on their behalf, "We wish him to make peace for us, since he once took part in [your] public affairs." Joncaire then delivered their gifts and speeches. When he had finished, a Jesuit missionary presented a belt from the Mission Iroquois calling on the governor to accept the Senecas' request.[97] Thus the formalities of a council held between France and multiple Native communities was conducted entirely between Frenchmen. To explain it, La Potherie concluded that Joncaire had "insinuated himself into [the Senecas'] mind so well, that they saw him as their most faithful friend, & like a man who had become naturalized among them."[98]

The ability of French officers to speak credibly on behalf of Natives was critical, observers claimed, to the negotiations that produced what they believed to be New France's grandest diplomatic achievement: the Great Peace of Montréal of 1701, which brought together more than a thousand members of some forty peoples to mark the end of the Beaver Wars.[99] Most Native communities sent headmen as representatives, but at times the Senecas and Onondagas chose adoptive French "sons" to speak for them—Joncaire for the Senecas and Paul Le Moine de Maricourt (known as Taouestaouis) for the Onondagas. In the fall of 1700 Joncaire and Maricourt led their delegations from Iroquoia to Montréal, met with Callières on the Natives' behalf, and conspired with the governor behind the scenes to ensure the smooth progress of the talks. The two officers' freedom to pass between French and Indigenous roles according to the needs of the moment allowed them to game the negotiations according to Callières's orders. For example, when the Iroquois arrived without the scores of Native captives they had pledged to bring with them, Joncaire, at the governor's urging, explained to France's outraged allies that the fault was entirely Maricourt's and his own, then pleaded with the Iroquois to rescue their "sons" from this "embarrassing predicament" by sending for the prisoners, which the Iroquois magnanimously agreed to do. The mutual fiction allowed all sides to sidestep a potential snag and proceed with the peace.[100] For the Senecas and Onondagas, appointing French-born sons as "Plenipotentiaries" in this moment may have represented a strategic choice to "hide in plain view" behind a European façade, either because several key headmen were absent or because they expected to receive better terms for it.[101] But to the French it showed that some Europeans could indeed know and represent Natives well enough to make actual Native voices superfluous.[102]

In staging the Great Peace, royal officers blended oratorical, musical, and balletic conventions meant to convey symbolically the patriarchal harmony Onontio had finally achieved with his enemies and allies. Callières, who had served under three different governors over nearly two decades, delivered a closing address infused with the indigenized imagery honed by his predecessors.[103] Once every orator had spoken and smoked, the governor arranged a performance designed "to confirm this great Alliance with something sensational": as soldiers distributed cuts of beef, three Frenchmen emerged from the audience to dance the *calumet,* singing and "stepping in rhythm, their faces animated, moving their bodies to match the vehemence of their words," which were punctuated by coordinated volleys of cannon, explosives, and musket fire.[104] The underlying claim that the French had mastered the art of Native diplomacy as well as any Native headman could not have been put more forcefully.

Performance and Paperwork

Amidst the noise of greetings, harangues, musket volleys, cannonades, drumbeats, *sassagouez*, and howls of pain or triumph, it is easy to forget that for French officials, the course of Franco-Native diplomacy was marked from beginning to end by the scratch of pens on paper. The written word defined their understanding and performance of Indianness. Indeed, it provided the essential medium through which they imagined what it meant to be Native, immersed themselves in a suitable persona, and explained the experience to others. In periodic flurries of written reports, instructions, and chronicles, royal administrators recorded and interpreted their face-to-face encounters with Indigenous peoples. During the five decades after 1663, their work became increasingly sophisticated, as the growing stakes and frequency of councils occasioned ever more ambitious levels of documentation on both sides of the Atlantic. To account for their own conduct and to help the minister and the king formulate policy, officials produced a vast body of written knowledge about Native peoples and the means necessary to govern them.

As the Onontio persona took root, the oral culture of diplomacy bled into the written culture of administration. Like the Jesuits, royal officials knew the importance of adhering to Native conventions of oratory, such as listening without interrupting, recapitulating what previous speakers had said, reciting the names and achievements of individual headmen, attaching meaning to specific wampum belts, and employing the correct metaphors and kinship terms. But keeping it all straight was virtually impossible without memory aids. The Jesuits had long addressed Native councils from written lists, which allowed them to recognize each headman present by his nation, band, and family, and to keep track of their own talking points.[105] Governors, fearing that their interpreters might misrepresent Onontio, followed suit. In the process they infused their own practices of speechwriting and reportage with the linguistic customs of their audience.

Governors took a direct hand in writing Onontio's speeches. Frontenac recorded his instructions to subordinates as complete orations written out in the "Native style." When he first addressed the Five Nations in 1673, he read from a piece of paper, which he then handed to his interpreter, "so that he may explain it to you, word for word."[106] In "terms adapted to their manner of speaking," the governor crafted a French-language address flavored with indigenized metaphors and locutions that he believed could be rendered directly into Iroquoian.[107] Frontenac may never have learned Iroquoian himself, but he did in a manner speak a Native language: the "style at Council," composed of "hyperboles, similes, and other figurative expressions." While some French observers found its conventions "elaborate" and "tiresome," Frontenac professed pride in matching an "eloquence, address, and finesse" he compared favorably to "the manners of the Venetian Senate."[108] His lieutenants and successors, Callières and Vaudreuil, would adopt similar speech patterns, and like Frontenac they would write their orations in an indigenized idiom that allowed their interpreters to translate the contents virtually word for word.[109]

French officials were immersed enough in the task of writing speeches to develop strong opinions about which phrases elicited the strongest emotional reaction from Native audiences. Terms of kinship were crucial, of course: Frontenac made it a point of emphasis to address all Natives as his children and to be addressed in turn as their father, and his successors scrupulously maintained the paternal front.[110] But filial forms of address comprised only a small portion of texts that abounded in vivid metaphors and rhetorical flourishes. After transcribing Callières's speeches to the Iroquois in October 1700, La Potherie explained the importance of the governor's overwrought expressions to the minister:

> "Bury the hatchet," "make a river pass over it," "weep for the dead," "strengthen the tree of peace" ... none of that deeply touches those who love only metaphors [i.e., Natives]. But "may the straps and all the instruments of war be buried with this hatchet," "may the earth be leveled over it," "may all the rivers become beautiful and clean," "may the blood of the dead on both sides go to the bottom of the water and the earth," "may the branches and leaves of this tree of peace provide a shade so thick that those who place themselves beneath it are not only cooled but also sheltered from all the storms that may threaten them"; that "Onontio has built the Council Hut, laid the mat, and lighted the fire of peace to warm all these children who will be united with their Father with whom they will make one body and smoke together peacefully." ... When all this has been stated in the sight of so many chiefs, there is no doubt that every one of them will be profoundly touched by it.[111]

Such evocative language seemed essential to pass as Onontio. Animated by physical cues and delivered "in the sight" of Indigenous headmen, La Potherie suggested, it aimed primarily to excite an emotional response. If the point of speeches was to move Native listeners to action, then speechwriting was largely a matter of deciding which rhetorical elements would most "profoundly touch" their hearts.

Composing speeches, like the act of delivering them, required the French to inhabit the Native persona they wished to project. In choosing Onontio's words, they reflected on his relationship to his audience, imposed order on the world around him, and imagined what he should say to his "children." Their speeches, supplemented by gestures and gifts, were carefully crafted to invest Onontio with personality and calibrated to express familiar desires and emotions in an alien tongue. What governors engaged in is not self-writing, as historians and anthropologists generally understand that term, since it was hardly constitutive of a modern sense of interiority, or a "true self."[112] But it did construct, through specific discursive practices, an individual whose thoughts, feelings, and expressions were conditioned by the expectations of his performers and his listeners.[113] As a cognitive exercise, then, it closely resembled the process of rhetorical learning, in which *collégiens* studied the words of ancient orators, practiced their written and spoken conventions, and then devised original speeches intended to persuade an imagined audience of Greeks and Romans.

The exercise of writing out speeches in the Native style compelled governors to pass back and forth between European and indigenized personae. Sometimes they ventriloquized the voice of the court, invoking the "grand Onontio" of France, or using orders from Versailles to help calibrate the terms and tone of their delivery.[114] At other times they switched pronouns or momentarily stepped out of character. They left traces of their movements in the documents themselves. When Frontenac dispatched Perrot to prevent the Odawa from making a separate peace with the English and the Five Nations in 1690, the governor wrote him a full address to be read out verbatim, in the first-person voice of Onontio; but for Perrot's eyes only he also included an instructive heading, "Speech that must be delivered to the Odawa..."[115]

As they read out Onontio's words, subordinate French officers not only passed between European and Native personae, but even from one indigenized role to another. Speaking in his absence, they claimed to act as neutral conduits for the unvarnished expression of his words and feelings—to temporarily embody him instead of their own Native "selves." In concluding an address to the Wendat on Frontenac's behalf in 1694, Cadillac insisted that his speech came directly from Onontio:

"There is my word, it is the spirit of Onontio, it is his voice, listen to it well."[116] As commandant at Detroit several years later, Lamothe Cadillac announced to his Odawa, Potawatomi, Wendat, and Mississauga listeners, "It is your father Onontio who convokes you, and who is about to speak to you through my mouth. All that you are about to hear comes from him alone."[117] In the same fashion, Perrot prepared a speech to the Odawa that explicitly acknowledged Onontio's authorship of the words before transitioning into the first person: "Listen, my children, our Father Onontio says; listen, he says; I regret to hear talk every year of the carnage committed in your lands ..."[118]

For French officials, the elaborate effort to encode themselves as Native entailed a parallel process of decoding Indigenous words and customs; like students of classical rhetoric, they studied Native oratory closely in order to grasp its meanings and master its conventions. That process began with the transcription of speeches by French scribes, which allowed governors to reference past talks faithfully wherever they went.[119] The mobile diplomatic archives they maintained were passed down from one administration to the next.[120] Texts of speeches seem to have circulated widely among officers and missionaries on the ground, who also kept written notes that they used to prepare memoranda about Native customs.[121] It was by collecting a vast number of these records that La Potherie was able to produce his history, which could be described more accurately as an annotated compendium of diplomatic speeches.

In transcribing speeches and sending them back to court, royal officials extended a well-established tradition of diplomatic reportage to New France, but their work involved an added level of cultural and linguistic interpretation.[122] After all, there had been little exposure to Native words at court before the 1660s, and what evidence exists suggests that the king and his ministers did not initially grasp their significance.[123] That changed in the ensuing decades in part because the perceived stakes and intensity of the Beaver Wars rose dramatically, but also because French governors claimed to derive much meaning from the words of headmen. They positioned themselves as interpreters of Native speeches, sprinkling their dispatches with Indigenous metaphors in order to explain the course of negotiations and to represent themselves as thoroughly versed in the ways of Natives. They couched Indigenous figures of speech in phrases such as "I am speaking Savage," "to use their terms," "as they put it," or "these are the terms ... I used in speaking to them," usually adding an explanation in idiomatic French ("that is to say ...").[124] Their efforts at translation extended to noting which Native "signatures" corresponded to the individual headmen and nations that formed part of their alliance—an attempt to impose schematic order on pictograms that were otherwise unintelligible to the French.

The interpretation of Native speeches took on added significance after Onontio's role shifted from war chief to keeper of the peace. No longer embroiled in constant bloodshed, the French were now absorbed in a ceaseless and widespread effort to prevent it. Speech transcripts served as the empirical basis not only for strategy and policymaking, but also for determining patronage and explicating Native customs. One report prepared by Vaudreuil in 1703 provides a case in point. After hosting Joncaire and several other Seneca emissaries to reaffirm the Peace of Montréal, he ordered his secretary to send copies of everyone's speeches to Versailles. When they arrived, an unnamed "specialist" at the Navy Ministry (likely the former intendant of New France Jean Bochart de Champigny) summarized them for the minister, who then made his own annotations in the margins. In the process the Iroquoian exchanges between Vaudreuil and Seneca headmen were transformed into idiomatic French, then into policy proposals, and finally into ministerial decisions: to promote Joncaire, for instance, and to request further information about Seneca adoption practices.[125] To be sure, the ministry's interpretation of the speeches flattened Indigenous desires and framed them within familiar political categories. Nevertheless the intellectual labor involved was sophisticated. Carried out from year to year and in a succession of similar documents, it defined for the minister who the various Native peoples were, what they wanted, and who among the French had the "character of mind" necessary to "manage" them.[126]

In this way, diplomatic speeches and the paperwork surrounding them became a burgeoning administrative ethnography of Natives controlled by the Crown. In the course of interpreting encounters with Indigenous peoples, royal administrators made definitive (if not always effective) claims about Native culture and how it should be manipulated to advance the king's interests. It was no accident that in this same period La Potherie (1703), Raudot (ca. 1709), Perrot (ca. 1715), and others all produced texts that sought to capture the essential "nature" of Indigenous peoples and identify the passions that governed their hearts. The anxious aim of their studies, these authors made clear, was to preserve France's hard-won preeminence. Their writings affirmed that knowing and mastering Natives was a matter of learning their ways and moving through the world as they did, however temporarily. In the preface to his volume on Indigenous customs, La Potherie aptly captured the conventional wisdom that cross-cultural performance and cross-cultural learning were intertwined processes. "No doubt you were surprised to learn of my metamorphosis," he announced, "it is but the strangeness and changeability of the human heart. I am now an Iroquois, & you will permit me to tell you a few facts about my nation."[127]

Conclusion

The aristocratic habits of performance and personation that helped condition French encounters with Natives remind us that cultural mobility was part and parcel of colonization. By the early eighteenth century, the self-conscious assumption of "Indigenous" personae, and the corresponding claim that such personae achieved real political mastery over Native peoples, had become utterly conventional. In fact, it was now a matter of policy. In subsequent decades, royal officials would request and receive advancement based on their perceived knowledge of Indigenous customs, and the instructions they received from court would make clear that the management of Natives was the "most essential... of all the areas of administration" entrusted to them.[128] Negotiators would even produce template speeches in the Native style, complete with rough-and-ready instructions about how to stage and administer councils.[129] By presiding over an alliance built around the performance of Indianness, officials believed, they had achieved the imaginative insight necessary to maintain the upper hand in their diplomacy with Natives. Their administrative culture reflected that conviction.

That is not to say that French negotiators were always (or often) successful in attaining their goals, that their conclusions were uncontested, or that their knowledge represented anything more than a sophisticated cultural construct—far from it. There were officers who failed to play the indigenized roles expected of them or failed to adapt to shifting political realities on Native ground. Throughout the final five decades of French rule in North America, moreover, the Crown would repeatedly intervene in damaging Indigenous wars that its agents neither understood nor controlled. The French never achieved the sort of total subjugation or assimilation of Natives that some officials thought possible and desirable; nor, of course, did they achieve complete or perfectly accurate knowledge of Indigenous peoples. The ideas that they developed were hardly reflections of some independent empirical reality. Instead, like performances of Indianness, they followed a logic conditioned by the cultural baggage their makers brought with them to the New World.

Nonetheless, as far as certain "truths" about Natives became rooted in French administrative discourses and practices, they had a profound impact upon the lives of Natives and Europeans alike. How French officials saw Indigenous peoples (and, no less important, how the latter saw the French) determined the conduct of war and peace. It guided royal decisions to court some nations and alienate others. As a result, it violently transformed identities, kinship ties, trading relationships, emotional bonds, and patterns of settlement and subsistence. It helped to produce and sustain dynamic ritual personae, above all Onontio, which provided a lasting basis for cultural exchange as well as conflict.[130] Most enduringly, it established a French conceit that they were uniquely suited to rule over Native peoples, and gave new grounds to write about them as colonial and racialized Others.[131]

In the long run, France's pursuit of Native alliances prefigured modern European attempts to manipulate the "hearts and minds" of Indigenous peoples through imitative practices of oratory and self-presentation. Father Jean Tailhan, a Jesuit priest who edited Perrot's writings for publication in 1864, drew an explicit analogy between Metaminens and the Arab Bureau chiefs of his own day, who immersed themselves in local dialects, customs, and conflicts in order to pacify the Muslim Algerian subjects of France's Second Empire.[132] Carefully orchestrated patterns of "going Native" became a common tool of governance and diplomacy in European empires.[133] Nearly two and a half centuries after Frontenac brandished the tomahawk and led the war dance, George Orwell wrote about the appalling necessity of the colonizer to "do what the 'natives' expect of him." The tendency of European officials to see themselves as "the leading actor of the piece" in colonial encounters, he observed, ignored the reality that their power was constrained by Indigenous expectations.[134] The same insight guided the French administrative manuals of his time, whose authors insisted that "reforming" *indigènes* could be achieved only by strategically accommodating their perceived customs and "political mentalities."[135] To the extent that early modern colonizers such as Frontenac and Perrot defined Onontio as a tool for the manipulation of Native peoples, they presaged the belief among their successors in France—and elsewhere in the West—that the governance of colonized subjects was largely a question of wearing the masks that Natives expected to see.

NOTES

1. In this essay I have used decolonized self-designations and widely embraced ethnonyms interchangeably, except in direct quotations from sources.

2. From the earliest years of French colonization in the early seventeenth century, French-Indigenous relations were predicated upon the kinship metaphors and reciprocal bonds of obligation that underpinned Aboriginal law and diplomacy. Over time both the fictive metaphors assigned to French governors ("brother," "father," etc.) and the implications for their alliances with Indigenous communities shifted in keeping with Native and French strategies and with the political landscape of northeastern North America, as I will explain in more detail below. For a close analysis of these changes as reflected in the ritual language surrounding Onontio, see Peter Cook, "Onontio Gives Birth: How the French in Canada Became Fathers to Their Indigenous Allies, 1645–1673," *Canadian Historical Review* 96, no. 2 (June 2015): 165–93.

3. In speeches delivered to Frontenac's subordinates at the French post of Michilimackinac (today's Mackinaw City, Michigan) the previous winter, some Odawa factions had criticized French weakness and seemed poised to seek a rapprochement with the Iroquois. Their "coolness" may in fact have been more of a negotiating tactic than a serious threat, but in the months since, the governor's emissaries had worked to convince them of French resolve, eventually persuading them to make the trek to Montréal. In their speeches preceding Frontenac's own, the Odawa and Nipissing still declared themselves uncertain of his intentions. Gilles Havard, *Empire et métissages: Indiens et français dans le Pays d'en Haut, 1660–1715* (Sillery, QC: Septentrion, 2003), 452–54; Claude-Charles le Roy "Bacqueville" de la Potherie, *Histoire de l'Amérique septentrionale* (Paris: Nyon, 1753 ed. [orig. 1702]), t. III: 60–70, 94–95; Charles de Monseignat, "Relation par Charles de Monseignat de ce qui s'est passé de plus remarquable au Canada depuis le mois de novembre 1689 jusqu'au mois de novembre 1690," 1690, Archives nationales d'outre-mer (ANOM), Colonies (COL), C11A, vol. 11, ff. 24v-25v.

4. According to the French colonial official and chronicler Claude-Charles Le Roy de la Potherie, "The *casse-tête* is a sort of hatchet that is the symbol of the War one wishes to declare. It is customary to present it with pomp in the midst of a dance, where everyone animates himself with all that the most frightening fury can inspire." La Potherie, *Histoire*, t. II: 157. On the long history and flexible meanings of the *casse-tête* in French-Indigenous relations, see Robert Englebert, "Colonial Encounters and the Changing Contours of Ethnicity: Pierre-Louis de Lorimier and Métissage at the Edges of Empire," *Ohio Valley History* 18, no. 1 (Spring 2018): 54–55; Havard, *Empire et métissages*, 448–54, 738–71; and Jean-François Lozier, "Lever des chevelures en Nouvelle-France: La politique française du paiement des scalps," *Revue d'histoire de l'Amérique française* 56, no. 4 (Spring 2003): 513–42. As recently as 1684 and 1686–87, Natives had refused or demurred when French envoys invited them to take up the hatchet against the Iroquois. Havard, *Empire et métissages*, 443–44.

5. Frontenac to Navy Minister Phélypeaux de Pontchartrain, 12 November 1690, reproduced in *Rapport de l'archiviste de la province de Québec* (1927–1928), ed. Pierre-Georges Roy (Québec: Proulx, 1928), 38.

6. Here La Potherie, who was not present at the scene or even in Canada until several years later, embellished upon the less florid contemporary account of Frontenac's secretary, Charles de Monseignat, but nonetheless lifted certain passages word for word. La Potherie, *Histoire*, t. III: 96–98; Monseignat, "Relation . . . de ce qui s'est passé de plus remarquable au Canada depuis le mois de novembre 1689 jusqu'au mois de novembre 1690," ff. 25–25v.

7. Historians disagree about precisely why and to what extent French culture(s) creolized in relation to Indigenous ones. For some recent or touchstone accounts that stress the mutability of French

(and Indigenous) cultures across different colonial contexts, see, in addition to the relevant works cited below, Richard White, *The Middle Ground: Indians, Empires, and Republics in the Great Lakes Region, 1650–1815* (New York: Cambridge University Press, 1991); Denys Delâge, "L'influence des Amerindiens sur les Canadiens et les Français au temps de la Nouvelle-France," Lekton 2, no. 2 (Fall 1992): 103–91; Tracy Neal Leavelle, *The Catholic Calumet: Colonial Conversions in French and Indian North America* (Philadelphia: University of Pennsylvania Press, 2011); Sophie White, *Wild Frenchmen and Frenchified Indians: Material Culture and Race in Colonial Louisiana* (Philadelphia: University of Pennsylvania Press, 2013); Doris Garraway, *The Libertine Colony: Creolization in the Early French Caribbean* (Durham, NC: Duke University Press, 2005); Shannon Lee Dawdy, *Building the Devil's Empire: French Colonial New Orleans* (Chicago: University of Chicago Press, 2008).

8. Until the 1980s, most historical writing on French-Indigenous relations in New France drew heavily upon metropolitan sources and emphasized the colony's apparent French (or proto-Canadian) qualities. Cornelius Jaenen, *Friend and Foe: Aspects of French-Amerindian Cultural Contact in the Sixteenth and Seventeenth Centuries* (Toronto: McClelland & Stewart, 1976); Louise Dechêne, *Habitants et marchands de Montréal au XVIIe siècle* (Paris: Plon, 1974); William J. Eccles, *France in America* (New York: Harper & Row, 1972); Gilles Paquet and Jean-Pierre Wallot, "Nouvelle-France/Québec/Canada: A World of Limited Identities," in *Colonial Identity in the Atlantic World, 1500–1800*, ed. Nicholas Canny and Anthony Pagden (Princeton, NJ: Princeton University Press, 1989), 95–114; Dale Miquelon, *New France, 1701–1744: A Supplement to Europe* (Toronto: McClellan & Stewart, 1987). The ethnohistorical turn of the 1980s and 1990s, however, witnessed an explosion of interest in Native agency, perceptions, and cultural logics; while some historians remained well-grounded in French history, others approached French-Indigenous encounters as a local story best told through colonial and ethnographic records. See, for example, Denys Delâge, *Bitter Feast: Amerindians and Europeans in Northeastern North America, 1600–1664* (Vancouver: University of British Columbia Press, 1993 [orig. 1985]); White, *Middle Ground*; James Axtell, *The Invasion Within: The Contest of Cultures in Colonial North America* (New York: Oxford University Press, 1986); and, among many others, Susan Sleeper-Smith, *Indian Women and French Men: Rethinking Cultural Encounter in the Western Great Lakes* (Amherst, MA: University of Massachusetts Press, 2001).

9. Some scholars have continued to build on the ethnographic literature, but lately others have sought to reintroduce metropolitan and imperial perspectives (and sources) more fully to the study of encounters. For an example of the former, see Michael Witgen, *An Infinity of Nations: How the Native New World Shaped Early North America* (Philadelphia: University of Pennsylvania Press, 2011). For examples of the latter, see Brett Rushforth, *Bonds of Alliance: Indigenous and Atlantic Slaveries in New France* (Chapel Hill: University of North Carolina Press, 2012); Céline Carayon, "Beyond Words: Nonverbal Communication, Performance, and Acculturation in the Early French-Indian Atlantic (1500–1701)," (Ph.D. diss., College of William and Mary, 2010); Lozier, "Lever des chevelures en Nouvelle-France," 513–42; Christian A. Crouch, *Nobility Lost: French and Canadian Martial Cultures, Indians, and the End of New France* (Ithaca, NY: Cornell University Press, 2014); Germaine Warkentin, *Pierre-Esprit Radisson: The Collected Writings*, 2 vols. (Montréal: McGill-Queen's University Press, 2012), I:3–104; Arnaud Balvay, "Tattooing and Its Role in French–Native American Relations in the Eighteenth Century," *French Colonial History* 9 (2008): 1–14; Gilles Havard, "Le rire des jésuites: Une archéologie du mimétisme dans la rencontre franco-amérindienne (XVIIe-XVIIIe siècle)," *Annales*.

Histoire, Sciences Sociales, 62e année, no. 3 (2007): 542–44, and *Empire et métissages*; Allan Greer, *Mohawk Saint: Catherine Tekakwitha and the Jesuits* (New York: Oxford University Press, 2005); and the list goes on.

10. Take, for instance, situations in which royal (or missionary) attempts to assimilate non-Europeans within an imperial framework ultimately served to fuel their racialization and colonization in the eyes of the French. Carayon, "Beyond Words," 277; Dominique Deslandres, ". . . Alors nos garçons se marieront à vos filles, & nous ne ferons plus qu'un seul peuple": Religion, genre et déploiement de la souveraineté française en Amérique aux XVIe-XVIIIe siècles—une problématique," *Revue d'histoire de l'Amérique Française* 66, no. 1 (2012): 5–35; Alexandre Dubé, "Les Amérindiens sous le regard des bureaux de la Marine (1660–1760): Quelque pistes de réflexion sur un objet administratif," in *Un continent en partage: cinq siècles de rencontres entre Amérindiens et Français*, ed. Gilles Havard and Mickaël Augeron (Paris: Les Indes savantes, 2013), 153–75; Saliha Belmessous, "Assimilation and Racialism in Seventeenth and Eighteenth-Century French Colonial Policy," *American Historical Review* 110, no. 2 (2005): 322–49; Crouch, *Nobility Lost*. Or from another perspective, situations where intercultural or interracial familial bonds foundered against institutionalized taboos distributed unevenly across imperial spaces. Jennifer Palmer, *Intimate Bonds: Family and Slavery in the French Atlantic* (Philadelphia: University of Pennsylvania Press, 2016).

11. David Bell, "English Barbarians, French Martyrs," in *The Cult of the Nation in France: Inventing Nationalism, 1680–1800* (Cambridge, MA: Harvard University Press, 2009), 78–106; "French Identities in Eighteenth-Century North America," in *Foreigners and Citizens: France, the Americas, and Europe, 18th–20th Centuries*, ed. Peter Sahlins and Laurent Dubois [unpublished]; David Armitage, *The Ideological Origins of the British Empire* (Cambridge: Cambridge University Press, 2000); and Linda Colley, *Britons: Forging the Nation, 1707–1837* (New Haven, CT: Yale University Press, 2005).

12. Given the sheer richness and diversity of encounters during this period, and the incoherent discourse about "Frenchness" in the metropole, it is hard to see how even careful scholars looking to draw general conclusions about French identity can do so without heavily limiting their source base. See, for instance, Brian Brazeau, *Writing a New France, 1604–1632: Empire and Early Modern French Identity* (Burlington, VT: Ashgate, 2009).

13. The notion that French identity was a fragile construct is problematic not only because it discounts the resilience of colonists' Old World "selves," but also because it presupposes fixed notions of Frenchness at a time when that category itself was still emerging. How can we measure the loss of French identity when the meaning of "French" had not yet become a subject of extended study and reflection, as would happen from the middle of the eighteenth century onward? On the limited usefulness of "identity" as a category of analysis, see Rogers Brubaker and Fred Cooper, "Beyond 'Identity,'" *Theory and Society* 29, no. 1 (February 2000): 1–47. On the comparative advantages of an approach that ignores "identity" in favor of closely analyzing the individual's dynamic relations with her surrounding social and cultural milieux, see Christopher Hodson, "Weird Science: Identity in the Atlantic World," *William and Mary Quarterly* 68, no. 2 (April 2011): 227–32 ("individual cultural adaptations" quote on 231–32). For scholarship that seeks to rescue identity as an analytical term by reducing its scope to the individual level and making its contours more supple, see François-Joseph Ruggiu, "A Way Out of the Crisis: Methodologies of Early Modern Social History in France," *Cultural and Social History* 6, no. 1 (2009): 65–85, and "Les notions d''identité,' d''individu' et de 'self' et leur

utilisation en histoire sociale," in *Identité, appartenances, revendications idéntitaires XVIe-XVIIIe siècles,* ed. Marc Belissa et al. (Paris: Nolin, 2005): 395–406; and Cécile Vidal, "Francité et situation coloniale: Nation, empire et race en Louisiane française (1699–1769)," *Annales. Histoire, Sciences Sociales* 64, no. 5 (September-October 2009): 1019–1050.

14. For an analysis of the early modern "self" as a dynamic sense anchored in one's external surroundings and social relations, see Guido Ruggiero, *Machiavelli in Love: Sex, Self, and Society in the Italian Renaissance* (Baltimore: Johns Hopkins University Press, 2008); and Lynn Enterline, *Shakespeare's Schoolroom: Rhetoric, Discipline, Emotion* (Philadelphia: University of Pennsylvania Press, 2012).

15. Here I build on Céline Carayon's argument that the "multimedia performance" of Native culture by French negotiators created a tension between mutual understanding (made possible by syncretic symbols and norms of communication) and mutual distrust (French belief that Native performances were "theatrical" and thus insincere). I am indebted to her work, but my emphasis is slightly different: I place greater weight on perceptions of theatricality for what they implied to the French about their own cultural superiority and ability to influence Natives than on its role in fueling French distrust. Carayon, "Beyond Words," esp. 278–88.

16. Here I take inspiration from John Jeffries Martin's concept of a "performative self" grounded in strategies of self-presentation, which assumed new intensity in European life from the early sixteenth century onward. Martin, "The Myth of Renaissance Individualism," in *A Companion to the Worlds of the Renaissance,* ed. Guido Ruggiero (Hoboken, NJ: Blackwell, 2007), 216.

17. In this sense of achieving influence through the intertwined interests of French agents and Indigenous communities, the decades covered here—from the 1660s to the early 1700s, primarily—witnessed the zenith of French-Native diplomacy in North America. The intercultural alliances that seemed stronger than ever at the Great Peace of 1701 (discussed below), however, showed mounting strain as Native migration and diplomacy created new communities outside the existing alliance structure, the Franco-British rivalry intensified, and the French struggled to incorporate western peoples beyond the Great Lakes. On this gradual and multicausal fragmentation in the decades preceding France's defeat in the Seven Years' War, see White, *Middle Ground,* 186–268; Witgen, *Infinity of Nations,* 215–314; Crouch, *Nobility Lost;* Rushforth, *Bonds of Alliance,* esp. 193–252; Denys Delâge, "Les Premières Nations et la Guerre de la Conquête (1754–1765)," *Les Cahiers des dix,* no. 63 (2009): 1–67.

18. Carayon, "Beyond Words," 270, 319.

19. On the importance of intercultural diplomacy to the survival of France's North American empire in particular, see Paul Cohen, "The Power of Apprehending 'Otherness': Cultural Intermediaries as Imperial Agents in New France," in *Encountering Otherness: Diversities and Transcultural Experiences in Early Modern European Culture,* ed. Guido Abbattista (Trieste: Edizioni Università di Trieste, 2011), 223–37.

20. As Robert Morrissey puts it, "Moving beyond the question of success or failure, a better question is: what was the nature of colonialism? . . . By recognizing the French government's inability to project power [in the way Versailles conceived it], we refocus our attention to the complex ways that the 'empire' built strength through alliance with Native peoples." Robert Michael Morrissey, *Empire by Collaboration: Indians, Colonists, and Governments in Colonial Illinois Country* (Philadelphia: University of Pennsylvania Press, 2015), 5.

21. Unless otherwise specified below, biographical information about royal officers comes from their individual entries in the *Dictionary of Canadian Biography*.

22. Not all royal officers attended a *collège* or seminary or received training in rhetoric. Namely, many of the fur traders and soldiers who served as go-betweens for the French on Native Ground left behind little trace of formal learning. The following is a list of governors-general, governors, and lesser officers (commandants, lieutenants, etc.) who were centrally involved in French-Native diplomacy during the period circa 1650–1710 and for whom there is evidence of a classical education received either from a *collège*, a seminary, or tutors: Charles Huault de Montmagny, Louis de Buade de Frontenac, Joseph-Antoine Lefebvre de La Barre, Daniel Graysolon Du Lhut, Charles Le Moyne de Longueuil et de Châteaugay, Antoine Laumet de Lamothe Cadillac, Nicolas Perrot, and Pierre Gaultier de Varennes et de La Verendrye. See their respective entries in the *Dictionary of Canadian Biography*. On the education of aristocratic boys in this period more generally, see Mark Motley, *Becoming a French Aristocrat* (Princeton, NJ: Princeton University Press, 1990); and L. W. B. Brockliss, *French Higher Education in the Seventeenth and Eighteenth Centuries: A Cultural History* (New York: Clarendon Press, 1987).

23. Charles Rollin, *Discours préliminaire au Traité des études* (1726), quoted in Georges Snyders, *La pédagogie en france aux XVIIe et XVIIIe siècles* (Paris: Presses Universitaires de France, 1964), 75; René Bary, *Méthode pour bien prononcer un discours et pour le bien animer* (Paris: D. Thierry, 1679), 71.

24. Snyders, *La pédagogie*, 123.

25. Anthony Grafton, "The Soul's Entrepreneurs," *New York Review of Books*, March 3, 1994.

26. Gustave Dupont-Ferrier, *Du Collège de Clermont au Lycée Louis-le-Grand (1563–1920)* (Paris: Boccard, 1925), 239–72; John W. O'Malley, *The First Jesuits* (Cambridge, MA: Harvard University Press, 1993), 221–25; Jennifer A. Herdt, *Putting on Virtue: The Legacy of the Splendid Vices* (Chicago: University of Chicago Press, 2010), 133–35 ("leader"); Bruna Filippi, "The Orator's Performance: Gesture, Word, and Image in Theatre at the Collegio Romano," in *The Jesuits II: Cultures, Sciences, and the Arts, 1540–1773*, ed. John W. O'Malley, S.J., Gauvin Alexander Bailey, Steven J. Harris, and T. Frank Kennedy, S.J. (Toronto: University of Toronto Press, 2006), 512–29.

27. For more on this topic, see James Farr, "The Death of a Judge: Performance, Honor, and Legitimacy in Seventeenth-Century France," *Journal of Modern History* 75, no. 1 (March 2003): 1–22.

28. On the ideal courtier as performer, see Nicolas Faret, *L'honneste-homme, ou l'art de plaire à la Court* (Paris: du Bray, 1630), 169; Jean de La Bruyère, "De la Cour," *Les Caractères, ou les Moeurs de ce siècle* ([1688; reprint; Paris: Librairie Ch. Delagrave, 1881), 168–200; Louis de Rouvroy, Duc de Saint-Simon, *Mémoires*, ed. Antoine de Boislisle, t. IV: 67–68. For the classic study of this topic under Louis XIV, see Orest Ranum, "Courtesy, Absolutism, and the Rise of the French State, 1630–1660," *The Journal of Modern History*, 52, no. 3 (1980): 426–451.

29. On the boon market for etiquette manuals during this period, see Robert Muchembled, *La société policée: Politique et politesse en France du XVIe au XXe siècles* (Paris: Seuil, 1998), 171.

30. On dancing as courtesy, see Thoinot Arbeau, *Orchésographie* (Lengres: J. Des Preyz, 1589), 2; and Pierre Rameau, *Le Maître à danser, qui enseigne la manière de faire tous les différens pas de danse dans toute la régularité de l'art, et de conduire les bras à chaque pas . . .* (Paris: Villette, 1725), viii-ix.

31. Herdt, *Putting on Virtue*, 134–35; and Richard Alewyn, *Das große Welttheater: die Epoche der höfischen Feste* (Munich: Beck, 1985).

32. François de Callières, *De la manière de négocier avec les souverains* (1716), reproduced in *François de Callières: L'art de négocier sous Louis XIV*, ed. Jean-Claude Wacquet (Paris: Presse de l'École Normale Supérieure, 2005), 189, 189n4, 195.

33. Callières, *Manière de négocier*, 195. For a similar use of theatrical metaphors to describe the art of diplomacy, see Abraham Van Wicquefort, *L'Ambassadeur et ses fonctions* (Cologne: Marteau, 1690), t. I: 5 and t. II: 3.

34. Jean de Lartigue, *La politique des conquérants* (Paris: 1664 ed.), 123–26; "La seconde partie de la politique des conquérans, accommodée au gouvernement de la France et à l'estat présent des affaires," Bibliothèque nationale de France, Manuscrits français 4164; "Inventaire après décès du Marquis de Frontenac" (22 April 1699), in *Nouvelles Archives de l'art français*, 3e série, vol. XV, *Revue de l'art français ancien et moderne* (Paris: Charavay, 1899), 225.

35. This claim is based upon their entries in the *Dictionary of Canadian Biography* and, in some cases, their personnel files in the Archives Nationales' Fonds Marine (C7), Paris, France, and the Archives Nationales d'Outre-Mer's Dossiers de Personnel (E), Aix-en-Provence, France.

36. See the examples cited in Havard, "Le rire des jésuites," 548–52, and Carayon, "Beyond Words," 277.

37. Those conventions include their stage design (*"mises en scène"*), scripts (*"manuscrits d'acteurs"*), and unity of setting (*"unités de lieu"*). François Moureau, *Le théâtre des voyages: Une scénographie de l'Âge classique* (Paris: Presses de l'Université Paris-Sorbonne, 2005). On the literature owned by officials in New France (mainly intendants, for whom more evidence survives), see Jean-Claude Dubé, "Les intendants de la Nouvelle-France et la République des Lettres," *Revue d'histoire de l'Amérique française* 29, no. 1 (1975): 31–48, and "Inventaire après décès... de Frontenac," *Nouvelles Archives*, 225.

38. Kathleen Lynch, "Staging New Worlds: Place and 'Le Theatre de Neptune,'" *Journal of Medieval and Early Modern Studies* 38, no. 2 (Spring 2008): 315–44.

39. Jean-Claude Dubé, *The Chevalier de Montmagny (1601–1657)* (Ottawa: University of Ottawa Press, 2005), 150, 215; Paul Le Jeune, *Jesuit Relations* (1640), 83–85; Jean Hamelin, "Charles Huault de Montmagny (c. 1583–1653)," in *Dictionary of Canadian Biography Online*. It was around this time that Montmagny himself became a character in Cyrano de Bergerac's *Voyage dans la Lune*, whose protagonist crash lands in Canada on his way to the moon. Cyrano de Bergerac, *Voyage dans la Lune* (1648; reprint: Paris: Flammarion, 1898), 47–64.

40. André Vachon, "René-Louis Chartier de Lotbinière," in *Dictionary of Canadian Biography*.

41. Denonville to Pierre Arnoul, ca. October 1685, BnF NAF 21430, f. 393.

42. Michael Wintroub, *A Savage Mirror: Power, Identity, and Knowledge in Early Modern France* (Stanford, CA: Stanford University Press, 2006); Henry S. Turner, *Early Modern Theatricality* (Oxford: Oxford University Press, 2013), 483–91; François Moreau, "American Aboriginals in the *Ballets de Cour* in Champlain's Time," in *Champlain: The Birth of French America*, ed. Raymond Litalien and Denis Vaugeois (Montréal: McGill-Queen's University Press and Septentrion, 2004), 43–49.

43. Ellery Schalk, *From Valor to Pedigree: Ideas of Nobility in France in the Sixteenth and Seventeenth Centuries* (Princeton, NJ: Princeton University Press, 1986), 115–16.

44. On emulation of the high nobility in everyday life, see Kristen Neuschel, *Word of Honor: Interpreting Noble Culture in Seventeenth-Century France* (Ithaca, NY: Cornell University Press, 1989).

45. La Potherie, *Histoire*, t. III: 198–99 ("*Scene*"), t. II: 116, t. 4: 199 ("*acteurs*").

46. La Potherie, *Histoire*, t. II: 115–17 ("gestures"), t. III: 198–99 ("*Scene*"), t. II: 116, t. 4: 199 ("*acteurs*"), t. II: 227 ("political skill"), t. IV: 83–84 ("eloquence"). "It is difficult to express the particulars of these kinds of Feasts unless one has seen them himself," La Potherie claimed; "I once found myself at a similar [war] banquet among the [Mission] Iroquois ... & it seemed to me that I was in the midst of Hell." La Potherie, *Histoire*, t. II: 117. On contemporary meanings of *sauvage*, see Cornelius Jaenen, "'Les Sauvages Ameriquains': Persistence into the 18th Century of Traditional French Concepts and Constructs for Comprehending Amerindians," *Ethnohistory* 29, no. 1 (1982): 46–47, and "Sauvage," in *Dictionnaire de l'Académie française* (1694).

47. In addition to its primary definitions as the space on a stage and a section within a theatrical piece where actors perform, the word *scène* denoted a prominent or public office: "We say, figuratively, that *A man appears on the stage*, to mean that he is in a post, in a position that draws the eyes of the world to him." "Scène," in *Dictionnaire de l'Académie française*.

48. As Stéphanie Chaffray has argued, European representations of Indigenous peoples during this period emphasized bodies over other, natural details (such as the surrounding landscape) not merely because they excited readers' curiosity, but also because the stereotypes they helped create advanced a broader effort to colonize those bodies and the New World spaces they represented. Stéphanie Chaffray, "Corps, territoire et paysage à travers les images et les textes viatiques en Nouvelle-France (1701–1756)," *Revue d'histoire de l'Amérique française* 59, no. 1–2 (Été–Automne 2005): 19, 35–37, 52.

49. Pierre Richelet, *Dictionnaire français* (Geneva: Widerhold, 1680), t. I: 371 ("geste") and t. II: 224 ("prononciation"). Gesture "refers principally to movements that accompany speech." "Geste," *Dictionnaire de l'Académie française* (1694). On Indigenous conceptions of gesture as an essential part of speech—and argumentative oratory in particular—see Céline Carayon, "'The Gesture Speech of Mankind': Old and New Entanglements in the Histories of American Indian and European Sign Languages," *American Historical Review*, 121, no. 2 (April 2016): 485–86.

50. The humiliated and defeated governor was subsequently recalled to France by the king. Lahontan, *Nouveaux voyages dans l'Amérique septentrionale* (The Hague: Frères Honoré, 1703), t. I: 51–56.

51. Jean Bobé, "Lettre de M. Bobé, missionaire," in La Potherie, *Histoire*, t. IV: 270. La Potherie, Lahontan, La Barre, Frontenac, Raudot, and the former commandant of Baie des Puants (today's Green Bay, Wisconsin), Nicolas Perrot, all agreed that Natives acted according to a keen perception of their own self-interest. La Potherie, *Histoire*, t. III: 1; Lahontan, *Nouveaux voyages*, t. II: 112; Nicolas Perrot, *Mémoire sur les moeurs, coustumes et religions des sauvages de l'Amérique septentrionale* (ca. 1715; Paris: Franck, 1864), 77–78; La Barre to Seignelay, 4 November 1683, Archives nationales d'outremer (ANOM), Colonies (COL), C11A, vol. 6, ff. 134–144, reproduced in Pauline Dubé, *La Nouvelle-France sous Joseph-Antoine Le Fevre de la Barre, 1682–1685: Lettres, memoires, instructions et ordonnances* (Montréal: Septentrion, 1993), 91; Frontenac to Pontchartrain, 30 April 1690, reproduced in *Rapport de l'Archiviste de la Province de Québec* (RAPQ) (Québec: Ls-A. Proulx, 1927–28), 30; Antoine-Denis Raudot, *Relation par lettres de l'Amérique septentrionale (années 1709 et 1710)*, ed. Camille de Rochemonteix (Paris: Letouzey et Ané, 1904), 3, 66.

52. Perrot, *Mémoire*, 69; La Potherie, *Histoire*, t. III: 28.

53. Perrot, *Mémoire*, esp. 69, 76–78.

54. Étienne Dubois de Bretteville, *L'éloquence de la chaire et du barreau* (Paris: D. Thierry, 1689), 315–17. When the French spoke of the "mind," or *esprit*, they could mean the rational faculties, but also

the humors, dispositions, or capacity for imagination that likewise arose from the soul. See "Esprit," *Dictionnaire de l'Académie française,* 1st ed. (1694).

55. Bretteville, *L'éloquence,* 317; Lamy, *La rhétorique,* 108; Marin Cureau de la Chambre, *Caractères des passions,* t. I: "L'art de connoistre les hommes" (Paris: 1648). On debates over the workings of the human heart and its passions, see Fay Bound Alberti, *Matters of the Heart: History, Memory and Emotion* (Oxford: Oxford University Press, 2010); and Susan James, *Passion and Action: The Emotions in Seventeenth-Century Philosophy* (New York: Oxford University Press, 1997), esp. 1–4. On the early modern preoccupation with reading the passions from bodily clues, see "Strange Alteration: Physiology and Psychology from Galen to Rabelais," in *Reading the Early Modern Passions: Essays in the Cultural History of Emotion,* ed. Gail Kern Paster, Katherine Rowe, and Mary Floyd-Wilson (Philadelphia: University of Pennsylvania Press, 2004), 272–94.

56. As Céline Carayon has found in her analysis of early European travel literature, Europeans tended to perceive Natives' nonverbal communications either as intentional (conveying a specific message) or as unconscious and thus revealing of the speaker's inner feelings or character. Carayon, "'The Gesture Speech of Mankind,'" 474.

57. La Potherie, *Histoire,* t. II: 256 ("brutal"), t. III: 28 ("violent feelings"). Mother Marie-Andrée Regnard Duplessis de Sainte-Hélène recalled witnessing one headman apologize to an intendant, "I beg you, do not be offended that I speak so loudly. Nature has given me this tone, and I mean you no disrespect by it." Regnard Duplessis de Sainte-Hélène to Hecquet de La Cloche, 17 October 1723, Library and Archives Canada, FR CHAN T, vol. 62, p. 6.

58. Raudot, *Relation,* 66.

59. La Potherie, *Histoire,* t. II: 262. The French obsession with Natives' supposed deceitfulness even extended to rendering Indigenous words in such terms, projecting a sincere/deceptive binary onto Native speakers. In his *Histoire de la Louisiane,* for instance, Antoine-Simon Le Page du Pratz reported the frustration of his friend, *Serpent-Piqué* (Tattooed Serpent), as follows: "Do the French have two hearts, a good one today and a bad one tomorrow? As for my brother and me, we have but one heart and one word . . ." Le Page du Pratz, *Histoire de la Louisiane,* (Paris: Bure, 1758): I:202–3. Such talk of the "heart" and its connections to one's "word" (or "mouth") served as a metaphor for individual trustworthiness—and, by extension, for the state of French-Native relations as a whole. Carayon, "Beyond Words," 273–77.

60. La Potherie, *Histoire,* t. III: 246. This comment follows his description of a war feast.

61. Samuel de Champlain, *Les voyages de la Nouvelle-France occidentale* (Paris: Collet, 1632), t. II: 148–49; Alain Beaulieu, "The Birth of the Franco-American Alliance," in *Champlain,* 153–61. Looking back nearly a century later, Perrot idealized the Champlain era as a period when "we began to make ourselves master of the savages, even though there were few French at that time." The key then, as at present, was to know their "nature" and traditions in order to "know how to manage them." Perrot, *Mémoire sur les moeurs,* 76–78, 96.

62. Le Jeune, *Jesuit Relations* 14 (1637): 98–99.

63. Le Jeune, *Jesuit Relations* 14 (1637): 67–69, 183–85. My interpretation here draws on Allan Greer's analysis of Native perceptions of Jesuit power. Greer, *Mohawk Saint,* 107.

64. James Axtell, *The Invasion Within: The Contest of Cultures in Colonial North America* (New York: Oxford University Press, 1986), 71–90.

65. Le Jeune, *Jesuit Relations* 5 (1633): 203–4.

66. Blackburn, *Harvest of Souls*, 85; Morrissey, "Terms of Encounter"; and Leavelle, *Catholic Calumet*, 132–33.

67. Axtell, *Invasion Within*, 84.

68. Historians continue to debate the extent to which northeastern Native communities were weakened and dislocated by warfare in the middle decades of the seventeenth century. Here I follow the prevailing account that many of the Native communities that moved into the Great Lakes region after ca. 1650 were composed of "refugees" fleeing disease and the pressures of a series of violent conflicts between European colonists and Native communities known alternately as the Iroquois Wars and the Beaver Wars. Others have used oral histories or case studies to suggest that these migrations westward were in fact "planned" by Natives and embedded in their culture. In this telling, the embrace of Onontio-as-father resulted from Native strategies conceived from a position of strength rather than one of weakness and desperation. See, for example, Witgen, *Infinity of Nations*, 29–64; Kathryn Magee Labelle, *Dispersed but not Destroyed: A History of the Seventeenth-Century Wendat People* (Vancouver: University of British Columbia Press, 2013); Michael McDonnell, *Masters of Empire: Great Lakes Indians and the Making of America* (New York: Hill & Wang, 2015), 9–10; and Heidi Bohaker, "Nindoodemag: The Significance of Algonquian Kinship Networks in the Eastern Great Lakes Region," *William and Mary Quarterly* 63, no. 1 (January 2006): 23–52.

69. Cook, "Onontio Gives Birth."

70. Cook, "Onontio Gives Birth," 191–92.

71. William J. Eccles, *Frontenac—The Courtier Governor* (Toronto: McLelland and Stewart, 1965), 233; Cook, "Onontio Gives Birth," 191–192; and Witgen, *Infinity of Nations*, 250–260.

72. Frontenac to Colbert, 13 November 1673, reproduced in *Rapport de l'archiviste de la Province de Québec pour* (1926–1927), 44.

73. Monseignat, "Voyage to Lake Ontario," in E. B. O'Callaghan, ed., *Documents Relative to the Colonial History of the State of New York*, vol. IX (Albany, NY: Weed, Parsons & Company, 1855), 104.

74. The Iroquois "gave me that which they have always refused to [previous] governors," he reported proudly to Colbert, "and which M[onsieurs] de Tracy and de Courcelles could not obtain from them, [even] after having defeated them and burned their villages." Frontenac to Colbert, 14 November 1674, reproduced in *RAPQ* (1926–1927), 65–66. Frontenac's claim to novelty was inaccurate: after negotiating with Tracy at Québec in 1667, several Mohawk headmen had left their "families as hostages"—presumably including children. Jon Parmenter, *The Edge of the Woods: Iroquoia, 1534–1701* (Lansing: Michigan State University Press, 2010), 130–31.

75. Eccles, *Frontenac*, 56.

76. Kristin E. Gager, *Blood Ties and Fictive Ties: Adoption and Family Life in Early Modern France* (Princeton, NJ: Princeton University Press, 2014), 20–36. Frontenac's accommodation may not have lasted long. Like other Native children taken into French custody during these years, the eight Haudenosaunee boys and girls he "adopted" were sent to the Jesuit and Ursuline seminaries for instruction. What became of them is unclear, but, to judge from similar cases at the time, they likely resisted the increasingly thorough form of "Frenchification" advocated by royal officials and subsequently escaped or were returned to their families. Frontenac to Colbert, 14 November 1674, ANOM COL C11A, vol. 4, ff. 163–64, 197–98; Duchesneau to Colbert, 13 November 1680, ANOM COL C11A, vol. 1, 178–79;

Mairi Cowan, "Education, *Francisation,* and Shifting Colonial Priorities at the Ursuline Convent in Seventeenth-Century Québec," *Canadian Historical Review* 99, no. 1 (March 2018): 3–7, 17–27.

77. On the costs of diplomatic gift-giving and their connection to Onontio's liberal paternal persona, see Catherine Desbarats, "The Cost of Early Canada's Native Alliances: Reality and Scarcity's Rhetoric," *William and Mary Quarterly* 52, no. 4 (October 1995): 609–14. Instances of Frontenac's hospitality toward Native emissaries are too numerous to cite here with any completeness, but they can be found throughout his correspondence as well as in the third and fourth volumes of La Potherie's history. Some examples include Lamberville to Frontenac, 9 September 1673 and 20 September 1682, in *Jesuit Relations* 57: 29 and 62: 149–51; "Memoire au Roy en réponse de sa depesche du dixiesme avril dernier," 13 November 1684, ANOM COL C11A, vol. 6, ff. 340–54, reproduced in Dubé, *La Nouvelle-France,* 256; La Potherie, *Histoire,* t. II: 320, t. III: 104–9, 137–38, 144–45, 218–19, t. IV: 91; Frontenac to Pontchartrain, 30 April 1690, in *RAPQ* (1927–1928), 30–31.

78. See, for example, his conduct among the Iroquois in 1673. Monseignat, "Voyage to Lake Ontario."

79. La Potherie, "An account of the most remarkable Occurences in Canada" (1697), reproduced in O'Callaghan, *Documents,* vol. IX: 685.

80. Rushforth, *Bonds of Alliance,* 155–64, 193–243.

81. In the decades after 1692, scalping became a specific and deliberate matter of French policy, which sought to mobilize an existing Indigenous custom for the purpose of encouraging France's Native allies to take up the hatchet when asked. Bounties for enemy scalps were paid at the governor's discretion. Lozier, "Lever des chevelures."

82. La Potherie, *Histoire,* t. III: 162.

83. See, for example, Adam Stueck, "A Place under Heaven: Amerindian Torture and Colonial Violence in New France, 1609–1729" (Ph.D. diss., Marquette University, 2012), 193–99. On the distinctions drawn by the French between European and Amerindian practices of torture, see Micah True, *Masters and Students: Jesuit Mission Ethnography in Seventeenth-Century New France* (Montréal: McGill-Queen's University Press, 2015), 83–112.

84. Antoine Laumet de Lamothe Cadillac to Pontchartrain, "Memorandum on the Peace Negotiations of Tareha," 1694, ANOM COL C11A, vol. 13, ff. 140–51v.

85. La Potherie, *Histoire,* t. IV: 11–12.

86. Havard, *Empire et metissage,* 741–47; Lozier, "Lever des chevelures."

87. La Potherie, *Histoire,* t. II: 297–98. "One must come to these extremes because otherwise [the Natives] would become convinced that we will be soft on them," he explained, after describing another incident in which Frontenac's lieutenant, the Chevalier de Vaudreuil, burned alive a party of Iroquois trapped in a house. La Potherie, *Histoire,* t. III: 135.

88. La Potherie, "An account of the most remarkable Occurences in Canada from the departure of the Vessels in 1695, to the beginning of 9ber 1696," in O'Callaghan, *Documents,* vol. X: 654.

89. Frontenac to Seignelay, 20 November 1690, ANOM COL C11A, reproduced in *RAPQ* (1927–1928), 44.

90. In addition to La Potherie's praise, see Bobé, "Lettre," in La Potherie, *Histoire,* t. IV: 268–69.

91. Perrot, for his part, claimed that his conduct had inspired "a great deal of confidence . . . and I was loved by them." Perrot, *Mémoire,* 119–22. For some of Perrot's exploits, see La Potherie, *Histoire,* t.

II: 87–90 (Perrot as god), 94–98, and 263–69 ("sorcerers"), 155–56 (dream-prophecy), 254 ("rodomontades"), 94–98, and 263–69 ("sorcerers"), 331.

92. Duchesneau to minister, 13 November 1681, ANOM COL C11A, vol. 5, ff. 313–313v.

93. Perrot, *Mémoire*; La Potherie, *Histoire*, t. II: 183–86 (Iowas), 186–87 (Fox), 218–19 (brandy), 227. For an example of governors invoking him in their speeches, see the speech preceding Frontenac's war dance in 1690. La Potherie, *Histoire*, t. III: 96–98. On Perrot's reputation among colonial officials, see "Perrot," *Dictionary of Canadian Biography*.

94. Lamothe Cadillac to Pontchartrain, "Memorandum on the Peace Negotiations of Tareha," 1694, ANOM COL C11A, vol. 13, f. 149.

95. La Potherie, *Histoire*, t. III: 252–53 ("secret").

96. Bobé, "Lettre," in La Potherie, *Histoire*, t. IV: 269–71.

97. La Potherie, *Histoire*, t. III: 249–50.

98. La Potherie, *Histoire*, t. III: 249. In fact, the strategic appointment of European-born "sons" as orators and representatives was neither unprecedented nor unusual among the Haudenosaunee during these years. See Parmenter, *Edge of the Woods*, 259–60, and below.

99. Whether the Great Peace should be seen as the high-water mark of French colonization in New France, a diplomatic triumph for the Iroquois, a successful example of cross-cultural politics, or a continuation of long-standing (if dynamic) forms of intercultural communications is still a subject of debate among historians, though most scholars agree that its outcomes were much more limited or ambivalent for the colony than French contemporaries believed. For examples of these differing views, respectively, see Havard, *Great Peace,* 179–83; José António Brandão and William A. Starna, "The Treaties of 1701: A Triumph of Iroquois Diplomacy," *Ethnohistory* 43, no. 2 (Spring 1996): 209–44; White, *Middle Ground,* 40; and Carayon, "Beyond Words," 347–50, 367–73.

100. Preliminary negotiations between Callières and Iroquois deputies, 18 July and 3 September 1700, ANOM COL C11A, vol. 18, ff. 81–88v; "Ratification de la paix faitte au mois de septembre dernier, entre la Colonie de Canada, les sauvages ses alliés, et les Iroquois . . ." (August and September 1701), ANOM COL C11A, vol. 19, ff. 41–44; La Potherie, *Histoire*, t. IV: 136–40, 148–58, 216–18.

101. The Great Peace built on months and even years of inter-Indigenous dialogue as well as prior negotiations between French and Haudenosaunee representatives. Maricourt and Joncaire had already served as interpreters in previous councils where many terms of the Peace were hammered out, so their presence at Montréal made them plausible and convenient scapegoats for the Iroquois's failure to uphold a key provision of the agreement. Moreover, given that the Seneca and Onondoga delegations were incomplete at this time and acting on their own behalf rather than in the name of the entire Confederacy, it may have been all the easier to allow Joncaire and Maricourt to speak for them, however temporarily (a state of affairs that would not persist when a more complete delegation of Haudenosaunee headmen and orators spoke for themselves the following year). Parmenter, *Edge of the Woods*, 232, 257, 259–60. On "hiding in plain view" as political strategy, see Susan Sleeper-Smith, *Indian Women and French Men,* 9, 116.

102. Pierre-François-Xavier de Charlevoix, *Histoire et description générale de la Nouvelle France* (Paris: Giffart, 1744), t. III: 414–16; La Potherie, *Histoire*, t. IV: 217–18, 229–36.

103. "Ratification de la paix," August and September 1701, ANOM COL C11A, vol. 19, ff. 41–42.

104. La Potherie, *Histoire,* t. IV: 240–53.

105. See, for example, Simon Le Moyne, *Relation 41* (1654), in *Jesuit Relations* 61: 108.

106. Monseignat, "Voyage to Lake Ontario," in O'Callaghan, *Documents,* vol. IX: 104. The same practice of reading from prerecorded speeches would be observed later, during the Great Peace of Montréal of 1701, by Governor Callières, Perrot, and several Jesuit interpreters who all spoke from copies of the same text. La Potherie, *Histoire,* t. IV: 241.

107. Monseignat, "Voyage to Lake Ontario," in O'Callaghan, *Documents,* vol. IX: 103–4.

108. La Potherie, "An account of the most remarkable Occurences in Canada from the month of September 1694 to the sailing of the vessels in 1695," in O'Callaghan, *Documents,* vol. IX: 605 ("tiresome"), 608 ("figurative expressions"); Frontenac to Colbert, 13 November 1673, reproduced in *RAPQ* (1926–1927), 62 ("Venetian Senate").

109. At the celebration of the Great Peace, Callières passed copies of his concluding address to his interpreters, to be read out verbatim. La Potherie, *Histoire,* t. IV: 240.

110. Frontenac to Colbert, 14 November 1674, reproduced in *RAPQ* (1926–1927), 65.

111. La Potherie to Pontchartrain, 16 October 1700, reproduced in Joseph-Edmond Roy, "Claude-Charles Le Roy de La Potherie," in *Proceedings and Transactions of the Royal Society of Canada,* series II, vol. 3 (Ottawa: Durie & Son, 1897): 19.

112. Isabelle Luciani, "Ordering Words, Ordering the Self: Keeping a *Livre de Raison* in Early Modern Provence, Sixteenth through Eighteenth Centuries," *French Historical Studies* 38, no. 4 (October 2015): 529–48; François-Joseph Ruggiu, "Une voix à soi? Autour du diaire de Michel Chartier de Lotbinière," in *Ecriture, récit, trouble(s) de soi: Perspectives historiques, France, XVIe-XX3 siècle,* ed. Isabelle Luciani and Valérie Piétri (Aix-en-Provence: Presses Universitaires de Provence, 2012), 159–85.

113. Michel Foucault, *Dits et écrits* (Paris: Gallimard, 1994), t. IV: 415–30, 783–813.

114. "Conference on the Intelligence received from the Iroquois," 23 March 1682, reproduced in O'Callaghan, *Documents,* vol. IX: 173; "Resume of speeches between 6 Iroquois deputies and Callieres," 18 July 1700, ANOM COL C11A, vol. 18, ff. 81v.

115. Frontenac, "Parole qui doit être dite à l'Outaouais pour le dissuader de l'alliance qu'il veut faire avec l'Iroquois et l'Anglais," ANOM COL C11A, vol. 11, ff. 130–33. For a similar example, see "Coppie des Instructions données par monsr le Gnal au sr de la Durantayes pour le voyage qu'il va faire aux Outaouax et Meamis (21 April 1683)," in Chevalier de Baugy, *Journal d'une expedition contre les Iroquois en 1687,* ed. Ernest Serrigny (Paris: Leroux, 1883), 165–67.

116. La Potherie, "An account of the most remarkable Occurences in Canada from the month of September 1694 to the sailing of the vessels in 1695," reproduced in O'Callaghan, *Documents,* vol. IX: 604–5.

117. La Potherie, "An account of the most remarkable Occurences in Canada from the month of September 1694 to the sailing of the vessels in 1695," reproduced in O'Callaghan, *Documents,* vol. IX: 704–5.

118. Perrot, *Mémoire sur les moeurs,* 153–54.

119. "*Acossen,* tell [the Iroquois] . . . what passed yesterday, which I caused to be written down in your presence, so that nothing may be altered," Frontenac ordered Le Moine on the second day of talks with the Iroquois in September 1682. "Conference between Count de Frontenac and a Deputy from the Five Nations," 12 September 1682, rep. and trans. in O'Callaghan, *Documents,* vol. IX: 185.

120. For instances of French officials reviewing the speeches of their predecessors, see La Barre, "Procès-verbal de l'assemblée convoquée par le Gouverneur La Barre pour discuter du péril Iroquois," 10 October 1682, ANOM COL C11A, vol. 6, ff. 68–70, reproduced in Dubé, *La Nouvelle-France sous*

Joseph-Antoine Le Febvre de La Barre, 48–49; "Commission donnée par Monsr le gnal au sr de la Durantayes pour aller a Missilimakina" and "Coppie des Instructions données par monsr le Gnal au sr de la Durantayes pour le voyage qu'il va faire aux Outaouax et Meamis," in Baugy, *Journal*, 168; Frontenac to Pontchartrain, 10 May 1691, reproduced in *RAPQ* (1927–1928), 62.

121. Perrot used his working notes to prepare extensive memoranda for Vaudreuil and Intendant Bégon; Louvigny did the same for Antoine-Denis Raudot; the Chevalier de Baugy likewise took notes to inform his letters to family in France. See Perrot, *Mémoire sur les moeurs*; Raudot, *Relation*; and Baugy, *Journal*.

122. On European practices of diplomatic reportage and archiving, see Filippo de Vivo, "Archives of Speech: Recording Diplomatic Negotiation in Late Medieval and Early Modern Italy," *European Historical Quarterly* 46 (July 2016): 519–44.

123. When Intendant Talon sent back a treaty concluded that year with several Iroquois "Ambassadors," Louis and Minister of Foreign Affairs Hugues de Lionne were amused and delighted by the appended "Explanation" of eleven gifts presented to Onontio, which summarized the speeches attached to each one while preserving the Iroquois's unfamiliar locutions and metaphors. "I will keep it as a very curious and well-done piece," Lionne assured Talon. "The King heard it read out to him with great pleasure." Lionne to Talon, 7 January 1667, reproduced in *RAPQ* (1930–1931), 62.

124. For instance, Frontenac to Pontchartrain, 10 October 1692, reproduced in *RAPQ* (1927–1928), 119; Vaudreuil to Pontchartrain, 4 November 1706, ANOM COL C11A, vol. 24, ff. 214–37, reproduced in *RAPQ* (1938–1939), 161; Vaudreuil and Raudot to Pontchartrain, 24 July 1707, ANOM COL C11A, vol. 26: ff. 54–61, reproduced in *RAPQ* (1939–1940), 380–81.

125. "Paroles des Sauvages au Sr de Vaudreuil et les réponses dudit sr de Vaudreuil en 1703" and "Paroles du Chef nommé Oronatyez Sonnontouan à Monsieur de Vaudreuil," 25 October 1703, ANOM COL C11A, vol. 21, ff. 68–86v.

126. For an excellent study of evolving administrative attitudes toward Natives visible in such documents, see Dubé, "Les Amerindiens."

127. La Potherie, *Histoire*, t. IV: 83.

128. The concentration of patronage in the hands of officers believed to possess special influence over Natives is reflected in the careers of the Vaudreuil and Joncaire families. See their entries in the *Dictionary of Canadian Biography*. For the centrality of Native governance in royal instructions, see "Mémoire du Roy pour servir d'instruction au Sr [Pierre de Rigaud] de Vaudreuil de Cavagnal, Capitaine de Vaisseau, Gouverneur et Lieutenant général de la Nouvelle-France," 22 March 1755, AN K 1232, pièce 50, and "Extrait des instructions données à Vaudreuil," ANOM COL C11A, vol. 100, ff. 50–51.

129. For imagined and template speeches, see Perrot, *Mémoire sur les moeurs*, esp. 143–56; Anonymous, "Moyens pour gagner du bien sans que personne en souffre," ca. 1726, Famille de Beauharnois Papers, Library and Archives Canada MG18-G6, vol. 1, pp. 11–15.

130. Onontio remained a fixture of intercultural diplomacy in North America until the British Conquest of New France in 1763; even decades afterward, Native headmen still invoked his memory in calling for the French to return to North America as a counterweight to British expansion. White, *Middle Ground*, 276–90.

131. On the French experience in New France as the origin of the "*génie colonial*" myth, see Jaenen, "'Les Sauvages Ameriquains,'"; Gregory Dowd, "Wag the Imperial Dog: Indians and Overseas Empires

in North America, 1650–1776," in *A Companion to American Indian History*, ed. Philip Deloria and Neal Salisbury (Oxford: Wiley-Blackwell, 2004), 55–56. Historians differ about the precise roots of French racial ideologies in colonial North America and the French Atlantic world, but most point to the later seventeenth and early eighteenth centuries as a decisive period in the spread and institutionalization of complexion-based racism; in recent years, scholarship has emphasized the ways in which modern conceptions of race emerged less from prefabricated metropolitan notions of "*race*" than from everyday contestations of power and privilege in the colonies, where various European attempts to coerce and control Africans and Indigenous peoples transformed long-standing but conditional prejudices into entrenched legal, social, and cultural systems of racialized exploitation. My argument here is that French performances of "Indianness," and the notion of cultural superiority that these performances seemed to substantiate, opened up important new terrain for racialized thinking. Cross-cultural performances on the ground and the essentially metropolitan, aristocratic lens of *personae* through which elite officers often interpreted them, however, were hardly the exclusive origin of colonial or racist attitudes toward Natives. See, for example, Guillaume Aubert, "'The Blood of France': Race and Purity of Blood in the French Atlantic World," *William and Mary Quarterly* 61, no. 3 (2004): 439–78; Pierre Boulle, *Race et esclavage dans la France de l'Ancien Régime* (Paris: Perrin, 2007); Sue Peabody, *"There Are No Slaves in France": The Political Culture of Race and Slavery in the Ancien Régime* (New York: Oxford University Press, 1996), and "A Nation Born to Slavery": Missionaries and Racial Discourse in Seventeenth-Century French Antilles," *Journal of Social History* 38, no. 1 (2004): 113–26; John D. Garrigus, *Before Haiti: Race and Citizenship in French Saint-Domingue* (New York: Palgrave Macmillan, 2006); Belmessous, "Assimilation and Racialism"; Cécile Vidal, "Francité et situation colonial: Nation, empire et race en Louisiane Française (1699–1769)," *Annales Histoire, Sciences Sociales*, 64e année, no. 5 (2009): 1019–50; Rushforth, *Bonds of Alliance*, esp. 299–382; White, *Wild Frenchmen*.

132. Perrot, *Mémoire*, vi.

133. For a recent overview of the literature on "going Native" in modern empires, see Ricardo Roque, "Mimesis and Colonialism: Emerging Perspectives on a Shared History," *History Compass* 13, no. 4 (2015): 201–11.

134. George Orwell, *Shooting an Elephant, and Other Essays* (1936; London: Harcourt, 1950), 6.

135. See, for example, Robert Arnaud, *L'Islam et la politique musulmane française en Afrique occidentale française* (Paris: Comité de l'Afrique Française, 1912); Ministre de la Guerre, *Manuel élémentaire à l'usage des officiers et sous-officiers chargés à commander des indigènes coloniaux (Indochinois-Sénégalais-Malgaches) dans la métropole* (Paris: Charles-Lavauzelle, 1923); Joseph-Simon Galliéni, *Madagascar de 1896 à 1905: rapport du Général Galliéni, Gouverneur Général au Ministre des Colonies*, 2 vols. (Tananarive: Imprimerie Officielle de Tananarive, 1905); Jacques Frémeaux, *Les Bureaux arabes dans l'Algérie de la conquête* (Paris: Denoël, 1993).

The Ancien Régime Culture of Labor Mobility and Migration to New France

LESLIE CHOQUETTE

Scholars often explain migration in economic terms, identifying various push-and-pull factors. Yet migration, as a form of cultural behavior, has a specificity of its own. As historian Jean-Pierre Poussou writes, "Migratory movements have their own laws, their internal logic, indeed, their own tradition." Regardless of the economic context, there is, in his words, "an inertia of migratory flows."[1] Viewed from the standpoint of migration history, the peopling of French North America in the seventeenth and eighteenth centuries was part of a larger ancien régime culture of work mobility. It occurred as a by-product of other, perennial French labor migrations such as the rural exodus, in which people abandoned the countryside to work in towns and cities, and interurban movements by people whose work took them from one city to the next. For an individual, Atlantic migration could be an accidental deviation from, or a simple extension of, established channels of labor mobility. An adventurous journeyman could cut short his traditional Tour de France for a lucrative colonial work contract; a hapless soldier could end up overseas as the involuntary consequence of a previous enlistment. In either case, colonial migration was at the confluence of familiar migratory flows.

In ancien régime France, the search for work gave rise to a whole range of population movements, from short to long distance and from short to long term. Peasants migrated seasonally from pockets of subsistence farming to adjacent areas of commercial agriculture to bring in the harvest; they also abandoned the countryside for temporary or permanent jobs in nearby towns and faraway cities. For centuries before the invention of the bicycle, journeymen set out on what was already called a Tour de France, moving from town to town in a loosely organized circuit to complete their artisanal training. Soldiers shuttled between garrison towns and battlefields during what were often long terms of service.[2]

Most migrants to New France were laborers—whether soldiers, indentured servants, or young women seeking work within the family economy of Canada's shops and farms. Further, most traditional forms of French labor mobility, from local to long-distance, contributed to the formation of the new, Atlantic migration stream.[3] At the local and regional levels, the secular and massive movements from country to town, and from small town to regional capital, sometimes spilled over, or were redirected, into the St. Lawrence Valley or Acadia. Among long-distance migrants, we find in New France mountain folk who had migrated annually to the big city and town dwellers with a tradition of complex interurban itineraries. Such were the journeymen of the Tour de France and the soldiers of the French army, dubbed by historian Jean-Claude Perrot a "school of mobility."[4]

Geographic mobility did not end with arrival in the colony. Between two-thirds and three-quarters of the migrants eventually returned to France.[5] The founding immigrants—those who remained—and their descendants became agricultural settlers, but they also traveled inland to trade, pioneering a French-Canadian continental diaspora that would last into the twentieth century. Jean Lamarre, a historian of nineteenth- and twentieth-century Canada, writes of the impact of geographic mobility upon French-Canadian identity formation: "The reliance on mobility constitutes a distinctive, and even recurrent, trait in the socioeconomic and cultural life of French Canadians. Its origins go back to the very beginnings of French colonization on the continent, and it must be carefully considered as a means of better understanding the nature of the solutions chosen by French Canadians in times of crisis."[6] Yves Frenette, holder of the Canadian Research Chair on Migrations, Transfers, and Francophone Communities, concurs, noting: "Geographic mobility is thus an important element of French-Canadian identity."[7]

Beyond the tradition of physical movement, did other aspects of French labor mobility influence the development of colonial societies and collective identities in French North America? Here the answer is less clear. Both soldiers and journeymen contributed, if not always permanently, to the peopling of New France, but their respective cultures left an uneven mark. Military customs and ethos went on to play a significant role throughout French North America; however, journeyman militancy and conviviality survived better in Louisbourg than in the towns of the St. Lawrence Valley.

The Ancien Régime Culture of Labor Mobility and Migration to New France

Traditional Patterns of Labor Mobility and Colonial Migration

LOCAL AND REGIONAL MOVEMENTS

Of the various types of French labor mobility, local harvest migrations were probably the least likely to lead to transatlantic movements. For instance, in 1698, the intendant of Alençon wrote that people from the neighboring province of Perche "seem sluggish, attached from father to son to the same work... do not like in the least to leave their country although unhappy, if not for a few who go help with the harvest in Beauce, which yields them some profits."[8] He went on to add, however: "Each one lives thus in his canton, such that for forty years, no one has gone to the Indies, Canada, Holland, England, or to sea, though the example of ten or twelve people who went to Canada at that time, where they established themselves very well, and three or four to the Islands, where they made a reasonable profit, ought to have excited others to leave their country to sample another."[9]

In fact, more than two hundred Percherons migrated to Canada beginning in 1634, when Robert Giffard, a Perche-based surgeon and apothecary, accepted a land grant in Beauport, northeast of Québec, to become one of the first colonizing seigneurs. Having traveled to Québec as a naval surgeon in the 1620s, Giffard had determined to settle there and solicited the seigneurie. Over the next several decades, he worked with fellow Percheron notables, the three Juchereau brothers, to recruit successful colonists from among the farmers and tradesmen of their province. The end of the movement coincided with the deaths, in Canada, of the two primary recruiters, Giffard and Jean Juchereau, in 1668 and 1672.

While the willingness of Percherons to emigrate probably had more to do with the social prestige of the recruiters than the tradition of seasonal harvest migration, we know of at least one instance where moving for agricultural work did inspire a colonial vocation. The fortuitous reference comes from the "testimonials of freedom at marriage," sworn statements required by Canadian bishops between 1757 and 1820 in hopes of preventing bigamy among migrants.[10] Prior to the 1757 marriage of André Guigné alias Bourguignon, a soldier from Auxerre, Abbé Briand wrote:

> Came before us Philippe Guillemin alias St Cyr, corporal in the company of Boishébert, native of Yssoudun in Berry, aged forty years, unmarried, in this country for eight, Who after having promised us under oath to tell the truth

assured us that the said Guigné is not married in France, and this for having worked for his father in the capacity of vineyard worker for three months, after which time at Candlemas they enlisted together for this country to which they came together.[11]

Philippe Guillemin had worked in Guigné's father's Burgundian vineyard, 175 kilometers from Issoudun, from All Saints until Candlemas. Who would have predicted that such a commonplace move would lead in the end to Canada?

We have more evidence about the links between local and regional urbanization movements and emigration to Canada. To begin with, the regional map of emigration closely resembles that of immigration into French towns and cities.[12] For example, emigrants to Canada from the present-day department of Loire-Atlantique came not only from Nantes, the major port city, but from the southeastern part of the diocese, the Loire Valley, and relay towns (*villes-relais*)—local towns serving as way stations along the route from countryside to metropolis. A handful also came from a line of parishes in the impoverished north, stretching from Riaillé through Blain to Saint-Gildas-des-Bois. According to historian Jacques Depauw, Nantes's demographic basin, the area of densest regional recruitment whose contours remain remarkably stable over time, consisted of precisely these places.[13] In southern Brittany, the cartography of emigration to Canada bore an undeniable resemblance to that of local urban arrivals.

If we consider the fifty-five Bretons, including three women, who are known to have moved in France before embarking for Canada, we discover that thirty-three had been born in Brittany, while nine came from neighboring provinces (Normandy, Maine, Anjou, Poitou). Thirty-two had left their native countryside for a town, and twenty had followed an interurban itinerary, usually from a small town to a larger one. All three women were Breton villagers whose interim destinations were port cities—Tréguier, Nantes, and Saint-Malo.[14]

Similar observations can be made regarding other regions, for example, the southwest. Besides Bordeaux, southwestern emigrants to Canada came from small groups of parishes known for their demographic ties to the port city—for example, the Dropt Valley villages of Duras, Auriac, Monteton, and Allemans-du-Dropt. Furthermore, specific regional migration currents that supplied Bordeaux with artisans also sent them on to Canada. Bordeaux's bakers and pastry cooks, for instance, came disproportionately from Périgord, Quercy, and Comminges.[15] In 1757 and 1761, the witnesses who came before Abbé Briand in Canada included pastry cooks Raymond Vert and Jean Pierre from Périgord and bakers Pierre La Chaume and Pierre Bonnet from Comminges. All had done their apprenticeships in Bordeaux before coming to Canada.[16]

Other examples from the testimonials of freedom at marriage demonstrate the importance of relay towns and urban hinterland villages for both urban immigration and emigration to Canada. Soldier Jacques Joseph Le Geay alias Printemps, "native of Noyon in Picardy and resident of Paris," and Emmanuel Bergeron, born in Saint-Germain-en-Laye and working as an apprentice baker on rue de la Draperie, had left their respective relay towns for the capital before shipping out to Canada.[17] Le Geay, who was thirty-nine years old and married at the time of his enlistment, probably conceived of his stay in Canada as temporary, a remedy for unemployment or means to amass a small nest egg. From the countryside around Paris came domestics and artisans for the city, and later Canada, such as cook Alexandre Picard from the village of Le Mesnil-Saint-Georges in Picardy, servant Jeanne Godin of Aunay near Vire in Normandy, and Ambroise Leguay alias La Grenade, "native to Coubron four leagues away from Paris, gilder."[18] Combining both of these types of mobility, from the countryside and the relay town, servant Suzanne Dionnet was born in rural Saintonge, worked for eight years in the small town of Tonnay-Charente, then immigrated to the port of Rochefort before leaving for Canada in 1751.[19]

LONG-DISTANCE MOVEMENTS

Long-distance work migrations also contributed to the peopling of New France, including the movements of fishermen and landlocked mountain folk. Seasonal cod fishing migrations to North America sometimes led to Canadian settlement, as one might expect. Temporary migrations of mountain folk did so as well, despite the lack of a maritime tradition, through various disruptions of the normal migratory process.

The migrations of Norman, Breton, and Basque fishermen to the Grand Banks were primarily seasonal in the seventeenth century but increasingly led to North American settlement in the eighteenth.[20] Temporary migrations remained important, as demonstrated by the testimonial of freedom at marriage of migrant Barthélemy Alis. A native of the village of Marcey in Normandy, Alis embarked for the Gaspé fishery in 1755, at the age of twenty-three, and he was still in Canada when he became engaged in 1771. But when urged to present witnesses who could attest to his freedom to marry, he could state only that "in the same ship, there had come a man named François Obu from the same parish ... [and that] others from his same parish had come the same year in different ships [but] are no longer in this province."²¹ Sometimes, permanent settlement took place only after multiple seasonal campaigns. Such was the case with François Hamel and François Frigot of Avranches, who both claimed to have "made several campaigns by sea as well as by land" before settling in Québec.²² A fourth migrant fisherman, Louis Alexandre of the village of Ronthon, continued the tradition of seasonal labor, while based in Canada instead of Normandy. After leaving home in 1751, at the tender age of twelve, he spent summers in Gaspé, then wintered upriver at La Rivière-Ouelle. He still resided on Québec's Côte-du-Sud at the time of his marriage fifteen years later, "going each summer to fish in Gaspé."²³

As for the mountain folk, their most typical migrations consisted of periodic descents into major cities to find work. Whether in Paris, Lyon, or Bordeaux, the arrival of these picturesque migrants, distinct in their appearance, speech, and manners, did not go unremarked. City dwellers noted the affinity of different groups of mountain folk to specific trades or jobs. Louis-Sébastien Mercier, in his *Panorama of Paris* in the eighteenth century, wrote that "the Auvergnats are almost all water carriers, the Limousin masons," and the Savoyards sweepers (*décrotteurs*), of chimneys especially.²⁴ As it happens, each of these specialized migratory currents, along with the Alpine tradition of peddling, could be found in Canada, having been diverted from a more traditional destination.

The Canadian Auvergnats included water carrier Pierre Rivet, son of a day laborer and proprietor from a village near Le Puy. Arriving in Paris at the age of seventeen, he had worked in the capital for ten years before going home for a two-week visit. He then worked in Paris for five more years until, tiring of his strenuous occupation, he enlisted in the Canadian troops. In the colony, he worked as a soldier and hired hand before becoming a tinker, another Auvergnat specialty. He married in Québec at the age of forty-eight.²⁵

Masons from the Massif Central, including Limousin, were appreciated in Canada, as shown by royal orders issued in 1720 to recruit masons, stonecutters, and carpenters for Île Royale (Cape Breton) "in the provinces of Le Puy-en-Velay, Auvergne, Bourbonnais, Limousin, and Poitou."²⁶ The Canadian odyssey of such mountain folk was not always the result of on-site recruitment. In 1721, when officials recruited nine more building workers in Paris for the Cape Breton fortifications, only two were native Parisians; five came from the Massif Central, including four Limousins: François Bonnet, François Lamarche, François Granjan, and Jean Buistre. According to the census records of Île Royale, two of the five, François Granjan and Jean Roche from the adjacent province of Marche, had become permanent residents by 1726.[27]

Masons from the Massif Central also made their way to Québec, as we learn from the testimonials of freedom at marriage. In 1758, prospective husband André le Comte alias Vadeboncœur, "mason by profession," told his story to Abbé Briand. A native of Azérables in Marche, he had come to Paris as a mason's helper in his early teens and lived for ten years on rue de la Mortellerie, convenient to the hiring market of La Grève, before enlisting in the Regiment of Languedoc. He married in Québec two years after his arrival.[28]

Like migrant masons, Savoyard chimney sweeps arrived in Canada both through the efforts of recruiters who valued their specialized skill and through more random, individual channels. In 1716, the general correspondence between officials in Québec and the naval ministry in France mentioned chimney sweeps, specifically, "six little Savoyards who would go over as soldiers."[29] In 1729 and again in 1730, Canadian administrators informed their French superior that "the two Savoyards who were sent by your orders a few years ago to this country [have] become too big and too fat to sweep chimneys. We entreat you . . . to send next year four others from twelve to fourteen years of age."[30] Though the naval minister refused this request on account of the expense, he acquiesced in 1749, informing Québec's intendant: "I have taken measures to have the six Savoyard chimney sweeps that you asked for assembled; and I expect that they will be able to be sent to the colony this year."[31] In contrast to such official recruitment, Pierre Pechereau, a chimney sweep from Saint-Clair in Upper Savoy, indentured himself for Canada along with a friend in the port of La Rochelle in 1755.[32]

Peddling was another occupational specialty of migrant mountain folk. In the High Alps, the region surrounding Le Bourg-d'Oisans and Briançon furnished peddlers to nearly all the towns in southern France.[33] Examining the origins of Alpine emigrants to Canada, we discover that they came from the same places known for their peddlers. Le Bourg-d'Oisans and a neighboring parish sent three, Briançon and nearby La Salle-les-Alpes four. Likewise, one emigrant from La Rochelle, merchant François Viennay-Pachot, was a native of Le Bourg-d'Oisans who had made his fortune at the age of twenty by marrying the widow of a hardware merchant from the port city.[34]

INTERURBAN MOVEMENTS

Not all long-distance labor migrants came from the coast or the mountains. As urban historian Jean-Claude Perrot noted of Caen, a Norman city of some thirty thousand inhabitants: "Two human networks connected the town to the outside; one was nourished by country sap, while the other, beyond rural Normandy, ran from town to town to the borders of France, and constituted the second homeland of the city folk." The "300,000 to 350,000 residents of large cities, in constant reciprocal relations,"[35] made up a population whose availability for work and adventure could be tapped to benefit the colonial enterprise. Parisian emigrants to Canada included several natives of provincial capitals: eight from Rouen, one from Bordeaux, etc. They represented a wide range of professions, from Étienne Mouillé, a Lyon silk worker who had worked in Turin before trying his luck in Paris, to Louis Artus de Sailly, a merchant from Amiens whose grandfather already belonged to the merchant community of that city.[36]

While many interurban migrations involved just one or two moves, others featured what could be called occupational hypermobility. Hypermobile migrants moved constantly over a period of years, working in a given town for days, weeks, or months before passing on to the next. In the case of both soldiers and journeymen on the Tour de France, urban hypermobility sometimes expanded to include colonial destinations.

Ancien régime military service was "incompatible with a home-bound state of mind," in the words of historian André Corvisier.[37] Soldiers moved constantly between garrison towns during the six or seven years of a typical enlistment, and three-fifths to two-thirds of them settled outside their community of origin upon finishing their service.[38] We know that the French army sent more than thirteen thousand emigrants to Canada, at least temporarily.[39] Some of these men were already professional migrants, as illustrated by the testimonial of freedom at marriage of Joseph Pusse alias La Lime, a foundry worker from Namur (Belgium) who arrived in Canada as a soldier in 1751. Appearing before Abbé Briand in 1757, Pusse presented as witnesses to his five-and-a-half years of service "in the troops of the Queen of Hungary": Julien Le Compte alias La Batterie from Beaumont-le-Vicomte, a small town in the province of Maine, who claimed to have seen him at Port-Louis, the Breton base of the East India Company; Martin Hainault, a cobbler from Paris; Pierre Bonnel alias La Lancette, a surgeon from Saint-Gilles in Languedoc, who said he had served with Pusse for four years "in Dutch country" (*chez les Hollandais*); and Joseph Tourelle of Saint-Claude in Franche-Comté, who swore to "having known him in Liège where they enlisted for Canada."[40]

In contrast, the hypermobility of journeymen (*compagnons*) was more structured, following timetables and itineraries imposed by tradition.[41] The journeymen of the Tour de France belonged to three semi-clandestine confraternities of artisans: the Enfants de Maître Jacques (Dévorants); the Enfants du Père Soubise (Bons Drilles); and the Enfants de Salomon (Gavots).[42] Artisans joined these societies in their late teens, after completing an apprenticeship, and could remain active members into their mid-twenties unless they married. Like soldiers, they chose nicknames for themselves, which they used practically to the exclusion of their family names. Journeyman nicknames, however, always included a geographical component, giving each young man a secure, regional identity as he set out on his travels. Among Gavots, the nickname consisted of a place name joined to a quality or flower: Parisien le Bienvenu (Welcome Parisian) or Bourguignon la Rose (Burgundian Rose). Dévorants coupled a given name with a place name, as in Pierre le Nantais (Pierre from Nantes). All journeymen wore "colors" in the form of cockades of multicolored ribbon, which they defended jealously. The five accepted colors were white, red, blue, yellow, and green.[43]

The heart of journeyman life was the Tour de France, a voyage enabling the young artisan to perfect his skills, see the world, and sow his wild oats. It had no fixed duration, but as a rule it lasted between three and seven years. Although itineraries varied according to the society and changed with the location of work, the Tour de France generally moved in a clockwise direction. From Paris, it followed the Seine, Saône, and Rhône River valleys to the Mediterranean; the coast, Canal du Midi, and Garonne Valley to Bordeaux; the Atlantic coast to Nantes; and the Loire Valley to Orléans before returning to Paris. The ideal route included the cities of Paris, Auxerre, Dijon, Lyon, Nîmes, Marseille, Toulouse, Agen, Bordeaux, Rochefort, La Rochelle, Nantes, Angers, Tours, Blois, and Orléans.[44] Journeyman mobility also extended beyond these *villes de devoir*, or focal points, of the Tour de France. In the eighteenth century, according to historian Émile Coornaert, traveling journeymen were to be found "in nearly all the towns of the kingdom, even in centers where they could not have been numerous."[45]

During their Tour, journeymen would move from town to town at irregular intervals, traveling by foot, stagecoach, or ferry as their budgets allowed. Upon arrival in a new town, they would descend on an inn affiliated with their society, accept the hospitality of its *mère des compagnons*, and make the acquaintance of the *rouleur*, or journeyman in charge of job placement. The length of their stay would vary from a few days to several months, depending on the labor market and their personal whims.[46] Working was typically accompanied by brawling with journeymen from other societies (for the three groups were bitter rivals), drinking in taverns, and sexual exploits. When it came time to move on, journeymen rarely departed alone, preferring the company of one or more traveling companions who might or might not have the same destination, and whom they felt free to abandon and rejoin at will.[47]

By its flexibility, the Tour de France was highly subject to short-cuts and detours; it could end elsewhere from where it began, either prematurely, or after extension of the normal period of mobility. An offer of marriage, an enlistment in the military, even a colonial indenture could break the normal circuit of the Tour and alter the journeyman's loosely structured itinerary.

The pioneers of New France included journeymen due to labor demand in the fledgling colony. Their arrival is a neglected aspect of an otherwise often-told story about early Montréal: the rescue of the struggling French settlement by the "great levy" (*grande recrue*) of 1653.

Founded as the missionary community of Ville-Marie in 1642, Montréal was on the verge of extinction ten years later from Iroquois raids. In a last-ditch attempt to save the outpost, Jérôme Le Royer de la Dauversière, procurator of the Société Notre-Dame de Montréal pour la conversion des sauvages en Nouvelle-France, recruited 121 new colonists for Ville-Marie in his small town of La Flèche in Anjou between March 23 and May 17, 1653. Most of these workers were peasants from the surrounding region, and only ten had journeyed to La Flèche from a considerable distance. Nonetheless, the first men to indenture themselves, a week before any of the peasants, were "Pierre Godin journeyman carpenter from the city of Chastillon sur Seine [Châtillon-sur-Seine], Paul Benoist also journeyman carpenter from the city of Nevers, René Bondy also journeyman carpenter from the city of Dijon, René Truffaut also journeyman carpenter from the city of Laval, and Fiacre Ducharme journeyman joiner from the city of Paris."[48] In all, ten journeymen contracted to emigrate from La Flèche: five natives of Maine and Touraine, two Parisians, and three men from Burgundy and Nivernais. These formal affiliates of the Tour de France made up about a quarter of the artisans recruited in La Flèche, including eight of eighteen in the building and woodworking trades, one of six in the garment trades, and one of the seven metalworkers. Although they signed a five-year labor contract, four of them settled permanently in Canada.[49]

To hear the voices of the Canadian journeymen themselves, we need to turn once again to the testimonials of freedom at marriage. In a typical story, a Parisian journeyman turned soldier named Antoine Boudin alias Saint-Germain explained to Abbé Briand in 1758 that he had lived with a Parisian master "for five years to learn there the trade of mason, after which having done his Tour de France for nearly three years, he enlisted in Bordeaux, From whence he returned to Paris to say farewell to his father, and from there went to Brest where he embarked for Canada."[50]

More unusual was the case of Antoine Griseau, who left his native town of Châlon-sur-Saône (on the road from Dijon to Lyon) "at about the age of fifteen for several towns of France, where he spent seven years in the capacity of journeyman confectioner" before embarking in Dunkerque for London, where he worked for ten months before leaving for Canada (now a British colony) in 1765.[51] Canadian journeymen rarely described their Tour de France in detail, but in a welcome exception, we have the 1759 testimonial of "Nicolas Lelat, native of Calais, mantle maker (*manchonnier*), aged twenty-eight, in Canada for two years as of September and away from his home country (*païs*) for three, and having worked in Rouen, Caen, Angers, Nantes, La Rochelle, and Bordeaux during the space of a year and a half, embarked for these countries."[52] Before shipping out of Bordeaux, Lelat had completed the full Atlantic segment of a traditional Tour de France.

⁓

In sum, despite age-old and well-worn itineraries, French labor migrations of all types spilled out in other directions, toward new horizons, to the benefit of New France. A migrant in a port city could decide, after a brief or extended stay, to try his or her luck in the colony. A soldier could embark, in a military or a civilian capacity, after shuttling between garrison towns for six or seven years. Even movements that were normally structured were vulnerable to rupture. Building workers from the Massif Central could interrupt their temporary migration to Paris to work on colonial fortifications, and footloose journeymen could cut short or prolong their Tour de France to practice their skills across the Atlantic. In these and other cases, traditional patterns of French labor mobility provided the means to people French Canada.

LESLIE CHOQUETTE

The Transatlantic Culture of Labor Mobility

Since traditional migration patterns were redirected to New France, what about other aspects of the ancien régime culture of labor migration? Certainly, labor migration remained an important feature of French-Canadian society, not just until the British Conquest but into the twentieth century; in 1901, nearly half of all French Canadians lived outside the province of Québec, over a third in the industrializing United States.[53] Beginning in the seventeenth century, the phenomenon of fur trade mobility (*mobilité pelletière*) contributed not only to the francophone continental diaspora, but to a "culture of circulation" critical to identity formation. The iconic figure of the *coureur de bois*, prototype for French North America's nomads and seekers, achieved mythical stature in French-Canadian culture. Writers of French-Canadian background from Joseph-Charles Taché (1820–1894) to Jack Kerouac (1922–1969) celebrated migration and wandering as the key to an intercultural space-time of new sensations and masculine liberty.[54]

Besides the economically and culturally significant legacy of physical movement, were migrant values and sociability or the cultures of specific groups of migrants transplanted to French North America? The evidence here is mixed. In the Canadian cod fishery, enough migrants probably settled or worked in local clusters to reproduce their home fishing cultures, at least temporarily. Cape Breton censuses from the eighteenth century show concentrations of settled Normans and Bretons from Mont Saint-Michel Bay as well as Basques.[55] On Scatarie, an island outpost near the easternmost tip of the large island, a dozen fishery proprietors employed a temporary labor force of around two hundred, most of them Normans. Scatarie's migrant workers in 1730 included brothers Mathurin and Charles Renaud, who decided to overwinter after several seasonal campaigns. Still, their ties to Normandy remained strong. In April 1731, Charles's wife Marie Joanne sent him a plaintive letter that began: "I let pass no occasion to inquire about your health which I pray God with all my heart is perfect as mine is good, thank God, and also that of our little girl who is doing well and who . . . has been walking since two months after you left." She continued, "All I ask is that you come home this year, for such a long absence is truly wearisome to me. Nothing has gone along well since you have been out." Sadly, both brothers had drowned at sea four months earlier.[56]

Basque fishermen formed communities with their own priests and tradesmen on Louisbourg's north shore and in outports such as Baleine, Fourché, Saint-Esprit, and Niganiche. The Superior Council in Louisbourg often needed to employ translators when they came before the court. Nonetheless, several families of successful Basque colonists, the Daccarrettes, Detcheverrys, and Hiriarts, for example, assimilated into the French-speaking population as they accumulated wealth and power.[57] The re-creation of regional fishing cultures in Canada was probably a short-lived phenomenon.

What of the many soldiers and journeymen who worked and settled in New France? To what extent did their distinct cultures travel across the Atlantic? As we shall see, the military establishment and its values came to play an even greater role in the colony than it had in the metropolis. In contrast, journeymen's organizations, which dominated the labor market in France,[58] failed to take root overseas, although traces of journeyman culture survived in the eighteenth-century garrison town of Louisbourg.

Assessing the "social, economic, and political significance" of the army in New France, historian William Eccles wrote: "The whole fabric of Canadian society was imbued with the military ethos."[59] For the duration of the colony (1604–1763), there were barely fifty years of peace. Soldiers made up a huge percentage of the colonial population in comparison to France, which nonetheless had the largest army in Europe under Louis XIV.[60] To this day, many families of French-Canadian descent bear soldiers' nicknames that have been passed down, instead of French family names.[61] Furthermore, after 1669, all able-bodied civilian males between the ages of sixteen and sixty were required to serve in the colonial militia. Given the frequency of fighting, most militiamen likely served on at least one campaign during their lifetime. "It was, however, among the dominant class, the colonial 'establishment,' or élite, that militarism and the military ethos took the firmest hold," Eccles noted.[62] Serving in the officer corps became a vehicle of social mobility for Canadians of humble extraction, who absorbed the martial and caste-like values of the French *noblesse d'épée* on their journey from commerce to nobility. Called to arms, the men of ennobled families like the Le Moynes and the Juchereaus managed quickly to forget their plebeian roots.[63]

French military culture thus journeyed successfully across the Atlantic, although it did not remain unchanged. As historian Christian Ayne Crouch has shown, the intercultural realities of New World warfare created a distinct Canadian martial culture, characterized by a willingness to engage in diplomacy and warfare on Native terms. During the Seven Years' War, Canadian martial culture even came into conflict with its French counterpart, as symbolized by the famous and fateful rivalry between Governor Vaudreuil and General Montcalm.[64]

The situation regarding journeyman culture is more ambiguous. There is some evidence that journeymen maintained an organized presence outside of France during the ancien régime. For example, Huguenot emigrants to Pennsylvania helped establish a craftsmen's society there, the Carpenters' Company of the City and County of Philadelphia, in 1724.[65] In New France, though, journeymen were unable to perpetuate their associations because of the hostile vigilance of colonial authorities. Beginning in 1677, Governor Frontenac made clear that "there is nothing more expressly forbidden than assemblies and conventicles that happen without permission, nor that could furnish more easily a pretext for all the Monopolies, Cabals, and Intrigues that malevolent individuals could intend to form." He continued, "We very expressly Prohibit and forbid all persons of whatever quality and condition to have in the future any assemblies, conventicles, and common signatures, of whatever nature and for whatever purpose, without our express permission."[66]

The governor's hostility to corporate organization was consistent with the attitude of authorities in France, who pursued a vigorous if less effective campaign against journeymen's associations throughout the seventeenth and eighteenth centuries. Metropolitan officials attempted repeatedly to dissolve the societies and control the mobility of individual journeymen through a system of passports.[67] French churchmen accused the societies of heterodoxy in 1639, leading to their condemnation by the ecclesiastical court in Paris and the theology faculty of the Sorbonne. Several religious figures who led the fight against the journeymen were also strong proponents of colonization, among them Abbé Jean-Jacques Olier and St. François de Laval. Abbé Olier, founder of the Order of Saint-Sulpice, personally engineered both the journeymen's condemnation by the Sorbonne and the creation of the Société Notre-Dame de Montréal pour la conversion des sauvages en Nouvelle-France. Monsignor Laval (canonized in 2014) became New France's first bishop in 1659. Under these circumstances, the procurator of the Société Notre-Dame, Jérôme Le Royer de la Dauversière, may have had a dual motive in recruiting journeymen for Montréal in 1653: saving the settlement by sending competent reinforcements and saving artisanal souls by converting them. According to St. Marguerite Bourgeoys, founder of the Congregation of Notre Dame, he succeeded on both counts. Writing of La Dauversière's recruits, the good sister exclaimed: "Shortly after their arrival in Québec, these ... men were changed like linen put to the wash."[68]

If the combined efforts of zealous churchmen and vigilant royal authorities kept journeymen's societies out of New France, did aspects of journeyman culture survive nevertheless? Along the St. Lawrence River, there is little evidence that they did. All the known craft rituals in early Québec and Montréal involved masters rather than journeymen. The organization of work was such that artisans were either isolated helpers in small-scale enterprises, often with the status of indentured servant, or independent masters. Since access to independent status was unrestricted, journeymen were free to set up shop upon arrival or, if indentured, upon expiration of their term of service. It was common for them to assume the title of master as soon as they received their first Canadian contract.[69]

Conditions were better in Louisbourg for the maintenance of journeyman militancy and conviviality. The town's elaborate fortifications required huge infusions of regimented labor, skilled as well as unskilled, with an emphasis on the building trades. The artisans most needed in Louisbourg were those that held pride of place in the journeymen's societies: stonecutters, joiners, locksmiths, carpenters, plasterers, and roofers.[70]

The militancy of Louisbourg's workers clearly scandalized administrators from the first to the final days of the settlement (1713–58). Already in 1714, they were striking over pay, much to the disgust of the major of the garrison: "When it was a question of working no one appeared," he wrote indignantly. "What is very sure is that these are very bad workers."[71] Strikes and insubordination continued in subsequent years, prompting the engineer to complain in 1720 that the workers, through "tumultuous contestations," had raised the daily rate in some ateliers from twenty to thirty or even thirty-five sous.[72] By the 1750s, according to the engineer, workers were "making the law." The twenty-nine masons and carpenters who arrived in 1754 were pocketing 2,060 livres of the king's money every month, an average daily wage of over fifty sous per person.[73]

For Louisbourg's workers, drinking rivaled striking as a favorite pastime; they were not only mutinous, but drunk.[74] Time after time, the taverns emptied out the workshops, to the prejudice of the *ouvrages du Roi*. On "Saint Monday," rainy days, even ordinary work days, workers seemed intent on pursuing what authorities could only term "a continuous disorder and debauchery."[75] A royal scribe wrote angrily in 1717, "It is impossible to have them for service, or even the most pressing needs without dragging them from the taverns which are in no greater number than there are houses."[76] Laments about artisanal drunkenness, coupled with wholly ineffectual attempts to regulate the spirits trade, were an omnipresent feature of the colonial regime.[77]

Of course, there is no guarantee that this turbulent behavior was the cultural legacy of the Tour de France. But in individual cases, Louisbourg's journeymen clung to their status with pride and obstinacy, as we learn from random documents that gave them voice. The judicial archives from 1743 and 1744 record the trial of a stonecutter named Valérien Louis, accused of stealing building materials from royal construction sites and fencing them to a long list of local artisans. Louis was a native of Dijon, an important stop on the Tour de France since the late fifteenth century.[78] The son and godson of stonemasons, he bore the nickname of a Gavot: Bourguignon La Verdure (Burgundian Greenery). In 1742, aged twenty-five, he made a three-year commitment to Louisbourg's entrepreneur in return for an annual salary of three hundred livres plus room, board, and return passage. He embarked for Louisbourg in La Rochelle, after a brief stay at an inn called Les Trois Chandeliers on rue du Marché.

Louis, or the Burgundian, as he was called throughout his trial, resisted attempts to treat him as an ordinary indentured servant at least as strongly as suggestions of his guilt. On at least five occasions, he informed the judge that he had come to Louisbourg as a "journeyman stonecutter," and when the judge seemed unimpressed, he adamantly stated that "he was not indentured in the capacity of domestic but clearly in that of journeyman."[79] In the end, his obstinate refusal to confess spared him the death penalty in favor of the galleys.

That other journeymen in Louisbourg took pride in their status is suggested by their appearance in the court records with unmistakable surnames and titles. In 1726, for instance, Hierome Dupuy gave testimony in a theft case as Bayonnais l'Aimable, "journeyman locksmith" in the workshop of blacksmith Jacques Frican.[80] Since this twenty-four-year-old Gavot never appeared in Louisbourg's census records, he must have returned home after his expanded Tour de France.

Court records also reveal that the daily life of journeymen in Louisbourg was organized in familiar ways. Master artisans, perhaps veterans of the Tour de France themselves, ran taverns and rooming houses for workers in their trades, with their wives acting as *mères*. The wife of Bayonnais l'Aimable's master Jacques Frican presided over one such establishment, gaining notoriety in 1737 for serving a thief along with her regular clients Prêt à Boire, La Terreur, and Sans Souci.[81] Other masters whose wives ran taverns and inns included Pierre Lelarge, a carpenter from outside La Rochelle; Jean-Baptiste Laumosnier, a stonecutter from Paris; and Pierre Morin, another stonecutter. In addition to workers from his atelier, Morin's inn housed visiting artisans like Armand Clavier alias L'Angevin, a tailor passing through Louisbourg after a stint in Québec.[82]

There are no archival examples of soldier-workers directly expressing pride in journeyman status, but there were few barriers between Louisbourg's military and civilian artisans. They drank together at the same workers' taverns, and sometimes they lodged together also. Although Louisbourg provided barracks for its soldiers from an early date, there were never enough beds for the entire garrison. One soldier-worker from Laumosnier's atelier, Germain le Parisien, also lived at his inn. He is known to us only by his nickname, that of a Dévorant.[83]

An episode that occurred in Laumosnier's tavern in 1733 suggests that a common journeyman culture was shared by all Louisbourg's artisans, whether they served in a civilian or a military capacity. The incident, recorded in the judicial archives, took place late in the afternoon on the last day of the Feast of the Epiphany. A soldier named Nicolas Lebègue alias Brûlevillage, a butcher by trade, entered the home of Dame Berruchon with an accomplice and stole a large quantity of multicolored ribbon. He then proceeded to Laumosnier's to find his friend Germain le Parisien, joining him for some *eau de vie* along with twelve or fifteen other soldiers. According to Laumosnier, "while drinking together the said Brûlevillage took from his pocket some ribbon of different colors to make cockades which the said Brûlevillage gave to the said soldiers, and they asked the wife of the witness to make them the cockades, which she did." Further testimony and physical evidence revealed the ribbon to be red, white, blue, and yellow, the first four of the journeyman's five colors.[84]

Although this story could be an expression of military particularism, since all the participants were soldiers, it makes equal sense to view it in relation to journeyman culture. It was not customary for soldiers of the period to wear cockades, but journeymen did so as a matter of course. Journeymen stonecutters, in specific, favored "flowery ribbons of various colors," just like those stolen from Dame Berruchon.[85] Laumosnier, moreover, ran an atelier for stonecutters, and his wife dispensed hospitality to his workers. In making cockades for the boys, she was behaving exactly like a good *mère des compagnons*.

In conclusion, the peopling of New France took place in large part by redirecting French labor migrants from traditional to untraditional destinations. From the local and regional movements of countryfolk into towns and cities to the long-distance mobility of fishermen, mountain dwellers, soldiers, and journeymen, colonial migration tapped into familiar networks and streams of labor migration. Individual migrants could either cut short or extend their usual work itineraries to travel westward across the Atlantic. To the extent that large, cohesive groups of labor migrants were transplanted to New France, elements of their respective work cultures likely survived intact. Fishermen from Normandy or the Basque country recreated local maritime communities in the Gulf of St. Lawrence, at least for a time. Soldiers and officers, always a disproportionate part of the colonial population, ensured the predominance of the French military ethos, although Canadian martial culture would evolve in response to the intercultural realities of colonial warfare. Unlike the military establishment, the organizational structures of journeymen were not recreated in New France; however, journeyman militancy and conviviality survived to some degree in Louisbourg due to the large-scale demand for labor on the fortifications. Regardless of specific cultural transfers, mobility and the idea of movement fundamentally shaped both the economic development of French-Canadian society and its collective identity, and they continued to do so well into the twentieth century.

NOTES

1. Jean-Pierre Poussou, "Réflexions sur l'apport démographique des études consacrées aux migrations anciennes," in *Migrations intérieures: méthodes d'observation et d'analyse, Actes du 4ᵉ colloque national de démographie du CNRS* (Paris, 1975), 148–49. All translations mine unless otherwise indicated.

2. For a detailed discussion of traditional patterns of French mobility, see Leslie Choquette, *Frenchmen into Peasants: Modernity and Tradition in the Peopling of French Canada* (Cambridge, MA: Harvard University Press, 1997), 181–99.

3. On migrants to New France, see also Hubert Charbonneau, *The First French Canadians: Pioneers in the St. Lawrence Valley* (Newark: University of Delaware Press, 1993); Yves Landry, ed., *Le peuplement du Canada aux XVIIᵉ et XVIIIᵉ siècles. Actes des premières journées d'étude du programme de recherche sur l'émigration des Français en Nouvelle-France (PRÉFEN)* (Centre de recherche d'histoire quantitative, Université de Caen Basse-Normandie, 2004); Peter Moogk, "Reluctant Exiles: Emigrants from France in Canada before 1760," *William and Mary Quarterly* 46, no. 3 (1989): 464–515; Marcel Trudel, *Catalogue des immigrants, 1632–1662* (Montréal: Hurtubise HMH, 1983). Canadian scholars have understandably focused on the "founding immigrants," those who stayed and founded families, giving rise to the French-Canadian population. I am interested in transatlantic movement, whether or not it was permanent, and I emphasize its relationship to patterns of internal migration in France. Similar links between internal and colonial migrations have been noted for the British Isles. For a comparative perspective, see Jean-Pierre Poussou, "Mobilité et migrations en France et dans les Îles britanniques à l'époque moderne," in Philippe Joutard and Thomas Wien with the collaboration of Didier Poton, eds., *Mémoires de Nouvelle-France: De France en Nouvelle-France* (Rennes: Presses

universitaires de Rennes, 2005), 27–50; Leslie Choquette, "Émigration et politique coloniale. Les cas français et anglais," in Joutard and Wien, 51–63.

4. Jean-Claude Perrot, *Genèse d'une ville moderne: Caen* (Paris: Mouton, 1975), vol. 1, 171. See also André Corvisier, "Service militaire et mobilité géographique au XVIIIe siècle," *Migrations. Annales de démographie historique* (1970): 185–204.

5. Demographer Mario Boleda tallies 33,500 French migrants in the St. Lawrence Valley during the French Regime, exclusive of Acadia and Louisiana. Of these, 9,300 were founding immigrants. See "Nouvelle estimation de l'immigration française au Canada, 1608–1760," in Landry, *Le peuplement du Canada*, 36.

6. Jean Lamarre, *The French Canadians of Michigan: Their Contribution to the Development of the Saginaw Valley and the Keweenaw Peninsula, 1840–1914* (Detroit: Wayne State University Press, 2003), 6.

7. Yves Frenette, *Brève histoire des Canadiens français* (Montréal: Boréal, 1998), 90. See also Christian Morissonneau, "Mobilité et identité québécoise," *Cahiers de géographie du Québec* 23, no. 58 (1979): 29–38. Morissonneau's emphasis on a "culture of mobility" (33) with roots in New France contrasted with earlier historiography focusing on agrarian settlement and rural social reproduction. Examining the continental diaspora of French Canadians from the seventeenth century onward, he argued that mobility has been more important than settlement as a defining trait of French-Canadian identity. In the decades since Morissonneau's article appeared, historians have tended to concentrate on either mobility or settlement. For recent works examining settlement, see Alain Laberge in collaboration with Jacques Mathieu and Lina Gouger, *Portraits de campagnes. La formation du monde rural laurentien au XVIIIe siècle* (Québec: Presses de l'Université Laval, 2010); Benoît Grenier, *Seigneurs campagnards de la Nouvelle-France. Présence seigneuriale et sociabilité rurale dans la vallée du Saint-Laurent à l'époque préindustrielle* (Rennes: Presses universitaires de Rennes, 2007).

8. "Extrait du mémoire de la généralité d'Alençon" (1698), Bibliothèque nationale de France, Nouvelles acquisitions françaises, vol. 231, fol. 26.

9. Cited in Louis Duval, *État de la généralité d'Alençon sous Louis XIV* (Alençon, 1890), 217–18. The former province of Perche corresponds to the eastern part of today's department of Orne, in the Normandy region. During the ancien régime, it was part of the generality of Alençon.

10. This period witnessed the settlement of soldiers from the four French regiments sent to Canada during the Seven Years' War. It is unfortunate that bigamy did not preoccupy Canadian bishops earlier, say, in 1665, with the arrival of the Regiment of Carignan-Salières. Nonetheless, the migratory circuits and short-circuits detailed in the testimonials were likely characteristic of the French Regime as a whole, rather than simply the middle years of the eighteenth century. They are a precious window onto an often undocumented but ubiquitous aspect of everyday life in early modern times.

11. "Témoignages de liberté au mariage," *Rapport de l'archiviste de la province de Québec* 32–33 (1951–1953): 22.

12. See Choquette, *Frenchmen into Peasants*, and "La mobilité de travail en France et l'émigration vers le Canada (XVIIe-XVIIIe siècles)," in Yves Landry et al., eds., *Les chemins de la migration en Belgique et au Québec du XVIIe au XXe siècle* (Louvain-la-Neuve: Éditions Académia, 1995), 195–208.

13. Choquette, *Frenchmen into Peasants*, 202; Jacques Depauw, "Immigration féminine, professions féminines et structures urbaines à Nantes au XVIIIe siècle," *Enquêtes et documents*, 2 (Nantes: Centre de recherches sur l'histoire de la France atlantique, 1972), 45–47, 60.

14. Choquette, *Frenchmen into Peasants*, 203–4.

15. Choquette, *Frenchmen into Peasants*, 225–28.

16. "Témoignages de liberté au mariage," 20–21, 121.

17. "Témoignages de liberté au mariage," 44; Testimonial of freedom at marriage, 12 September 1766, Archives du Séminaire de Québec (ASQ), ms. 430.

18. "Témoignages de liberté au mariage," 45, 67.

19. "Témoignages de liberté au mariage," 5.

20. Eric Krause, Carol Corbin, and William O'Shea, eds., *Aspects of Louisbourg* (Sydney: University College of Cape Breton Press, 1995), 169–208.

21. Testimonial of freedom at marriage, 1771, ASQ, ms. 430.

22. "Témoignages de liberté au mariage," 150–51.

23. Testimonial of freedom at marriage, 12 September 1766, ASQ, ms. 430.

24. Louis-Sébastien Mercier, *Le tableau de Paris*, ed. Jeffrey Kaplow (Paris: Maspero, 1979), 144.

25. Testimonial of freedom at marriage, 12 September 1766, ASQ, ms. 430.

26. Archives nationales d'outre-mer (ANOM), Series B, vol. 42, fol. 175, 466.

27. ANOM, Series G1, vol. 466.

28. "Témoignages de liberté au mariage," 43–44.

29. Françoise Mournard, "Les Allobroges au Canada," *Revue des questions historiques* 62 (1934): 104.

30. ANOM, Series C11A, vol. 53, fol. 205.

31. ANOM, Series B, vol. 55, fol. 491; vol. 89, fol. 25 [227].

32. ANOM, Series F5B, vol. 57.

33. *Entre faim et loup, problèmes de la vie et de l'émigration sur les hautes terres françaises au XVIIIe siècle* (Clermont-Ferrand: Institut d'études du Massif Central, 1976), 24–30.

34. Choquette, *Frenchmen into Peasants*, 244.

35. Perrot, *Genèse d'une ville moderne*, vol. 1, 176.

36. The archives of the cathedral chapter of Amiens contain a "Lease by the chapter to Louis Artus and Nicolas Choquet, merchants in Amiens, Saint-Leu parish, of a mill appropriate for fulling serge," dated 16 October 1598. Archives départementales de la Somme, Série G, vol. 1423. Just as the elder Artus's grandson immigrated to Canada, so did the great-grandson of his partner, Nicolas Choquet.

37. Corvisier, "Service militaire," 185.

38. Corvisier, "Service militaire," 193.

39. Mario Boleda, "Nouvelle estimation de l'immigration française au Canada, 1608–1760," 34. This figure does not include French soldiers stationed outside the St. Lawrence Valley. The Louisbourg garrison alone numbered 3,700 at the time of the British Conquest.

40. "Témoignages de liberté au mariage," 13–14. In the mid-eighteenth century, the city of Namur was ruled by Austria (hence the reference to Maria Theresa, the Queen of Hungary); its citadel was controlled by the Dutch. Liège was an independent prince-bishopric allied with France.

41. Of the many works dealing with the journeymen of the Tour de France, see Pierre Barret and Noël Gurgand, *Ils voyageaient la France. Vie et traditions des compagnons du Tour de France au XIXe siècle* (Paris: Hachette, 1980); Jean-Pierre Bayard, *Le compagnonnage* (Paris: Payot, 1977); Luc Benoist, *Le compagnonnage et les métiers* (Paris: Les Presses universitaires de France, 1966); Émile Coornaert, *Les compagnonnages du Moyen Âge à nos jours* (Paris: Éditions ouvrières, 1966); Raoul Dautry, *Compag-*

nonnage par les compagnons du Tour de France (Paris: Plon, 1951); E. Martin de Saint-Léon, *Le compagnonnage. Son histoire, ses coutumes, ses règlements et ses rites* (1901; Paris: Librairie du Compagnonnage, 1977); Agricol Perdiguier, *Le livre du compagnonage* [sic] (Paris, 1841); Daniel Roche, ed., *Journal de ma vie: Jacques-Louis Ménétra, compagnon vitrier au XVIIIe siècle* (Paris: Montalba, 1982).

42. In journeyman folklore, the sponsors of the three societies—Master Jacques, Father Soubise, and King Solomon—were associated with the building of the first temple in Jerusalem.

43. Martin de Saint-Léon, *Le compagnonnage*, 263; Perdiguier, *Livre de compagnonage*, 60–61.

44. Bayard, *Le compagnonnage*, 177–78. On the northwestern fringe of this circuit, Rouen was also an important stop on the Tour de France. See Coornaert, *Les compagnonnages*, 142.

45. Coornaert, *Les compagnonnages*, 47–48.

46. Michael Sonenscher, *Work and Wages: Natural Law, Politics, and the Eighteenth-Century French Trades* (Cambridge: Cambridge University Press, 1989), 158, 165.

47. For a firsthand account of an eighteenth-century Tour de France, see Roche, ed., *Journal de ma vie*, 46–108. Ménétra's memoir is the only surviving autobiography by an eighteenth-century journeyman.

48. Cited in Maria Mondoux, "Les hommes de Montréal," *Revue d'histoire de l'Amérique française* 2 (1948–49): 62–64. See also Roland Auger, *La grande recrue de 1653* (Québec: Société généalogique canadienne-française, 1955); Dany Fougères and Roderick MacLeod, eds., *Montréal: The History of a North American City* (Montréal: McGill-Queen's University Press, 2017), vol. 1, 91.

49. See Leslie Choquette, "Compagnonnage in Eighteenth-Century New France," in A. J. B. Johnston, ed., *Essays in French Colonial History: Proceedings of the 21st Annual Meeting of the French Colonial Historical Society* (East Lansing: Michigan State University Press), 75–91.

50. "Témoignages de liberté au mariage," 48. My punctuation.

51. Testimonials of freedom at marriage, 1772, ASQ, ms. 430.

52. "Témoignages de liberté au mariage," 65.

53. Yves Roby, *Histoire d'un rêve brisé? Les Canadiens français aux États-Unis* (Sillery, QC: Septentrion, 2007), 7. See also Yves Frenette, Étienne Rivard, and Marc St.-Hilaire, eds., *La francophonie nord-américaine* (Québec: Presses de l'Université Laval, 2012), 106–205; Bruno Ramirez, "Migrants canadiens-français dans l'espace nord-américain, 1830–1930: Une synthèse critique," in Thomas Wien, Cécile Vidal, and Yves Frenette, eds., *De Québec à l'Amérique française: Histoire et mémoire* (Québec: Presses de l'Université Laval, 2006), 267–82; Bruno Ramirez, *On the Move: French-Canadian and Italian Immigrants in the North Atlantic Economy, 1861–1914* (Toronto: McClelland & Stewart, 1991); Bruno Ramirez, *La ruée vers le Sud: Migrations du Canada vers les États-Unis, 1840–1930* (Montréal: Boréal, 2003).

54. The first *coureurs de bois* were French laborers, an interesting twist tying French labor mobility patterns to their New France counterparts. Such connections will be further explored by the collaborators of Yves Frenette, holder of the Canada Research Chair on Migrations, Transfers, and Francophone Communities at Université de Saint-Boniface, who received a partnership grant from the Social Sciences and Humanities Research Council of Canada in 2019 for the project "Three Centuries of Francophone Migrations in North America (1640–1940)." On fur trade mobility, see Robert Englebert, "Merchant Representatives and the French River World, 1763–1803," *Michigan Historical Review* 34, no. 1 (2008): 63–82; Jay Gitlin, *The Bourgeois Frontier: French Towns, French Traders, and*

American Expansion (New Haven, CT: Yale University Press, 2010); Gilles Havard, *Histoire des coureurs de bois: Amérique du Nord, 1600–1840* (Paris: Les Indes Savantes, 2016); Carolyn Podruchny, *Making the Voyageur World: Travelers and Traders in the North American Fur Trade* (Lincoln: University of Nebraska Press, 2006). Taché was the author of *Forestiers et voyageurs* (1863); Kerouac's *On the Road* was published in 1957. On the importance of Kerouac's bilingualism and French-Canadian ethnicity to his "nomadic morality and identity" (63), see Hassan Melehy, *Kerouac: Language, Poetics, and Territory* (New York: Bloomsbury, 2016).

55. Censuses of Île Royale, ANOM, Series G1, vols. 408–409, 466.

56. Cited in Christopher Moore, *Louisbourg Portraits: Life in an Eighteenth-Century Garrison Town* (Toronto: Macmillan, 1982), 141. Moore's translation.

57. Moore, *Louisbourg Portraits*, 130, 136.

58. The different societies conveniently forgot their rivalries where labor relations were concerned, and they cooperated frequently to boycott workshops or even entire towns. Striking a town was known as a *damnation* or *mise en interdit*. See Luc Benoist, *Le compagnonnage et les métiers* (Paris: Les Presses universitaires de France, 1966), 35; Coornaert, *Les compagnonnages*, 7; Martin de Saint-Léon, *Le compagnonnage*, 87–91.

59. W. J. Eccles, "The Social, Economic, and Political Significance of the Military Establishment in New France," in *Essays on New France* (New York: Oxford University Press, 1987), 110. See also Louise Dechêne, *Le peuple, l'état et la guerre au Canada sous le Régime français* (Montréal: Les Éditions du Boréal, 2008).

60. After Louis XIV sent the Regiment of Carigan-Salières to Canada in 1665, the colony's 1,300 soldiers made up over a third of the total population (Eccles, *Social, Economic, and Political Significance*, 111). Later in Louis's bellicose reign, France had 500,000 soldiers in a population of 21 million. On the French army during the ancien régime, see André Corvisier, *L'armée française de la fin du XVIIe siècle au ministère de Choiseul: Le soldat* (Paris: Presses universitaires de France, 1964), 2 vols.; Jean Chagniot, *Paris et l'armée au XVIIIe siècle. Étude politique et sociale* (Paris: Éditions Economica, 1985).

61. Such names include Sansoucy, Laliberté, LaChance, LaFleur, and a great many others.

62. Eccles, *Social, Economic, and Political Significance*, 114.

63. Pierre Le Moyne d'Iberville, founder of Louisiana, and his brother Jean-Baptiste Le Moyne de Bienville, who established New Orleans, were grandsons of an innkeeper from Dieppe in Normandy. Louis-Antoine Juchereau de Saint-Denis, founder of Natchitoches in northwestern Louisiana, descended from a well-to-do peasant in Tourouvre-au-Perche.

64. See Christian Ayne Crouch, *Nobility Lost: French and Canadian Martial Cultures, Indians, and the End of New France* (Ithaca, NY: Cornell University Press, 2014). A recent case study of two officers serving in the Seven Years' War, one French and one Canadian, complicates this picture. See Joseph Gagné, *Inconquis: Deux retraites françaises vers la Louisiane après 1760* (Québec: Septentrion, 2016).

65. Bayard, *Le compagnonnage*, 172, 181; Coornaert, *Les compagnonnages*, 146.

66. "Ordonnance de M. De Frontenac portant défense aux habitants de s'assembler sans permission (23 mars 1677)," *Rapport de l'archiviste de la province du Québec* (1927–1928), facing xvi.

67. Barret and Gurgand, *Ils voyagaient la France*, 343; Benoist, *Le compagnonnage*, 32; Germain Martin, *Les associations ouvrières au XVIIIe siècle (1700–1792)* (1900; Geneva: Slatkine-Megariotis Reprints, 1974), 47.

The Ancien Régime Culture of Labor Mobility and Migration to New France

68. Cited in Ed. de Lorière, "Quelques notes sur les émigrants manceaux et principalement fléchois au Canada pendant le XVIIe siècle," *Annales fléchoises* 9 (1908): 24.

69. On artisan life in the St. Lawrence, see Marius Barbeau, "Confrérie des menuisiers de Madame Sainte-Anne," *Archives du folklore* 1 (1946): 72–96; Russel Bouchard, *Les armuriers de la Nouvelle-France* (Québec: Ministère des Affaires culturelles, 1978); Jean-Pierre Hardy et Thierry Ruddel, *Les apprentis artisans à Québec, 1660–1815* (Montréal: Les Presses de l'Université du Québec, 1977); Édouard-Zotique Massicotte, "La communauté des cordonniers à Montréal," *Bulletin des recherches historiques* 24 (1918): 126–27; Peter Moogk, *Building a House in New France: An Account of the Perplexities of Client and Craftsman in Early Canada* (Toronto: McClelland & Stewart, 1977), and "In the Darkness of a Basement: Craftsmen's Associations in Early French Canada," *Canadian Historical Review* 57 (1976): 399–439.

70. Benoist, *Le compagnonnage*, 38–39; Dautry, *Compagnonnage*, 101–4.

71. Letter of L'Hermite to the Minister, 1 December 1714, ANOM, Series C11B, vol. 1, fol. 83.

72. Letter of Verville to the Navy Council, 19 June 1720, ANOM, Series C11B, vol. 5, fol. 235.

73. Letters of Franquet to the Minister, 13 October 1750, 9 November 1754, ANOM, Series C11B, vol. 29, fol. 314; vol. 34, fol. 226, 228.

74. Letter of Soubras to the Navy Council, 1717, ANOM, Series C11B, vol. 2, fol. 258.

75. Letter of Soubras to the Navy Council, 13 April 1717, ANOM, Series C11B, vol. 2, fol. 9. See also Letter of Verrier to the Minister, 1 November 1738, ANOM, Series C11B, vol. 20, fol. 227; Letter of Duquesnel to the Minister, 2 June 1741, ANOM, Series C11B, vol. 23, fol. 43.

76. Letter of La Forest to the Navy Council, 12 November 1717, ANOM, Series C11B, vol. 2, fol. 274.

77. Complaints about taverns appeared in the administrative correspondence in 1714–18, 1720–22, 1738–39, 1741–42, 1749, and 1753–54. This list is not exhaustive.

78. See Paul Labal, "Notes sur les compagnons migrateurs et les sociétés de compagnonnage à Dijon à la fin du XVe siècle et au début du XVIe siècle," *Annales de Bourgogne* 22 (1950): 187–92.

79. Superior Council of Louisbourg, Trial of Valérien Louis alias Le Bourguignon for theft, 1743–1744, ANOM, Series G2, vol. 187, fol. 128–334. As Steven Kaplan and Ulrich-Christian Pallach have shown, this issue had long been a prickly one for journeymen. Steven Kaplan, "Réflexions sur la police du monde du travail, 1700–1815," *Revue historique* 261 (1979): 23; Ulrich-Christian Pallach, "Fonctions de la mobilité artisanale et ouvrière: Compagnons, ouvriers et manufacturiers en France et aux Allemagnes (XVIIe-XIXe siècles)," *Francia* 11 (1983): 396, 404.

80. Superior Council of Louisbourg, Trial of Jean-Baptiste Lahaye, François Dubois, Raymond Aulier alias Saint-Louis, and Charlotte Dumesnil for theft, 1726, ANOM, Series G2, vol. 179, fol. 129–428.

81. She testified that she served them "a quart of *eau de vie*, that after having drunk the said *eau de vie* they drank another two jugs or five bottles of wine." Superior Council of Louisbourg, Trial of Mathurin Bunau for theft, 1737, ANOM, Series G2, vol. 184, fol. 454–517.

82. Superior Council of Louisbourg, Trial of Louis Davory for theft, 1740, ANOM, Series G2, vol. 186, fol. 228–322.

83. Superior Council of Louisbourg, Trial of Nicolas Lebègue alias Brûlevillage and Thomas Béranger alias La Rozée for theft, 1733, ANOM, Series G2, vol. 182, fol. 148–357.

84. Trial of Nicolas Lebègue and Thomas Béranger. According to the different witnesses, somewhere between eight and twenty soldiers had been drinking at the inn during the incident.

85. Perdiguier, *Livre de compagnonage*, 37. Accounts of the ceremonial life of ancien régime journeymen often mention large quantities of brightly colored ribbon. Michael Sonenscher has called attention to the ribbons of the journeymen leather dressers of Troyes, Germain Martin to those of journeymen in Orléans: Michael Sonenscher, "Mythical Work: Workshop Production and the Compagnonnages of Eighteenth-Century France," in Patrick Joyce, ed., *The Historical Meanings of Work* (Cambridge: Cambridge University Press, 1987), 38–39, 265–66; Martin, *Les associations ouvrières au XVIIIe siècle*, 110.

A French Huguenot's Career as a British Colonial Administrator in Acadie/ Nova Scotia/Mi'gma'ki, 1710–1750

GREGORY KENNEDY AND VINCENT AUFFREY

In 1710, a British military expedition captured Port Royal, the administrative center of the French colony of Acadie. Three years later, the French formally ceded Acadie "*dans ses anciennes limites*" as part of the Treaty of Utrecht ending the War of the Spanish Succession. Unfortunately, nobody agreed on what the boundaries of British Nova Scotia were; the French argued that they had only given up what is today the peninsula of Nova Scotia, while the British claimed that the ceded territory included the entire region from the Gaspé Peninsula in what is now Québec to the frontier of Maine. A joint commission was created to study the question. In the meantime, effective British control was limited to a small garrison at newly baptized Annapolis Royal, and a fishing station at Canso. The British created a council composed of military officers to administer the colony until such time as a civil government could be created. In the absence of British colonists, and with potentially hostile French Acadian and Indigenous Mi'kmaq populations, the British relied on the military to enforce its claims to the region. Not surprisingly, most of these men adopted a hardline attitude toward those whom they saw as a threat.

As Jeffers Lennox has recently written, talking about Acadie, Nova Scotia, or Mi'gma'ki in the eighteenth century is to "engage in an act of imagination."[1] Territorial claims were fluid and mutable, shifting with policies, wars, and negotiations, even as settler communities grew and became increasingly fixed around the Bay of Fundy and on the Atlantic coast. Many people were actively looking for stability and security, even as they sought to achieve personal and professional ambitions as heads of household, farmers, tradesmen, officials, and community leaders. Indigenous communities including the Mi'kmaq, who lived throughout much what is now Atlantic Canada, and the Wolastoqiyik (Maliseet), who inhabited the region around what Europeans called the Saint John River in what is now the Province of New Brunswick, sought recognition of their rights and lands. This general search for collective order relied in part on ambitious individuals actively pursuing professional mobility and willing to cross oceans, imperial boundaries, and linguistic divides. Speaking of the French Atlantic, Laurent Dubois emphasized the ways that colonies like Acadie were "a destination for the more adventurous or determined ... driven less by misery than by a desire to continue to go beyond the opportunities available to them within France."[2] Similarly, Elizabeth Mancke has noted that by the eighteenth century, a new "imperial state" was emerging in the British Atlantic that created new opportunities through civil government and royal service.[3]

Paul Mascarene was one of these highly mobile and ambitious people. Born in France, he found his place in the British Army and is widely viewed by scholars today as the best of the military men sent to administer Nova Scotia between 1710 and the deportation of the Acadians that began in 1755. Naomi Griffiths noted his intelligence, self-reliance, and bilingualism, making him "of immense value."[4] The first professional historian to write about Acadie, Rameau de Saint-Père, lauded Mascarene's "character" and "elevated spirit" as well as his ability "to rise above the difficulties of his situation."[5] Barry Moody's detailed biographical study remains the most thorough treatment. He wrote that Mascarene was "a person of considerable ability and competence ... struggling almost alone against insuperable odds" and serving "faithfully and quietly during a crucial transitional period in the development of Nova Scotia. Britain did nothing during this period to warrant or to reward such stewardship."[6]

This essay offers a new lens of professional mobility and the quest for power to reconsider the relatively well-known life and career of Paul Mascarene in Mi'gma'ki/Acadie/Nova Scotia. While historians tend to highlight his diplomatic abilities, they often pay less attention to his personal bravery and professional ambitions. There was more to him than protocol and polite exchange; Mascarene understood the importance of appealing to all through the vectors of trusted agents and his own presence. The first part of his career as a member of the British Council at Annapolis Royal up to 1740, marked largely by disappointment, demonstrates the limits for advancement in a frontier outpost and the intense competition among rivals. A detailed look at Mascarene's actions and relationships with the local inhabitants during that same period will explore the foundations of his good standing with them; indeed, working with the British could provide social and professional mobility for some Acadians as well. Historians have tended to focus most on Mascarene's role as lieutenant-governor during the War of the Austrian Succession (1740–48), when he was unexpectedly thrust back into the spotlight. While some have credited him for helping keep the Acadian population neutral, this essay will conclude with a reconsideration of these difficult years, which left this career officer disenchanted and ready to retire from public life. While most scholars agree that Mascarene's approach demonstrated that diversity and accommodation were possible in Nova Scotia and in the wider British Atlantic, few have considered to what extent the discrediting of his administration, even in his own mind, added strength to those advocating more drastic measures. John Mack Faragher emphasizes that Mascarene's legacy would soon be forgotten in a "horrifying cascade of events" aimed at nothing short but the destruction of the Acadian population.[7]

Looking back, Mascarene's career was an incredible story of professional mobility. Scion of a prominent Huguenot family from Castres, Languedoc, France, Paul (baptized Jean-Paul) was born in 1685, the same year that Louis XIV revoked the Edict of Nantes, which had afforded certain protections to the Protestant minority community. Mascarene came into the world in a cottage in the mountains near Noves, nearly three hundred kilometers away from his family home, as his parents were hiding out from the *dragonnades*—the troops sent by the king to force the Huguenots to abjure their faith. Like many other Huguenot families, the Mascarenes made a break for it. They headed toward Bordeaux to find passage by ship to a friendly country but were captured along the way. His father, Jean, was tried, imprisoned, and ultimately expelled from France, while his mother, Marguerite, abjured and was reinstated with the family property. This was not the end of the story. Jean's grandmother managed to smuggle an eleven-year-old Paul to Geneva in 1696. There, Paul was hosted by the Rapin family and introduced to the classics and Latin. In 1698, Paul set off for Utrecht to find his father, but sadly, Jean had died from illness just two days before his arrival.

The young Mascarene completed his education with the continued support and hospitality of the Rapins. Two of Paul's uncles, as well as members of the Rapin family, had fought for William III during the Glorious Revolution, so Mascarene found patronage and support in London in 1706, joining the British Army.[8] As Guy Rowlands has shown using the example of Louis XIV's army, it was not unusual for young men at this time to seek service in other dynastic states.[9] In the case of the

Mascarenes, as with other Huguenots, it was a way to make a living, gain prestige, and also support their religion at a time when they were not welcome in France. Indeed, Paul was initially assigned to an infantry regiment composed principally of French Huguenots. In 1708, he was detached for overseas service with the expedition of Samuel Vetch assigned to conquer French Acadie. Vetch's men traveled first to Boston, where they met up with colonial troops, gathered supplies, and rested after their oceanic voyage. During the subsequent months, Mascarene made a new home for himself in Boston; like many British military officers who served in the Northeast, he preferred to live there as much as possible. Forty years later, Mascarene retired with the rank of brevet colonel and the title of Lieutenant-Governor of Nova Scotia. These were remarkable achievements for a foreign exile uprooted and transient for much of his early life.

In other ways, Mascarene's life demonstrates the degree to which early modern people were in fact rooted in communities, identities, and reputations as well as constrained by political imperatives and professional structures. Paul spent much of his early life looking for a home and settled on Boston as a place to create a family. The relationships and alliances that he made came to define his standing in Massachusetts society and the British Atlantic World. When the influence of his patrons and friends was waxing, Mascarene could look forward to promotions and opportunities in the army and in civil society. When his allies fell from grace, however, Mascarene found himself on the wrong side of many disputes and decisions. Perhaps most telling, much of Mascarene's professional tenure occurred during an extended period of peace between France and Great Britain. While undoubtedly positive for civil populations throughout the Northeast, including that of Nova Scotia,[10] this period of peace was characterized by neglect and disinterest from colonial authorities, and limited opportunities for advancement for military men. Mascarene's many requests went unheeded in London, and he suffered from the perennial assumption that as a Frenchman himself, his judgement and impartiality toward the French Acadians remained in doubt. What is more, the communities around him showed little interest in mobility. Massachusetts families would not come to Nova Scotia, and the Acadians and Mi'kmaq who did live there showed little inclination to support British authority and also refused to leave. On a personal level, Mascarene became rooted by his family obligations in Boston, particularly after the death of his wife in 1729 left him responsible for his four young children. On a professional level, Mascarene was mired in an impossible status quo in Nova Scotia in which his position was constantly contested by peers and rivals in the

British Council, while the lack of investment and serious action left that same body incapable of exercising true authority outside the walls of Fort Anne.

Mascarene's career demonstrates the opportunities and limits of professional mobility in the Northeast and more broadly in the Atlantic World. He also played a crucial role in the colonial administration of Nova Scotia, negotiating with Indigenous and French Acadian communities in an effort to maintain peace and respect for British sovereignty. He genuinely believed that with time and proper guidance, some of the Acadians could become true British subjects, just as he had done as a young French exile. This view of a kind of imperial mobility was not shared by most of his colleagues and superiors, but it made him uniquely suited to the challenges of administering a diverse and contested colony on the frontier of the British Empire. When put to the test during the War of the Austrian Succession, Mascarene's effectiveness seems obvious in hindsight, as most of the Acadian population chose not to support the French despite their bonds of language, culture, and faith. At the time, however, his rivals were quick to point out the limits of his policies. Mascarene even came to doubt himself, particularly when it appeared that his trusted agents had turned against him. The war proved to be not only the end of Mascarene's career, but a defining turning point in the events leading up to the *Grand Dérangement*.

Mascarene the Military Man

Barry Moody wrote that "army life would prove basically incompatible with Mascarene's temperament,"[11] yet Paul displayed conspicuous courage in Vetch's campaign against Acadie in 1710. He was part of a large enterprise, composed of 3,400 men and 39 ships, and was undoubtedly aware that the two previous expeditions against Port Royal had failed miserably.[12] The army provided outlets to employ his considerable intelligence and education. For example, upon arrival in Boston in 1709, Lieutenant Mascarene was given the responsibility of training a small cadre of artillery troops from the colonial volunteers in the use of siege cannons and mortars, and he was soon promoted to captain.[13] Mascarene led the grenadier troop that stormed the French defenses, earning the honor of taking possession of the fort after the French surrender as well as a field promotion to the rank of brevet major.[14] Those heady days after the fall of Port Royal in 1710 must have left an indelible mark on his memory. In fact, most historians, in their focus on Mascarene as colonial administrator, have underestimated the degree to which his sense of self as a military officer contributed to his outlook.

Mascarene was also selected to lead the delegations sent to the Acadian communities near Port Royal and in the Minas Basin after the French capitulation. Although this choice was undoubtedly motivated in part by his ability to speak French, it is important to emphasize that Mascarene was there as a conqueror, arriving at the head of a column of troops and requiring contributions of labor, food, furs, and money from the inhabitants. In his instructions to Mascarene, Vetch, who commanded the new garrison at Annapolis Royal and was soon appointed governor of Nova Scotia, directed him to "acquaint them by the fate of war they are become prisoners at discretion and that both their persons and effects are absolutely at the disposal of the conquerors and had I not interposed to protect them the army would have plundered ravaged carried away destroyed all they now have."[15] Since previous English attacks on Acadie had resulted in considerable pillage of the town and its inhabitants, this was not simple bravado.[16]

In addition to forging Mascarene's reputation as a courageous and skilled officer, the campaign against Acadie also served to create several key relationships. These included friendship with Vetch, who quickly relied upon Mascarene for advice and to translate his instructions into French, as well as with Colonel William Tailer, who commanded a regiment of colonial troops during the expedition and was appointed lieutenant-governor of Massachusetts from 1711 until 1716, and Jonathan Belcher, a prominent Massachusetts merchant who helped supply the expedition and a future governor of Massachusetts (1730–41). Vetch clearly trusted Mascarene, appointing him one of four military officers to act as a magistrate for courts martial and also as a kind of court of appeal for anything involving the civilian population.[17] Mascarene returned as a hero to Boston with Vetch, and in 1714 he married Elizabeth Perry, who was related to Tailer and brought considerable wealth and commercial interests to the new household. In general, it seemed that his French ancestry was "no barrier to entry into British colonial society."[18] The following year he was elected a vestryman at the prestigious King's Chapel Anglican Church. It is worth noting that Mascarene had chosen to join the Church of England and not the French Protestant Calvinist congregation. He certainly would not have been brought up in the Church of England while in France, Geneva, or Utrecht. Mascarene's choice to serve in his monarch's official religion instead of pursuing his Calvinist heritage was a clear sign of his earnest belief in royal service.

Mascarene's rising prospects were challenged by shifting political factions in

London and Boston that only intensified after the death of Queen Anne in 1714 and the accession of George I. Vetch lost, regained, and then lost definitively the governorship of Nova Scotia in 1717. He spent several years as an adviser on colonial affairs, but was increasingly marginalized. He died in 1732 in a London debtor's prison. Francis Nicholson, Vetch's initial replacement in 1712, led an inquiry into the former governor's financial affairs and attempted to implicate Mascarene on corruption charges. Although he ultimately seems to have cleared him from wrongdoing, Nicholson then tried to transfer his subordinate to Plaisance, Newfoundland. Mascarene dodged this "exile" by relying on his Massachusetts connections. Tailer advocated for him and the Council of Massachusetts Bay passed a resolution in 1715 naming him engineer to repair the fort at Penobscot, a much closer posting in Maine.[19] There is no evidence that Mascarene had any formal engineering training, but this position was subsequently leveraged to gain a new appointment as official engineer of the Board of Ordnance. Soon after, Mascarene visited London in search of a promotion. In this he was to be disappointed.

Named captain in 1717 in the newly formed 40th Regiment of Foot under the new governor of Nova Scotia and Newfoundland, Richard Phillipps, Mascarene was consigned to a subordinate position. Tailer had a falling out with Belcher, and Belcher—a fervent Congregationalist—became more hostile to the Church of England, in which Mascarene was a prominent member. When the dust settled, Mascarene emerged as a respected but somewhat marginalized figure in the Northeast. He continued to exercise duties as a member of the British Council of Nova Scotia and as a royal engineer, but his ambitions to rise even higher in the army and in the colonial administration had been frustrated. This did not prevent him from working diligently; his report to Phillipps on the state of Fort Anne described in detail the various breaches in the walls as well as the temporary measures that Mascarene had undertaken to repair them. He concluded, however, that "it would be madness" to rely on this and that it should be "easily perceived that the whole must be rebuilt anew."[20] But the governor spent little time in Nova Scotia, and the Board of Ordnance was not inclined to spend the money. Increasingly, Mascarene found himself alongside the other members of the Council, holed up in Annapolis Royal with little to do but to squabble among themselves over precedence and private interests. He spent as much time as he could in Boston with his family.

Mascarene wrote a detailed report on the state of the colony for Phillipps in 1720, and this often-cited document reveals the thoroughly military mindset of this young officer anxious to serve his king. Although he commented on the potential to develop agriculture, trade, fishing, and mining, he reserved most of his remarks for a detailed evaluation of the military means needed to secure the colony against French aggression as well as repeated insistences that the French population needed to eventually be replaced by loyal British inhabitants. Mascarene warned that the Acadians could muster "a thousand men under arms" and posed a significant threat to Nova Scotia.[21] Indeed, he recommended no further delays in forcing them to swear unconditional allegiance or to quit the colony, asking for six hundred regular troops to be sent to carry out these instructions as soon as possible. Aware of the costs in such a deployment, Mascarene argued forcefully that the future benefits to the colony would be considerable, encouraging new British colonists, increasing trade, and providing security so that "in a little time, a small force of regular troops would be able to defend it."[22] Concerned with the dilapidated state of Fort Anne, Mascarene nevertheless argued that the primary effort should be made at Minas, where there was a larger French population and also Indigenous communities. Mascarene advocated for an expedition of three to four hundred troops and the construction of a fort, initially with earth redoubts, ditches and palisades, and several cannons which would "command the meadow, which is their treasure" as well as control entry from the Bay of Fundy into the Minas Basin.[23] Mascarene further recognized the strategic importance of the isthmus of Chignecto and the Acadian community of Beaubassin, through which the French corresponded and traded regularly with all of the French inhabitants and had also already staged the migration of two hundred families to Saint John Island (Prince Edward Island). Another small fort with a garrison of 150 troops would be necessary to cut these key supply lines.[24]

In his 1720 report, Mascarene is dismissive of the threat posed by First Nations, noting that "it is well known the Indians are but a handful in this country" and that their "mischief" was incited by the French.[25] Like most Europeans, he assumed that Indigenous peoples did not have their own agency and were easily dominated by missionaries and military officers. However, rising tensions between the British and the Wabanaki Confederacy, a loose association of several First Nations in the Northeast that included the Mi'kmaq living in Nova Scotia, began to shift this perception. The hostilities were caused largely by British encroachment on Wabanaki lands. After an initial raid on the fishing post at Canso, Mascarene was sent to construct basic defenses. War was officially declared in 1722 and, before long, Indigenous warriors gathered near Minas and then laid temporary siege to Annapolis Royal, causing considerable damage to the outer town and some of the farms. Mascarene creatively extended the fort's main defenses, notably with a series of sturdy blockhouses that functioned as skirmishing positions outside the walls. His efforts ensured that the fort itself would not come under threat, as the Mi'kmaq lacked artillery, and also that the inhabitants would be better defended in the future.[26]

After several destructive raids, hostage-takings, and other acts of violence, both sides agreed to peace negotiations in 1725. Massachusetts took the lead, but Mascarene was sent to represent Nova Scotia at the proceedings. He arranged for the Mi'kmaq and Wolastoqiyik leaders to visit Annapolis Royal the following year, and he helped Lieutenant-Governor Doucett draft the Treaty of Peace and Friendship.[27] Although the interpretation of this document remains contested, in general terms it allowed both sides to save face, recognizing British rights to govern Nova Scotia as well as Indigenous rights to live, hunt, and travel in their lands. The agreement became known as Mascarene's Treaty, suggesting that Indigenous and British leaders alike recognized his pivotal role as commissioner in the negotiations.[28]

Despite his success in defending the colony and as a diplomat, Mascarene's career prospects were significantly undermined during the 1720s by his disputes with an underling from the Board of Ordnance, Lieutenant Washington. This culminated in an investigation of mismanagement of garrison funds during his work on the fortifications, and it led to Mascarene's removal as royal engineer. As with Nicholson's inquiry, Mascarene had been directly implicated in financial wrongdoing, and whether fairly or unfairly, the damage to his reputation appears to have been considerable.[29] Mascarene's work with First Nations and his time in Boston also led to extended absences from Nova Scotia, during which other officers profited from his absence. When Governor Phillipps returned to the colony in 1729, he appointed Major Alexander Cosby as president of the Council, despite Mascarene having greater seniority.[30] After Phillipps's departure in 1731, Lieutenant-Governor Lawrence Armstrong took over the colony's administration. His abrasive manner and rigid approach soon alienated the other members of the Council and the local inhabitants alike.[31] During Armstrong's tenure, Mascarene spent most of his time in Boston, and in 1732 he was assigned the task to work with Andrew Le Mercier, the pastor of the French Protestant church, to recruit families for Nova Scotia.[32] This recruiting project failed to attract anyone, and one might wonder if the Anglican military man Mascarene was really the right man for the job. For his part, Mascarene cited "the quit rent, the absence of a House of Representatives, and the perception that the Acadians already possessed all the good land," as the reasons behind the disappointing results.[33]

These numerous setbacks might explain why Mascarene's erstwhile friend and patron Jonathan Belcher, now governor of Massachusetts, failed to get him appointed as lieutenant-governor of that colony.[34] The rest of the 1730s were marked by further petty disputes and relative isolation. Certainly, many of his colleagues must have resented the rapid rise of this foreign exile, while the political defeats of some of his patrons and friends diminished his support in Boston and London. Moody argues that Mascarene was "in some ways an odd fish in the imperial backwater of Annapolis Royal" and did not fit in.[35] This section on Mascarene's military career suggests that it was not that Mascarene was ill-suited to the army, it was rather that he was too much a military man, which explains his ultimate inability to secure higher positions in colonial administration up to 1740. His skills as a leader were best suited to battlefield preparation, combat, and the negotiating table, where policies and allegiances were clear and he could act with confidence to serve his king. But promotions within the army were limited because the next step was reserved for the commanding officer of the 40th Regiment. This path was not possible due to the overlap between military and civilian administration and Mascarene's compromised standing. At the same time, the prolonged peace after the Treaty of Utrecht stymied Mascarene's potential for military advancement through other regiments and expeditions. If his story had ended there, we might remember him quite differently, and focus on the limits to professional mobility in a colonial backwater. The sudden death of Lieutenant-Governor Lawrence Armstrong in 1739 put Mascarene back in charge as president of the Council, and the subsequent death of his long-time rival Alexander Cosby in 1742 cleared the way at last for his promotion to lieutenant-colonel, just as hostilities were reopening with France in the lead up to the War of the Austrian Succession. Passed over multiple times while in his prime, Mascarene, now nearing sixty years of age, found himself entrusted with military command and civil leadership of the colony at its most difficult time.

Mascarene and the Acadians to 1740

Historians, relying largely on his actions after 1740, have generally underlined Mascarene's positive and effective measures to collaborate with the local French inhabitants; for example, John Grenier called him "the closest thing to a friend that the Acadians had among the British."[36] Indeed, Mascarene's policies are often credited for preserving the colony during the War of the Austrian Succession.[37]

Barry Moody emphasized his "tact in dealing with the Acadians and his basic sense of fairness, both lifelong attributes of the man."[38] Before looking at this later period in more detail, it is worth briefly reviewing Mascarene's interactions with the Acadians before 1740. While others have focused on the administration of loyalty oaths, here I will look more specifically at Mascarene's actions and relationships.[39]

As we have seen, after the fall of Port Royal in 1710, Mascarene was dispatched to Minas to collect "contributions" from the local inhabitants. Their status was unclear as the capitulation of the French governor had only included those living in the vicinity of the fort, and the Treaty of Utrecht ceding Acadie to Great Britain was not yet signed. Mascarene quickly discovered that the Acadians knew how to negotiate. They first asked for time to choose representatives and to bring people in from outlying communities. Next, they condemned the "tyranny" of the French regime, which had left many of them impoverished and "actually beggars." As a result, they could offer only half of what Mascarene had required, which Mascarene thought "I could not refuse."[40] The inhabitants further requested that Mascarene provide "some show of power" with his troops, ostensibly so that everyone would be pressured into contributing. In reality, this was likely so that they would have grounds to justify these payments as under duress should the French and their Mi'kmaq allies return. Significantly, one of the men chosen as a representative of Minas was Alexandre Bourg, with whom Mascarene eventually formed a close and lasting relationship.

Although Mascarene later characterized them as one homogeneous group loyal to France and to their priests, earlier documents indicate that he was acutely aware that the French population was divided in their approach to the British. There were known inflammatories like "Le Basque" as well as a group of "bandits" who seized Peter Capon, an Englishman sent from the fort to "get corn from the inhabitants" upriver. There were also more helpful people. Pierre LeBlanc arranged Capon's release by paying a ransom. Pierre Goudreau used his sloop to transport foodstuffs from Minas to Annapolis Royal both for the garrison and for the needs of the local population. Mascarene credited the "quietest part of the inhabitants" for intelligence on the plots of the "mutinous part," a group that appears to have grown bolder after the defeat of a British patrol at the Battle of Bloody Creek in 1711. This intelligence was crucial in the organization of raids that dispersed a group of would-be rebels hiding out in the homes upriver from the fort.[41] Mascarene further left detailed records of his work as a civil magistrate, which consisted largely of registering property transactions and other private matters among the local inhabitants.⁴² In short, many Acadians appeared prepared to accept the new British government. Mascarene's insistence on paying for the lodging of his soldiers during his visits and compensating those who had helped facilitate trade demonstrated his fairness and that there were economic as well as political incentives for cooperation.

The British Conquest created new opportunities for professional mobility for some Acadians. Too often we consider the local inhabitants as passively resisting British authority; as Chris Hodson has emphasized, some Acadians actively "sought connection" with power for pragmatic and personal reasons.⁴³ For example, Prudent Robichaud became a leading figure in Annapolis Royal, representing the community and trading with the garrison.⁴⁴ In Minas, Alexandre Bourg filled a similar role, aided by recommendations from Paul Mascarene. In his fruitless efforts to get the Minas Acadians to take the oath of allegiance in 1720, Bourg was the first Acadian proposed by Governor Phillipps to serve as a community representative.⁴⁵ After the war with the Wabanaki, Phillipps tried again, and after securing a conditional oath, he appointed several Acadians as public officials, including Alexandre Bourg as notary, rent-gatherer, and king's attorney for the Minas Basin.⁴⁶ Given the importance of registering land claims and sales, as well as marriage contracts and wills, the role of notary was particularly influential.

British correspondence with Bourg indicates that the positions came with considerable benefits and prestige that placed him above other community representatives. Bourg collected 5 percent on all quitrents gathered for the council and could also pay himself with fees for his notary and legal work. One letter from Lieutenant-Governor Armstrong mentions an advance of two hundred pounds paid against this future salary, while another speaks to reimbursement for travel fees between Minas and Annapolis Royal.⁴⁷ This at a time when the entire revenue of the colony was reported as only a few pounds in quitrents!⁴⁸ The letters also mention that Bourg had petitioned for land after receiving a promise of support from Governor Phillipps, despite the fact that no Acadian was officially permitted to acquire new lands. Armstrong even provided information on who was making complaints against Bourg, suggesting that the latter should "look after" these "refractory people."⁴⁹ Armstrong eventually became dissatisfied with Bourg's service, accusing him of neglect as a rent-gatherer and replacing him with François Mangeant in 1737.⁵⁰ However, both Bourg and Mangeant, as well as Constable Louis Maufils, continued to be employed in ever-expanding roles around Minas, such as reporting on strangers arriving in the area and conducting surveys for disputed land claims.⁵¹ When Mascarene returned after Armstrong's apparent suicide in 1739, one of his first acts as president of the British Council at Annapolis Royal was to reinstate his old acquaintance to the position of notary and rent-gatherer for Minas.[52]

Mascarene's actions and writings balance a general sense of duty and obligation with a specific concern for the importance of individual choice. When sent to collect contributions from the inhabitants after the fall of Port Royal, Mascarene negotiated, worked through chosen delegates, and ensured to make cooperation appear as the best option. He continued this practice while working as a magistrate and diplomat, both with Acadians and with First Nations. Even his 1720 report that argued so forcefully against allowing disloyal French inhabitants to remain rested on the premise that the latter had to choose; it was their refusal to declare themselves openly that rankled him. He wrote, "It would be therefore necessary for the interest of Great Britain ... not to delay any longer the settling of it, but to go about it in good earnest."[53] Mascarene's actions in Nova Scotia indicate that he genuinely believed some would choose to become British subjects; he cultivated relationships with those who appeared amenable, including Alexandre Bourg, to mutual benefit. It is noteworthy that Paul Mascarene was the only senior British officer to visit Minas and Beaubassin between 1710 and 1744. This tour, in 1735 and at the head of a small column of soldiers, was intended to remind the local population that they were British subjects.[54] While it is doubtful that the tour had much impact on the Acadians, which may be why most historians do not mention it, this remarkable event nevertheless demonstrated Mascarene's personal courage and the relative goodwill that he had created. As an exile who had seen his parents split over religious loyalty and then had chosen foreign service and a new religion himself, he believed that cultural mobility within the Atlantic World was possible.

Mascarene and His Network, 1739–1743

Passed over on several occasions for senior appointments, Paul Mascarene was suddenly thrust into action as president of the British Council in 1739. His approach built on his previous career as well as on the ideals defined by his classical education and military culture. It featured a curious mix of idealism and pragmatism. Mascarene continued to emphasize that the inhabitants must choose, and that their actions had consequences. In a letter to Bourg, Mascarene reminded him that "those who rebel against this government's orders will not be safe" but "happy are those who are well-intentioned for the common peace and fulfill their duty, for they can easily be distinguished from those who seem to only bring trouble."[55] So great was Mascarene's faith in reason that he took the trouble to correspond extensively with the French priests serving as missionaries in Acadie in an effort to convince them to help their Acadian and Mi'kmaq flocks respect British authority. This is perhaps surprising given his earlier evaluation that "these missionaries have their superiors at Canada or Cape Breton, from whom it is natural to think, they will receive such commands as will never square with the English interest."[56] Evidently, Mascarene did not feel that this correspondence was a waste of time, as he not only argued for the priests' help in keeping the peace, but even engaged them in debate over spiritual doctrine. His life had been profoundly touched by religious differences, and he seemed to genuinely enjoy the opportunity to converse with other educated people, remaining respectful, and sometimes quite earnest in his letters; he even exchanged books with some of the missionaries who wrote back.[57]

Griffiths has observed that Mascarene's inclination to accept "diversity of opinion" was unusual and valuable for a colonial administrator and military officer of the time.[58] But there were limits to this accommodation, and Mascarene was clear that he would not allow the priests "to challenge British civic rule."[59] When Mascarene received word that Father Claude de Saint-Poncy, who had previously been expelled from Annapolis Royal by Armstrong for refusing orders, had returned to Beaubassin, he wrote to Bourg that if Saint-Poncy did not depart immediately, the inhabitants "would suffer."[60] The fact that Mascarene was even aware of the priest's presence serves as a reminder that even in the communities furthest from Annapolis Royal, he had informants among the Acadians. Mascarene also protected his agents, expelling a different priest who had excommunicated the constable Louis Maufils. Mascarene was wary of new priests sent by the bishop of Québec, including the Sulpician Jean-Pierre de Miniac. He was concerned that Miniac's title of "vicar-general" of Acadie would provide a new ecclesiastical authority and rallying point for the French in the colony.[61] However, Miniac would prove to be reasonable, and along with Charles de la Goudalie and Claude-Jean-Baptiste Chauvreulx, the Sulpicians in the colony appear to have consistently argued for peace with the British.

Mascarene was aware that his reach from Annapolis Royal was limited, but instead of accepting the status quo, he actively sought to employ his agents to influence events. For example, Mascarene was concerned about the conduct of the French in Beaubassin and, more broadly speaking, around the isthmus of Chignecto. He had identified this area as strategically important back in 1720, and in the 1740s it had become a center for trade between the Acadians, Louisbourg, and Québec. Armstrong had appointed a local inhabitant named Bergereau to work as notary and rent-gatherer for the Chignecto region, but Mascarene did not trust him, probably because repeated requests for the rent revenue and a report on the "state and feeling of the inhabitants" had gone unanswered.[62] So the lieutenant-governor turned to Alexandre Bourg in Minas, requesting him to secure the rents from Bergereau and also those collected by the missionary Jean-Louis Le Loutre, responsible at that time for the area from Cobequid to Tatamagouche on the Baie Verte. He further sent Bourg letters intended for Bergereau and the deputies of Chignecto, asking Bourg to direct them to someone "you can confide in at that place" so that the letters would get into the hands of the right people.[63] A year later, Mascarene wrote another confidential letter to the deputies in Chignecto and to Bergereau, calling them out for their long "state of disobedience" and requesting them to restore order, provide up-to-date lists of land sales and accounts of quit-rents. He further invited Bergereau to visit him in Annapolis Royal in order to clear up the "suspicion" that the latter had entered into "foreign trade."[64]

Mascarene would do all that he could to prevent Acadian trade with the French. In one rather ironic letter to Bourg, Mascarene asked him to "acquaint" one Charles Dugas that he "cannot at this time" accept the latter's offer to become involved in illicit trade outside the colony, since he "prefers the discharge of his duty to private interest."[65] While it is unclear precisely what kind of offer was made, that an Acadian at Minas would approach Mascarene directly with a trade proposal is once again revealing both of the willingness of some Acadians to work with the British and of the standing that Mascarene seems to have held. Enforcing trade restrictions was one thing, as it was directly related to hindering the French, but Mascarene also advocated for the Acadians at times, for example, recognizing that British policy preventing the Acadians from acquiring new lands was flawed. In a letter to the Duke of Newcastle, Mascarene pressed for changes because "the inhabitants who from the subdivision of their lands in each family now want room to make new settlements for the increase of their children, which occasion many of them to look out for lands and make settlements thereon contrary to the orders often repeated to restrain them."[66] On top of the question of gaining title to new lands, much of his correspondence with the Acadian deputies involved sorting out existing property rights. In one letter to Bourg at Minas, Mascarene mentions four different ongoing disputes that had been brought to him and, significantly, he asks for the deputies at Pisiquid (near modern-day Windsor, Nova Scotia) to work with Bourg to find amicable solutions.⁶⁷ Mascarene understood that assuring property rights and inheritances was a fundamental aspect of civil governance and of the transition of the Acadians and their children to become loyal British subjects.

Mascarene's network also helped in diplomacy with the local Mi'kmaq communities. Raids on fishing vessels and cargo ships had been an ongoing issue in the colony since the end of the French regime. In 1742, an English merchant named Trefry was "plundered" near Minas just before he was to set sail for Boston. He sent a complaint and a detailed inventory of his cargo to Annapolis Royal. Bourg, Mangeant, two of the other Minas deputies, and two Mi'kmaq representatives all responded quickly. They were able to secure the return of much of the cargo, and an Acadian called "Sapin" was compensated for lending his vessel to the unlucky merchant. Mascarene "highly approved" of this conduct and promised that the Mi'kmaq could "depend on the friendship of His Majesty's subjects as long as they refrain from molesting them."⁶⁸ This is a very significant affirmation because it suggests that Mascarene, who had played a crucial role in the Treaty of Peace and Friendship of 1726, recognized the autonomy of the Mi'kmaq in Nova Scotia.

Mascarene believed that he was on the right track in his administration of Nova Scotia. He requested a raise and the official appointment of lieutenant-governor, noting his many years of service abroad, his impartial administration of justice, and his knowledge of the "temper" of the French inhabitants.⁶⁹ The death of Cosby cleared the way, and Mascarene also received a promotion to the rank of lieutenant-colonel. He knew that there was still much work to be done, writing to the Secretary of State and the Lords of Trade that "the inhabitants cannot be depended upon for assistance in case of a rupture with France" but he did expect that "we can keep them from joining with the enemy... especially by making them sensible of the advantage and ease they enjoy under the British Government thereby to wean them from their old masters. But as to do this effectually a considerable time will be required."⁷⁰ Mascarene felt confident in part because he had built a network of agents throughout the colony. Some of these men, including Alexandre Bourg, were prominent community leaders. Mascarene did more than any other British officer after the Treaty of Utrecht to cultivate these relationships. This "awareness of the need to govern with the general support of the governed"⁷¹ goes a long way to explaining how he was able to extend British influence beyond Annapolis Royal, especially in the brief period of peace between his return in 1739 and the outbreak of open hostilities in 1744. His support from the local population was about to be put to the test.

Mascarene, Bourg, and the Duvivier Expedition

With war declared, Mascarene tried to convince his superiors to send him more troops, ships, and supplies.[72] Realizing that he would likely find no help there, Mascarene turned to William Shirley, governor of Massachusetts. Shirley was a political opponent of the previous governor, Mascarene's old patron, Jonathan Belcher. However, Mascarene the military man understood that Massachusetts was the most likely place from which to get support quickly. In an initial letter in May 1744, Mascarene asked for help in case of an attack on Annapolis Royal. Three weeks later, he advised Shirley that the British outpost at Canso had been captured and burned, and that he had reliable reports that the French were on their way. Mascarene "recommended the Province to your Excellency's care till they think fit at home to take proper notice of us."[73]

Mascarene prepared the defenses and was ready when the French arrived. The French commander, François Du Pont Duvivier, lacked artillery and so had to rely on raids to try and break into the fort. Mascarene reported casualties from sniper fire and significant damage to the town caused by one such attack, "but our artillery and small arms in little time dislodged them." Although outnumbered and encircled, Mascarene rallied his small garrison and relied on the walls and superior firepower to keep his adversary out. He was further encouraged by the absence of Acadian support—"the French inhabitants of this River have kept hitherto in their fidelity and no ways joined the Enemy." After a month of ineffectual skirmishing, reinforcements from Shirley arrived. Discouraged, the Mi'kmaq broke camp, and this forced Duvivier to retreat to Minas.[74]

Mascarene and the French authorities in Canada credited (or blamed) Acadian neutrality for the failure of the attack. Duvivier wrote in his journal that only a handful of Acadians joined his force, and that he was surprised to discover that even his requests for food, labor, and intelligence often required intimidation and threats.[75] The neutrality preached by the missionaries was also a key factor in keeping most of the Acadians at home. Indeed, it appears that Chauvreulx may have even excommunicated those of his parishioners who took up arms for the French.[76] Mascarene could count on other kinds of direct support from the Acadian population including, most critically, information. He learned of the outbreak of war and the organization of Duvivier's expedition from his informants in the Chignecto region. Fully advised of his adversary's progress toward the fort, Mascarene could plan the deployment of his soldiers accordingly. After Duvivier's retreat, he continued to receive information from the local inhabitants. One woman sent word that she had observed a group of strange Frenchmen "coming out of the woods at the upper end of the River," which notified Mascarene that his adversary was again moving toward Annapolis Royal. His informants also relayed news about the French fleet expected to arrive in Chedabucto as well as on gatherings of Mi'kmaq and Abenaki warriors.[77]

Mascarene understood that Duvivier would place demands on the French inhabitants. In his correspondence after the attack on Annapolis Royal, he accepted the deputies' reports that they had done their best to stay neutral and only provided supplies when forced to do so. He responded that they must serve the British as best as they can, such as providing labor to help repair the fort, and guides for the navigation of British ships.[78] However, Mascarene felt betrayed when he learned that Joseph LeBlanc, known as "Le Maigre" and also Alexandre Bourg's son-in-law, had carried out a brisk livestock trade with Duvivier and also sent sheep and cattle directly to the French fortress of Louisbourg on Île Royale (Cape Breton Island). Some of the deputies from the outlying communities in the Minas Basin further reported that Bourg had not delivered orders from the British Council related to the war and the prohibition of trade with the enemy. Mascarene normally could see through the disputes between the different factions within the Acadian communities, but Bourg's apparent betrayal shook him to the core. Writing in the immediate aftermath of the siege, Mascarene wrote to Bourg that his actions "giving me an unexpected surprise I therefore in friendship to you desire you may send me your reasons . . . and in hope you are not shaken in your allegiance to our Sovereign the King."[79]

Bourg had other compelling problems, notably dealing with the French officers, troops, and warriors who were still gathered in Minas. In October, a group of deputies from the communities of the Minas Basin wrote to the French commander requesting that he withdraw immediately, noting that "we live under a mild and tranquil government, and we have all good reason to be faithful to it." That Bourg was one of the primary spokespeople can be gleaned from the fact that the French commander's response accepting their request was addressed specifically to him.[80] Bourg finally wrote back to Mascarene in November, but by then the British Council was not interested in his "many excuses" and a short time later officially relieved him of his duties. Mascarene then ordered Bourg, Le Maigre, and Amand Bugeaud (who had also traveled to Louisbourg) to appear in Annapolis Royal to answer charges of collaboration with the enemy.[81]

There is something poignant in the two former friends facing off. Their relationship dated back to 1710, and neither of them were young men anymore. In 1744, Mascarene was fifty-eight, while Bourg was seventy-three. Mascarene, the military man, expected that his subordinates would be loyal and work as tirelessly as he did. Mascarene believed that he had been betrayed, and that Bourg had been proven false. The long delay in hearing from Bourg only intensified this belief. Bourg, the community leader facing impossible demands from all sides, needed Mascarene to be reasonable and balanced in his expectations. Bourg believed that he had done his best to support the British government and his community. Standing up to the French commander and asking him to withdraw was no small action. The Council asked several questions relating to Bourg's apparent negligence in not delivering orders, in not stopping his family from participating in "unlawful commerce," and in not giving a proper account of his conduct as soon as possible. Bourg's answers were short and give the impression that he was confused by the sudden turn of his standing. They were also the answers of an old man who had been through a considerable ordeal. Bourg explained that the orders were distributed but seized by French officers and that he had faced constant threats from Duvivier because his work for the British was well known. Between the French presence, his age, and the difficult weather of the autumn season, he had not been able to come to Annapolis Royal before then.[82] Retrospectively, it seemed unusually unreasonable of Mascarene that he did not accept these answers and support Bourg. On the other hand, in the aftermath of an attack on the fort and under scrutiny from people like William Shirley, Mascarene probably felt pressure to be firm. His relationships with certain Acadians were a boon when they served the British interest but could be criticized when the colony came under attack. In this case, his principal agent in Minas was charged with colluding with the enemy. The fracturing of his long-standing friendship with Bourg in the crucible of war was symbolic of the difficulties of professional mobility in a contested frontier, particularly when most officials believed that the inhabitants were disloyal.

In the same month that Bourg was relieved of his duties and interrogated at Annapolis Royal for his supposed collaboration with the French, Mascarene wrote to his superiors crediting his victory over Duvivier to the neutrality of the inhabitants.[83] But Shirley advised that there was a "danger of too much tenderness" in Mascarene's conciliatory approach.[84] Bourg's apparent betrayal and political pressure from above pushed Mascarene to make uncharacteristic decisions. For example, he sent Gorham's Rangers to build blockhouses in Minas and Chignecto.

True to their fearsome reputation, they caused panic among the local inhabitants, burning the homes of some of those deemed disobedient as an example and murdering families to intimidate the Mi'kmaq.[85] As the war dragged on, distrust and anger mounted. In February 1747, a battalion of New England militia stationed at Grand Pré were attacked by French troops as they slept. Some of the inhabitants had clearly provided intelligence to facilitate the attack, and at least a few had actively participated. This bloody setback irrevocably discredited Mascarene's claims about Acadian neutrality. His 1748 letter to Shirley reads as an attempt to blame others, notably his colleagues, for what amounted to professional failure and a complete loss of standing.[86]

After the defeat at Grand Pré, Griffiths notes that "even Mascarene wondered whether eviction [of the Acadians] might not be considered."[87] For Grenier, the fighting convinced Mascarene "that the British possessed little real authority over the Acadians and Indians, and all his careful and fair handling of them had resulted in only a miniscule level of obedience without allegiance."[88] Some historians criticize Mascarene for allowing Shirley and his more aggressive policies to take hold in Nova Scotia. Rawlyk notes that as early as November 1745, the majority of the British Council at Annapolis Royal voted in favor of Shirley's proposal to deport the French population.[89] For Robert Rumilly, Mascarene's grudging support to Shirley's plan was nothing short of "hypocrisy," but it is worth noting that Mascarene had acknowledged the need to remove disloyal subjects among the Acadian population as early as 1720.[90] By the end of the war, Mascarene was simply no longer in a position to stand firmly against plans for widespread deportation and seems to have lost faith in the inhabitants. He nevertheless continued to advocate for humane measures; for example, in 1748 he tried to arrange additional food, salt, and "other necessaries" to be shipped to the Acadian communities in Minas and Chignecto.[91]

Conclusion

After the war, a new governor, Edward Cornwallis, was sent to Nova Scotia. He founded Halifax as the new capital, and Mascarene again found himself in a subordinate position. Sent to renew treaties with the First Nations in 1751, Mascarene thereafter remained in Boston and entered retirement. Looking back on his career, he "took pride in what he called his mildness."[92] This was echoed by the governor of New France during the war, who noted Mascarene's "mild measures" and called them so "extraordinary" that "we do not clearly perceive [his] motives."[93] Mascarene certainly deserves the praise of those historians who observed his intelligence and his "basic sense of fairness."[94] Before the war, Mascarene must have felt as though he was achieving his goal of creating loyal British subjects. He had visited the outlying communities in person, the system of deputies was in place and functioning, and several Acadians were performing duties as British officials. In addition to the neutrality adopted by most of the inhabitants during the war, some of the Acadians brought key intelligence, trade goods, and labor to the British garrison. By any reasonable standard, Mascarene's policies and approach as lieutenant-governor were successful.

The discrediting of Mascarene's approach and his own disenchantment are revealing of the difficulties of colonial administration and the limits of professional mobility on the frontiers of empire. After Duvivier's attack on Annapolis Royal, Mascarene wrote to his superiors that "I humbly refer to be considered at home since a twelve month is past since we have received anything particularly relating to this garrison."[95] He did not have the troops or the resources necessary to do everything that he felt was needed. In this, he was no different from any number of French and British colonial officials. But Mascarene's experience was also quite unique, being a French Protestant in service to the king, and at least some of his superiors and peers questioned his suitability for high office.[96] Perhaps in appreciation for the opportunities he was given as a foreign exile, he was a fully committed military man, putting the monarchy and service to the empire above other considerations. His personal courage was exemplary, whether leading the attack on Port Royal in 1710, negotiating with potentially hostile Acadian and Mi'kmaq communities, or defending his fort in the face of a numerically superior enemy. His political acumen is more suspect in retrospect. Mascarene struggled to wade through the morass of petty rivalries and private interests that engulfed Nova Scotia during this period. He suffered numerous betrayals and disappointments, even from men he trusted. Samuel Vetch had fallen into disgrace and left questionable accounts that implicated Mascarene in corruption charges. Francis Nicholson tried to exile him to Newfoundland. Richard Phillipps passed over Mascarene to give promotions to his less experienced son-in-law, Cosby. The Board of Ordnance revoked his position as royal engineer due to questionable charges brought by an unreliable junior officer. Jonathan Belcher failed to get Mascarene appointed as lieutenant-governor of Massachusetts, undoubtedly his most cherished ambition.

In fact, Mascarene was finally awarded promotions and appointments commensurate with his abilities only after the untimely deaths of those who had been put above him. He took on the administration of Nova Scotia with vigor, undoubtedly convinced that this was his chance for vindication and recognition. But then, everything seemed to unravel during the War of the Austrian Succession. Even those whom he had trusted, like Alexandre Bourg, seemed to have turned on him. His network of agents let him down again when the French successfully ambushed the militia battalion sent to winter in Grand Pré. These actions must have hurt Mascarene deeply, as they were directed not only at him but at his legacy. Paradoxically, Mascarene lost faith in his ideals at a time when they seemed to be demonstrating their value. The evidence suggests that Bourg had not betrayed him and, apart from a few well-known partisans, the missionaries and the other French inhabitants not only stayed neutral but, in many cases, tried their best to support the British and get the French to withdraw. This surprised the British and the French alike. But this was not the interpretation of events that survived the war; the Battle of Grand Pré and the phantom menace posed by a growing French population loomed much larger in British collective memory, emboldening those who had always believed that a more drastic solution was necessary.

This detailed examination of Mascarene's career and his relationship with Alexandre Bourg suggests that loyalty was perhaps less fluid and contingent in Mi'gma'ki/Acadie/Nova Scotia than sometimes asserted. Professional mobility required risk-taking and commitment, and people became defined by their choices. For better or for worse, these choices had consequences. Nobody could predict the future, such as the disgrace of a patron, the death of a rival, or the coming of war. Accusations of wrongdoing could dog a person's reputation, particularly when that individual already appeared as a possible misfit standing out from his peers. Both Mascarene and Bourg sometimes prospered and sometimes suffered in relation to colleagues. Service to civil government had created opportunities for both of them, and their relationship suggests ways that the Acadians and the British government could have and did at times coexist. Diversity was possible in the British Atlantic World and, what is more, the ability to create connections among far-flung and disparate communities—British, French, and Indigenous—was crucial to making empire work. Mascarene was living proof that people could become loyal British subjects, when given the right incentives and through personal relationships. He wielded his cultural capital effectively in pursuit of personal power and influence.

A French Huguenot's Career as a British Colonial Administrator in Acadie

His Protestantism gave him the possibility of entrance to Anglo-American society in Boston, while his French language and background allowed him to do what few others could have done in building trust among the Acadians. Unfortunately, the war made his connections with Acadians seem like a liability. The charges against Alexandre Bourg and the attack at Grand Pré further discredited Mascarene's approach and provided easy ammunition for those already convinced that he was unreliable. This discredited legacy directly contributed to a culture that allowed less charitable men, including William Shirley, Edward Cornwallis, and ultimately, Charles Lawrence, to advocate and effect the Acadian deportation as part of their own strategies of professional mobility.

NOTES

1. Jeffers Lennox, *Homelands and Empires: Indigenous Spaces, Imperial Fictions, and Competition for Territory in Northeastern North America, 1690–1763* (Toronto: University of Toronto Press, 2017), 3.

2. Laurent Dubois, "The French Atlantic," in Jack P. Greene and Philip D. Morgan, eds., *Atlantic History: A Critical Reappraisal* (New York: Oxford University Press, 2009), 141.

3. Elizabeth Mancke, "Chartered Enterprises and the Evolution of the British Atlantic World," in Elizabeth Mancke and Carole Shammas, eds., *The Creation of the British Atlantic World* (Baltimore: John Hopkins University Press, 2005), 254–62.

4. N. E. S. Griffiths, *From Migrant to Acadian: A North American Border People, 1604–1755* (Montréal: McGill-Queen's University Press, 2004), 239.

5. Edmé Rameau de Saint-Père, *Une colonie féodale en Amérique: l'Acadie, 1604–1710*, Tome II (Paris: Didier, 1877), 72.

6. Barry Moody, "A Just and Disinterested Man: The Nova Scotia Career of Paul Mascarene," (Ph.D. diss., Queen's University, 1976), 398.

7. John Mack Faragher, *A Great and Noble Scheme: The Tragic Story of the Expulsion of the French Acadians from their American Homeland* (New York: W. W. Norton, 2005), 243.

8. The details of Mascarene's early life come from Barry Moody's outstanding treatment in "A Just and Disinterested Man," as well as from Maxwell Sutherland's article on Paul Mascarene in the *Dictionary of Canadian Biography online* (DCB).

9. Guy Rowlands, "Foreign Service in the Age of Absolute Monarchy: Louis XIV and His *Forces Étrangères*," *War in History* 17, no. 2 (2010): 141–65.

10. N. E. S. Griffiths, "The Golden Age: Acadian Life, 1713–1748," *Histoire sociale—Social History* 17, no. 33 (1984): 21–34.

11. Moody, "A Just and Disinterested Man," 20.

12. Léopold Lanctôt, *L'Acadie des origines* (Montréal: Les éditions du fleuve, 1988), 101.

13. George A. Rawlyk, *Nova Scotia's Massachusetts: A Study of Massachusetts-Nova Scotia Relations, 1630–1784* (Montréal: McGill-Queen's University Press, 1973), 114.

14. Sutherland, "Paul Mascarene," *DCB online*.

15. Vetch to Mascarene, 16 Nov 1710, Government at Annapolis Royal: memorials of Captain (and Major) Paul Mascarene, Private Letter Book and Journal also other letters, Transcripts from the Brown Collection, British Museum, Volume 9: 1710–1753, Public Archives of Nova Scotia (PANS) Halifax.

16. Gregory M. W. Kennedy, *Something of a Peasant Paradise? Comparing Rural Societies in Acadie and the Loudunais, 1604–1755* (Montréal: McGill-Queen's University Press, 2014), 57.

17. Moody, "A Just and Disinterested Man," 35.

18. Geoffrey Plank, *An Unsettled Conquest: The British Campaign against the Peoples of Acadia* (Philadelphia: University of Pennsylvania Press, 2001), 102.

19. Moody, "A Just and Disinterested Man," 47–48.

20. Mascarene, Acting Royal Engineer, to Governor Phillipps on the condition of Fort Anne, 1720, Transcripts from the Brown Collection, Volume 9, PANS.

21. Cited in Thomas B. Akins, *Selections from the Public Documents of the Province of Nova Scotia*, vol. 2 (Public Archives of Nova Scotia, 1869), 41–42.

22. Akins, *Public Documents*, 43.

23. Akins, *Public Documents*, 46.

24. Akins, *Public Documents*, 47–48.

25. Akins, *Public Documents*, 42.

26. John Grenier, *The Far Reaches of Empire: War in Nova Scotia, 1710–1760* (Norman: University of Oklahoma Press, 2008), 62.

27. Grenier, *The Far Reaches of Empire*, 68–72.

28. The text in full can be read here: http://www.danielnpaul.com/TreatyOf1725.html. Daniel N. Paul has written extensively about the British lack of regard for the Mi'kmaq, including their non-respect of treaties, in *We Were Not the Savages: A Micmac Perspective on the Collision of European and Aboriginal Civilizations* (Nimbus, 1993). Further analysis of this treaty is provided in William Wicken, *Mi'kmaq Treaties on Trial: History, Land and Donald Marshall Junior* (Toronto: University of Toronto Press, 2002), 110–17.

29. Moody, "A Just and Disinterested Man," 80–83.

30. Sutherland, "Paul Mascarene," *DCB online*.

31. Griffiths, *From Migrant to Acadian*, 316–19.

32. Plank, *An Unsettled Conquest*, 102.

33. Rawlyk, *Nova Scotia's Massachusetts*, 133.

34. Moody, "A Just and Disinterested Man," 98–99.

35. Sutherland, "Paul Mascarene," *DCB online*.

36. Grenier, *Far Reaches of Empire*, 100.

37. Robert Sauvageau, *Acadie: La guerre de cent ans des Français d'Amérique aux Maritimes et en Louisiane, 1670–1769* (Paris: Berger-Levrault, 1987), 194.

38. Moody, "A Just and Disinterested Man," 33.

39. A. J. B. Johnston, "Borderland Worries: Loyalty Oaths in Acadie / Nova Scotia, 1654–1755," *French Colonial History* 4 (2003): 31–48.

40. Major Mascarene to Francis Nicholson, 6 Nov 1713, Transcripts from the Brown Collection, Volume 9, PANS.

41. Memorial to Nicholson, 6 Nov 1713.

42. RG 1 Vol 8 1711–1713 Letters and orders relating to Affairs of Annapolis Royal, 6 Jun 1711 to Oct 1713 while under Governor Samuel Vetch, PANS.

43. Christopher Hodson, *The Acadian Diaspora: An Eighteenth-Century History* (New York: Oxford University Press, 2012), 204.

44. Kennedy, *Something of a Peasant Paradise*, 201.

45. Phillipps to the Inhabitants of Minas, 28 April 1720, Governor's Letter Book, Annapolis, 1719–1742, p. 165, PANS.

46. Commission as King's Attorney for Alexandre Bourg, 10 December 1730, Commission Book, 1720–1741, p. 180, PANS.

47. Armstrong to Alexandre Bourg of Minas. 21 September 1731, Commission Book, 1720–1741, p. 185, PANS; Armstrong, Directions as to Plaintiffs and Defendants, January 1743, Commission Book, 1720–1741, p. 187, PANS.

48. Griffiths, *From Migrant to Acadian*, 325.

49. Armstrong to Alexandre Bourg of Minas. 21 September 1731, Commission Book, 1720–1741, p. 185, PANS.

50. Armstrong, Order Deposing a Rent-Gatherer, 28 December 1737, Commission Book, 1720–1741, p. 216, PANS.

51. Order to Maufils, Constable, to assist Mangeant in Gathering the Rents at Minas. 1737. December 28; Order to Bourg Regarding Mangeant's Grant. 1738. May 5; Order to Bourg and Mangeant to Visit Chippody. 1738. May 5. Commission Book, pp. 217–21, PANS.

52. Commission Book, 7 May 1740, p. 236, PANS.

53. Cited in Akins, *Public Documents*, 43.

54. Lanctôt, *L'Acadie des origines*, 124.

55. Mascarene to Bourg, 17 September 1740, Governor's Letter Book, p. 139, PANS.

56. Cited in Akins, *Public Documents*, 41.

57. Lanctôt, *L'Acadie des origines*, 124; Robert Rumilly, *Histoire des Acadiens*, vol. 1 (Ottawa, 1955), 288.

58. Griffiths, *From Migrant to Acadian*, 334.

59. Lennox, *Homelands and Empires*, 114.

60. Mascarene to Bourg, 4 September 1740, Governor's Letter Book, p. 140, PANS.

61. Mascarene to the Lords Commissioners of Trade and Plantations, 3 Dec 1742, Private Letter Book and Journal of Paul Mascarene then Governor of the Province of Nova Scotia, PANS.

62. Mascarene to Bergereau, 24 March 1740, Governor's Letter Book, PANS.

63. Mascarene to Bourg, 7 January 1741, Governor's Letter Book, PANS.

64. Mascarene to the Deputies of Chignecto; Mascarene to Bergereau, 11 January 1742, Governor's Letter Book, PANS.

65. Mascarene to Bourg, 16 July 1741, Governor's Letter Book, p. 153, PANS.

66. Mascarene to the Duke of Newcastle, undated (1742), Private Letter Book and Journal of Paul Mascarene then Governor of the Province of Nova Scotia, PANS.

67. Mascarene to Bourg, and Mascarene to the Deputies of Pisiquid, 19 April 1742, Governor's Letter Book, pp. 162–163, PANS.

68. Mascarene to Bourg, 12 April 1742 and Mascarene to Momquaret and Wouito, 13 April 1742, Governor's Letter Book, pp. 161–162, PANS.

69. Mascarene to the Duke of Newcastle, undated (1742), PANS.

70. Mascarene to the Secretary of State and the Lords of Trade, 1 December 1743, Private Letter Book and Journal of Paul Mascarene then Governor of the Province of Nova Scotia, PANS.

71. Griffiths, *From Migrant to Acadian*, 333.

72. Mascarene to Secretary of State and Lords of Trade, 1 December 1743, Governor's Private Letter Book, PANS.

73. Mascarene to Shirley, 21 May 1744, 9 June 1744, and 13 June 1744, Governor's Private Letter Book, PANS.

74. Mascarene to Secretary of War, 2 July 1744; Mascarene to William Young, 27 July 1744, Governor's Private Letter Book, PANS.

75. Bernard Pothier, *Course à l'Accadie: Journal de campagne de François Du Pont Duvivier en 1744* (Éditions d'Acadie, 1982).

76. Micheline D. Johnson, "Claude-Jean-Baptiste Chauvreulx," *DCB online*.

77. Mascarene to the Lords of Trade, undated (June 1744); Mascarene to Shirley, 28 July 1744; Mascarene to the Secretary of War and the Lords of Trade, 22 September 1744, Governor's Private Letter-Book, PANS.

78. Lennox, *Homelands and Empires*, 128–29.

79. Mascarene to Bourg, 27 July 1744, cited in Akins, *Public Documents*, 130–31.

80. From the Inhabitants of Minas, Canard River, Pisiquid, and the surrounding rivers to Monsieur De Gannes, chevalier, as well as his response, 13 October 1744, translated from the French and cited in Akins, *Public Documents*, 135–36.

81. Minutes of the British Council at Annapolis Royal, 17 December 1744, cited in Akins, *Public Documents*, 152–54.

82. Minutes of the British Council at Annapolis Royal, 25 January 1745, cited in Akins, *Public Documents*, 56–60.

83. Lanctôt, *L'Acadie des origines*, 125.

84. Sutherland, "Paul Mascarene," *DCB online*.

85. Grenier, *Far Reaches of Empire*, 131–32.

86. Faragher, *A Great and Noble Scheme*, 242.

87. Griffiths, *From Migrant to Acadian*, 349.

88. Grenier, *Far Reaches of Empire*, 140.

89. Rawlyk, *Nova Scotia's Massachusetts*, 185.

90. Rumilly, *Histoire des Acadiens*, 293.

91. Mascarene to Shirley, 31 May 1748, Brown Collection, document 15, PANS.

92. Plank, *An Unsettled Conquest*, 104.

93. Rawlyk, *Nova Scotia's Massachusetts*, 183.

94. Moody, "A Just and Disinterested Man," 33.

95. Mascarene to William Young, Secretary, 27 July 1744, Private Letter Book, PANS.

96. The question of naturalizing foreign Protestants, especially Frenchmen, was controversial in Great Britain, leading to a series of bills that were enacted, then repealed. Catherine Naeve, "Natural-

izing Refugees: How Foreign Protestants Became British in the Eighteenth Century," *H-France Salon* 9, no. 25 (2017): 2. For Huguenot integration into British colonies, also see Owen Stanwood, "Between Eden and Empire: Huguenot Refugees and the Promise of New Worlds," *American Historical Review* 118, no. 5 (2013): 1319–1344.

The Trials of Brother Chrétien
A Case of Ruin and Redemption in the French Atlantic

CHRISTOPHER HODSON

As the early modern French Atlantic World has emerged as a viable field of study over the past two decades, something strange has emerged along with it: a near-ritualistic invocation, repeated in a great many books and articles, of the field's shortcomings. This invocation suggests that, especially in relation to more mature scholarship on the British and Iberian Atlantics, histories of the French Atlantic have been—and often continue to be—shaped not by the human and political geographies of the early modern period, but by the national boundaries of the more recent past. To wit: past scholars of New France (often Canadians) have tended to stick to New France, scholars of Louisiana have tended to remain ensconced in the Lower Mississippi Valley, scholars of the French Caribbean have tended to cling to the major islands, and scholars of France itself have tended not to notice anything beyond the so-called hexagon—and this to say nothing of the historiographical isolation imposed on distant, poorly understood places such as Guiana, the Illinois Country, Saint-Vincent, and the like.[1]

Although at least partially reflective of insecurities common among French Atlanticists, who can feel like small fry in the vast sea of better-established literatures, this invocation also speaks to a real interpretive problem worth solving. And indeed, swimming against the current of anachronism has forced historians to seek out new connections among peoples and continents, pulling themselves from the grip of regional and national frameworks. In doing so, they have complicated two venerable visions of the French presence in the Atlantic World. The first, championed mostly by French scholars in the mid-twentieth century, saw the French Atlantic as hamstrung by an overbearing and omnipresent absolutism that choked out the independent, capitalist impulses that might have resulted in a more successful (read: British-style) empire.[2] The other took the opposite tack, blaming the French state's inability to see beyond European affairs, a willful myopia that yielded underdeveloped colonies with tenuous links to each other and to the metropolis—a curio of vaguely French local worlds adrift in Atlantic space.[3]

Recently, however, historians have maneuvered out of these cul-de-sacs with big thinking. A capacious view of what constitutes the state has resulted in new histories of a robust, if idiosyncratic, French Empire whose influence reached deep into the lives of Indigenous people and colonists alike from the Sénégal Valley to the plains of North America.[4] New work on commerce and French political culture has produced histories that reconstruct the deadly entanglement of ancien régime capitalism, Caribbean sugar, African slavery, and revolution.[5] Expansive studies of Native American confrontations with French emissaries and missionaries have revealed racial relations and hybridized religious practices that bound diverse peoples in an embrace at once transcontinental and transatlantic.[6] In sum, it has become clear that the movement of people, as well as the exchange of goods and ideas, knit the early modern French Atlantic—as maddeningly intricate as it seemed from the perspective of Versailles, and as disparate as its outposts may seem to our modern eyes—into an integrated whole.

With an eye on the vast migratory, commercial, and imperial forces that fostered that integration, however, this essay, like others in this collection, suggests the benefits of thinking small. Indeed, by lingering in the borderland between microhistory and biography, we can get a better glimpse of the torturous decisions and face-to-face interactions which, braided together by the thousands, created a coherent French Atlantic. To that end, I aim to tell two intertwined stories about a man known as Brother Chrétien. The first took place during his life, in the early to mid-eighteenth century; it deals in faith, fraud, and a flight from the snows of Montréal to the shores of Saint-Domingue. The second took place some thirty-five years after Chrétien's death in 1755; it deals in charm, charity, and a chapter, long since forgotten, in the intellectual life of a Franco-Caribbean racist-turned-revolutionary.

Brother Chrétien's story—or rather, the story that a modern historian such as myself can now reconstruct—illuminates the means by which seemingly minor eighteenth-century actors and institutions cemented links between France and its colonies. Put straightforwardly, it suggests that the French Atlantic was indeed something more than a handy bit of modern terminology. As Chrétien himself lived it, the French Atlantic was a distinctive, evolving configuration of interests and loyalties generated by the movement of people and capital, and by the Bourbon monarchy's attempts to channel those movements to geopolitical ends. It was also, in his moments of optimism, a godly community in the making.

But modern historians such as myself are not Brother Chrétien's only chroniclers. Indeed, in 1790, as France and its empire were buffeted by revolution, another searcher attempted to tell Brother Chrétien's story. Like his subject, this author was himself on the move in the French Atlantic, even as the French Atlantic shape-shifted beneath his feet. He strained to revive the long-dead Brother Chrétien and to craft a wide-ranging narrative of his life and pious works that doubled as a solution to the most pressing political issue of his day. Grasping for meaning amid ceaseless motion, his efforts reveal that even in the eighteenth century, those who inhabited the French Atlantic were already interpreting the strange history of its integration.

"A Great Deal of Virtue but Little Talent for Administering": The Rise and Fall of Brother Chrétien

As the autumn of 1687 faded into a typically cruel Montréal winter, François Charon de la Barre believed his days were numbered. Feverish and frail, the thirty-three-year-old fur trader summoned a notary to his rented house on the rue Saint-Paul and, on November 26, dictated his last will and testament. Week after frigid week went by, however, and Charon slowly regained his strength. By March 1688, he was confident enough in his survival to revoke the will, and grateful enough for such an obviously divine intercession to reassess his life's purpose.

Ablaze with newfound piety, Charon wasted no time. During the next few months, he gathered a trio of merchant-partners, launched a fundraising drive, and cajoled the seigneurs of Montréal Island into giving him a nine-acre plot on Pointe Saint-Charles on the eastern tip of present-day Lachine, just beyond the town's defensive palisade. He there built a three-story stone almshouse to care for Montréal's destitute, crippled, and aged men. By 1701, it boasted (if that is the right word) "a ward full of poor people . . . well cared for" by Charon and his followers. New France's leaders sang the institution's praises, convincing Louis XIV to promise a thousand livres annually for its upkeep. Better still, the bishop of Québec agreed to place Charon at the head of a new religious community, the Frères hospitaliers de la Croix et de Saint-Joseph. Clad in plain black habits adorned with a woolen cross, the Brothers Charon, as they were known, not only cared for Montréal's needy but also volunteered for missionary voyages as far afield as the Illinois Country while planning a system of schools and workshops to be run by their ambitious new brotherhood.[7]

That brotherhood was, of course, dwarfed by the great Catholic orders whose preaching, service, and economic clout were crucial to the expansion of the French Empire—the Jesuits, Franciscans, Sulpicians, and Ursulines, among others. But Montréal's smaller religious communities, from the Brothers Charon to the mission-minded Chanoinesses hospitalières de Saint-Augustin and the uncloistered nuns of the Congrégation de Notre-Dame, played an understated, but no less key role in the integration of their frontier town with both the colonial and Indigenous worlds that surrounded it and with metropolitan France itself. And they did so, often as not, by getting into trouble.[8]

The Brothers Charon, for example, ran afoul of the increasingly devout Louis XIV in 1707, when they received word from Versailles that their order's vows were, in the king's eyes, illegitimate. Protesting that they had no desire "to be monks, but only to establish a house of charity," the brothers sent Charon to Paris to plead their case, and to resecure their thousand-livre royal annuity.[9] He spent five fruitless years there before returning to Montréal to hatch yet more plans designed to keep the brotherhood afloat: missionizing Natives near new French outposts at Détroit and Niagara, and at last founding a series of parish schools. The former plan languished, but the latter was funded in 1717—by the post–Louis XIV regency government, less pious than its predecessor—to the tune of three thousand livres annually, prompting Charon to head for France in search of teachers.

In 1718, on his second recruiting trip, he met Louis Turc de Castelveyre, a thickset thirty-year-old from Martigues on the Mediterranean coast. He evidently made quite an impression, for as Charon lay dying—this time for real—aboard the *Chameau* en route to North America, he declared that Turc was to succeed him as superior of the Brothers Charon. Although Canadian officials knew only that the *Chameau*'s crew "said much good" about Turc, they had little choice but to accept Charon's wishes; with "the poverty of the colony growing each day," disrupting the brotherhood's work at the hospital could prove disastrous.[10]

Once in Montréal, Turc took the name Brother Chrétien and lurched into a checkered career as an administrator. He began, boldly enough, by angling to use the three thousand livres earmarked for Charon's schools to pay down the order's debts and to support the hospital's normal operations. New France's intendant suggested a compromise (giving 1,500 livres to the hospital and 1,500 to the schools), but the Crown refused, demanding that the full amount be applied to teacher salaries, and that each parish priest produce a report certifying that instruction had in fact taken place.[11] Even as this squabble played out, Chrétien hurtled into a series of lawsuits. Early in the 1720s, he tangled with François Darle and André Souste, two silk and woolen manufacturers hired by Charon to build a workshop near the almshouse.[12] Before the hard-scribbling royal clerks of Montréal, he railed against the merchant Jacques Charbonnier, who had recently convinced the Superior Council in Québec that he, and not the Brothers Charon, was the real inheritor of a house on the Pointe Saint-Charles that had once belonged to the order's founder.[13] Chrétien even went to both Québec's lower *prévôté* court and the Superior Council to settle a dispute over the estate of Charon's sister-in-law, willed to the hospital in 1699 but claimed by her descendants upon her death in 1724.[14]

Chrétien's propensity for expensive lawsuits contributed to the perception that the Brothers Charon were sliding toward insolvency. The governor-general and intendant of New France thought so as early as 1720, when they told ministers at Versailles that Brother Chrétien possessed "a great deal of virtue but little talent for administering" his order's affairs.[15] By 1723, Brother Chrétien had determined to solve the hospital's financial woes by returning to France, and by turning on the charm that had worked so well on François Charon de la Barre. Over the next year, he cultivated—perhaps disingenuously—a cozy relationship with the aging bishop of La Rochelle, the Atlantic port most directly implicated in Canadian trade.[16] Bonding over shared disgust with the education given to Catholic children in their towns, the men resolved to found a school for aspiring teachers; the bishop agreed to donate a house in La Rochelle, while staffing and, fatefully, fundraising fell to the Brothers Charon. Emboldened, Chrétien headed for Paris, where he managed to borrow some forty thousand livres from a host of well-heeled benefactors, from merchants to the widow of a royal apothecary.[17] But when the bishop died late in 1724, this project fell into limbo. Pestered by creditors, hounded by the suspicious bishop of Québec, and badgered by his hand-wringing brethren back in Montréal, Chrétien buckled under the rising pressure.[18]

And so he walked away, straight onto the deck of a ship headed from La Rochelle to the Caribbean colony of Saint-Domingue. While a journey to the tropics was a bold step for Chrétien, he followed a well-worn path. France's religious orders had a long-standing presence in the Caribbean, and as Saint-Domingue's population of planters, poor whites, and African slaves rose during the first quarter of the eighteenth century, Catholic clerics and laymen trailed them across the Atlantic.[19] Many felt called to fill the spiritual void described by Pierre-François-Xavier de Charlevoix, a Jesuit who toured Saint-Domingue early in the 1720s. Charlevoix lamented that while slaves held religion "in the greatest esteem," their "irreligious masters" gave "little care ... to the instruction of these unfortunates," perpetuating a cycle of cruelty and impiety that only evangelization across the racial divide could break.[20]

Religious orders with more modest aims founded hospitals. As in Canada, such orders valued Caribbean almshouses as sites for Christian service, while colonial officials liked that they provided such service at little cost to the state. What might now be called public-private partnerships proliferated. For example, the chevalier de la Rochalar, Saint-Domingue's governor-general during the 1720s, teamed up with the Cordeliers of La Rochelle to open a hospital in Petit-Goâve on the colony's southern peninsula.[21]

Familiar as he was with Saint-Domingue's charitable institutions, Rochalar knew exactly where to look when, early in 1726, he received a letter from Versailles, asking on behalf of the bishop of Québec if someone called Brother Chrétien had turned up in the colony.[22] Indeed he had, Rochalar replied. Although Chrétien had appeared "in the guise of a true zealot for the public good" upon his arrival in 1725, the governor-general wondered if he alone had not been duped. After reaching the town of Léogane, Chrétien had apparently cajoled its priest into founding a hospital. Then, as was his habit, he started sweet-talking local donors: the widow Castaing offered land, plus an annuity of one hundred pistoles until her death; planters Chaveau and Delafond chipped in sixteen thousand livres; local carpenters agreed to work on the building for free.[23] "Little by little," Rochalar reported, Chrétien "became the proprietor of these funds by applying them to his own affairs," until suspicions arose and the threat of an "in-depth examination" of the hospital's finances loomed. And then Chrétien took his most desperate journey yet: "deserting" to the Spanish side of Hispaniola, leaving Rochelar with no leads and a clutch of pious creditors high and dry.[24]

Scattered throughout the French Empire, those creditors stewed for nearly two years, until word reached Versailles of an unexpected development. Chrétien, Rochalar wrote from Saint-Domingue in May of 1728, "must have gotten bored" in exile, for he had suddenly materialized in Bayaha, a town on the colony's eastern border.[25] Rochalar had him arrested and shipped to La Rochelle, whose authorities hustled him back to Québec, where the bishop gleefully removed him as superior of the Brothers Charon and stashed him in a convent to await trial.[26]

It soon became clear, however, that bringing Brother Chrétien to justice would be no straightforward task. Gilles Hocquart, New France's newly appointed intendant—the office charged with overseeing the colony's courts—learned just how tricky the case would be when, late in 1729, he received a letter penned by the Québec lawyer Nicolas de Villerme on behalf of nearly forty of Chrétien's French victims. Having already taken their case before the Châtelet, the preeminent court in Paris's knotty judicial system, Villerme's defrauded clients described themselves as "creditors" not only of Brother Chrétien, but of the bishop of Québec and the Brothers Charon as well. From these parties, they demanded repayment of their investments, which added up to over fifty thousand livres. For his part, the ever-litigious Chrétien countersued the Brothers Charon while claiming that a Québec merchant, Claude Morillonnet *dit* Berry, owed *him* over nine thousand livres.

Hocquart threw up his hands. With "proceedings pending in different jurisdictions" and Versailles breathing down his neck, the intendant declared that it was in everyone's best interest that the case be decided by "a single judge." To that end, he tapped Louis-Guillaume Verrier, attorney general of the Superior Council in Québec.[27] The Brothers Charon hurled every procedural roadblock they could imagine in Verrier's path, fearful that a judgment against them might bankrupt the order. In 1730, for instance, they lodged an appeal with Hocquart, claiming that the attorneys for Chrétien's French creditors had no right to view the order's internal documents. Hocquart dismissed it, but the case continued to limp along, hamstrung by stall tactics, the sluggish pace of transatlantic communication, and the tedium of combing through reams of evidence.[28]

Finally, in April 1735, Verrier made his ruling. The debts racked up in France during the previous decade were Chrétien's own, the attorney-general wrote, but the Brothers Charon and Claude Morillonet *dit* Berry did indeed owe the former superior money and goods totaling over thirty thousand livres.[29] Hocquart's relief at the resolution of Chrétien's unpleasant case was palpable. "Frankly, Verrier is the only man in this country who could have unraveled it," he wrote to Versailles, pleading for a salary bonus to keep the Superior Council's star attorney happy.[30]

Brother Chrétien promptly turned his winnings over to his French creditors and told them that he intended to return to Saint-Domingue, where "he hoped to make some income with a brewery he wanted to build there."[31] Keen to get their hands on that income, the creditors made no objection, and since Hocquart was eager to shoo his most bothersome subject away, Chrétien sailed for the Caribbean. He left devastation in his wake. Donors turned heel and the Brothers Charon went bankrupt. By the late 1740s, their derelict hospital had been turned over to a female religious order, the Sisters of Charity (known as the Grey Nuns), whose zeal and efficiency drew acclaim from all quarters.[32] Brother Chrétien's name, by contrast, became a byword for corruption. As late as 1748, the abbé de l'Isle-Dieu, vicar-general over all religious orders in New France, clung to his belief in the ex-superior's guilt. Chrétien had never really acted on behalf of the Brothers Charon, the abbé insisted, but had instead funneled investors' money to his own "crazy and extravagant enterprises" in Saint-Domingue—operating what was, in effect, an eighteenth-century Ponzi scheme.[33]

But from Montréal to Québec, Chrétien's culpability hardly seemed to matter to most people. What mattered was that he was gone.

Hardscrabble: Brother Chrétien's French Atlantic World

Nearly three centuries after Brother Chrétien's final flight from New France, we would do well to emulate these hard-luck Canadians in one respect: by resisting the temptation to revisit Chrétien's guilt or innocence. Instead, while steeping in the mystery of his bizarre habits of borrowing and spending, we might instead reflect, in the best microhistorical tradition, on what his story reveals about the transatlantic context in which it occurred.

Let us begin where Louis Turc de Castelveyre's connection to the French Atlantic did—with the Frères hospitaliers de la Croix et de Saint-Joseph, the scrappy fraternity that eventually took on the name of its founder, François Charon de la Barre. Such orders get short shrift in histories trying to tackle French Atlantic integration. Jesuits, the boldest of the missionaries to France's Indigenous allies in the *pays d'en haut* and the Illinois Country, simply make better avatars for the cultural negotiations that allowed for the expansion of Louis XIV's empire into the west; so do the Ursulines of New Orleans, whose complex relations with Natives and enslaved peoples did much to shape French Louisiana beginning in the 1720s.[34]

By comparison, the Brothers Charon, laser-focused as they were on local poverty in Montréal, seem better aligned with antiquarianism than with the capacious scope of Atlantic history. And yet, precisely because of their penury, and thus their perpetual scramble for patronage and resources, the brotherhood was driven to engage with the mother country in creative ways. Charon's teacher-seeking journeys to Paris and southern France, like Brother Chrétien's later stay in La Rochelle, suggest that while we have rightly paid attention to Catholicism as a point of connection between Frenchmen and Native Americans (and to a lesser extent, between Frenchmen and West Africans), we have perhaps glossed over the links it created, and the capital it moved, between the French Atlantic's constituent parts.

Still, Brother Chrétien *was* on trial. So if, as I have suggested, we embrace the fruitlessness of overparsing his guilt or innocence, what can we say about the convoluted legalities that shaped his time at the helm of the Brothers Charon? The history of law in the French Atlantic is, for very good reasons, dominated by the notion of legal pluralism. Replicating and complicating the "baroque patchwork of distinct jurisdictions" that made up early modern France, the French Atlantic was scored by ill-defined legal boundaries and characterized by multiple sources of legal authority.[35] Cases like Brother Chrétien's, which crossed those boundaries and implicated many such authorities, were waking nightmares for men like Gilles Hocquart. While French leaders did leverage this fragmentation to suit their own interests, Hocquart took an absolutist tack. His selection of Guillaume Verrier to cut the Gordian knot of jurisdictional conflicts at the heart of Chrétien's case echoed, if only faintly, the impulse toward uniformity in law that had emanated from the monarchy since the medieval period, and which had been amplified by Louis XIV in particular. Although the true reach and efficiency of French absolutism has been overblown by both modern scholars and Hocquart's contemporaries, Verrier's one-man judicial task force does suggest the ways in which Atlantic complexities could produce absolutist results.

Brother Chrétien's story, then, is not so much about identifying the man as a wide-eyed incompetent, a con artist, or an outright villain. Instead, it offers us a series of snapshots of the ancien régime's French Atlantic, and of the French Empire that sought to bring its constituent parts to heel. Chrétien's travels, as well as the flows of money, personnel, and legal claims those travels provoked, illuminate a transoceanic underworld that is rarely glimpsed in full—a realm of poor, covetous religious orders, of well-meaning, clear-eyed Catholic philanthropists, of incipient bonds between Montréal, La Rochelle, and Saint-Domingue, and of royal officials out for quick solutions to thorny problems.

This, however, is just one interpretation of those faded eighteenth-century snapshots—one that responds to a very modern set of sensibilities and intellectual imperatives. There were others.

"A Secret Charm": Resurrecting Brother Chrétien

Sometime in 1790, the Royal Society of Arts and Sciences of Cap-Français, the newest (and, as it turned out, last) learned society to be chartered by Louis XVI and the only such institution in Saint-Domingue, received a document by post. It bore no return address and no indication of authorship, only a sealed envelope bearing the epigraph "Charity is a heavenly gift." Recognizing the delivery as an entry in one of the society's literary competitions, members of the prize committee read it and agreed that it merited a gold medal—an easy decision, as the essay was the only submission they had received since opening this particular contest nearly five years earlier.[36]

Breaking the envelope's wax seal and peering inside, they discovered that the author was the Martinique-born jurist, intellectual, and slave owner Médéric-Louis-Élie Moreau de Saint-Méry. First as a lobbyist for Caribbean planters and later as president of the electors of Paris, Saint-Méry had played an outsized role in the early French Revolution, keeping up a manic pace as he did so. Late in 1789, even as he hurled himself into the maelstrom of Parisian politics, he managed to complete a massive, racially charged work of scholarship that would eventually be published as the *Déscription topographique, physique, civile, politique, et historique de la partie française de l'isle Saint-Domingue.* Then, in 1790, he was elected to represent his home island in the Constituent Assembly, the legislature tasked with writing France's first constitution and managing relations between emboldened radicals and the Crown. And yet, busy though he was with the wholesale remaking of France, Saint-Méry had carved out time to cobble some of his research from the *Déscription topographique* into a new essay and send it off to Cap Français for the Royal Society's none-too-competitive contest. Remarkably, his subject was Brother Chrétien.

Dredging up an obscure drifter-turned-grifter in a moment of world-altering change would seem an odd choice, but Saint-Méry had his reasons. Having spent years burrowing into the French archives, he had picked up and followed the faint traces of Chrétien's story, from his first meeting with Charon to his tumultuous years in New France to a Caribbean plot-twist in the final act. Now Saint-Méry aimed to repurpose that story to suit an auspicious, dangerous new epoch in the history of France's Atlantic empire.

Saint-Méry's *Eulogy of M. Turc de Castelveyre* began with hagiographical boilerplate: notes on Chrétien's family of minor but altruistic nobles, his 1687 birth in Martigues, his burgeoning "feelings of charity for the poor," the rise in his heart of an insatiable desire for the personal virtue that would become the "food of his soul." Then came the tricky parts. Saint-Méry first toured his readers through Chrétien's days at the helm of the Montréal hospital; he blamed its bankruptcy on the superior's surfeit of apostolic zeal and an inability, born of sheer innocence, to say no to pious but costly "speculations" such as the teachers' school in La Rochelle.

The author then turned to Saint-Domingue, where Chrétien had fled in 1725 not to escape his order's debts, Saint-Méry insisted, but to pay them off by selling beer and trafficking in Canadian fish. And yet, Saint-Méry admitted, "as soon as [Chrétien] disembarked at Léogane, he abandoned his profit-making ideas and his concern for the Brothers Charon, turning instead to the creation of another 'asylum for the poor.'" Tracked down by Saint-Domingue's governor, however, Chrétien had indeed yielded to what Saint-Méry excused as "weakness" and fled to the Spanish side of the island. Weighed down by shame, he recrossed the border and surrendered in 1728, spending the next seven years in Canada atoning for his error and defending his name. Vindicated by Verrier, Chrétien left New France in 1735 and, as far as anyone there knew, simply wandered into the void. But, as Saint-Méry had learned, a "secret charm" had guided Chrétien's steps toward a "new existence."[37]

The charm steered him to Saint-Domingue—not to Léogane, where "painful memories" (and, presumably, still-angry locals) abounded, but to Cap Français, the colony's busiest port. The city was growing fast and had the pains to prove it. At the turn of the century, Le Cap had consisted of little more than three hundred or so log houses with palm-frond roofs and a lone Catholic church featuring an open-air nave; one visiting cleric described its white residents as "naked savages" who laughed and swore during his sermon.[38] Over the next three decades, however, Le Cap boomed as sugar and indigo cultivation, and the brutal slavery that attended them, took root on the plateau above town. In 1730, a visitor to the "Northern Plain" was stunned by the "immense revenues" of his host, who ran "two magnificent sugar works, each of which brought in 80,000 livres" each year.[39] By the late 1730s Le Cap's hinterland was marked by a racial imbalance unmatched just about anywhere else on earth. A paltry 739 white men capable of bearing arms, along with 362 boys and 132 mixed-race and free black men, watched over the Northern Plain's 18,000 slaves.[40] White migrants were in fact coming, but they were often trapped in Cap Français, blocked from acquiring land in a superheated market or stripped of health and resources by the rigors of the transatlantic journey.

Such people caught Chrétien's eye. Although ostensibly in town to (again) start a brewery and pay off his debts, he turned to the charitable life in a flash.

Clad in an old monk's habit, Chrétien began haunting the docks and alleyways of Le Cap, searching for down-and-out migrants and orphans. Taking them by the hand, he marched these rag-draped souls to the doorsteps of some of Le Cap's wealthiest residents, demonstrating in a vivid way the need for "public charity." Alternately guilt-provoking and ingratiating, Chrétien wormed his way into high society. Claude Desmé Dubuisson, a wealthy merchant married into a Northern Plain planter family, became a key patron, while the Jesuits of Le Cap, Saint-Méry labored to explain, "were not indifferent witnesses of such generous zeal."[41]

Before he knew it, Chrétien was again spending other people's money. With funds from donors and a last-minute bump from members of the Superior Council, he purchased a small estate just inside the city's new wall. By 1740, Chrétien was ready to open a combination almshouse-workshop for Le Cap's poor children, old and sickly men, and "those who, arriving from France, find themselves without shelter or relief."[42] Memories of Montréal, however, gave him pause. The thought of once again having "business to conduct" and "property to attend to," Saint-Méry wrote, drove Chrétien to "confide to more able hands" the financial administration of the new institution.[43]

Freed from such onerous responsibilities, Chrétien named his almshouse "Providence" and set to work. He became a fixture on Le Cap's waterfront, "awaiting those brought forth from Europe by curiosity, poverty, [or] imprudence." He then led them to Providence, bound their wounds, lived alongside them, and browbeat his rich patrons into doling out jobs to help newcomers find their footing. In Saint-Méry's telling, money—and the demands of his creditors from France to Léogane—no longer concerned him. While planting fruit trees in the garden at La Providence, neighbors predicted that Chrétien would be robbed. "Ah," he replied, "then I will plant so many that there will be enough even for the thieves."[44]

For the next fifteen years, Brother Chrétien pursued an "active and laborious life" of service before dying in 1755 at the age of sixty-seven. To be sure, there were hard moments and false friends. Saint-Méry reserved special venom for the white former employee who accused Chrétien of "appropriating a female slave, and of having with her an illicit affair," describing the claim as a fraud whose mastermind was saved from prison only by Chrétien's merciful intercession with the judges. Such hiccups notwithstanding, Providence proved its worth repeatedly, and not just in terms of local charity. During the War for American Independence, the almshouse would play host to over nine hundred injured and sick French soldiers, providing crucial service to Louis XVI's campaign to dismember the British Empire. From Saint-Méry's perch in 1790s Paris, no one in Cap Français had a more salutary effect on the town, the colony of Saint-Domingue, or the French Empire than the pug-nosed exile from Canada.[45]

Indeed, so successful was his almshouse that imitators abounded. In Port-au-Prince, for instance, a coalition of clerics, planters, and merchants launched their own hospital for indigent migrants, modeling it explicitly on Chrétien's Providence. François Dolioules, a master mason in Cap Français, was so moved by Chrétien's example that he donated his own fine house to the "disgraced poor women" of his town. Known, unoriginally, as Women's Providence, the almshouse opened its doors in the early 1740s, pulling in donations from planters and merchants in Chrétien's fundraising network.[46]

In 1756, the year after Chrétien's death, another mason began work on a dormitory on one of Providence's back lots, toiling alongside twelve of his slaves to construct a separate refuge for "individuals of his class." Born on Africa's Gold Coast and himself sold into slavery in 1736, Jasmin had learned the trade from his first owner. After a second master freed him ten years later, he married a fellow Gold Coast native named Marie-Catherine; together they amassed a small fortune (that included those twelve slaves) and, having witnessed the suffering of freed men and women, hoped to ease it. Nearly eighty years old as Saint-Méry told his tale in 1790, Jasmin still offered "continual proof of his compassionate virtue" in the shadow of Providence.[47]

"The Bonds That United the Two Worlds": Brother Chrétien in the Age of Revolutions

For Saint-Méry, the import of Chrétien's second act in Saint-Domingue was clear. As he shipped his essay off to Cap Français in 1790, the dissolution of the empire Chrétien had traversed seemed like a real possibility. New France, of course, had been lost to the British during the Seven Years' War, and now the tumult of revolution threatened to shake France's tropical islands loose. The slave owners who inhabited them, and whose interests Saint-Méry represented in Paris, had always shown an independent streak; as early as the 1760s, Louis XV himself suspected that Caribbean planters, keen to market their sugar to the kingdom's rivals, had in mind "to one day, and perhaps soon, escape from France."[48] By 1790, relations between those same planters and the revolutionary government in Paris had become so strained that an islander independence movement—or worse, a mass planter defection to the British—seemed more likely than ever.

At issue, of course, were the (to the planters) ominous implications of the emerging revolution, with its disruption of social hierarchies and its high-toned talk of rights, freedom, and equality. They had already felt an impact. Convinced that Louis XVI had in fact freed them, slaves on Martinique revolted in 1789, while whites in Saint-Domingue fretted as the same rumor made the rounds of that colony's plantations. That summer, slaves in Cayenne on the South American coast reminded officials that "if each slave took up a rock, it would be enough to annihilate them all."[49] And to the planters' dismay, the revolutionaries seemed intent on making matters worse. Many of the liberal aristocrats who drove the events of 1789—the abbé Siéyès, the marquis de Condorcet, the comte de Mirabeau among them—had honed their politics in the Société des amis des noirs, France's first abolitionist society. Antislavery language infused the revolution's earliest proclamations, and planters, along with the coastal merchants who did business with them, worried that policy might follow rhetoric.[50]

Their fears seemed on the cusp of realization when, in November 1789, word leaked that the comte de Mirabeau, among the revolution's most gifted orators, planned to introduce a motion to abolish slavery in the new Legislative Assembly. Saint-Méry swung into action. As a key member of the newly formed proslavery lobbying group known as the Club Massiac, he quickly mobilized as many allies as he could to counter Mirabeau's "seductive eloquence."[51] Absentee planters in Paris leaned on legislators, while chambers of commerce across coastal France launched a letter-writing campaign to bombard revolutionary government with warnings: of "the inevitable fall of our American trade and the rapid decline of the national, to which it is intimately linked," of "a multitude of bankruptcies," and of the broad "misfortune" sure to sweep France if Mirabeau's measure passed.[52] Legitimated by the abolitionism of the Amis des noirs, the "spirit of insubordination and revolt that reigns among the Blacks" guaranteed "irreparable losses" to France's economy—whether from a postslavery nose-dive in Caribbean production (and the resulting drop in Atlantic commerce that, according to one Frenchman, sustained a "world of workers" throughout the kingdom) or from a break for independence by disaffected white islanders, no one knew.[53]

Saint-Méry and France's proslavery forces won the day. On March 8, 1790, as Mirabeau bellowed objections, the Legislative Assembly passed a law allowing each French colony to craft a constitution regulating its own internal affairs, including slavery. The immediate threat of abolition thus passed, but as Saint-Méry saw it, real threats to the integrity of the empire endured, slave revolt chief among them. To that looming problem, there was an obvious solution. The new French government should, many argued, undo the many laws that discriminated against the Caribbean's *gens de couleur*—free people of mixed-race ancestry who, notwithstanding their precarious legal standing, had for decades formed the backbone of the sugar islands' internal police force. Although no small number of white planters supported a new, pragmatic alliance with the gens de couleur, others considered any breach in the wall between white and black to be a veritable invitation to slave rebellion.

In June 1790, this dispute over race erupted into violence on Martinique. After being denied the honor of marching behind the national flag during the Corpus Christi procession in the town of Saint-Pierre, three white officers from a mixed-race militia unit accosted the enslaved tambourine player of an all-white unit. What began as a street brawl turned into a running battle that ended with the deaths of the three white officers and fourteen of their mixed-race militiamen.[54] Competing narratives of the Corpus Christi riot flooded into Paris, triggering a crisis at the empire's very heart. A fragile coalition of planters and Amis des noirs continued to support better treatment for the gens de couleur; others, including Saint-Méry's Club Massiac and France's chambers of commerce, so feared the prospect of giving rights to anyone with any African ancestry that for the rest of 1790 they attempted to bar any ship bearing a mixed-race passage from leaving a French port, lest the contagion of racial confusion spread.[55]

This, then, was the context in which Saint-Méry deployed the strange story of Brother Chrétien. For him, the fugitive-turned-saint served as a symbol of the virtues and practices that once promoted imperial integration, and that could do so again. His initial 1724 flight to Saint-Domingue to La Rochelle, Saint-Méry argued, was not a flight at all, but rather a self-conscious move to promote connections among outposts of French civilization. "Brother Chrétien wished to unite Canada, France, and Saint-Domingue by charity," he explained, and in spite of moments of weakness and the misguided attacks of enemies, it worked—Chrétien had indeed "tightened the bonds that united the two worlds!" His Cap Français almshouse had not only served the poor, but had functioned as a kind of showcase for the French Empire's best self. "He wanted to demonstrate," Saint-Méry declared, "that the French, whether they live in France or America, form one people and one family."[56]

In Saint-Méry's mind, however, integration came with conditions. Brother Chrétien, he noted, "had founded ... a hospital particularly destined for Europeans."⁵⁷ Indeed, non-Europeans cropped up only twice in the *Éloges:* first when Saint-Méry refuted the charge that Chrétien had violated a female slave, and again when he described Jasmin and Marie-Catherine's construction of a copycat Providence for their fellow freedmen and women. These were, however, crucial elements of the story Saint-Méry wished to tell. For him, the suddenly ubiquitous debates over race and the political status of the gens de couleur were a mere sideshow. Whatever mixed-race people or their allies among the Amis des noirs might say, Saint-Méry believed, racism and segregation were inevitable outgrowths of the extraction of labor from enslaved Africans. Caribbean whites had obviously given the African ancestors of mixed-race people their freedom. Rather than militate for some unnatural form of equality, he believed, such people would be best served by continuing to count on white benevolence, and by doing all they could to defend slavery, the empire's lifeblood, while sweeping racial issues aside. Jasmin and Marie-Catherine's imitation of Chrétien's charity, after all, was only made possible by the twelve African slaves the Gold Coast natives themselves possessed.⁵⁸

So in the end, Brother Chrétien's story served Saint-Méry as a window onto a future in which revolutionary conceptions of self-rule, Atlantic capitalism, and racism harmonized to sustain a French Empire integrated by the profits bled from African slaves in the "the most brilliant of our colonies."⁵⁹ The charitable impulses of Catholic Christianity did much of the heavy lifting. Chrétien's own efforts to unify the French across Atlantic space were, according to Saint-Méry, driven by his godly concern for the white poor, while Jasmin, he explained in a footnote, had been mentored by Chrétien himself as well as a kindhearted Jesuit in Cap Français.⁶⁰ Tailored to suit the onrushing events of 1789 and 1790, Brother Chrétien's story was, in the end, one in which guileless piety mediated the racial complexities and vast distances of life in the French Atlantic.

The years to come would reveal the degree to which Saint-Méry's thinking was hopelessly wishful. Relations among Caribbean planters, the gens de couleur, and metropolitan revolutionaries continued to worsen until, in August 1791, their debates were interrupted by the largest slave revolt in modern history. By 1794, the French revolutionaries, fearful of losing their Caribbean possessions to the British or Spanish, put an end to slavery throughout their empire, crossing their fingers that the new republic's newest citizens would defend the islands on which they had once lived as human property. By then, Saint-Méry had fled France for Philadelphia, driven into exile by the revolution's radical turn. There, while operating a bookstore in the American capital, and later after returning to France in 1798, he wrote of many things: bare-knuckles boxing, horse-breeding, and, ruefully, the Caribbean. But Brother Chrétien, and the French Atlantic his story might have helped save, remained firmly in his past.[61]

In spite of Saint-Méry's best wishes for his subject ("May your memory, for too long dishonored, receive from the most distant posterity a tribute of tenderness and gratitude that you have so well merited"), and in spite of his best hopes for the French Atlantic, a great many people followed his example by forgetting that either had existed.[62] Brother Chrétien appears in a few histories of New France, usually as a foil for the Grey Nuns, whose charitable activities in Montréal contributed much to that city's early history.[63] Otherwise, he has slipped into obscurity. The French Atlantic in which he lived faded away as well. Anglo-Americans, of course, needed no excuse to ignore their old rivals, focusing instead on the history of the victorious British Empire, or of the United States that succeeded it. On the French side, eclipsed as it was by the Napoleonic Empire, and by France's nineteenth-century invasions of Africa, southeast Asia, and the Pacific, the early modern French Atlantic became something of a national disgrace—so many imperial defeats, so many lost colonies, as well as the shame of having participated so eagerly in the enslavement of so many Africans, led generations of French scholars to gloss over Brother Chrétien's world, at best confining themselves to one or another of its regional elements.[64]

This essay's reconstruction of Brother Chrétien's life, however, reveals a French Atlantic that did in fact encompass and bind those elements. To be sure, the oceanic system in which he circulated was, on some level, born of grand imperial designs hatched in the *bureaux* of Versailles and of the adaptations made when those designs collided with the imperatives of French merchants, Native Americans, and West Africans, both enslaved and free. But the French Atlantic was also made of less monumental stuff. As Brother Chrétien's career as an administrator suggests, penurious and half-baked institutions like the Frères hospitaliers de la Croix et de Saint-Joseph played an underappreciated role in its integration, triggering flows of capital and knowledge that coursed between France and the colonies. The plight of the Brothers Charon also pulled the diverse legal systems and sources of authority that characterized the ancien régime into close contact with one another. The result was not the legal uniformity the Bourbon kings wanted, but rather compromises, accommodations, and rulings that incrementally eroded the barriers between New France, Saint-Domingue, and the mother country. Although not in the way he had imagined, Saint-Méry was right: Brother Chrétien had in fact "tightened the bonds that united the two worlds," whether out of criminality, incompetence, or both.[65]

Saint-Méry's invocation of the mid-century French Atlantic in a moment of late-century revolutionary stress, of course, merits a careful reading. A chronicler of laws, an observer of West African and creole culture among the enslaved, and a French-educated ally of merchants and planters, Saint-Méry knew well that a French Atlantic existed because he lived in it, steeping in its heightened tensions over race and colonial rights. His rehabilitation of Brother Chrétien—and with him the commemoration of a rose-tinted empire that he envisioned as a faith-cure for the revolution's ills—should, on one hand, give us pause. After all, modern historians too have been accused of fabricating Atlantic and even global systems to function as ancestors for our own political claims: as an antecedent of NATO, for instance, or more recently as a precursor to the neoliberal cosmopolitanism that seemed to dominate the early twenty-first century. In interpretive terms, perhaps we are more like him than we care to admit.[66]

On the other hand, Saint-Méry's biography of Brother Chrétien arose from the archives, and with documents that made recourse to an ocean-spanning past both inescapable and useful. By Saint-Méry's lights, the interconnected French Atlantic that shaped Brother Chrétien (even as he inadvertently shaped it) was simply too real *not* to use as a balm in divisive times. Yes, as the Haitian Revolution would prove, he was hopelessly naïve about the capacity of Christian charity to paper over the injustices of slavery and racism, or to reconcile warring Parisian factions. And yet in restoring Brother Chrétien to a world defined by the ceaseless transit of people, laws, and do-gooder capital, Saint-Méry did manage to capture, if in gauzy terms, a lost French Atlantic that, alas, could not save his own.

NOTES

1. See Cécile Vidal, "The Reluctance of French Historians to Address Atlantic History," *Southern Quarterly* 43, no. 4 (2006): 153–89; Sylvia Marzagalli, "The French Atlantic," *Itinerario* 23, no. 2 (1999): 70–81; Robert Englebert and Guillaume Teasdale, "Introduction," in Englebert and Teasdale, *French and Indians in the Heart of North America, 1630–1815* (East Lansing: Michigan State University Press, 2013), xx–xxiii; Christopher Hodson and Brett Rushforth, "Absolutely Atlantic: Colonialism and the Early Modern French State in Recent Historiography," *History Compass* 7 (2009): 1–17.

2. See, for example, Pierre Pluchon, *Histoire de la colonisation française, tome I: Le premier empire coloniale des origines à la restauration* (Paris: Fayard, 1991).

3. See James Pritchard, *In Search of Empire: The French in the Americas, 1670–1730* (New York: Cambridge University Press, 2004); Philip P. Boucher, *France and the American Tropics to 1700: Tropics of Discontent?* (Baltimore: Johns Hopkins University Press, 2008).

4. See Cécile Vidal and Gilles Havard, *Histoire de l'Amérique française* (Paris: Flammarion, 2003); Robert Michael Morrissey, *Empire by Collaboration: Indians, Colonists, and Governments in Colonial Illinois Country* (Philadelphia: University of Pennsylvania Press, 2015); Brett Rushforth, *Bonds of Alliance: Indigenous and Atlantic Slaveries in New France* (Chapel Hill: University of North Carolina Press, 2012); Shannon Lee Dawdy, *Building the Devil's Empire: French Colonial New Orleans* (Chicago: University of Chicago Press, 2008).

5. See, among many others, Trevor Burnard and John Garrigus, *The Plantation Machine: Atlantic Capitalism in French Saint-Domingue and British Jamaica* (Philadelphia: University of Pennsylvania Press, 2016); Paul Cheney, *Revolutionary Commerce: Globalization and the French Monarchy* (Cambridge, MA: Harvard University Press, 2010); Paul Cheney, *Cul de Sac: Patrimony, Capitalism, and Slavery in French Saint-Domingue* (Chicago: University of Chicago Press, 2017); Jeremy Popkin, *You Are All Free: The Haitian Revolution and the Abolition of Slavery* (New York: Cambridge University Press, 2010); see too the essays in Suzanne Desan, Lynn Hunt, and William Max Nelson, eds., *The French Revolution in Global Perspective* (Ithaca, NY: Cornell University Press, 2013).

6. See Sophie White, *Wild Frenchmen and Frenchified Indians: Material Culture and Race in Colonial Louisiana* (Philadelphia: University of Pennsylvania Press, 2012); Tracy Neal Leavelle, *The Catholic Calumet: Colonial Conversions in French and Indian North America* (Philadelphia: University of Pennsylvania Press, 2012); Kathleen Duval, *The Native Ground: Indians and Colonists in the Heart of the Continent* (Philadelphia: University of Pennsylvania Press, 2004).

7. These paragraphs are based on Albertine Ferland-Angers, "Charon de la Barre, François," *Dictionary of Canadian Biography*, vol. 2, University of Toronto/Université Laval, 2003-present, accessed October 25, 2017, http://www.biographi.ca/en/bio/charon_de_la_barre_francois_2E.html.

8. See Leslie Choquette, "'Ces Amazones du Grand Dieu': Women and Mission in Seventeenth-Century Canada," *French Historical Studies* 17, no. 3 (Spring 1992): 627–55.

9. François Charon de la Barre to Ponchartrain, [1707], Archives Nationales d'Outre-Mer (ANOM), série C11A, vol. 27, 138.

10. L'Eveque de Québec to Conseil Supérieur, 20 April 1720, ANOM, C11A, vol. 41, 264v, 262.

11. Vaudreuil and Bégon to conseil de la Marine, 8 October 1721, ANOM, série C11A, vol. 43, 410v.

12. Procés entre François Darle et André Souste, ouvriers fabricants de bas de soie et de laine, demandeurs, et le supérieur Louis Turc de Castelveyre, frère chrétien, défendeur, pour un marché d'engagement," 21 March 1720, Bibliothéque et Archives Nationales de Québec (BANQ), TL4, S1, D2461.

13. "Opposition par Sr. Louis Turc dit Chrétien contre Le Sr. Charbonnier," 18 February 1721, BANQ, TL4, S1, D2608.

14. See documents in "Procès en appel entre Philippe Damours, sieur de la Morandière, requérant, et Michelle Mars, veuve de Joseph Riverin, et les frères hospitalières de Montréal, intimés, pour le réglement d'une succession," in BANQ, TL4, S1, D3395.

15. Vaudreuil and Bégon to minister, 6 November 1720, ANOM, C11A, vol. 43, 91v.

16. See Dale Miquelon, *Dugard of Rouen: French Trade to Canada and the West Indies, 1729–1770* (Montréal: McGill-Queen's University Press, 1978); John G. Clark, *La Rochelle and the Atlantic Econ-*

omy during the Eighteenth Century (Baltimore: Johns Hopkins University Press, 1981); J. F. Bosher, *The Canada Merchants, 1713–1763* (New York: Oxford University Press, 1987).

17. "Gilles Hocquart chevalier Conseiller du Roy en ses conseils, commissaire general de la Marine, ordonnateur faisant les fonctions d'Intendant dans la Nouvelle France," 3 December 1729, ANOM, série F3, vol. 81, n.p.

18. See Albertine Ferland-Angers, "Turc de Castelveyre, Louis," *Dictionary of Canadian Biography*, vol. 3, University of Toronto/Université Laval, 2003-present, accessed November 3, 2017, http://www.biographi.ca/en/bio/turc_de_castelveyre_louis_3E.html.

19. See Sue Peabody, "'A Nation Born to Slavery': Missionaries and Racial Discourse in the Seventeenth-Century Antilles," *Journal of Social History* 38, no. 1 (2004): 113–26.

20. Pierre-François-Xavier de Charlevoix and Jean-Baptiste le Pers, *Histoire de l'Isle Espagnole, ou de S. Domingue* (Amsterdam: 1733), IV: 364. See also Sue Peabody, "'A Dangerous Zeal': Catholic Missions to Slaves in the French Antilles, 1635–1800," *French Historical Studies* 25, no. 1 (Winter 2002): 53–90.

21. Chevalier de la Rochalar to [?], 25 May 1728, ANOM, série C9A, vol. 28, n.p.

22. Ministre to chevalier de la Rochalar, 19 March 1726, ANOM, série F3, vol. 81, n.p.

23. Chevalier de la Rochalar to ministre, Petit-Goâve, 28 September 1726, ANOM, série F3 81, n.p.; on Chrétien's donors, see Louis-Elie-Médéric Moreau de Saint-Méry, *Déscription topographique, physique, civile, politique et historique de la partie Française de l'Isle Saint-Domingue* (Philadelphia: 1798), II: 467.

24. Chevalier de la Rochalar to ministre, Petit-Goâve, 28 September 1726, ANOM, série F3, vol. 81, n.p.

25. Chevalier de la Rochalar to ministre, Petit-Goâve, 24 May 1728, ANOM, série F3, vol. 81, n.p.

26. See Ferland-Angers, "Turc de Castelveyre, Louis."

27. "Gilles Hocquart chevalier conseiller du Roy en ses conseils, commissaire, general de la Marine, ordonnateur faisant les fonctions d'Intendent dans la Nouvelle France," 3 December 1729, ANOM, série F3, vol. 81, n.p.

28. "Ordonnance de Gilles Hocquart, faisant les fonctions d'intendant," BANQ, E1, S1, P2217.

29. "Jugement rendu par les commissaires Charles de Beauharnois, Gilles Hocquart," 22 April 1735, ANOM, série C11A, vol. 107, 95–222v; see also Ferland-Angers, "Turc de Castelveyre, Louis."

30. Hocquart to minister, 7 October 1735, ANOM, série C11A, vol. 64, 94v.

31. Beauharnois and Hocquart to minister, 3 October 1735, ANOM, série C11A, vol. 107, 93–94v.

32. See William Henry Foster, *The Captors' Narrative: Catholic Women and Their Puritan Men on the Early American Frontier* (Ithaca, NY: Cornell University Press, 2003), 90–106.

33. Abbé de l'Isle-Dieu to minister, 11 October 1748, ANOM, série C11A, vol. 92, 407–410v; l'Isle-Dieu to minister, 6 September 1748, ANOM, séfie C11A, vol. 92, 401v.

34. See Dominique Deslandres, *Croire et faire croire: Les missions françaises aux XVIIe siècle (1600–1650)* (Paris: Fayard, 2003); Rushforth, *Bonds of Alliance*; Morrissey, *Empire by Collaboration*; Richard White, *The Middle Ground: Indians, Empires, and Republics in the Great Lakes Region, 1650–1815* (New York: Cambridge University Press, 1991); Emily Clark, *Masterless Mistresses: The New Orleans Ursulines and the Development of a New World Society, 1727–1834* (Chapel Hill: University of North Carolina Press, 2007); on religion and cultural exchange in Louisiana, see also Jennifer M. Spear, *Race, Sex, and Social Order in Early New Orleans* (Baltimore: Johns Hopkins University Press, 2009), and of course

Daniel Usner, *Indians, Settlers, and Slaves in a Frontier Exchange Economy: The Lower Mississippi Valley before 1783* (Chapel Hill: University of North Carolina Press, 1992).

35. For quote, see Brett Rushforth, *Bonds of Alliance: Indigenous and Atlantic Slaveries in New France* (Chapel Hill: University of North Carolina Press, 2012), 77; on legal pluralism in the early modern period generally, see Lauren Benton and Richard J. Ross, *Legal Pluralism and Empires, 1500–1850* (New York: New York University Press, 2013).

36. *Prospectus des travaux que la Société Royale des Sciences et des Arts du Cap-François se proposoit de présenter dans la séance publique, que devoit avoir lieu le 17 août 1790* (Cap Français: Imp. du Cap, 1790), 2–3. On the Royal Society, heir to the creole intellectual society known as the Cercle des Philadelphes, see James E. McClellan III, "L'historiographie d'une académie colonial: Le Cercle des Philadelphes (1784–1793)," *Annales historiques de la Révolution française* 320 (June 2000): 1–10.

37. Médéric-Louis-Élie Moreau de Saint-Méry, *Éloges de M. Turc de Castelveyre et de M. Dolioules, Fondateurs des deux Hospices appelés Maisons de Providence, au Cap-Français, Isle Saint-Domingue* (Paris: Rochette, 1790), 1–18.

38. Jean-Baptiste Labat, *Nouveau voyage aux Isles de l'Amérique* (La Haye, 1724), II: 221–23.

39. Nicolas-Louis and Pierre-Jean-Baptiste Nougaret Bourgeois, *Voyages intéressants dans les différents colonies françaises, espagnoles, angloises, etc.* (Paris, 1788), 120–21.

40. "Recensement general de l'isle de Saint-Domingue de l'année mil sept cent trente neuf," ANOM, série G1 509, 22. My thanks to Rob Taber for this source.

41. On Dubuisson, see Trevor Burnard and John Garrigus, *The Plantation Machine: Atlantic Capitalism in French Saint-Domingue and British Jamaica* (Philadelphia: University of Pennsylvania Press, 2016), 155.

42. See Moreau de Saint-Méry, *Loix et constitutions des colonies françoises de l'Amérique sous le vent* (Paris, 1784–85), III: 645.

43. Saint-Méry, *Éloges de M. Turc de Castelveyre et de M. Dolioules*, 20.

44. Saint-Méry, *Éloges de M. Turc de Castelveyre et de M. Dolioules*, 22–23.

45. Saint-Méry, *Éloges de M. Turc de Castelveyre et de M. Dolioules*, 23.

46. Saint-Méry, *Éloges de M. Turc de Castelveyre et de M. Dolioules*, 26, 34.

47. Saint-Méry, *Éloges de M. Turc de Castelveyre et de M. Dolioules*, 27–28.

48. Jean Tarrade, *Le commerce colonial de la France à la fin de l'Ancien Régime: L du régime de l'Exclusif de 1763 à 1789*, vol. 1 (Paris: Presses universitaires de France, 1972), 370.

49. David Geggus, "The Slaves and Free Coloreds of Martinique during the Age of the French and Haitian Revolutions," in Robert L. Paquette and Stanley L. Engerman, eds., *The Lesser Antilles in the Age of European Expansion* (Gainesville: University Press of Florida, 1996), 285; Bourgon to minister, 23 December 1789, Cayenne, ANOM, AC, série F3 22, n.p.

50. See, for instance, Jeremy Popkin's assessment of antislavery language in the *cahiers de doléances* of 1788 and 1789 in Popkin, "Saint-Domingue, Slavery, and the Origins of the French Revolution," in Thomas E. Kaiser and Dale K. Van Kley, *From Deficit to Deluge: The Origins of the French Revolution* (Stanford, CA: Stanford University Press, 2011), 220–48.

51. Les Députés extraordinaires des Manufactures & du Commerce de France to the Chambre de commerce de Marseille, 20 November 1789, Chambre de commerce et d'industrie de Marseille, H44, n.p.

52. Directeurs du Chambre de Commerce de la province de Guienne to Chambre de Commerce de Marseille, 9 December 1789, CCIM, H44, n.p.

53. *Addresse de la commune d'Honfleur, a Nosseigneurs les deputes a l'Assemblée Nationale* (Honfleur: Faure, 1789), 2, 4; *Ville du Havre-de-Grace, Addresse a l'Assemblée Nationale* (Le Havre: 1789), 2, in CCIM, H44; for "world of workers," see Paul Cheney, *Revolutionary Commerce: Globalization and the French Monarchy* (Cambridge, MA: Harvard University Press, 2010), 184.

54. *Récit des évenemens arrives a la Martinique, depuis le 3 juin, jusqu'au 9, contradictoirement a la relation publiée par MM. Ruste et Corio, deputes de St. Pierre* (Paris: Imprimerie Nationale, 1790), 4, 7.

55. Gouy, Reynaud, and Chabanon to Chambre de commerce de Marseille, 9 August 1790, CCIM, H44, n.p.

56. Saint-Méry, *Éloges de M. Turc de Castelveyre et de M. Dolioules*, 12, 31.

57. Saint-Méry, *Éloges de M. Turc de Castelveyre et de M. Dolioules*, 30.

58. On Saint-Méry, race, and the gens de couleur, see Laurent Dubois, *Avengers of the New World: The Story of the Haitian Revolution* (Cambridge, MA: Harvard University Press, 2004), 83; John Garrigus, *Before Haiti: Race and Citizenship in French Saint-Domingue* (New York: Routledge, 2006), 242.

59. Saint-Méry, *Éloges de M. Turc de Castelveyre et de M. Dolioules*, 31.

60. Saint-Méry, *Éloges de M. Turc de Castelveyre et de M. Dolioules*, 27.

61. For a recent treatment of Saint-Méry, see François Furstenberg, *When the United States Spoke French: Five Refugees Who Shaped a Nation* (New York: Penguin, 2014).

62. Saint-Méry, *Éloges de M. Turc de Castelveyre et de M. Dolioules*, 31.

63. See, for example, Robert Rumilly, *Histoire de Montréal* (Montréal: Fides, 1970), I: 325–333; Foster, *The Captors' Narrative*, 92.

64. Vidal, "The Reluctance of French Historians to Address Atlantic History," 153–189.

65. Saint-Méry, *Éloges de M. Turc de Castelveyre et de M. Dolioules*, 12.

66. See Bernard Bailyn, *Atlantic History: Concepts and Contours* (Cambridge, MA: Harvard University Press, 2005), 28; Mary Eyring, Christopher Hodson, and Matthew Mason, "Introduction: The Global Turn and Early American Studies," *Early American Studies* 16, no. 1 (Winter 2018): 1–6.

Family Formation, Race, and Honor in Colonial Haiti's Free Communities, 1670–1789

ROBERT D. TABER

"Wife?" (*Laughing.*) "A word the whites use. We never had a priest, nor papers, either."
—JEAN-JACQUES DESSALINES TO AZELIA, AUGUST 1791, IN
LANGSTON HUGHES, *THE EMPEROR OF HAITI*, 1936

In *The Emperor of Haiti*, black American author Langston Hughes deploys a semifictional presentation of Haitian revolutionary Jean-Jacques Dessalines to explore key themes of the revolution, including why Dessalines, the victorious leader of the Haitian Armée Indigène, continued the plantation system and court life after the country's 1804 declaration of independence. Performance is a recurring theme in the play—court dances, hillside drumming, ritual banter, cultures of fighting and dueling, and the marks of labor discipline—but there is one particular performance that is crucial for delineating the boundaries and mechanics of racialization, social acceptance, and accessing the power of the state in colonial Haiti: the appearance before a priest for the creation of paperwork.[1] The priest would note whether a resident was a *négresse* or a *mulâtresse* or a *quarteronne* or the nothing that signified whiteness; they would also decide if someone should be called *Dame* or *Demoiselle* or *la nommée* and *la ditte*, indicating their social standing. Such moments of racialization, and bestowal of honor, were, for people of color, demonstrations of participation in the colonial process and of performance as colonial subjects.

What's more, the state imbued these parish documents with legal significance, making them part of what William Brown calls "administrative ethnography."[2]

In the late colonial period, the state used baptismal and other sacerdotal records to determine free status and the ability of subjects to access the benefits of full acceptance, including professional positions, militia and military commissions, and liberty from a humiliating law placing limits on what kinds of clothes they could wear.[3] Residents of color, free and enslaved, responded in part by using these documents and colonial laws to assert and protect their own freedom and that of their families, and their access to the benefits of colonialism, including profits of the plantation complex.[4] The social constructions of race and honor in colonial Haiti—constructions that had legal ramifications—resided to a significant extent in the hands of the missionaries and parish priests who performed sacraments in the colony's many port towns. The stakes of these documents rested in their abilities to prove individual freedom and civil and community status and thus escape what Brett Rushforth calls in his epilogue the "physical brutality of slavery" and the "psychic brutality of having to argue for one's full humanity."[5] Security depended on the ability to claim Frenchness, and the passive connotation of *affranchi*—to be "made French" through the "gift" of freedom—made it a suitable slur for white colonists to use against free people of color to push back against their claims of full French identity by asserting they could never escape the stain of slavery.[6]

To examine the way colonial society interwove race and honor, this essay brings to bear the largest longitudinal analysis to date of the colony's marriage records, with information from six of the colony's approximately fifty parishes. It also includes microhistories of two women of color and their families to illuminate the possibilities for the cultural mobility of residents of color, who in turn used the law to assert their own gains. What these explorations show is that while elite discourse mirrored the hopes of administrators, and of many planters and white settlers, for orderly discrimination and maintenance of a racial regime, it does not reflect the social realities within the colony. Instead, what becomes clear is that the great change wrought by European colonialism in the eighteenth century—the forging of a deep antithesis between social honor (or standing) and blackness—was haphazard at best, even in colonial Haiti. As Hughes's Dessalines reminds us, however, these opportunities for legal participation and subversion remained limited, so many of the enslaved, laughing wryly at the way the colonial state excluded them from paths of social and cultural mobility, chose resilience, flight, and/or revolution.[7]

The growth of the sugar economy, colonial expansion into the southern Caribbean, and avenues opened by the Age of Atlantic Revolutions all offered possibilities to free people of color in the Caribbean to claim freedom, status, national belonging, and citizenship.[8] The women and men of color pursuing these openings had to navigate a shifting legal landscape. In so doing, they shaped and reshaped cultural understandings and expectations, including what it meant to be "French." Fear, along with "greed, longing, and restlessness," guided their pursuit of security for themselves and their families.[9] During the Haitian and French revolutions, this cultural mobility would generate famous examples, including the admission of the formerly enslaved Jean-Baptiste Belley as a deputy to the French Directory. It would also inspire fierce backlash, including from the government of Napoleon Bonaparte.[10]

Before the revolutionary era, however, the white elite in colonial Haiti engaged in a moral panic over the growth of the free population of color and the group's apparent wealth, often engaging in the propagation of tropes that had little connection to truths. They centered much of this panic on fears and assumptions about the sexual behavior of women of color and the threat these women posed to the cultural development of young white men. For example, the plantation manager Jean-Baptiste Corbier worried his son would be turned into "another of the 'human monsters'" by life in the colony.[11] To justify their sexual commodification of and violence against women of color, white writers stereotyped free women of color as Jezebels financially dependent on white men.[12]

This moral panic extended to aspects of the law, as honor became synonymous with whiteness. This differs somewhat from Canada, where questions of honor usually centered on maintaining respect for nobility or other assertions of social status within the white community. In Canada, white settlers of middling rank used insults, rumor, and slander to police hierarchy.[13] Young men would also engage in charivari, or a ritual of mocking protest, against couples they found in violation of social norms—often older men who married younger women.[14] Slander, insult, and the resulting court cases were the tactics used by wealthier white men in Louisiana to establish their relative status, particularly during times of social flux or when French and Canadian officers had to work in close proximity to one another.[15] In the later colonial period, however, the Louisiana elite used the law to build a system in which honor was determined based on being born in wedlock, proving European ancestry, and manifesting respectability and religious devotion.[16] In colonial Haiti, Corbier, the French-born but common plantation manager, found himself accepted by the nobility present in the colony.[17] Meanwhile local poorer whites who were anxious about their social status could, and did, use extrajudicial violence and the backing of the colonial courts to assert a social supremacy to free people of color.[18]

Many free people of color responded by securing legal and sacerdotal documents that stated their free status, described their property, and protected their heirs' claims. The French colonial state, expanding its reach during the eighteenth century, likewise insisted on documentation, closing opportunities for an informal *liberté de savane* (liberty of the field).[19] Residents of color therefore engaged in the performative paperwork of colonialism so the colonial state would protect their property and status. More people married than found themselves in lawsuits. Examining marriages sheds greater light on the constructions of race and honor, while also elucidating the pervasiveness of the slaveholding strategy and the tactical creativity of residents who discovered that they were "of color." A broad exploration of parish records illustrates what the polemicists of the day in their panic got right and got wrong about marriage, race, and honor in colonial Haiti.

As colonial Haiti became more important to France for economic and military reasons, white authors sought to inform the metropole of its history and its needs. These polemics often involved discussion of race and family life, impressions rooted in the authors' own experiences and biases, but generally involving the Jezebel trope. Men of color responded by asserting that they could guarantee the stable family life seen by the elite as necessary for proper economic development, a response that both subverted and reified the moral panic over women of color, sexuality, and cultural mobility.

In 1750, the white colonial lawyer Emilien Petit framed his *Patriotisme américain* as a continuation of earlier chronicles, capturing the development of colonial Haiti into a significant part of France's colonial system. In this descriptive polemic written for the purpose of securing greater state investment in the colony's governance and security, Petit devoted large sections to the role of people of color and to methods of increasing the colony's white population. As seen below, the middle of the eighteenth century was a time of flux during which some people of color achieved high social status. Petit viewed growth of the free population of color as a problem derived from male planters' manumission of concubines. Manumission, he felt, should therefore be limited to those enslaved workers who were loyal and had worked for many years in the colony's fields.[20] Petit held a special scorn for enslaved artisans trained in France and then freed for, in his view, undercutting the free labor market for white colonists, overburdening the town hospitals and charities, and causing disruptions because of their familiarities with white residents.[21] Much of Petit's scheme to "populate" the colony likewise focused on replacing enslaved artisans and domestics with French men and women.[22] Petit's prescription for the colony—revitalizing white marriages, discouraging interracial marriage, replacing enslaved labor with white colonists working for wages—was based on his analysis that the free population was at a demographic tipping point and that the French state needed to rescue the colony for settlement by white families.

As John Garrigus, Gene Ogle, and others have shown, and as the parish records underscore, the years after Petit's *Patriotisme américain* witnessed further conflation of whiteness with honor. To Petit's chagrin, the free population of color continued to grow and marriages between two people of color became a larger share of all marriages. It was in this setting that the often-hyperbolic lawyer and Enlightenment thinker Hilliard d'Auberteuil wrote his *Considérations sur l'État Présent de Saint-Domingue*. The work is perhaps best known for the way d'Auberteuil deploys geographic determinism—he argued that the heat made all of the colony's creole residents oversexed.[23] D'Auberteuil also insisted that marriage was "rare" in the colony: French men arrived to seek fortune, white women and women of color were mostly concubines, the marriages that did occur were unstable or suffered as spouses were on opposite sides of the Atlantic for decades.[24] These geographic tropes, however, had little foundation in truth.

While it is difficult to determine the stability or happiness of colonial marriages, marriage itself was not rare within the free population, white and of color. Hilliard d'Auberteuil (probably over) estimated this free population in 1775 at 40,000 persons. During the decade of the 1770s, just in Léogane, Saint-Marc, and Ouanaminthe, three of the colony's approximately 47 parishes, 371 marriages occurred. Supporting this, in 1783 alone, 380 marriages occurred across the colony, or one marriage for about every 40–50 free residents.[25] D'Auberteuil's push for reenslavement of free *noirs* and for forcing all free *mulâtres* to serve in the *maréchaussée* (rural police) came in response not only to the growing free population of color but also to the increasing number of marriages between two people of color, marriages that granted some legal protection to these households and, in some cases, freed enslaved partners and children.[26]

The most famous polemicist representing the interests of well-off free people of color was Julien Raimond. During the late colonial and early revolutionary periods Léogane residents Hillaire Jouette and Pierre Labuissonnière (Raimond's brother-in-law), among others, also wrote key letters.[27] Raimond spent a considerable portion of his 1785 letter discussing various discriminatory practices (*coutumes*) that disrupted family life among free people of color. Raimond blamed whites for these disruptive practices.[28] Despite the discrimination, or perhaps as a response to it, free people of color married in increasing numbers during the 1780s, making up the majority of all marriages in several of the examined parishes. Finally, Raimond argued that poor white women came to the colony in large numbers in the mid-1740s only to find their chances for marriage stymied by women of color from wealthy families better able to offer a large inheritance.[29]

Petit, Hilliard d'Auberteuil, and Raimond each tried to prescribe an order for colonial society while explaining its complexity.[30] However, tens of thousands of free people of color had to navigate the new laws, the discrimination, and the expanding slave economy.

One of the most powerful tools in the arsenal of the colonial state was to make doing their paperwork appear worthwhile. This included legal documents such as concessions (land grants), deeds, final testaments, marriage contracts, leases, manumissions and bills of sale. Thanks to laws that made ecclesiastical documents acceptable proof of free status, it could also include baptisms and marriage records. These are still found in a file in the French colonial archives named the "état civil" (civil status). After the mid-1770s, priests and notaries were subject to laws requiring them to note race and proof of free status.[31] Doing this paperwork meant taking part in a covenant between subject and state in which state was granted authority in exchange for legal and, if necessary, forceful, protection. Although neither white colonists nor free people of color in colonial Haiti had access to representative assemblies, they worked within the colony's laws and economy to find ways to use laws and social expectations to secure honor and a livelihood. These maneuvers had limits—most free residents were either directly or indirectly dependent on enslaved labor and the sale of sugar, coffee, indigo, or cotton.[32] Residents also had differing access to legal protection based on their race, sex, social status, history of enslavement, age, and family and social connections. Notaries and priests were the men who judged and inscribed these details of a resident's life. The notaries and priests therefore filled the archives with the paperwork of colonialism, inscribing the results, and their judgments, of performances of subjecthood, followed particular legal and/or ecclesiastical strictures.[33]

As the notaries, priests, and missionaries wrote critical documents that memorialized and officially recognized key moments of family formation, including marriage and baptism, they distilled community attitudes, suspicion, and knowledge. They then attached particular markers of honor and/or race to each name: *la nommée, sieur, le nommé, dame, nègre, mulâtresse, blanche*, etc.[34] Microstudies of two women of color and their families illuminate the connection between race, honor, and freedom in the everyday of colonial Haiti. The stories show that the colony had its own landscapes of patriarchy and racialization that differed from metropolitan France or mainland Spanish America due to official efforts to use race as a social organizer in a colonial society where 90 percent of the population was enslaved.

In late September 1780, Marie Françoise (née Cosquière) Dubreuil of Léogane appeared in front of a local notary. Anxious about the enforcement of new laws demanding that free people of color prove their free status, Dubreuil employed a legal tool common among Léogane's freeborn population of color: a white male witness testifying on her behalf. David Belloc, a *habitant* on the plain of Léogane and president of the Port-au-Prince Chamber of Agriculture, stated that Marie Françoise Dubreuil had been born free. This was one of eight such acts drawn up in Léogane between 1779 and 1784 for different individuals needing to prove their free status.[35] This act was sufficient to prove her freedom and to give her the right to engage in legal tussling to protect her property. A few months later she and her husband, Mathurin, filed a protest against an unjust survey involving their land.[36]

The story of increasing racial discrimination in the late colonial period is a familiar one, but material from Léogane's parish registers sheds additional light on the honor previously accorded to Marie Françoise's family.[37] When Marie Françoise married Mathurin in 1759, the priest listed her mother as "Dame Bouché, *négresse libre*." *Dame* and the male equivalent *sieur* are honorifics, signifying full community acceptance as capable adults worthy of respect, and are functional opposites of *le/la nommé(e)* (the so-called). Despite being the daughter of a woman called "*dame*" and a white "*sieur*," Marie Françoise received no similar honor from the priest officiating the ceremony.[38] Our understanding of the suddenness and sharpness in Marie Françoise's apparent loss of community standing—from being the daughter of a *sieur* and *dame* to having to depend on a local notable to prove her free status—is aided by supplementing the notarial record with material from the parish, an emerging path in studies of colonial Haiti.[39] Different observers made different judgments of the same family at different points in the colony's history.

Marie Rose was an enslaved woman in Léogane who received her freedom in August 1785 by virtue of her marriage to her owner, Romain Rivière, a man of color from the Spanish portion of Hispaniola but long living in the area of Léogane. Rivière had purchased Marie Rose and their three children at the start of that month.[40] At a point in the early 1760s, the free people of color and the enslaved of Léogane had begun using a previously ignored clause of the 1685 Code Noir, the main legal text governing slavery in the colony. The clause granted freedom to enslaved women and men who married their owners, as well as to any of their children then owned by the master. When Marie Rose married Romain Rivière, it was the thirty-fourth time a free/slave couple in Léogane had used the 1685 law in this way, with every occurrence happening after 1762.[41] During the opening years of the Haitian Revolution, whites criticized the allowance of "manumission by marriage" and the growth of the free population of color it enabled.

Marie Rose's manumission, however, was not her first experience with liberty. In November 1763, she gave birth to a baby girl. The next month she presented the baby to the priest Antoine for baptism. She stated that she herself was a *mulâtresse libre*, that the father was unknown, but that the baby should be named Marie Louise, a name the child shared with her godmother.[42] When Marie Louise married a *nègre libre* man in 1787, two years after her mother's manumission, she used the copy of the 1763 baptismal record to prove her own free status, a claim the notary and the priest accepted. The notary, however, also identified her mother, Marie Rose, as the wife of (*femme de*) Romain Rivière, and Rivière as the bride's stepfather.[43]

Five possible explanations exist for the incongruity between Marie Rose's status as free in 1763 and enslaved in 1785. She may have initially passed as free. She may have been a polygamous partner of Romain. The notary may have provided a baptismal certificate that would benefit Marie Rose and Marie Louise but did not, in fact, belong to the child. Marie Rose may also have been placed back into slavery for harboring someone fleeing slavery; or perhaps she sought additional proof of a "liberty" she had long enjoyed. Together the possibilities illustrate the way individual efforts to navigate colonial laws and practices, including slavery, in order to create a family and provide for children intersected with and indeed shaped local, colonial, and imperial politics. And as such, longer explanations of each possibility follow.

First, Marie Rose may have passed as free in 1763, using the denser population of the town to mask her true legal status in a temporarily successful performance. During this time, she might have begun her relationship with Romain Rivière, which led to the birth of their first child around 1774. At some point, however, administrators discovered her fugitive status and placed her back in slavery, but not before Marie Rose placed her daughter Marie Louise with a guardian who continued to raise her as free.

It is also possible that Romain Rivière practiced polygamy and maintained relationships with two women named Marie Rose, one in slavery and one free from birth.[44] Romain served as a godfather at least nine times in the late 1780s, a relationship some historians suggest was an acknowledgment of paternity outside of legally recognized marriage.[45] The same notary, however, drew up the marriage contracts for both Marie Rose and Marie Louise, and if the Marie Rose involved in the first was a different person than the Marie Rose witnessing the second, he made no note of it, which suggests that if Romain was practicing polygamy, the notary was either complicit in the performance or did not notice it.

A third explanation centers on the notary, Jean-Charles Razond, using the parish records to carry out an identity theft to benefit Marie Rose and Marie Louise. Of the seven notaries active in late colonial Léogane, Razond conducted the most business with Léogane's free people of color, and he wrote all seven of the surviving notarized documents involving Romain Rivière. Beginning in 1778, notaries in the west and south provinces had to, by law, identify the documents that proved the freedom of free people of color, and Léogane's notaries followed this rule assiduously.[46] Typically, the notary used a baptismal record showing birth to a free mother or the record of the person's manumission. On occasion, they used a sworn statement by prominent colonists, or, if the person had been identified in several notarized acts, the previous acts. Razond would have gained a familiarity with the Léogane parish registers as he conducted business on behalf of Rivière and Marie Rose. It is possible that Marie Rose gave birth to Marie Louise while enslaved, but Razond noticed a baptismal record with the same, very common, names and similar racial descriptors. He then told the illiterate Rivière family about the record that could retroactively "prove" Marie Louise's freedom.[47] This way, she could have the same liberty as her half-siblings freed by the marriage between their owner/father and their mother, creating an archival performance.

Furthermore, it is possible that Marie Rose had been legally free but then convicted for harboring a fugitive slave. A 1705 decree had established that free people of color who hid runaways or fenced stolen goods for them could, with their family, be sold back into slavery.[48] Indeed, in 1768, the Council of Le Cap, with jurisdiction over the colony's North Province, republished the 1705 decree as it condemned a free black man named Hercule to be sold back into slavery for harboring an unknown number of runaway slaves.[49] The provision that the condemned person be sold with their family, however, suggests that in this scenario, Marie Rose would have passed Marie Louise to other free guardians so the latter could stay out of slavery.

Finally, it may be that Marie Rose perceived the shifting demands to "prove" a freedom she had long claimed and sought additional proof of a free status the state doubted. Recent work by Sue Peabody and others has highlighted the contested nature of free and enslaved statuses in the colonial and revolutionary eras.[50] It is significant that Rivière paid her previous owner, supporting the owner's claims to her life and labor, and also that Marie Rose stopped pursuing additional archival support for her liberty after her marriage to Rivière, signifying a newfound perception of security in her free status. Although each of these possibilities is unlikely, one of them is correct.

Whether Marie Rose successfully passed as free, was a polygamous spouse of Romain Rivière, had a notary's assistance in stealing another woman's identity, was sold back into slavery for harboring a fugitive, or was seeking proof for a liberty she had long claimed, her daughter Marie Louise came of age during a period when families of color in the colony navigated colonialism and increasing official discrimination to establish their children as beneficiaries of the slave society and plantation economy. When Marie Louise married her free black husband, Marie Rose and Romain Rivière promised the newlyweds a slave man and woman "forming a couple" (*formant un ménage*) from the next slave ship to arrive at Léogane.[51]

Economic, social, and cultural mobility in the years before 1789 required ownership of the enslaved, and so family tactics were oriented around the purchase and use of enslaved Africans, even among newly free families of color. To engage in these purchases and transfers residents of color had to prove or perform their freedom for those creating the state's archives. Stepping back into a colony-wide view illustrates the use of markers of race and honor over the eighteenth century and provides an important corrective to the generalizations made by colonial polemicists.

The final section of this essay therefore examines markers of race and honor for marriages in six of colonial Haiti's fifty or so colonial parishes: Léogane and Saint-Marc in the west, Ouanaminthe and Le Cap in the north, and Saint-Louis and Fond des Nègres in the south (table 1). These parishes were selected due to the extensive nature of their parish records as well as the diversity of geography and historical development found in each. The information presented here is the most extensive analysis to date of the marriages in colonial Haiti's parish records.[52] The Léogane parish registers stretch back to 1669, providing an on-the-ground view of the complicated links between concepts of racialization and notions of honor. Material from five other parishes provides additional context and highlights regional particularities. Concepts of honor and race developed with the growth of the eighteenth-century colonial slave society. Whiteness and honor, while highly correlated by 1789, were not perfectly so.

Table 1. Chronology and Number of Surviving Marriage Records, by Selected Parish

Parish	Dates of Records	Number of Marriages
Léogane	1669–70, 1672, 1675–85, 1692–1705, 1708–9, 1711–89	1,459
Saint-Marc	1726–88	637
Ouanaminthe	1731–53, 1762, 1766, 1770–88	203
Cap Français	1777–88	620
Saint-Louis-du-Sud	1703–31, 1743–88	146
Fond des Nègres	1716–18, 1722–89	161

Sources: Centre des Archives d'Outre-Mer, Dépôt des Papiers Publics des Colonies, État civil, Léogane, 1669–70, 1672, 1675–85, 1692–1705, 1708–09, 1711–1789; Saint-Marc, 1726–88; Ouanaminthe, 1731–53, 1762, 1766, 1770–88; Cap Français, 1777–88; Saint-Louis-du-Sud, 1703–31, 1743–88; Fond des Nègres, 1716–18, 1722–89.

These marriage records enable a view of how honor in the colony gradually became associated with whiteness. The two had been strongly linked before, but not every *marchand* or cooper who came to the colony in the late seventeenth century was a *"sieur." Demoiselle* and *dame* also reflected a hierarchy of status. Middling whites—wealthy enough to marry, at least eventually, but too poor to be a *dame* or a *sieur* in France—received these titles in the colony on an increasingly frequent basis by the 1750s. Even then it was not total: Alexandre David, a French-born cook, received no such honorific when he married Demoiselle Honorée Caisene, a young widow from Provence, in Le Cap in 1786, and neither did the fisher Laurent Joachim Duc, who married in Saint-Marc in 1778.[53] During the pre-1750 period, poor and middling whites could also be listed as *"le nommé,"* or "the so-called," as was Vallone, the son of a laborer, who married a local sixteen-year-old in Saint-Marc in 1744, an indication of the disrespect connoted by the term.[54] Yet, even as priests became more diligent about identifying race, a few free people of color, like Marie Françoise Dubreuil's mother the Dame Bouché, could still receive honorifics in official records (table 2).[55]

Table 2. Date of Last Instance of Free Person of Color
Receiving an Honorific in a Marriage Record

Parish	Year	Honorific	Racial Designation
Léogane	1759	*Dame*	*Négresse*
Saint-Marc	None	None	N/A
Ouanaminthe	1780	*Sieur*	*Mulâtre*
Cap Français	1788	*Sieur*	*Nègre*
Saint-Louis-du-Sud	1751	*Dame*	*Mulâtresse*
Fond des Nègres	1743	*Sieur*	*Mulâtre*

Sources: Centre des Archives d'Outre-Mer, Dépôt des Papiers Publics des Colonies, État civil, Léogane, 1669–70, 1672, 1675–85, 1692–1705, 1708–09, 1711–1789; Saint-Marc, 1726–88; Ouanaminthe, 1731–53, 1762, 1766, 1770–88; Cap Français, 1777–88; Saint-Louis-du-Sud, 1703–31, 1743–88; Fond des Nègres, 1716–18, 1722–89.

Not every parish included people identified as being of color and also receiving an honorific, nor does this combination go back to the start of the eighteenth century. The first example from Ouanaminthe appeared in 1746. In the older Léogane, the first appeared in 1728. The other aspect of this smattering of individuals who received honorifics and racial descriptions is worth noting: priests identified few as *quarterons* (one-quarter African) and none were *tiercerons* (one-third African, generally assumed to be the child of a *quarteron[ne]* and a *mulâtre[sse]*)—most were *nègre(sse)s libres* or *mulâtre(sse)s libres* who had gained community standing, most likely through ownership of enslaved workers.

There is often an assumption, stemming from Turner's frontier thesis, or Bailyn's "contested marchlands" of the Atlantic, or Breen and Innes's work on Antonio Johnson, or borderlands theory, that racialization and the provision of social status are more mutable in earlier periods, or in places where the colonial state has a lighter footprint.[56] While the colonial parish records suggest that may be true in terms of avoiding racialization or passing, the lasting flexibility that occurs in Cap Français, a highly urbanized colonial capital, is notable, while Fond des Nègres, a rural parish on the southern peninsula, appears to have ended flexibility much earlier. In Léogane, the first example of a racialized person receiving an honorific in a marriage record occurred in 1728, over forty years after the establishment of the parish's first sugar plantation and at a time when at least three-quarters of the parish's population was enslaved.[57]

Léogane served as the first site of sugar cultivation under French governance in colonial Haiti and as a primary location for the colonial government before the founding of Port-au-Prince. It also offers the longest continuous run of records of any parish in the colony. Its longevity as a slave society led to an early emergence of a free population of color. Léogane served as a prime place for weddings until the establishment of Port-au-Prince in 1750. The historical geography of the parish reveals occasional sharp decreases in the number of marriages solemnized in Léogane each decade between 1690 and 1750 as neighboring parishes were established. The number of marriages solemnized in Léogane did not reach 1690s levels again until the 1780s.[58] The data from Léogane show a tremendous growth in "uncertain" marriages during the takeoff of plantation slavery, the gradual but steady categorization of almost everyone by the end of the eighteenth century, a sliver of interracial marriages, and a tremendous growth in the percentage (and number) of marriages between people of color, driven in part by manumissions by marriage (figure 1).[59]

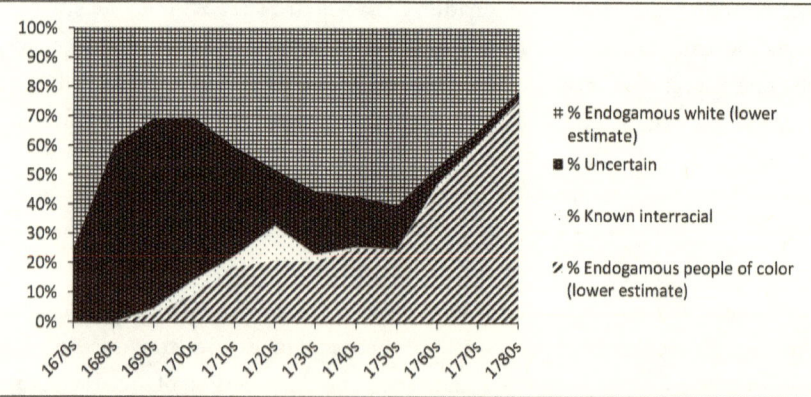

Figure 1. Marriages in Léogane by Racial Endogamy, 1669–1789

Source: EC, Léogane, 1669–70, 1672, 1675–85, 1692–1705, 1708–09, 1711–1789.

Saint-Marc, the port and local court for the Artibonite Valley, one of the last refuges of buccaneer culture on the island, was settled in part by migrants from Léogane during the 1710s and 1720s. Although it was founded later than many of the colony's port towns, it grew rapidly from midcentury as cotton and indigo cultivation boomed in the Artibonite Valley, as did coffee on the nearby mountains. The free population of color was smaller in Saint-Marc than it was in Léogane, and perhaps because of fewer opportunities for endogamous marriage among free people of color, interracial marriage happened at a steadier, if not a great, clip. Of particular note, many of the "uncertain" marriages during the 1740s involved a white male immigrant marrying a local woman listed with neither racial descriptor nor honorific. Saint-Marc also did not have a single case of someone listed with a racial descriptor and also an honorific, and its priests and notaries were slower than Léogane's to follow a late colonial law requiring racial descriptors and evidence of free status to always be included. A boom and then a steadily decreasing rate for "uncertain" after the widespread adoption of plantation agriculture and widespread African slavery (figure 2) has parallels to the history of marriage in Léogane.

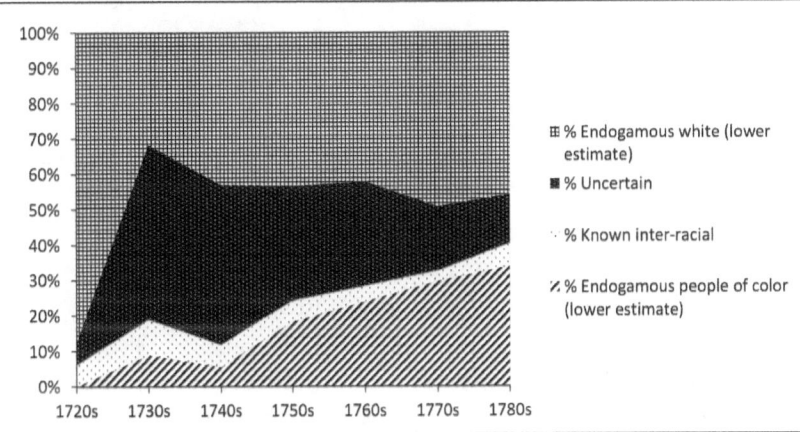

Figure 2. Marriages in Saint-Marc by Racial Endogamy, 1726–1788

Source: EC, Saint-Marc, 1726–1788.

Ouanaminthe, a small border town in the colony's far northeast, enjoyed close ties with the Spanish colony of Santo Domingo, home to many free of people of color, some of whom married French subjects in the town. The proximity to the long-settled Spanish colony and the greater age of the settlement before the start of surviving parish registers are probably both factors that led to the high proportion of marriages between two people of color in the 1730s. The erratic nature of the middle section of the chart (figure 3) is probably due to only three years surviving from the 1750s and two from the 1760s. The "uncertain" portion shrunk more than in Saint-Marc though not as much as Léogane, and the number of declared inter-racial marriages remained small throughout the century.

Figure 3. Marriages in Ouanaminthe by Racial Endogamy, 1731–1788

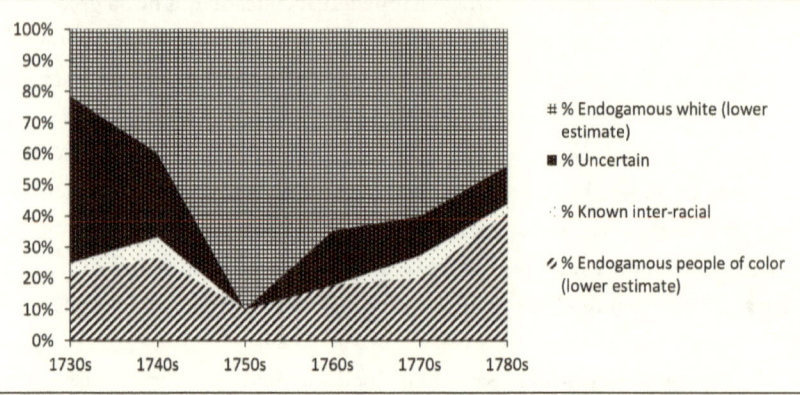

Source: EC, Ouanaminthe, 1731–1753, 1762, 1766, 1770–1788.

Cap Français, one of the two colonial capitals and often called by colonizers "the Paris of the Antilles," does not have a long run of parish records, but thanks to its sizable population, it does have a large set of marriages, enabling a meaningful year-by-year analysis. The late 1770s and early 1780s saw a trough in endogamous marriages among free people of color (figure 4), which may have been due to mobilization for the US War of Independence. As in Léogane, marriages between free and enslaved people of color formed a significant portion of marriages between people of color.

Figure 4. Marriages in Cap Français by Racial Endogamy, 1777–1788

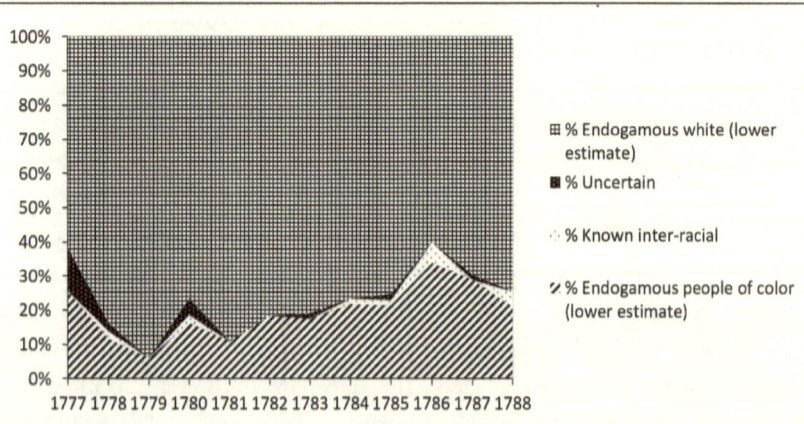

Source: EC, Cap Français, 1777–1788.

Saint-Louis-du-Sud, on the south coast of the colony, was the center of activities carried out by the Compagnie de Saint-Domingue during the first part of the eighteenth century. The Compagnie gave approval for at least two of its enslaved workers to marry one another in the 1710s: François Gamoly and Marie Marosse. Of note, the officiant did not provide a place of birth for either Gamoly or Marosse and referred to Gamoly as *dit* (the "so-called"), presaging later treatment of free people of color in the colony.[60] Like Léogane, but unlike Saint-Marc or the other parishes analyzed here, Saint-Louis-du-Sud experienced a period with a higher percentage of interracial marriages (figure 5), albeit later than Léogane. The comparative delay was probably due to the later transition to becoming a slave society. The lack of data available for the 1730s makes it difficult to link the period of Compagnie administration with later colonial history, but it is probable that marriages between free people of color began to be solemnized in this decade.

Figure 5. Marriages in Saint-Louis-du-Sud by Racial Endogamy, 1703–1788

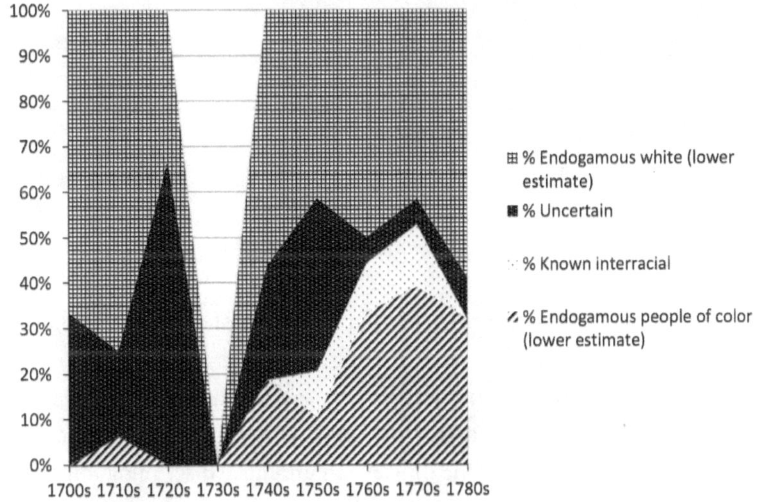

Source: EC, Saint-Louis-du-Sud, 1703–1731, 1743–1788.

Fond des Nègres is the most rural parish under analysis here, and one that long boasted a large free populace of color. Despite the largest proportion of people of color in the free populace, the rate of interracial marriage was no larger than in other parishes and often lower (figure 6). That may be due to the small size of the white population. Only once did someone in a marriage record receive an honorific and a racial marker: a priest referred to a *mulâtre* groom in 1743 as "sieur." More detailed study is needed to determine whether the shift in the 1770s and 1780s is due to growth within a defined population of color or the arrival of a new priest who racialized a larger proportion of the parish's residents.

Figure 6. Marriages in Fond des Nègres by Racial Endogamy, 1716–1789

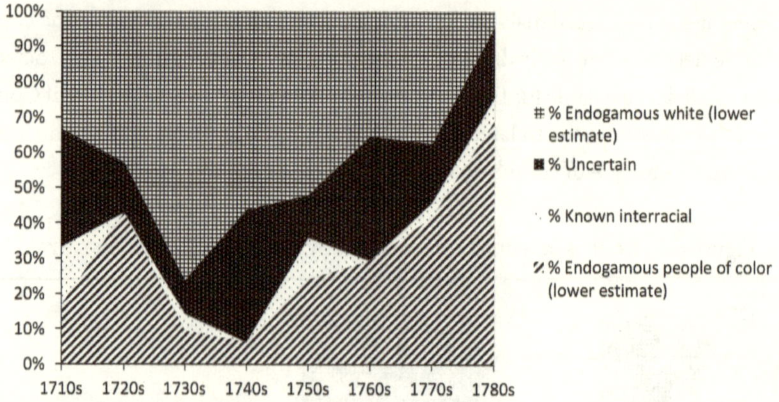

Source: EC, Fond des Nègres, 1716–18, 1722–1789.

Conclusion

In colonial Haiti elite male writers viewed questions of gender, sexuality, race, honor, and social stability as part of an interconnected whole, with white male writers using tropes to blame "tropical temptresses" (or the tropical heat) for what they considered to be a degradation of French culture. Prominent free men of color responded by criticizing the official and unofficial discrimination they felt disrupted family life; they also argued for their own virtue and economic productivity and expressed frustration that avenues of social and civil acceptance into the elite were closed to them. The microhistories of Marie-Françoise Dubreuil and Marie Rose Rivière show the many ways women of color used the law to protect themselves, and by extension, their families, securing freedom though not honor. Finally, longitudinal evidence from the parish records provides important new context for these efforts and arguments, showing that the assumptions of writers often had little basis in the lived reality of free people of color in the colony.

The parish records do not support Raimond's famous 1791 synopsis of the history of marriage in the colony. As seen above, rates of known interracial marriages remained low throughout the eighteenth century and in Léogane interracial marriage hit a nadir in the 1740s. The best support for the Raimond thesis is 1740s Saint-Marc, where many white immigrant men married locally born women listed with neither honorific nor racial descriptor. Even if all of the "unknown" marriages followed the pattern asserted by Raimond, along with the 6 percent of marriages known to be interracial, they would constitute a bare majority of marriages in one parish. In 1740s Léogane and Ouanaminthe, white immigrant men married local women listed without racial signifiers or honorifics only a smattering of times. Fond des Nègres featured a similar pattern. In the late 1750s and early 1760s. Saint-Louis-du-Sud provides partial support for Raimond's thesis, with seven out of forty-five marriages during the 1740s and 1750s potentially being matches between recent French immigrants and local women, but there were many more marriages between white men and white women in the parish during those years. Marriages being solemnized and recorded by the local parish would have been a crucial component of the tactic Raimond outlined, as the groom's end goal would be for him or his children to inherit the bride's family's wealth.

In conclusion, this analysis of long runs of parish records and the individual biographies provides important context for the polemical arguments, showing that they were rooted in perceptions, stereotypes, and political needs rather than analysis. The microhistories and the parish records also illuminate aspects of colonial Haitian life that have heretofore received little discussion, including the longitudinal changes in the relationship between race and honor, the general importance of marriages between people of color in the 1780s as a tactic of economic and cultural mobility, and the regional variation within the colony. Much remains to be determined regarding the role this ritual performance, the creation of vital records, played in fashioning families, preserving property claims, and inscribing race and honor in colonial Haiti as free people of color rebutted official claims that they were somehow not full legal persons, not fully French. Finally, as Hughes's Dessalines reminds us, not every family saw this sort of performance as significant, choosing to mask the rituals they found sacred to them and to pursue direct counter-plantation strategies through self-liberation. But for many colonial residents, including many families of color, these cultural and legal performances were crucial tactical moments for taking part in the colony's grand strategy of slaveholding and commodity export. The "power imbalances inherent in document collection" are a key challenge in writing the histories of enslaved families, particularly those families the colonial state did not recognize as such or for whom they did not prioritize the preservation of documents. These are obstacles that must be overcome as we seek to illuminate the lives of marginalized individuals.[61] Attention to the quantitative material available from across the eighteenth century is crucial for illuminating the way colonialism unfolded at the grassroots for French Atlantic families such as those of Marie Françoise Dubreuil and Marie Rose Rivière.

NOTES

Epigraph: Quote from Leslie Catherine Sanders and Nancy Johnston, eds., *The Plays to 1942: Mulatto to Sun Do Move* (Columbia: University of Missouri Press, 2002), 286.

1. I use "colonial Haiti" throughout in lieu of "Saint-Domingue" to emphasize the presence, experiences, and cultures of the enslaved majority and the realities of the colonial system. Haiti is unique among independent states in the Americas in that the former colonizer insisted on calling it by its colonial name for two decades after it achieved de facto independence. The term "Haïti," or in the Northern kingdom "Hayti," and in present-day Kreyòl "Ayiti," is derived from one of the original Taíno names for all or part of the island English speakers presently call "Hispaniola." Haïti or variations thereof was in use during the seventeenth and eighteenth centuries, though "Saint-Domingue" predominated during the 1700s. The victors who declared Haitian independence in 1804 selected "Haïti" as a symbol of their solidarity with the Taíno against colonialism and slavery. See David Geggus, *Haitian Revolutionary Studies* (Bloomington: Indiana University Press, 2002), chap. 13. I opt for "Haiti" rather than "Haïti" to preserve clarity for an Anglophone audience.

2. See William Brown's essay in this collection.

3. Yvan Debbasch, *Couleur et liberté: Le jeu du critère ethnique dans un ordre juridique esclavagiste* (Paris: Librairie Dalloz, 1967); Garrigus, *Before Haiti: Race and Citizenship in French Saint-Domingue* (New York: Palgrave Macmillan, 2006), 162–64; Dominique Rogers, "Les libres de couleur dans les capitales de Saint-Domingue: Fortune, mentalités et intégration à la fin de l'Ancien Régime (1776–1789)" (Ph.D. diss., Université de Bordeaux III, 1999), 241–46; Yvonne Fabella, "Inventing the Creole Citizen: Race, Sexuality, and the Colonial Order in Pre-Revolutionary Saint-Domingue" (Ph.D. diss., Stony Brook University, 2008), 36–39.

4. I use "residents of color" or "people of color" interchangeably to refer to all who are described in the documents as *gens de couleur,* and will provide specific racial labels (*noir, mulâtresse,* etc.) when available. The individuals using these documents include the "man of letters" often discussed in Caribbean intellectual history and the creative women highlighted by Sara Johnson. See Johnson, *The Fear of French Negroes* (Berkeley: University of California Press, 2012), 123.

5. See Brett Rushforth's epilogue to this collection.

6. For the uses of *affranchi*, see Garrigus, *Before Haiti*, 167, 170, 234.

7. Although the baptismal records of the colony can provide a wealth of information regarding informal family formation—*concubinage* in the parlance of the eighteenth century, "unions" in the contemporary sociology of Haiti—this essay focuses on marriage for three overlapping reasons. Marriage involved a household seeking legal recognition from the colonial state and having to conform to the state's parameters, making marriage records radar blips of the interaction between society and the colonial state. Marriage records also, unlike baptismal records, require the presence, and therefore include information about, both sides of the family, including (usually) the couple's places of birth and their parents. Finally, seeing who could marry, when the number of bans was reduced, and when couples married, helps illuminate the ways the rules of colonial governance influenced the everyday. For a discussion of the different relationships in Haiti today, see James Allman, "Sexual Unions in Rural Haiti," *International Journal of Sociology of the Family* 10, no. 1 (January 1980): 15–39. For an extended discussion of how these relationships function in urban settings, see M. Catherine Maternowska, *Reproducing Inequities: Poverty and the Politics of Population in Haiti* (New Brunswick, NJ: Rutgers University Press, 2006). Concubinage was the preferred term of the colony's legal writers, including Moreau de Saint-Méry.

8. Robert D. Taber and Charlton W. Yingling, eds., *Free Communities of Color and the Revolutionary Caribbean: Overturning, or Turning Back?* (New York: Routledge, 2018). The literature on cultural mobility and people of color in the Age of Revolutions is vast. Two notable recent examples are Jane G. Landers, *Atlantic Creoles in the Age of Revolutions* (Cambridge, MA: Harvard University Press, 2011); Kit Candlin and Cassandra Pybus, *Enterprising Women: Gender, Race, and Power in the Revolutionary Atlantic* (Athens: University of Georgia Press, 2015).

9. Robert D. Taber, "'The Issue of Their Union': Family, Law, and Politics in Western Saint-Domingue, 1777 to 1789" (Ph.D. diss., University of Florida, 2015), 43–47. Quote from Stephen Greenblatt, "Cultural Mobility: An Introduction" in Stephen Greenblatt, ed., *Cultural Mobility: A Manifesto* (New York: Cambridge University Press, 2010), 2.

10. Margaret Crosby Arnold, "A Case of Hidden Genocide? Disintegration and Destruction of People of Color in Napoleonic Europe, 1799–1815," in Taber and Yingling, eds., *Free Communities of Color*, chap. 6.

11. Paul Cheney, *Cul de Sac: Patrimony, Capitalism, and Slavery in French Saint-Domingue* (Chicago: University of Chicago Press, 2017), 98.

12. The presentation of women of color by white writers in colonial Haiti correlates with what is now regarded in black studies as the Jezebel stereotype, which seeks to justify sexual violence against black women by positing their sexual promiscuity. Patricia Hill Collins, *Black Feminist Thought: Knowledge, Consciousness, and the Politics of Empowerment*, 2nd ed. (New York: Routledge, 2009), 89–93. Marlene Daut describes this as the "trope of the tropical temptress": Marlene Daut, *Fictions of Haiti: Race and the Literary History of the Haitian Revolution in the Atlantic World, 1789–1865* (Liverpool: Liverpool University Press, 2015), 197–219. For more on rape, sexual coercion, and concubinage in colonial Haiti, see Arlette Gautier, *Les soeurs de Solitude: La condition féminine dans l'esclave aux Antilles du XVIIe au XIXe siècle* (Paris: Editions Caribéennes, 1985), 152; Fabella, "Inventing the Creole Citizen," chap. 4. For a broader view, see Sasha Turner, *Contested Bodies: Pregnancy, Childrearing, and Slavery in Jamaica*

(Philadelphia: University of Pennsylvania Press, 2017), chap. 2; Marissa Fuentes, *Dispossessed Lives: Enslaved Women, Violence, and the Archive* (Philadelphia: University of Pennsylvania Press, 2016), chap. 4; Sharon Block, "Lines of Color, Sex, and Service: Comparative Sexual Coercion in Early America," in Martha Hodes, ed., *Sex, Love, Race: Crossing Boundaries in North American History* (New York: New York University Press, 1999), 141–63. Jennifer Morgan focuses instead on masters' discussion of enslaved women's capacity to produce children: Jennifer Morgan, *Laboring Women: Reproduction and Gender in New World Slavery* (Philadelphia: University of Pennsylvania Press, 2004), 75–87.

13. Peter N. Moogk, "'Thieving Buggers' and 'Stupid Sluts': Insults and Popular Culture in New France," *William and Mary Quarterly* 36, no. 4 (October 1979): 524–47.

14. Allan Greer, *The Patriots and the People: The Rebellion of 1837 in Rural Lower Canada* (Toronto: University of Toronto Press, 1993), 69–86.

15. Shannon Lee Dawdy, *Building the Devil's Empire: French Colonial New Orleans* (Chicago: University of Chicago Press, 2008), 172–73.

16. Louisiana was a Spanish possession from 1763 until shortly before its annexation by the United States in 1803. During that time, Spanish officials introduced the centuries-old concept of *limpieza de sangre*, which mediated questions of honor through ancestry, "occupation, faith, and respectability." Jennifer M. Spear, *Race, Sex, and Social Order in Early New Orleans* (Baltimore: Johns Hopkins University Press, 2009), 133.

17. Cheney, *Cul de Sac*, 36–40.

18. Gene Ogle, "Policing Saint Domingue: Race, Violence, and Honor in an Old Regime Colony" (Ph.D. diss., University of Pennsylvania, 2003).

19. Garrigus, *Before Haiti*, 43.

20. Emilien Petit, Le *Patriotisme américain ou Mémoires sur l'établissement de la partie française de l'isle de Saint-Domingue, sous le vent de l'Amérique* (N.p.: 1750), 30–34.

21. Petit, *Patriotisme américain*, 39–41.

22. Petit, *Patriotisme américain*, 108–111.

23. Hilliard d'Auberteuil, *Considérations sur l'état présent de la colonie française de Saint-Domingue*, vol. II (Paris: Chez Grangé, 1777), 29–33.

24. D'Auberteuil, *Considérations*, II: 44–46.

25. Depending on the size of the population. With a free population of 30,000, it would be 1 in 39; with a free population of 40,000, it would be 1 in 53. Marriage data for 1783 from *Affiches Américaines*, Feuille du Cap Français, 26 March 1785.

26. D'Auberteuil, *Considérations*, II: 78–84, 88.

27. Moreau de Saint-Méry collected many of these letters and memoranda, and they are currently catalogued in CAOM F3 series 91 "Gens de couleur." For a discussion of Labuissonnière's letter, see Taber, "'The Issue of Their Union,'" conclusion.

28. CAOM F3 91, 177–79.

29. Julien Raimond, *Observations sur l'origine et les progrés du préjugé des colons blancs contre les hommes de couleur; sur les inconvéniens de le perpétuer; la nécessité, la facilité de le détruire; par M. Raymond, homme de couleur de Saint-Domingue* (Paris, 1791).

30. Taber, "'The Issue of Their Union,'" conclusion.

31. John Garrigus, *Before Haiti*, chap. 5. While the French colonial state would use the Church's paperwork, there were still several conflicts between the Church and the state in the French Caribbean, particularly over the creation of black congregations in Martinique and Guadeloupe. Sue Peabody, "'A Dangerous Zeal': Catholic Missions to Slaves in the French Antilles," *French Historical Studies*, 25, no. 1 (Winter 2002): 53–90.

32. Michel de Certeau, *The Practice of Everyday Life*, xviii; Taber, "'The Issue of Their Union,'" introduction.

33. The role of the notary and other official scriveners has drawn significant attention in the historical literature on ancien régime France and early Spanish America, as well as from John Garrigus and Dominique Rogers, cited above. See Julie Hardwick, *The Practice of Patriarchy: Gender and the Politics of Household Authority in Early Modern France* (State College: Pennsylvania State University Press, 1998); Jennifer Palmer, "What's in a Name? Mixed-Race Families and Resistance to Racial Marginalization in Eighteenth-Century La Rochelle," *French Historical Studies* 33, no. 3 (2010): 357–85; Kathryn Burns, "Notaries, Truth, and Consequences," *American Historical Review* (April 2005): 350–79; Michael C. Scardaville, "Justice by Paperwork: A Day in the Life of a Court Scribe in Bourbon Mexico City," *Journal of Social History* 36, no. 4 (Summer 2003): 979–1007. For similar ideas in the colonial context of nineteenth-century Dutch East Indies, see Ann Laura Stoler, *Along the Archival Grain: Epistemic Anxieties and Colonial Common Sense* (Princeton, NJ: Princeton University Press, 2010).

34. Garrigus, *Before Haiti*, 168.

35. Centre d'Archives d'Outre Mer, Dépôt des papiers publics des colonies, notariat, Saint-Domingue (hereafter SDOM) 396, 29 September 1780; SDOM 396, 27 February 1779; SDOM 396, 30 March 1779; SDOM 396, 17 April 1779; SDOM 396, 25 April 1780; SDOM 396, 3 June 1780; SDOM 396, 21 March 1780; SDOM 1530, 30 October 1784. All witnesses were men, all but one of whom were white. All but one of the individuals having their freedom stipulated were female.

36. SDOM 1528, 19 February 1781; SDOM 1528, 2 April 1781.

37. Dominique Rogers, "Les libres de couleur dans les capitales de Saint-Domingue: Fortune, mentalités et intégration à la fin de l'Ancien Régime (1776–1789)" (Ph.D. diss., Université de Bordeaux III, 1999); John Garrigus, *Before Haiti*; Stewart R. King, *Blue Coat or Powdered Wig: Free People of Color in Pre-Revolutionary Saint-Domingue* (Athens: University of Georgia Press, 2001); Fabella, "Inventing the Creole Citizen"; Doris Garraway, *The Libertine Colony: Creolization in the Early French Caribbean* (Durham, NC: Duke University Press, 2005).

38. Centre des Archives d'Outre-Mer, Dépôt des papiers publics des colonies, État civil (hereafter EC), Léogane, 1759, f. 6. Very few notarial records survive for colonial Haiti prior to the mid-1770s, and it is unknown if Marie Françoise and Mathurin signed a marriage contract. Generally, scholars of colonial Haiti have examined either parish marriages or notarized marriage contracts but not both. One exception is for Léogane, Saint-Domingue, in the 1780s. Sixty-three percent of free-slave marriages in 1780s Léogane do not have surviving marriage contracts, compared with 36 percent of marriages involving at least one person of color but not an enslaved partner and 26 percent (11/42) of marriages between two white colonists. Taber, "'The Issue of Their Union,'" 132.

39. The major studies of notarial documents conducted by Rogers, Garrigus, and Stewart King did not incorporate parish registers in a systematic way, and Jacques Houdaille's quantitative analysis

of parish registers did not correlate findings with specific individuals from notarial records. Scholars have drawn occasional linkages, typically in the pursuit of biographies of prominent individuals. See Philippe Girard, *Toussaint Louverture: A Revolutionary Life* (New York: Basic Books, 2016); Terry Rey, *The Priest and the Prophetess: Abbé Ouvière, Romaine Rivière, and the Revolutionary Atlantic World* (New York: Oxford University Press, 2017).

40. Centre d'Archives d'Outre Mer, Dépôt des papiers publics des colonies, notariat, Saint-Domingue (hereafter SDOM) 1530, 22 August 1785; Centre des Archives d'Outre-Mer, Dépôt des papiers publics des colonies, État civil (hereafter EC), Léogane, 1785, f.f. 24.

41. Out of 315 marriages between 1762 and 1785. EC, Léogane, 1669–1785. It is possible that some marriages between an enslaved person and their owner were recorded in the separate, lost, register for sacraments for the enslaved, but there is no indication that such is the case.

42. EC, Léogane, 1763, f.f. 20.

43. SDOM 1532, 15 October 1787; EC, Léogane, 18 December 1763.

44. For an overview of polygamy in the early Americas, see Sarah M. S. Pearsall, "'How Many Wives' in Two American Revolutions: The Politics of Households and the Radically Conservative," *American Historical Review* 118, no. 4 (2013): 1000–1028.

45. EC, Léogane, 1785, f.f. 15, 21; EC, Léogane, 1786, f.f. 15, 40; EC, Léogane, 1787, f.f. 3, 13, 27; EC, Léogane, 1788, f.f. 19; EC, Léogane, 1789, f.f. 22; King, *Blue Coat or Powdered Wig*, 13. In only two cases, however, does it seem at all probable that Romain Rivière was the child's biological father, as the other entries either named fathers, often married to the mothers, or the racial designations did not match with the baptized child's having a black father. See EC, Léogane, 1786, f.f. 15, and EC. Léogane, 1789, f.f. 22. At least once, Marie Rose, "spouse" of Romain Rivière, served as godmother as he stood as godfather: see EC, Léogane, 1787, f. 3.

46. Conseil du Port-au-Prince, "Arrêt du Conseil du Port-au-Prince, touchant les Actes qui concernent les Gens de couleur se disant libres," 9 January 1778, in Médéric Louis Élie Moreau de Saint-Méry, *Loix et constitutions des colonies françoises de l'Amérique sous le vent* (Paris: Quillau, Méquignon jeune, 1784–90), vol. 5, 807–8.

47. Neither Romain Rivière nor Marie Rose could sign their names. While they may have been able to read, they would not have enjoyed the same access to the Léogane parish records as the notary Razond.

48. Louis XIV, "Ordonnance du Roi, contre les Nègres libres, qui facilitent aux Esclaves les moyens de devenier Marons," 10 June 1705, in Moreau de Saint-Méry, *Loix et constitutions*, vol. 2, 36–37.

49. Council of Le Cap, "Arrêt du Conseil du Cap, qui ordonne que le nommé Hercule, Nègre libre, sera vendu au profit du Roi, pour avoir récélé des Esclaves, et qu l'Arrêt ensemble l'Ordonnance de Sa Majesté du 10 June 1705, seront imprimés, publiés et affichés," 23 March 1768, in Moreau de Saint-Méry, *Loix et constitutions*, vol. 5, p. 165.

50. Sue Peabody, *Madeleine's Children: Family, Freedom, Secrets, and Lies in France's Indian Ocean Colonies* (New York: Oxford University Press, 2017); Rebecca J. Scott and Jean M. Hébrard, *Freedom Papers: An Atlantic Odyssey in the Age of Emancipation* (Cambridge, MA: Harvard University Press, 2014); Miranda Spieler, "Abolition and Reenslavement in the Caribbean: The Revolution in French Guiana," in Suzanne Desan, Lynn Hunt, and William Max Nelson, eds., *The French Revolution in Global Perspective* (Ithaca, NY: Cornell University Press, 2013), 132–47. Jennifer Palmer graciously shared with

me work-in-progress on Marie Victoire Morisseau and her efforts to secure recognition of her freedom that prompted this possible interpretation, for which I thank her.

51. SDOM 1532, 15 October 1787. "Ménage" had a complex meaning in the eighteenth century, but one aspect focused on marriage and family life. To place a woman *en ménage* was a familiar way of saying that she was married. It also referred to the *meubles,* or moveable goods, needed for the proper functioning of a household. The common colonial practice of providing newly married couples with a ménage of slaves, therefore, meant adding a slave household/family to the free one and giving the free newlyweds human chattel to labor for their economic benefit. Definitions from *Dictionnaires d'autrefois,* http://artflsrv02.uchicago.edu/cgi-bin/dicos/pubdico1look.pl?strippedhw=ménage, accessed 13 April 2015.

52. Jacques Houdaille read through a sample of 10 percent of the burial records for the colony for "Quelques donnés sur la population de Saint-Domingue au XVIIIe siècle" *Population* 28, nos. 4–5 (1973): 859–72. He earlier examined three small parishes, including Fond des Nègres. Houdaille, "Trois paroisses de Saint-Domingue au XVIIIe siècle: Étude démographique," *Population* 18, no. 1 (1963): 93–110. A later article sampled material from seventeen parishes but only included information on 697 families and only provided colony-wide conclusions regarding age at marriage, fertility, and infant mortality. Houdaille, "Reconstitution des familles de Saint-Domingue (Haiti) au XVIIIe siècle," *Population,* 46, no. 1 (1991): 29–40.

53. EC, Cap Français, 1786, f. 45; EC, Saint-Marc, 1778, f. 3.

54. EC, Saint-Marc, 1744, f. 4.

55. Compare this history with the literature on honor and whiteness in the circum-Caribbean, especially Ann Twinam, *Purchasing Whiteness: Pardos, Mulattos, and the Quest for Social Mobility in the Spanish Indies* (Stanford, CA: Stanford University Press, 2015). As far as can be determined, granting of honorifics rested directly in the hands of notaries and priests in colonial Haiti without additional petitions required but also without the legal recourse available in the Spanish circum-Caribbean.

56. Frederick Jackson Turner, *The Frontier in American History* (LaVergne, TN: Scholar Select, 2016); Bernard Bailyn, *Atlantic History: Concepts and Contours* (Cambridge, MA: Harvard University Press, 2005); T. H. Breen and Stephen Innes, *"Myne Owne Ground": Race and Freedom on Virginia's Eastern Shore, 1640–1676* (New York: Oxford University Press, 2004); Juliana Barr, *Peace Came in the Form of Woman: Indians and Spaniards in the Texas Borderlands* (Chapel Hill: University of North Carolina Press, 2007).

57. ANSOM G1509, 11, 20.

58. This is in terms of surviving entries in the parish register. All the records from 1690 and 1691 are missing, and more marriages probably happened in the Léogane of the 1690s, a center of colonizing efforts, than in the Léogane of the 1780s, a middling periphery of Port-au-Prince.

59. Taber, "'The Issue of Their Union,'" chap. 3.

60. EC, Saint-Louis-du-Sud, 1715, f. 1.

61. Ashley Farmer, "In Search of the Black Women's History Archive," *Modern American History,* 1, no. 2 (July 2018): 289–93; Fuentes, *Dispossessed Lives,* introduction.

From Voyageurs to Emigrants
Leaving the St. Lawrence Valley for the Detroit River Borderland, 1796–1846

GUILLAUME TEASDALE AND KAREN L. MARRERO

In 1846, French-Canadian lawyer and intellectual François-Xavier Garneau (1809-1866) published a sweeping history of Canada and French Canadians, with surprisingly little information about its immediate western hinterland—the Detroit River borderland. Garneau, who never visited Detroit, acknowledged that the French had established Detroit and that the French language was still spoken in the city despite the fall of New France in 1760 and the regime changes that ensued. However, he did not elaborate further nor did he mention anything about the enduring connections between Lower Canada (Québec) and the Detroit River borderland.[1] Historical publications by nineteenth-century French-Canadian elites, usually men working in liberal professions in Montréal or Québec City, suggest that knowledge regarding the Detroit River borderland (part of the former *pays d'en haut* of the New France era) was limited among the pioneers of French-Canadian historiography.[2] Meanwhile, thousands of French-Canadian men who did not belong to the elite were well acquainted with the French River World of the interior of North America because of their work as voyageurs for Montréal-based British merchants.[3] The vast majority of these men were illiterate and did not write any personal diaries about their travels. Such diaries would have probably helped historians like Garneau draw a more complete picture of French North America.[4] Still, these nineteenth-century French-Canadian elites' lack of knowledge regarding the interior of the continent remains difficult to explain considering the persisting economic and cultural connections between Lower Canada and the Detroit River borderland. This essay invites historians of French North America to revisit the theme of French-Canadian emigration outside of Québec, to pay greater attention to the decades that preceded the construction of railways, and to embrace a continental perspective of the history of Lower Canada.⁵ In other words, this essay represents one of the early attempts to generate a historiography on French-Canadian emigration out of the St. Lawrence Valley between the British Conquest and the Industrial Revolution.⁶

In 1796, Britain surrendered present-day Michigan to the United States and, as a result, the Detroit River region was divided into two separate jurisdictions.⁷ The local French-Canadian settlers, who still made up the largest demographic group at the time, had for generations used the Detroit River to visit friends and relatives who lived on the other side.⁸ This was substantiated in 1825 by Father Gabriel Richard (1767-1832), a native of France and priest in Detroit for more than three decades, who calculated that there were more than four thousand Catholic parishioners in southeast Michigan (Wayne, Monroe, Macomb, and St. Clair Counties; essentially the only parts of the territory parceled out) and that almost all of them were "*Français originaires du Canada.*"⁹ These parishioners were divided between four parishes, St. Anne's (est. 1701) being the oldest and by far the most important of them.¹⁰ The significant presence of French Canadians in the Detroit area probably explains why, in 1827, the Territory of Michigan agreed to pay Philippe Lécuyer and Jean-Baptiste Vallée "for translating into the French language certain congressional and territorial laws."¹¹ Up until the 1830s, despite efforts by American authorities to enforce the newly established border, the Detroit River borderland remained a place where, as Karen L. Marrero explains, "loyalty to nation was in flux and where alternative forms of community developed."¹² Regarding the Upper Canada side of the Detroit River (Essex County), Joseph Bouchette (1774-1841), a native of Lower Canada and Surveyor-General of British North America, appeared surprised to "discover" a strong French-Canadian presence so far away from the St. Lawrence Valley when he traveled through Upper Canada in the late 1820s. In particular, he noted the resemblance between the land organization of the settlements of this French-Canadian population (long and narrow strips of land) and the seigneuries of the St. Lawrence Valley:

> The settlements in this part of the Western District, the most remote of any in this province, originated when Canada was yet under the domination of France, and are therefore composed chiefly of French Canadians. The distribution of the lands in narrow elongated slips, the consequent contiguity of the farms, the mode

of cultivation, and the manners of the people are strongly contrasted with the same features in other settled parts of Upper Canada; but they bear so striking an analogy to the character of the seigniorial settlements in the sister province, that it would be easy to fancy ourselves in one of its many flourishing parishes, were it not for the superiority of the Detroit fruits that would dissipate the illusion.[13]

No doubt, such landscape also looked familiar to French-Canadian voyageurs from Lower Canada who traveled through the Detroit River borderland in the early nineteenth century.

Between 1784 and 1844, the population of Lower Canada grew from approximately 110,000 to 700,000. By contrast, Michigan's population amounted to less than 400,000 in 1850.[14] At the time, industrialization had not yet begun in Lower Canada and the vast majority of French Canadians lived on individual tracts of land (*censives*) within seigneuries, ribbon farm lots in old feudal districts, most of which fronted the St. Lawrence River. Due to this significant demographic growth, it became more and more difficult for younger generations to access farming lands in the St. Lawrence Valley; this reality contrasted sharply with the New France era, when many lands were still available.[15] French-Canadian historians have already discussed how, according to the French civil law (*la coutume de Paris*), a family censive was to be distributed equally to all children upon the passing of its holder; in Lower Canada, this component of the French civil law was not altered until the 1840s.[16] However, in actual fact, as early as the second half of the eighteenth century, parents in some parts of the St. Lawrence Valley became less and less able to further subdivide the family property and split it equally.[17] As a result, in the 1790s it was already common for some children to have to look for new lands outside of the seigneurie.[18] Also, during the first three decades of the nineteenth century, many seigneuries of Lower Canada were hit by an agricultural crisis that deeply affected the lives of thousands of French Canadians. These economic difficulties together acted as push factors that enticed many French Canadians away from the St. Lawrence Valley, beyond the boundaries of Lower Canada, into the interior of North America.[19]

For a great number of young French-Canadian men who had reluctantly joined the voyageur world, for lack of other opportunities, and who still hoped to find a more stable way of life, the St. Lawrence Valley of the early nineteenth century had little to offer. In stark contrast, the Detroit River borderland was clearly a desirable destination. In fact, it had everything a young man could dream of. In the early nineteenth century, tracts of land along the Detroit River and other watercourses of the area were regularly available for purchase, and numerous transactions took place between long-established French-Canadian families and newly arrived French Canadians. Furthermore, the agricultural settlements of the Detroit River borderland were attractive places for single voyageurs in search of potential brides. Catholic Church records show that for generations local couples living on farms generally had between ten and twenty children. Therefore, the community of the Detroit River borderland included a significant number of French-Canadian women, and many of them married voyageurs from the St. Lawrence Valley in the early nineteenth century.

This essay illustrates that French-Canadian emigration from Québec did not begin with the construction of railways in northeast North America (including the Midwest) in the mid-nineteenth century, as often portrayed by the historians of French Canada who have studied the emigration waves of the period 1840s–1920s. It argues that French-Canadian emigration began much earlier as push factors were already in place in the St. Lawrence Valley by the early nineteenth century. This emigration was connected to the French River World of preindustrial North America, which contained the Detroit River borderland and its agricultural settlements. The pioneers of French-Canadian historiography overlooked this world in their writings because they were not acquainted with it, and so did the subsequent generations of French-Canadian historians.[20]

French-Canadian families did leave Lower Canada in the early nineteenth century; however, this essay focuses on single men. It discusses the multiple circumstances which help in understanding the reasons for the departure of young men from the St. Lawrence Valley, why they chose to settle at Detroit, and the means by which some of them transformed an economically modest life as a voyageur into that of a landowner. Men who had little prospect of acquiring land in the St. Lawrence Valley found at Detroit French-Canadian families who were in possession of extensive tracts of land, resulting from a freehold land system that had developed after 1760. By marrying French-Canadian women of the Detroit River borderland, the newly arrived men were able to acquire not only land held by these established families but a standard of living that exceeded the typical socioeconomic parameters of a career as voyageur. As Marrero explains, "women of early Detroit had traditionally played pivotal roles in their families' business activities and would have contributed to their husband's economic successes in a multitude of ways," including helping them get access to the land.[21]

This essay is divided into three sections. The first examines the nature of the French-Canadian presence in the Detroit River borderland with regard to land occupation. The second deals with the historiography of the fur trade, more specifically how some recent works by Canadian historians have helped us to understand the context of relocation of voyageurs from Lower Canada to the Detroit River borderland. Finally, the last section delves into the lives of three French-Canadian men who are noteworthy examples of the larger history of retired voyageurs who established roots in the Detroit River borderland. The evidence presented in this essay will demonstrate the importance of studying the social history of Lower Canada through a continental perspective in order to fill historiographical gaps that cannot be filled through an inward perspective that focuses solely on the St. Lawrence Valley itself.

Land without a Lord

In 1842, the Legislative Assembly of Canada East (Lower Canada's name since 1840) launched a commission to enquire into the possibility of abolishing seigneurialism in the province by transforming all seigneurial land tenures into freeholdings; this process began in 1854 and was gradually completed by 1940.[22] During those twelve years between 1842 and 1854, the Legislative Assembly sponsored investigations to gather information about how seigneurialism had developed in Canada since the seventeenth century. During that time, the Legislative Assembly published a number of its findings, including an old report penned by seigneur and politician Charles-Louis Tarieu de Lanaudière (1743-1811) in 1790. Tarieu de Lanaudière stated that Detroit was once a *seigneurie directe*, that is to say a seigneurie under the direct authority of the king of France (as opposed to seigneuries owned by individuals; see below). The report went on to note, "With exception to the house-lots in the Towns of Quebec and Three Rivers, there are only a few Royal grants *en censive* in Canada, except at Detroit, where all the grants [were] issued by His Majesty in *roture*, as well in the Town and Country."[23] In other words, Detroit was the only location in the Great Lakes region where French authorities had implemented a standardized land granting and land occupation system directly under the authority of the king during the New France era. For the last century and a half, historians of French North America have failed to examine seigneurialism in the Detroit River region, its impact on the local development of agricultural settlements after the fall of New France, and the ways it helped to maintain cultural and economic connections with the St. Lawrence Valley well into the nineteenth century.[24]

In ancien régime France, most lands were owned by *seigneurs particuliers* (nobles, Catholic orders, etc.) whereas the king owned the remaining land holdings as seigneuries directes. In other words, there existed no land without a lord. Peasant farmers (*censitaires* or *roturiers*) who cultivated individual tracts of land within seigneuries did not "own" property, but rather "held" their lots and shared ownership with their seigneur, their manorial lord.[25] Censitaires were required to pay dues to their lord every year and could sell their lots, but they had to share the profit from those sales with the seigneur. This land tenure system was implemented in the St. Lawrence Valley in the seventeenth century and continued until 1854; in France it collapsed following the outbreak of the French Revolution in 1789. However, whereas seigneurialism in the St. Lawrence Valley survived the British Conquest of 1760, it did not in the Detroit River region. After the fall of New France, the local settlers, who had received land grants directly from the king of France through the commanders of Fort Pontchartrain (in today's downtown Detroit) and the governor-general of New France between 1734 and 1760, found themselves in a difficult position. British authorities did not recognize the king of France as owner of a seigneurie directe at Detroit and, as a result, refused to honor the land titles of the local French. As the French Canadians at Detroit were no longer able to receive land grants as they had before the change in regime, another major problem developed. To circumvent this difficulty, many families adapted by acquiring illegal "Indian deeds" from their Aboriginal neighbors (namely the Odawa, Potawatomi, and Ojibwe). In this way, they continued to further develop agricultural settlements that resembled the seigneuries of the St. Lawrence Valley, minus the presence of seigneurs. These Indian deeds (more than three hundred were granted between 1765 and 1796) not only contributed to the expansion of the French-Canadian land occupation along the Detroit River, but also along other watercourses (River Rouge, Clinton River, River Raisin, etc.).

During the last decades of the eighteenth century, land tenure in the Detroit River region evolved into a freeholding system.[26] To live on a farm in the Detroit River borderland in the early nineteenth century meant to live in a place where there was, in fact, "land without a lord." The situation was much different in the St. Lawrence Valley between 1760 and 1854. The seigneurs continuously raised the dues they required from their censitaires. They also increased the number of mandatory tasks that new censitaires were obliged to perform as yearly service to the seigneur as per new land grant contracts. Eventually, it became common for seigneurs to refuse to grant parts of their seigneuries that were still available. Instead these sections were kept for speculative purposes.[27]

Following the fall of New France, despite its ambiguously defined land market (difficulty to have land titles acknowledged, acquisition of new lands through illegal Indian deeds, etc.), Detroit became a place where it was somewhat easy to acquire land and where there were no obligations to any seigneurs. In the early nineteenth century, once British and American authorities had finally regulated the land market on their respective side of the border, the stark disjunction between land markets and regulations in the Detroit River borderland and Lower Canada served as an incentive for migrations to the western hinterland.[28]

Voyageurs, Merchants, Notaries, and Contracts

As Carolyn Podruchny explains, "the voyageurs were the 'proletarians' of the Montreal fur trade from the 1680s until the 1870s," and their primary task consisted in transporting by canoe "vast quantities of furs and goods between Montreal and posts in the far western and northern reaches of North America [on behalf of merchants]."[29] In the first decades of the nineteenth century, thousands of French-Canadian men from the St. Lawrence Valley still worked in the fur trade and traveled the interior of the continent.[30] However, as Podruchny remarks, "it is impossible to measure their precise numbers because their contracts signed in Montreal have not all survived, nor were contracts made in the pays d'en haut collected in a systematic manner."[31] The vast majority of the contracts produced in Montréal that have survived have been included in the Voyageur Contracts Database, created by Nicole St-Onge and Robert Englebert.[32] This database contains more than 35,000 contracts, yet we know that many more contracts were actually produced, either in Montréal or elsewhere. As St-Onge writes, "forays into the collections of notaries who practiced in smaller centers such as Trois-Rivières and Sorel or even notaries based in traditional voyageur-recruitment villages such as L'Assomption and Laprairie revealed the existence of hundreds of additional contracts not entered into the database."[33] Englebert has calculated that between 1763 and 1805, "six hundred contracts were issued for voyageurs headed to Detroit."[34]

This number does not include contracts in which the destination is not clearly stated or contracts which were produced after 1805.

The Voyageur Contracts Database, which also includes contracts from the 1810s, 1820s, and 1830s, is very helpful in tracking down many of the voyageurs who put down roots in the Detroit River borderland between 1796 and 1846. Due to the disappearance of many contracts, not all these voyageurs show up in the database. Luckily, other sources can often help fill in the blanks: Christian Denissen's *Genealogy of the French Families of the Detroit River Region, 1701-1936*; the publications of the French-Canadian Heritage Society of Michigan (namely, its magazine *Michigan's Habitant Heritage*); the database of Université de Montréal's Programme de recherche en démographie historique; and Walter Lowrie's *American State Papers*, which details all land ownership claims by French Canadians in southeast Michigan during the first decade of the nineteenth century.[35]

Three Emigrants

Lower Canada was not isolated from the rest of North America, far from it. In the context of the French River World, many voyageurs became emigrants by choosing to put down roots in the interior of the continent and never returning to Lower Canada. The stories of Charles Rouleau, Michel Cadieux, and Pierre-Claude Cartier are three examples of French-Canadian men from Lower Canada who married into French-Canadian families of the Detroit River borderland, where they established deep roots.

CHARLES ROULEAU IN RIVER ROUGE

On July 22, 1793, British Indian Affairs officer Thomas Duggan wrote from Fort Detroit to his superior, Alexander McKee, that Charles Rouleau was on his way to meet him at the Miami Rapids.[36] A century later, Detroit historian Silas Farmer wrote of Charles Rouleau: "Mr. Roulo, came from Quebec, and was one of the early explorers of Indiana. He afterwards settled in Detroit, on what is known as the old Roulo farm, now owned by Dr. Broman. He built the first water-power grist mill on Roulo Creek, and lived and died on the old homestead. He married Miss Chovin, by whom he had a large family of children, Charles being the eldest."[37] Born in 1761 in the parish of Saint-Laurent, on the island of Orleans, just east of Québec City, Charles was raised on the family farm that his father, Charles Sr., had received from his own parents a decade earlier.[38] It is not clear whether or not he officially worked as a voyageur prior to being mentioned in Duggan's letter, for he does not appear in the Voyageur Contracts Database. He does not seem to belong to a family in which working in the fur trade was a tradition. Still, somehow, Charles had moved to the Detroit River region sometime in the early 1790s. Not much is known about the context of his departure from the island of Orleans other than he apparently did not inherit the family's property. Between 1763 and 1777, Charles's parents had nine children.[39] Therefore, it is not impossible that Charles realized that he would not have access to family land (whether through inheritance or purchase) any time soon, if he were to ever have that option. At the time, it was common for aging landholders in the St. Lawrence Valley to retire from farming activities by ceding their property to one of their children (*donation à cause de vieillesse*).[40] This did not happen with Charles. His parents were still raising his younger siblings in 1793, when he was traveling from Fort Detroit to the Miami Rapids. Purchasing a tract of land from a neighboring family was not an option either for Charles, because there were no lands left for sale on the island of Orleans in the late eighteenth century.[41] At the time, Charles had one older brother and three younger brothers. Three of them married in nearby parishes on the mainland and his younger brother, Antoine, married in the parish of Saint-Laurent. This suggests that Antoine may have been the one who inherited the family's property.[42] Still, it is interesting that Charles did not pursue the path of his brothers who moved to nearby seigneuries, and instead settled on a tract of land near Detroit.

In 1796, census takers Gabriel Godfroy, Jean-Baptiste Beaugrand, and John Cissney listed Charles Rouleau as a resident of River Rouge, southwest of Detroit.[43] This agricultural settlement had been established in the 1770s, when French settlers acquired lands through illegal Indian deeds, more specifically deeds from the local Potawatomi. In 1797, Rouleau married Jeanne Chauvin at St. Anne's Church in Detroit before priest Gabriel Richard. That same year the couple had their first child at River Rouge. They had fourteen more children between 1799 and 1828.[44] Not surprisingly, Charles Rouleau appeared on the 1799 voters' list for Wayne County.[45] In 1805, in the records of the US commission on private claims in southeast Michigan, he claimed ownership over a long and narrow tract of land along the north shore of River Rouge (today, this lot would be located on the border between Detroit's neighborhood of Springwells Village and the city of Dearborn). In his claim, we learn who his neighbors were, the size of his property, and how much of it was under cultivation:

No. 567. CHARLES ROULEAU.—The Board took into consideration the claim of Charles Rouleau to a tract of land, situate on river Rouge, which was entered with the former Commissioners of the Land Office at Detroit, in vol. 1, page 298, under the date of 4th February, 1805. This tract contains, by estimation, one hundred and twenty arpents, it being three arpents in front by forty in depth, bounded in front by river Rouge, in rear by the old Pattawatamie road, on one side by lands of Pierre Dumay, and on the other by lands of John Cissne. Whereupon, Theophile Demers was brought forward as a witness in behalf of the claimant, who, being duly sworn, deposed and said, that, previous to the 1st July, 1796, the claimant was in possession and occupancy of the premises, and has continued so to this day; a house and a shop are erected thereon: and about eighteen arpents are cultivated. And therefore it does appear to the commissioners that the claimant is entitled to the above described tract of land.[46]

This tract of land was still in the Rouleau family in 1891.[47] During the commission, Charles also claimed private property over a tract of land he had recently purchased, presumably as a method to expand his family's properties. This tract was also located near the River Rouge, although it did not front onto the river.[48] In 1827, Charles was again listed in the census of River Rouge.[49] He and Jeanne were now parents of eleven children, five boys and six girls (not including three children that had died at a young age). All but one of their children later married into other local French-Canadian families. As for their grandchildren, almost all of them found a bride or groom within French-Canadian families from the Michigan side of the Detroit River borderland.[50]

It is not clear how Charles and Jeanne passed these two properties down to their children, but it appears that one of their sons, Pierre, born in 1820, continued to reside on a tract of land along the north shore of the River Rouge well into the second half of the nineteenth century, before retiring from farming and giving part of his property to his sons. According to Elaine Walters Raymo, who researched the history of Detroit's Holy Cross Cemetery (established in 1840 near the rear end of former lot No. 29), "three sons of Peter Roulo, Charles, Edward, and Joseph, inherited a fraction of their father's land through a decree of partition granting them ownership in 1879." She adds that "they sold this fraction of land to Henry Ford on August 30, 1915, to become part of the Ford Rouge Plant."[51] The youngest of these sons, Édouard, married Joséphine Livernois at St. Anne's church in 1878; Joséphine's parents, Daniel Livernois and Émilie Riopel, both belonged to French-

Canadian families that had been present on the north shore of the Detroit River for generations.[52] Édouard and Joséphine, like many other members of the Rouleau and Livernois families of River Rouge, were buried in Holy Cross Cemetery.[53]

To Charles Rouleau, southeast Michigan appeared to be an ideal place to settle down, to replicate the sedentary way of life in which he had grown up, and to raise a family. His story, far from unique, shows that marrying into a local French-Canadian family was perhaps the best way to ease his integration into the French-Canadian community of the Detroit River borderland. With his bride, he got access to a tract of land and worked to develop a *patrimoine familial* (family patrimony). Charles chose the settlement of River Rouge, but there were other settlements where French-Canadian newcomers could put down roots in the early nineteenth century. Grosse Pointe, known as the Côte du Nord-Est in the eighteenth century, was another favorite site.

MICHEL CADIEUX IN GROSSE POINTE

On April 1, 1818, in front of Montréal notary John Gerbrand Beek, Michel Cadieux signed a three-year contract (*"hiverner trois années"*) to travel through the interior of North America. Born on September 22, 1799, in the parish of Saint-Louis-de-Terrebonne, north of Montréal, Michel was only eighteen years old when he signed that contract.[54] His lack of experience was confirmed not only by his young age but also by the fact that he was assigned to the position of *milieu* or middleman in the canoe.[55] In the hierarchy of the voyageur world, a milieu stood near the bottom. Therefore, men appointed to that position always earned significantly less than the more experienced members of their brigade.[56] Michel grew up in the seigneurie of Terrebonne. Since the New France era, this seigneurie had been one of the most important recruitment pools for Montréal merchants looking for young men to work in the fur trade.[57] In the early nineteenth century, the seigneurie of Terrebonne still had deep connections with the interior of the continent, mainly through Montréal's North West Company (and, to some extent, the Hudson's Bay Company).[58] Between 1802 and 1804, the seigneur of Terrebonne was Scottish merchant and fur trade marquis Simon McTavish (1750–1804), who had previously lived at Detroit and at other locations in the Great Lakes.[59] During the next ten years, the seigneurie was in the hands of McTavish's heirs, until it was sold to Scottish merchant Roderick Mackenzie (1761–1844). Like McTavish, Mackenzie had also been involved in the fur trade through the North West Company and other companies for several years. He had also lived in the Great Lakes region, where he fathered three children by an Aboriginal woman.[60] These Scottish seigneurs, who maintained connections with the fur trade world after establishing roots in Terrebonne, did not have to look very far for voyageurs. Michel was just one of many local young men willing to paddle and portage, for three years, into the Great Lakes and beyond.

The Cadieux family of the seigneurie of Terrebonne was one of those French-Canadian families in which every generation of young men worked in the fur trade, and several of Michel's ancestors appear to have visited Detroit during the eighteenth century. Michel had unquestionably heard about the Detroit River borderland before visiting the area. Like many other voyageurs from Lower Canada, he eventually decided to put down roots and return to an agricultural way of life. He did so not in his home parish or nearby, but in Detroit.

On August 10, 1830, Michel married Archange Gouin at St. Anne's Church. Her parents were Charles-Nicolas Gouin (born in 1776 at an unknown location in the Great Lakes region, probably in present-day northern Ohio or Indiana, and baptized at St. Anne's Church in 1778) and Élizabeth Labadie (baptized in 1784 at Assumption Church, on the south shore of the Detroit River). Archange's father was of mixed ancestry, for he was born to a Miami woman named Louiliracatias. However, it seems that Charles-Nicolas Gouin was raised primarily in the French-Canadian community of the Detroit River region, for his own father, Joseph-Nicolas Gouin, remarried at St. Anne's Church in 1781. This time he wed a French-Canadian woman, Marie-Archange Boyer, with whom he had three children between 1781 and 1789; this suggests that Louiliracatias had died, had been abandoned, or had refused to settle in Detroit. Archange's mother belonged to French-Canadian families who had been established in the area since the French regime.[61]

Michel and Archange had twelve children, seven boys and five girls. For decades, they owned an old French farm in Grosse Pointe, Michigan. Michel died in 1865 and was buried in the cemetery of St. Paul's Church, now located within the city of Grosse Pointe Farms.[62] As for Archange, she passed away much later, in 1891. Archange's obituary in the *Detroit Free Press* reads as follows:

> Archange Cadieux, widow of the famous Indian trader, Michael Cadieux, and daughter of Bapt. Chas. W. Gouin, died Saturday, January 17, at her residence in Grosse Pointe.... Archange died on the same farm where she was born and raised, eighty-one years ago.... The deceased was an uncompromising Catholic.

... She was the mother of thirteen children, seven of whom survive her.... The funeral of the deceased will take place Tuesday morning at 9:30 o'clock from S.S. Peter and Paul's Church, Grosse Pointe.[63]

The same year, William C. Sauer mentioned in his *Detailed Official Atlas of Wayne County, Michigan*, that two descendants of Michel and Archange lived on lots No. 300 and No. 564 of the US commission on private claims.[64] In 1850, Isidore Cadieux, one of the six sons of Michel and Archange, had built a house on lot No. 300. At the turn of the twentieth century, this lot developed into Cadieux Road. However, unlike virtually all other "old French houses" in southeast Michigan, Isidore's house was never demolished. In 2014, as part of the expansion project of a nearby hospital, the "Cadieux Farmhouse" was moved a few blocks away to be preserved.[65]

Although he hailed from a different region of the St. Lawrence Valley, the story of Michel Cadieux is similar to that of Charles Rouleau. Both were young and single when they came to the Detroit River borderland. They did not settle in the same agricultural settlements, but both rapidly established deep roots and stayed on the same property for many years. This was not always the case with the French-Canadian newcomers. In the early nineteenth century, the Detroit River was a very fluid international border and, as mentioned earlier, local residents often readily disregarded it when opportunities arose on the other side.

PIERRE-CLAUDE CARTIER ON BOTH SIDES OF THE BORDER

Pierre-Claude Cartier was born in the parish of Saint-François, near Trois-Rivières, in 1790. In 1806, at the age of sixteen, he signed his first voyageur contract, as a milieu, to travel to unspecified locations south of the Great Lakes. In 1810, he signed another contract, this time to travel to Michilimackinac and Missouri, again as a milieu.[66] Not much is known about Pierre-Claude's family. His parents and grandparents were from the same parish, and presumably lived within the seigneurie of Saint-François-du-Lac. Pierre-Claude was the oldest of six children (not including two children who died before reaching the age of one), all boys. It is not known if any of Pierre-Claude's five brothers also worked in the fur trade. The parish of Saint-François had provided voyageurs for decades, so it is very likely that Pierre-Claude grew up in an environment in which many young men offered their services to merchants to work as voyageurs.

After his second contract, Pierre-Claude decided to put down roots along the south shore of the Detroit River (British side of the border). He had very likely visited the area as part of one of his voyageur contracts, perhaps both. During the War of 1812, he was listed as a member of Upper Canada's Second Regiment Essex Militia, which was almost entirely made up of local French-Canadian settlers, and he was wounded at the Battle of River Raisin (Michigan Territory) on January 23, 1813.[67] In the early 1820s, he was living across the border, at River Raisin.[68] On January 13, 1823, Pierre-Claude, now thirty-two years old, married Marie-Florence Chauvin at Ste. Anne's Church. The bride belonged to a French-Canadian family with deep roots in the Detroit River region, on both sides of the border. Marie-Florence's ancestors had lived in the area since her great-grandfather, Charles Chauvin, had received a tract of land from the king of France northeast of Fort Pontchartrain (Côte du Nord-Est) in 1734.[69] Many of her ancestors were listed in the US commission on private claims in southeast Michigan. Today, there are also many Chauvins on the Canadian side of the border. Pierre-Claude had only one child by Marie-Florence, who unfortunately died around 1830. In 1833, again at St. Anne's Church, Pierre-Claude married Catherine Dubé. His second bride also belonged to a French-Canadian family long established in the Detroit River region. Her father, Joseph Dubé, who was born in Detroit in 1777, had claimed a tract of land at L'Anse Creuse (near today's Mount Clemens, Michigan) in 1808 (lot No. 165).[70] Pierre-Claude had two children by Catherine, a son and a daughter; it is not clear where exactly in southeast Michigan the couple raised their children. Pierre-Claude passed away in 1840, while Catherine died in 1858. Both were buried in the cemetery of St. Anne's Church.[71]

One of Catherine's sisters, Félicité, also married a man from Lower Canada, at St. Anne's Church in 1844. Her husband, Alexandre-Célestin Dumontier, was born in 1812 in the parish of L'Ange Gardien, on the north shore of the St. Lawrence River, across from the island of Orleans.[72] Félicité and Alexandre-Célestin died in 1894 and 1895, respectively. Like Pierre-Claude and Catherine, they were both buried in the cemetery of St. Anne's Church.[73]

Conclusion

Decades before the first railways were built in North America, French Canadians were already seeking opportunities for a stable way of life beyond the boundaries of the St. Lawrence Valley. These migrations undoubtedly occurred because of the lack of opportunities for younger generations within the seigneuries of the valley.

Access to the land became increasingly difficult, and this problem was compounded by an agricultural crisis that affected thousands of French Canadians during the same period. To fully understand these migrations, it is essential to grasp the extent of the continuing connections between the St. Lawrence Valley and the interior of North America during the first half of the nineteenth century—the persisting French River World. English-Canadian fur-trade historians have already demonstrated the significance of these connections. However, a deeper understanding of the unique history of French-Canadian land occupation in the Detroit River region between the 1730s and 1810s is also important. The fact that seigneurialism disappeared in the Detroit River region following the British Conquest of New France, resulting in local land tenure evolving into a freeholding system, appealed to voyageurs from Lower Canada, who saw an alternative to living under the authority of a seigneur. The agricultural settlements of the Detroit River region had been home to hundreds of French-Canadian women for several generations by the early nineteenth century and this became another pull factor for many single voyageurs. Charles Rouleau, Michel Cadieux, and Pierre-Claude Cartier are merely three examples among many other young men from Lower Canada who put down roots in the Detroit River borderland between 1796 and 1846. In the future, more research on these preindustrial migrations beyond the boundaries of the St. Lawrence Valley will help to further enrich our understanding of the social history of the Detroit River borderland, Lower Canada, and, more broadly, French North America.

NOTES

The research for this article was supported by the Social Sciences and Humanities Research Council of Canada through an Insight Development Grant. The authors would like to thank their research assistants: Adam Drouillard, Jason Lavin, John-Michael Markovic, and Shane Miller. They would also like to thank Robert Englebert for his insightful comments on previous drafts of this essay.

1. François-Xavier Garneau, *Histoire du Canada depuis sa découverte jusqu'à nos jours*, volume 2 (Québec: N. Aubin, 1846), 19.

2. In his 1844 *Histoire du Canada et des Canadiens, sous la domination anglaise*, which focuses on the period 1760–1838, Michel Bibaud (1782–1857) only briefly mentions Detroit when discussing the events of 1837–38, without providing any information about the local French population. Although he grew up on a farm on the island of Montréal, Bibaud attended Montréal's Collège Saint-Raphaël and became a teacher and journalist. Michel Bibaud, *Histoire du Canada et des Canadiens, sous la domination anglaise* (Montréal: Lovell & Gibson, 1844); Céline Cyr, "Michel Bibaud," in *Dictionary of Canadian Biography*, vol. 8, University of Toronto/Université Laval, 2003-, http://www.biographi.ca/en/bio

/bibaud_michel_8F.html (accessed June 27, 2018). This shortcoming about the Detroit River borderland in the early French-Canadian historiography can also be noticed in historical works authored by French-Canadian priests educated at the Petit Séminaire, in Québec City, during the nineteenth century. Charles-Honoré Laverdière (1826–1873) is a good example. Between 1840 and 1851, he studied at the Petit Séminaire. In 1869, he published *Histoire du Canada à l'usage des maisons d'éducation*, intended for teachers across Québec. In his book, Laverdière does not include any information about the French Canadians in the Detroit River borderland. Charles-Honoré Laverdière, *Histoire du Canada à l'usage des maisons d'éducation* (Québec: Augustin Côté, 1869); Michel Paquin, "Charles-Honoré Laverdière," in *Dictionary of Canadian Biography*, vol. 10, University of Toronto/Université Laval, 2003-, http://www.biographi.ca/en/bio/laverdiere_charles_honore_10E.html (accessed June 27, 2018).

3. Robert Englebert coined the term "French River World." Robert Englebert, "Merchant Representatives and the French River World, 1763–1803," *Michigan Historical Review* 34, no. 1 (2008): 66. See also Robert Englebert, "The Legacy of New France: Law and Social Cohesion between Quebec and the Illinois Country, 1763–1790," *French Colonial History* 17 (2017): 35–66.

4. Joseph-François Perrault (1753-1844), who visited Detroit, St. Louis, and New Orleans in the 1770s, was an exception. Born into a merchant family connected to the famous Bâby family through his mother's side, Joseph-François was educated at the Petit Séminaire and went on to work in several liberal professions in present-day Québec. Between 1791 and 1836, he published several works, including a five-volume history of Canada entitled *Abrégé de l'histoire du Canada*. Unfortunately, and for unknown reasons, Perrault did not elaborate on the French-Canadian presence along the Detroit River in these volumes. See, for instance, Joseph-François Perrault, *Abrégé de l'histoire du Canada, première partie, depuis sa découverte jusqu'à sa conquête, par les Anglais, en 1759 et 1760* (Québec: Thomas Cary, 1832); *Abrégé de l'histoire du Canada, seconde partie, depuis sa conquête, par les Anglais, en 1759 et 1760, jusqu'à l'établissement d'une Chambre d'assemblée, en 1792* (Québec: Thomas Cary, 1832). On the life of Perrault, see Claude Galarneau, "Joseph-François Perrault," in *Dictionary of Canadian Biography*, vol. 7, University of Toronto/Université Laval, 2003-, http://www.biographi.ca/en/bio/perrault_joseph_francois_7F.html (accessed June 27, 2018).

5. Some historians of Lower Canada have used a continental perspective, but almost exclusively to study the intellectual history of the 1837–1838 rebellions. There is also a need for a combination of continental and social history approaches. On the Lower Canada rebellions and the idea of liberty in the intellectual context of the Atlantic world revolutions, see Allan Greer, *The Patriots and the People: The Rebellion of 1837 in Rural Lower Canada* (Toronto: University of Toronto Press, 1993); Michel Ducharme, *Le concept de liberté au Canada à l'époque des révolutions atlantiques, 1776–1838* (Montréal: McGill-Queen's University Press, 2010).

6. It is not the first attempt, however. See Jennifer Constantin, "Canots, terres et fourrures en Haute-Louisiane: Les voyageurs de Ste-Geneviève convertis à la sédentarité (1763–1803)," (MA thesis, University of Ottawa, 2011). Also, historian Yves Frenette, from Université de Saint-Boniface in Winnipeg, Manitoba, is leading a new group of scholars working on French migrations in North America between 1760 and 1914. Although the group has so far mainly focused on the second half of the nineteenth century, it intends to further expand its investigation to the preindustrial era over the next few years. For more information about this research group, see https://ustboniface.ca/crc-mtcf/contact-yves (accessed June 28, 2018). A few other works have looked at French-Canadian migrations

to the interior of North America, but they have focused on the French regime. See, for instance, Renald Lessard, Jacques Mathieu and Lina Gouger, "Peuplement colonisateur au Pays des Illinois," *Proceedings of the Meeting of the French Colonial Historical Society* 12 (1988): 57–68; Lina Gouger "Migrer à Détroit au XVIIIe siècle: La part du monde rural dans le peuplement d'une zone de frontière," in *Les exclus de la terre en France et au Québec, XVIIe-XXe siècles: La reproduction familiale dans la différence*, edited by Gérard Bouchard, John A. Dickinson, and Joseph Goy (Sillery, QC: Septentrion, 1998); Lina Gouger, "Le peuplement colonisateur de Détroit, 1701–1765," (Ph.D. diss., Université Laval, 2002).

7. In 1796, present-day Michigan became part of the US Northwest Territory. Between 1803 and 1805, Michigan was briefly integrated into Indiana Territory. It became a territory of its own in 1805, until it reached statehood in 1837.

8. See Catherine Cangany, "'The Inhabitants of both Sides of this Streight constitute a french Colony': The Detroit River and the Politics of International Milling, 1796–1837," in *Une Amérique française, 1760-1860: Dynamiques du corridor créole*, edited by Guillaume Teasdale and Tangi Villerbu (Paris: Les Indes Savantes, 2015); Guillaume Teasdale, *Fruits of Perseverance: The French Presence in the Detroit River Region, 1701–1815* (Montréal: McGill-Queen's University Press, 2018), chap. 7.

9. Association de la propagation de la Foi, ed., *Annales de l'Association de la Propagation de la Foi*, tome 3 (Lyon: Librairie de Rusand, 1828), 326–27.

10. The three other parishes were: Saint-Antoine de la Rivière-aux-Raisins (est. 1788), Saint-François-de-Sales à la Rivière-aux-Hurons (est. 1824; the Huron River was later renamed Clinton River), and Saint-Paul in Grosse Pointe (est. 1825). See also Guillaume Teasdale, "Les débuts de l'Église catholique américaine et le monde atlantique français: Le cas de l'ancienne colonie française de Détroit," *Histoire et missions chrétiennes* 17 (2011): 35–58. In the 1830s and 1840s, other priests from France also had a mission for French-Canadian settlers further north, along the St. Clair River, on the north shore of Lake St. Clair, on the Michigan side of the border. Société historique de Saint-Boniface, Winnipeg, Manitoba, Relevés des registres sacramentaux de la mission de St. Clair River, Michigan, 1832–1841, no. 0001/1777/3012. Father Richard's calculation did not include the few thousand French who lived across the border, in Upper Canada, part of a separate Catholic diocese since 1796. In 1825, there were two parishes on the British side of the border: Assomption de la Pointe de Montréal (present-day Windsor; est. 1767) and Saint-Pierre (present-day Tilbury East; est. 1802). A third parish, Saint-Jean-Baptiste (Amherstburg), was established in 1827; many more were established during the following decades. See Société franco-ontarienne d'histoire et de généalogie régionale Windsor-Essex, *Le Sud-Ouest ontarien à la recherche de ses ancêtres* (Belle-Rivière, ON: Société franco-ontarienne d'histoire et de généalogie régionale Windsor-Essex, 2001), xvi. On the arrival of priests from France to southeast Michigan in the first decades of the nineteenth century, see George Paré, *The Catholic Church in Detroit, 1701–1888* (Detroit: Gabriel Richard Press, 1951), 352–75. For an overview of the establishment of French-Canadian Catholic parishes in present-day Ontario before 1826, see Gaétan Gervais, "Les paroisses de l'Ontario français, 1767–2000," *Cahiers Charlevoix* 6 (2005): 114–17. For a biography of Jean-Baptiste Marchand, priest of the parish of Assomption de la Pointe de Montréal between 1796 and 1825, see Bruno Harel, "Jean-Baptiste Marchand," in *Dictionary of Canadian Biography*, vol. 6, University of Toronto/Université Laval, 2003-, http://www.biographi.ca/en/bio/marchand_jean_baptiste_6E.html (accessed June 29, 2018). On the history of the parish, see George F. MacDonald, "Forgotten Facts about Assumption Parish, Sandwich, Ontario," *CCHA Report* 18 (1951): 39–45.

11. *Laws of the Territory of Michigan* (Detroit: Sheldon & Wells, 1827), 603.

12. Karen L. Marrero, "'Borders Thick and Foggy': Mobility, Community, and Nation in a Northern Indigenous Region," in *Warring for America: Cultural Contests in the Era of 1812*, ed. Nicole Eustace and Fredrika J. Teute (Chapel Hill: University of North Carolina Press, 2017), 420. On the efforts by American authorities, see Lawrence B. A. Hatter, "The Jay Charter: Rethinking the American National State in the West, 1796–1819," *Diplomatic History* 37, no. 4 (2013): 693–726. On the development of "colonial borderlands" into "modern borderlands" in the Great Lakes region, see Randy William Widdis, "Migration, Borderlands, and National Identity: Directions for Research," in John J. Bukowczyk et al., *Permeable Border: The Great Lakes Basin as Transnational Region, 1650–1990* (Pittsburgh: University of Pittsburgh Press, 2005), 152–74.

13. Joseph Bouchette, *The British dominions in North America, or, A topographical and statistical description of the provinces of Lower and Upper Canada, New Brunswick, Nova Scotia, the Islands of Newfoundland, Prince Edward, and Cape Breton including considerations on land-granting and emigration: to which are annexed, statistical tables and tables of distances, &c.* (London: H. Colburn & R. Bentley, 1831), 106-7. For more information on Joseph Bouchette, see Claude Boudreau and Pierre Lépine, "Joseph Bouchette," in *Dictionary of Canadian Biography*, vol. 7, University of Toronto/Université Laval, 2003–, http://www.biographi.ca/en/bio/bouchette_joseph_7F.html (accessed March 21, 2018).

14. *Censuses of Canada, 1665 to 1871*, vol. 4 (Ottawa: Printed by I. B. Taylor, 1876), 74, 144; http://legislature.mi.gov/(S(ppormflktwzeosnrvzabovaj))/documents/2017-2018/michiganmanual/2017-MM-P0003-p0019.pdf

15. Historian Benoît Grenier writes: "Sous le régime français, le peuplement des seigneuries demeure très limité. À l'intérieur des fiefs, il reste encore de vastes espaces non concédés tandis que des seigneuries entières n'ont fait l'objet d'aucune mise en valeur." Benoît Grenier, "Le régime seigneurial au Québec," *Bulletin d'histoire politique* 23, no. 2 (2015): 145.

16. Yves F. Zoltvany, "Esquisse de la Coutume de Paris," *Revue d'histoire de l'Amérique française* 25, no. 3 (1971): 379; Gilles Paquet and Jean-Pierre Wallot, "Stratégie foncière de l'habitant: Québec (1790–1835)," *Revue d'histoire de l'Amérique française* 39, no. 4 (1986): 557.

17. Sylvie Despatie, "La transmission du patrimoine dans les terroirs en expansion: un exemple canadien au XVIIIe siècle, *Revue d'histoire de l'Amérique française* 44, no. 2 (1990): 171–98.

18. Jacques Mathieu, Pauline Therrien, and Rénald Lessard, "Mobilité et sédentarité: Stratégies familiales en Nouvelle-France," *Recherches sociographiques* 28, no. 2–3 (1987): 218. Some historians have argued that rise in wealth inequality among *censitaires* in Lower Canada at the turn of the nineteenth century resulted in the wealthier censitaires being able to find nearby lands for their children while the children of poorer censitaires were often being pushed out of the area. On this emerging social hierarchy, Gilles Paquet and Jean-Pierre Wallot write: "On voit même se reproduire de cette façon toute une hiérarchie sociale: les gros habitants établissent tous leurs enfants sur des terres de bonne dimension alors que les plus pauvres n'y parviennent pas et doivent les envoyer ailleurs." Paquet and Wallot, "Stratégie foncière de l'habitant," 558.

19. On the Lower Canada agricultural crisis and the historiographical debate that it involved, see Alain Laberge, "Crise, malaise et restructuration: l'agriculture bas-canadienne dans tous ses états," in *Érudition, humanisme et savoir: Actes du colloque en l'honneur de Jean Hamelin*, ed. Yves Roby and Nive Voisine (Sainte-Foy, QC: Presses de l'Université Laval, 1996). It should be noted that the historians

involved in this debate have not contemplated the possibility that the crisis pushed French Canadians out of Lower Canada.

20. Despite the publication, during the second half of the nineteenth century, of two works on the French-Canadian presence in the Detroit River borderland, French-Canadian historians have continued to overlook that topic until very recently. These two publications are Edmé Rameau de Saint-Père (historian from France who visited Windsor), *Notes historiques sur la colonie canadienne du Détroit: Lecture prononcée par Mr. Rameau à Windsor sur le Détroit, comté d'Essex, C.W. le Lundi 1er avril 1861* (Montréal: J. B. Rolland & fils, Libraires-éditeurs, 1861); and Télesphore Saint-Pierre (Québec journalist who lived in Detroit and Windsor), *Histoire des Canadiens du Michigan et du comté d'Essex, Ontario* (Montréal: Typographie de la Gazette, 1895).

21. Karen Marrero, "Women at the Crossroads: Trade, Mobility, and Power in Early French America and Detroit," in *Women in Early America*, ed. Thomas A. Foster (New York: New York University Press, 2015), 180.

22. Benoît Grenier, "L'Église et la propriété seigneuriale au Québec (1854–1940): continuité ou rupture?," *Études d'histoire religieuse* 79, no. 2 (2013): 21–39.

23. Legislative Assembly of Canada East, *Titles and Documents Relative to the Seigniorial Tenure, Required by an Address of the Legislative Assembly, 1851* (Québec: E. R. Fréchette), 36. Emphasis in original. In French, this excerpt reads as follows: "Hors des emplacemens des maisons des villes de Québec et Trois-Rivières, il n'y a eu que peu de concessions royales en Canada en censive, excepté au Détroit, où toutes les concessions relèvent de Sa Majesté en roture, soit de ville, soit de campagne." Assemblée législative du Canada East, *Pièces et documents relatifs à la tenure seigneuriale, demandées par une adresse de l'Assemblée législative, 1851* (Québec: E. R. Fréchette, 1852), 16. For more information on Charles de Lanaudière, see Yves Beauregard, "Charles-Louis Tarieu de Lanaudière," in *Dictionary of Canadian Biography*, vol. 5, University of Toronto/Université Laval, 2003-, http://www.biographi.ca/en/bio/tarieu_de_lanaudiere_charles_louis_5F.html (accessed March 28, 2018).

24. See Teasdale, *Fruits of Perseverance*, chap. 2.

25. Benoît Grenier, *Brève histoire du système seigneurial* (Montréal: Boréal, 2012), 38. Annie Antoine writes, regarding French peasants in ancien régime France: "Qu'il soit locataire ou propriétaire, le paysan vit dans le cadre d'une seigneurie, il a donc le statut de tenancier (holder)." Annie Antoine, "Les paysans en France de la fin du Moyen Âge à la Révolution: Propriétaires? tenanciers? locataires?," in *Ruralité française et britannique, XIIIe-XXe siècles*, edited by Nadine Vivier (Rennes: Presses universitaires de Rennes, 2005). On the concept of "tenancier" (holder), see also Zoltvany, "Esquisse de la Coutume de Paris," 372.

26. Between the 1760s and 1790s, land transactions in the Detroit River region were carefully recorded by French-Canadian or British notaries. Library and Archives Canada, Fonds Notaires de Détroit; Burton Historical Collection, Detroit Public Library, Detroit Notarial Records; Wayne County Register of Deeds, Libers 1, 2, A, B, and C.

27. Christian Dessurault, "L'évolution du régime seigneurial canadien de 1760 à 1854: Essai de synthèse," in *Le régime seigneurial au Québec 150 ans après: Bilans et perspectives de recherches à l'occasion de la commémoration du 150ᵉ anniversaire de l'abolition du régime seigneurial*, ed. Alain Laberge and Benoît Grenier (Québec: Centre interuniversitaire d'études québécoises, 2009), 29.

28. On the regulation of the land market in the Detroit River borderland at the turn of the nineteenth century, see Lawrence B. A. Hatter, "The Transformation of the Detroit Land Market and the Formation of the Anglo-American Border, 1783–1796," *Michigan Historical Review* 34, no. 1 (2008): 83–99; Teasdale, *Fruits of Perseverance*, chap. 5.

29. Carolyn Podruchny, *Making the Voyageur World: Travelers and Traders in the North American Fur Trade* (Lincoln: University of Nebraska Press, 2006), 4.

30. Some of these men traveled as far as the Pacific Coast. See, for instance, Nicole St-Onge, "Blue Beads, Vermilion, and Scalpers: The Social Economy of the 1810–1812 Astorian Overland Expedition's French-Canadian Voyageurs," in *French and Indians in the Heart of North America, 1630-1815*, ed. Robert Englebert and Guillaume Teasdale (East Lansing: Michigan State University Press, 2013); Melinda Marie Jetté, *At the Heart of the Crossed Races: A French-Indian Community in Nineteenth-Century Oregon, 1812–1859* (Corvallis: Oregon State University Press, 2015).

31. Podruchny, *Making the Voyageur World*, 4.

32. This digital database is hosted by the Société historique de Saint-Boniface, Manitoba, and can be accessed at no cost.

33. Nicole St-Onge, "The Persistence of Travel and Trade: St. Lawrence River Valley French Engagés and the American Fur Company, 1818–1840," *Michigan Historical Review* 34, no. 2 (2008): 18–19.

34. Englebert, "Merchant Representatives," 65.

35. Other helpful sources include Germaine Chiasson and Carmen MacLeod, *Mariages: Paroisse l'Assomption de Windsor, Ontario, 1700-1985* (Ottawa: Société franco-ontarienne d'histoire et de généalogie, 1985); Juliette St-Pierre, *Sépultures: Paroisse l'Assomption de Windsor, Ontario, 1768–1985* (Ottawa: Société franco-ontarienne d'histoire et de généalogie, 1986).

36. Michigan Pioneer and Historical Society, *Michigan Pioneer and Historical Collections*, 2nd ed. (Lansing, MI: Wynkoop Hallenbeck Crawford Co., 1908), 12: 71. Rouleau is sometimes spelled Roulot or Roulo. The Miami Rapids are located near present-day Toledo, Ohio, where the British built a fort in 1794, during the Indian Wars of the Old Northwest.

37. Silas Farmer, *History of Detroit and Wayne County and Early Michigan: A Chronological Cyclopedia of the Past and Present* (Detroit: Silas Farmer & Co., 1890), 1292.

38. Programme de recherche en démographie historique de l'Université de Montréal (hereafter abbreviated PRDH), #193175, Charles Rouleau; Bibliothèque et Archives nationales du Québec à Québec (BAnQQ), Fonds Cour supérieure, District judiciaire de Québec, cote CR301,P3417, Donation par Gabriel Roulleau (Rouleau) et Geneviève Petitclerc, mari et femme; à Charles Rouleau, leur fils, 28 juin 1751; BAnQQ, Fonds Prévôté de Québec, cote TL1,S11,SS1,D99,P385, Lecture d'un contrat de donation passé devant maître Pichet, notaire, le 28 juin 1751, par lequel Gabriel Rouleau et Geneviève Petitclerc, son épouse, font donation à Charles Rouleau, leur fils, d'une terre sise à Saint-Laurent, 21 septembre 1751.

39. PRDH, #30415, Famille de Charles Rouleau et Geneviève Gosselin.

40. Lise Langlois, "Reproduction sociale à l'Île d'Orleans: Stratégies, transmissions du patrimoine et migrations sous le régime français" (MA thesis, Université de Sherbrooke, 1997), 62.

41. Langlois, "Reproduction sociale à l'Île d'Orleans," 41; Claude Boudreau, "La représentation cartographique du monde rural québécois au XIXe siècle: L'exemple de l'île d'Orléans," *Proceedings of the Meeting of the French Colonial Historical Society* 12 (1988): 12–13.

42. François Rouleau (1807-1897), one of the sons of Antoine Rouleau and his wife, Geneviève Godbout, studied at the Petit Séminaire de Québec and became a lawyer. According to David Gosselin, François was the first lawyer from the parish of Saint-Laurent, which reveals that he grew up at that location and that his father had likely inherited the family farm from his own father (also Charles's father) in the early nineteenth century. David Gosselin, *Pages d'histoire ancienne et contemporaine de ma paroisse natale, Saint-Laurent, Île d'Orléans* (Québec: Dussault & Proulx, 1904), 87.

43. Donna V. Russell, ed., *Michigan Censuses, 1710–1830: Under the French, British, and Americans* (Detroit: Detroit Society for Genealogical Research Inc., 1982), 64.

44. Christian Denissen, *Genealogy of the French Families of the Detroit River Region, 1701-1936*, 2nd ed. (Detroit: Detroit Society for Genealogical Research, 1987), 1102–1103.

45. Pioneer Society of the State of Michigan, *Michigan Pioneer and Historical Collections*, 2nd ed. (Lansing, MI: Wynkoop Hallenbeck Crawford Co., 1907), 8:509; Télesphore Saint-Pierre, *Histoire des Canadiens français du Michigan et du comté d'Essex, Ontario*, 2nd ed. (Sillery, QC: Éditions du Septentrion, 2000), 192.

46. Walter Lowrie, ed., *American State Papers: Documents, Legislative and Executive, of the Congress of the United States, from the First Session of the First to the Third Session of the Thirteenth Congress, Inclusive: Commencing March 3, 1789, and Ending March 3, 1815* (Washington, DC: Gales & Seaton, 1832), 1:485–86.

47. William C. Sauer, *Detailed Official Atlas of Wayne County, Michigan* (Detroit: William C. Sauer, 1893), 5.

48. Lowrie, ed., *American State Papers*, 310.

49. Russell, ed., *Michigan Censuses*, 154.

50. See Jack Bibean and Marianne Dibean, "Wayne County, Michigan Dibean Marriage Index," http://files.usgwarchives.net/mi/wayne/vitals/marriages/dbn/wayne-dbn-dec2013-r.txt. In the 1840s and 1850s, the old French community of the Detroit River region was rapidly being divided between two separate French communities, that of southwest Ontario and that of southeast Michigan. See Teasdale, *Fruits of Perseverance*, chap. 7.

51. Elaine Walters Raymo, *Detroit's Holy Cross Cemetary* (Charleston, SC: Arcadia Publishing, 2009), 31.

52. Denissen, *Genealogy of the French Families*, 1103. For primary sources on the early history of the Riopel family in southeast Michigan, see William L. Clements Library, University of Michigan, Ann Arbor, Riopelle Papers.

53. Most of the graves of these families, including that of Édouard and Joséphine, are still standing today and can be viewed online on a website like https://www.findagrave.com/.

54. PRDH, #567773, Michel Cadieux.

55. Société historique de Saint-Boniface (hereafter abbreviated SHSB), Voyageur Contracts Database, "Michel Cadieux, contract date: 18180401."

56. Carolyn Podruchny writes: "The wages paid to voyageurs varied according to their position.... Within the canoe paddlers called middlemen, or *milieux*, were subject to the authority of the foreman and steersmen, or *devant* and *gouvernail*, collectively called *bouts*, who usually acted as canoe and brigade leaders. Bouts could earn from one third to more than six times as much as milieu." Podruchny, *Making the Voyageur World*, 40. Emphasis in original.

57. Suzanne Boivin Sommerville, "Re: Michael, Baptized as Michel, Cadieux: Correction to Several Online Data Bases and other Publications," *Michigan's Habitant Heritage* 34, no. 3 (2013): 152.

58. See Robert Englebert, "Diverging Identities and Converging Interests: Corporate Competition, Desertion, and Voyageur Agency, 1815–1818," *Manitoba History* 55 (2007): 18–24.

59. Fernand Ouellet, "Simon McTavish," in *Dictionary of Canadian Biography*, vol. 5, University of Toronto/Université Laval, 2003-, http://www.biographi.ca/en/bio/mctavish_simon_5E.html (accessed March 22, 2018).

60. Roderick Mackenzie's ownership of the seigneurie of Terrebonne was actually challenged by the heirs of McTavish after the transaction: "In 1814 Mackenzie purchased the seigneury of Terrebonne from the McTavish estate, agreeing to pay £8,000 plus £1,200 per year until the total, £28,000, had been attained. He planned to continue McTavish's commercial development of the property and wrote of raising the annual revenue from £1,000 to £3,000. He never became a seigneur, however, and had to leave the property in 1824 after a court action, initiated by McTavish's widow, cancelled his purchase because the executors had exceeded their authority in making the sale. He nevertheless continued to live in Terrebonne." Peter Deslauriers, "Roderick Mackenzie," in *Dictionary of Canadian Biography*, vol. 7, University of Toronto/Université Laval, 2003-, http://www.biographi.ca/en/bio/mackenzie_roderick_7E.html (accessed March 22, 2018).

61. Diane Wolford Sheppard, "Detroit River Region métis Families—Part 5—G," http://www.habitantheritage.org/yahoo_site_admin/assets/docs/m%C3%A9tis_Families_-_Part_5_-_G.20434256.pdf (accessed March 23, 2018); Denissen, *Genealogy of the French Families*, 172, 540, 616–8.

62. http://www.gphistorical.org/pdf-files/funstuff/stpaulscemetery.pdf (accessed March 18, 2018).

63. *Detroit Free Press*, January 19, 1891.

64. During the commission, these two lots had been claimed by men named Michel Rivard and Jean-Baptiste Rivard, respectively; At the time, several other members of the Rivard family, which was present on both sides of the border, had claimed ownership over tracts of land in southeast Michigan. Sauer, *Detailed Official Atlas of Wayne County*, 3. In addition to Michel Rivard and Jean-Baptiste Rivard, François Rivard (lot No. 180), Antoine Rivard (lot No. 181), Charles Rivard (lot No. 299), and Nicolas Rivard (lot. Not. 656) also claimed private property rights: Lowrie, ed., *American State Papers*, 356–57, 395, 452, 485, 515, 522.

65. Eric D. Lawrence, "Cadieux Farmhouse Reconstruction a Work in Progress," *Detroit Free Press*, April 30, 2015, https://www.freep.com/story/news/local/michigan/wayne/2015/04/30/work-continuing-cadieux-farmhouse/26668531/ (accessed March 23, 2018).

66. SHSB, Voyageur Contracts Database, "Pierre Cartier, contract date: 18060505"; SHSB, Voyageur Contracts Database, "Pierre Cartier, contract date: 18100113."

67. Diane Wolford Sheppard, "Essex and Kent County, Ontario Militia Rolls for the Period 25 December 1812 to 24 January 1813," *Michigan's Habitant Heritage* 33, no. 4 (2012): 233.

68. Sharon A. Kelley, Patricia A. Miller, and Gail F. Moreau-DesHarnais, eds., *Marriage Records Ste. Church Detroit 1701–1850* (Detroit: Detroit Society for Genealogical Research, 2001), 92.

69. Christian Denissen, *Genealogy of the French Families*, 264–68; Bibliothèque et Archives nationales du Québec-Québec, Fonds Intendants, cote E1,S3,P268, Acte de concession par Charles de Boische, Marquis de Beauharnois, et Gilles Hocquart, gouverneur et intendant de la Nouvelle-France, au sieur Chauvin, 16 juin 1734.

70. Denissen, *Genealogy of the French Families*, 409–10; Lowrie, ed., *American State Papers*, 350–51.

71. The St. Anne's cemetery was originally located in the heart of today's downtown Detroit, where St. Anne's Church used to be located, until it was moved further west in the 1880s. However, due to urbanization, the cemetery was relocated twice, in 1817 and 1869. For this reason, the graves of Pierre Cartier and Catherine Dubé do not exist anymore. See Sherry Somerset and Suzanne Boivin Sommerville, "Remembering Those Buried in 1869 at Mt. Elliott Cemetery," *Michigan's Habitant Heritage* 31, no. 2 (2010): 92–94.

72. Denissen, *Genealogy of the French Families*, 410, 440; PRDH, #80268, Famille de Joseph Guyon Després Dion Dumontier et Euphrosine Pépin Lachance. Alexandre-Célestin Dumontier does not show up in the Voyageur Contracts Database. Denissen provides the following information about Alexandre-Célestin: "Alexander went to NY as a young man remained there 5 yrs worked 2 yrs in MA from there to MI and Macomb Co at the time of his marriage." Denissen, *Genealogy of the French Families*, 440.

73. Their graves still exist today. See https://www.findagrave.com/memorial/156962236/felicitas-dumontier (accessed March 31, 2018) and https://www.findagrave.com/memorial/156962117/alexander-dumontier (accessed March 31, 2018).

Making Indians in the American Backcountry
Récits de voyage, *Cultural Mobility, and Imagining Empire in the Age of Revolutions*

ROBERT ENGLEBERT

It was an inauspicious beginning to a very short chapter in an otherwise storied career. The newly appointed governor of Guadeloupe, Georges-Henri-Victor Collot, arrived on the small Caribbean island amid growing political and racial tensions in 1793.[1] A veteran of the American War for Independence who had served under Marshal Rochambeau, Collot had risen through the ranks, navigating the revolutionary zeal and horror that had gripped his homeland and brought so many of his compatriots to ruin. And yet this decorated French general, seemingly adept at negotiating the political minefield of the early French republic, was ill-prepared to fully grasp the shifting geopolitical landscape and the social ramifications of racially charged policies in the Caribbean.[2]

Upon his arrival in Guadeloupe, Collot was quickly confronted with a slave revolt, imperial miscommunication, and the prospect of British invasion. With few appreciable resources at his disposal, the governor reacted to events on the fly. Nowhere was this more evident than in Collot's decision to arm *gens de couleur* and slaves in defense of the colony. Overturning the colonial racial social order to cobble together a defense force further split the already fractious white planters, and when the British attacked in March of 1794, French royalists sided with France's longtime imperial rivals. Defeated and deflated, Victor Collot surrendered Guadeloupe to the British, who then remanded him to the United States.[3]

The story of Collot's short tenure in Guadeloupe clearly elucidates the widening social and political fissures that threatened to tear France's Atlantic empire apart. Notions of race, nation, and citizenship were all being redefined, and the prospect of a new world order must have been unsettling for this moderate republican. Collot would tell his own version of events from America, what historian Laurent Dubois has interpreted as a selective and sanitized account, meant to expunge all sense of personal culpability or transgression.[4] Writing to the French minister of the marine, he framed his all-too-brief governorship as an impossible task, determined by forces greater than himself, and he prefaced his *compte rendu* with the disclaimer, "I governed the island of Guadeloupe at a time when it was nearly impossible to do any good, and very difficult to prevent evil."[5] In this no-win scenario the governor and, by proxy, the empire were the ultimate victims of circumstance.

Collot's *compte rendu* is most assuredly revisionist, but also highly imaginative, weaving an idealized French Atlantic empire as backdrop against which insurrecting slaves, Jacobin threats, and treasonous monarchists are explicated. Of course, the backdrop, subtle as it is, is a fiction. Collot's version of imperial governance more closely resembles a romanticized ancien régime France, replete with references to benevolent governors and unified loyal—read tepid and docile—subjects.[6] His notion of French order, moreover, belied the reality of terror and political strife, even while regularly referencing a homeland in shambles. These inaccuracies, however, are beside the point. Contradictory and self-serving as it was, Collot's *compte rendu* was an act of imperial imagining.

Building on a legacy of colonial writing, Collot sought to elicit his own particular vision of empire. But while his account of Guadeloupe fabricated an elusive imperial ideal meant to salvage a French Atlantic empire that was seemingly crumbling all around him, Collot's next œuvre imagined a new French Empire, built on the foundations of lost colonies in the heart of North America. By 1795, Collot found himself paroled in Philadelphia and facing a lawsuit for damages over the loss of a merchant's ship while still governor. Faced with the prospect of a lengthy stay in America, he then struck an agreement with the French ambassador, Pierre-Auguste Adet, to embark on a voyage to survey the western territories.[7] In much the same manner that Louis-Antoine de Bougainville's *Voyage autour du monde* had attempted to set a new vision for French imperialism following the loss of New France a generation earlier, Collot's account of the American backcountry offered the prospect of remaking the French Empire.[8] And he was not alone in this endeavor.

The late eighteenth century was a period of heightened French cultural mobility. People, goods, and ideas diffused throughout the Atlantic World, informing and reacting to the rampant sociopolitical change that historians have come to call the

Age of Revolutions. Revolution-turned-terror in France prompted an exodus of political refugees of varying stripes, from monarchists to early revolutionaries and moderate republicans. Approximately 25,000 French émigrés entered the United States during the early 1790s, with scores ending up in Philadelphia. The result was a robust and vibrant expatriate community, where the intellectual currents of the Enlightenment and the American, French, and Haitian revolutions intermingled.[9]

Escaping the summer heat of Philadelphia, a number of these French expatriates ventured into the Pennsylvanian and New York hinterland to speculate and report on newly established towns of French émigrés. Men like François-Alexandre-Frédéric, duc de La Rochefoucauld-Liancourt; Constantin-François de Chasseboeuf, comte de Volney; Louis-Marie, vicomte de Noailles; and Charles-Maurice de Talleyrand-Périgord drew inspiration from their own cultural and political baggage and attempted to reconcile their understandings of nation and empire with the stark reality of new surroundings and less-than-ideal circumstances. Making these "new Frances" was a highly imaginative process, which François Furstenberg keenly notes, was "not just an economic transformation; it was also a cognitive one."[10] Frontier towns of French émigrés like Asylum, he explains, "fired liberal imaginations across the Atlantic world."[11]

Some Frenchmen traveled further still, to the farthest reaches of the American backcountry, where the trans-Appalachian West met the Mississippi River. Men like Victor Collot, French engineer Nicolas de Finiels, and the comte de Volney had all spent time in Philadelphia and went on to chronicle the historic Illinois Country, which included portions of the Ohio, Illinois, Wabash, and Mississippi river valleys. Unlike émigrés who gave accounts of their compatriots at new towns like Asylum, Gallipolis, and Castorland, these Frenchmen visited a region of older colonial settlements and came face-to-face with the legacy of France's ancien régime in the heart of North America. Edward Watts suggests that French expatriates contrasted sharply with those they encountered, having no formal ties to a defunct French Empire in North America, and differentiated politically and ideologically by the French Revolution.[12] While there are limits to how far these distinctions may have actually played out on the ground, French chroniclers of Illinois Country conceptualized the francophones they happened upon as distinct from themselves.[13] The result was a manifestation of imperial imagining, the invention of francophone colonial others made into new Indians and measured against fictional notions of Frenchness.[14]

French travel accounts and reports of the American backcountry were epistemologically grounded in the evolving tradition of the *récit de voyage*, a complex literary form that combined history, geography, and ethnography with fantastic storytelling.[15] A hybrid of fictional and nonfictional genres, with deep roots dating back to antiquity, French travel literature exploded in the seventeenth century as France pursued imperial expansion.[16] Missionaries, colonial officials, military officers, and merchants recorded their travels and wrote reports, which were then edited and published for public consumption.[17] Academic scholarship has traditionally interrogated *récits de voyage* regarding the America backcountry as early ethnographies of Indigenous peoples, but have largely eschewed these writings as French ethnographies of a preexisting francophone population shaped by post–French Revolutionary imperial imaginings.

During the eighteenth century, *récits de voyage* took on a more instructive quality for popular audiences, and explanations of *mœurs étrangères* (ethnographies of foreign social and cultural mores) increasingly contributed to an introspective intellectual voyage, where the reader learned about herself by reading about distant lands and peoples.[18] In producing such narratives, however, authors also underwent their own voyage of personal discovery;[19] travel engendered a collision of expectations and circumstances, which elucidated sense of self in relation to a colonial other.[20] As literary scholar Réal Ouellet puts it, the traveler's perception "comes from the encounter between his culture and an experience with a reality that he has trouble grasping."[21]

Authors drew inspiration from previous travel writings, imitating writing styles and copying excerpts, sometimes even entire sections. Jean-Baptiste Truteau's account of a voyage up the Missouri River (1794–96) borrowed liberally at times from Louis Hennepin's *Description de la Louisiane nouvellement decouverte au sud'Oüest de la Nouvelle-France* (1683) and Louis-Armand de Lom d'Arce, Baron de Lahontan's *Mémoires de l'Amérique septentrionale* (1702).[22] In similar fashion Victor Collot and Nicolas de Finiels adopted Truteau's early writings into their own reports on the Missouri, while François-Marie Perrin du Lac's published travels were lifted almost wholesale from Truteau.[23]

Coming to grips with imperial leftovers in Illinois Country, French expatriates displayed a certain nostalgia for a lost empire, and fashioned ethnographic portrayals of francophones rooted in literary traditions and colonial debates. By discussing overlapping characteristics, commonalities, and contradictions, French authors cast and recast francophones in order to adhere to their own preconceived notions of empire and suit new imperial imaginings.[24] The colonial others that emerged from these narratives were thus familiar, and at the same time very foreign.[25]

Canadiens as Imperial Legacy

Early colonial settlement in Illinois Country consisted mostly of fur trade merchants, *engagés* (indentured laborers), and *coureurs de bois* (illicit traders) who married local Indigenous women to create a populace defined by Native kinship and pronounced *métissage* (racial/cultural hybridity).[26] Many of the first francophone arrivals did not settle permanently, but instead cycled through seasonally in accordance with fur trade migration patterns. By the 1730s, however, a settler colonial population had taken root, made up largely of *Canadiens*—those from the St. Lawrence Valley.[27] Settlers from France and Louisiana also came to Illinois Country, along with the forced migration of enslaved people of African descent and enslaved Indigenous people.[28] During the latter half of the eighteenth century, Spanish, British, and American colonial officials arrived in the region, along with Anglo-American settlers and Indigenous peoples from the Ohio Valley.[29] By the late eighteenth and early nineteenth centuries, the Illinois Country had become a complex multiethnic mélange.[30]

Irrespective of the heterogeneous population they encountered, French chroniclers of Illinois Country fixated on *Canadiens* and *métissage* to account for France's imperial legacy. Comte de Volney's *Tableau du climat et du sol des Etats Unis d'Amérique*, for instance, evokes a particular *canadien* archetype, where French creoles from the St. Lawrence Valley sought liberation and freedom from imperial control by regularly intermarrying and mixing with Indigenous peoples.[31] Louis Dubroca's writing, however, presents *métissage* as far more compatible with French imperialism, the likely result of Napoleon's renewed interest in the American West. Dubroca depicted a region settled by a combination of military figures and strong robust men from Canada, and he noted that "the custom they [the French] had adopted in Canada of living with the *sauvages* encouraged them [the French in Upper Louisiana] to marry the daughters of the Arkansas without difficulty, and those alliances enjoyed the happiest of outcomes."[32] He argued, moreover, that the close relationship between Native and newcomer was the by-product of years of peaceful coexistence in Canada and the role that *Canadiens* had played in defending the Illinois against Iroquois raids during the seventeenth century.[33]

Volney and Dubroca's interpretations are replete with historical inaccuracies of *canadien* migration and settlement seemingly bent on legitimizing French imperial claims by harkening back to a period of perceived French colonial possession.[34] Other authors, of course, were hardly more consistent, and certainly not any more accurate in recalling the legacy of empire in the heart of North America.[35] Berquin Duvallon, for example, described the Illinois Country as having been settled only fifty years earlier by "une peuplade de Français Canadiens,"[36] while Nicholas de Finiels recounted a more recent *canadien* migration of fur trade merchants and *engagés*.[37] Most accounts, however, consistently painted *canadien* migration to Illinois Country as antecedent to contemporary events, which served as a reminder of France's failed imperial project in America while at the same time justifying imperial renewal.

Nicolas de Finiels differed somewhat from most of his contemporaries in that he described ongoing *canadien* migration and its impact on the cultural landscape of the region.[38] A French military engineer who had served the Spanish regime in Louisiana, de Finiels remained in the colony following its retrocession to France in 1800, and he wrote a report on Upper Louisiana with an eye toward rekindled imperial interest. De Finiels characterized *Canadiens* as possessing a widespread reputation for stories: "[Creoles] lie for nothing, but rather to joke than to deceive. They owe this failing to the *Canadiens* who have settled among them. Their penchant for telling tales is generally so recognized that in Louisiana one calls everything that appears questionable or concocted *Canadienne*."[39] He explained, moreover, that these lovable tricksters had a marked effect on language and customs, merging Native idioms with *la langue de Molière* to create a unique patois.[40] But as influential as *Canadiens* may have been, de Finiels clearly saw linguistic and cultural differences between *Canadiens* and the French, and there was little room for the former in his imperial vision for the future.[41] Noting the steady stream of American settlers to the region and fierce commercial competition from British merchants in the north, he posited that any hope of French imperial renewal meant first and foremost tightening trade regulations and securing the region from Anglo-American incursions. Like many French chroniclers of the interior of North America, de Finiels saw *Canadiens* as an integral part of a historic imperial golden age in America that lay within memory; it bestowed a certain legitimacy to new imperial claims, but that historical legacy was degraded and fading away.[42]

Collot's Canadiens: *A Means to Imperial Revival*

Like de Finiels, Victor Collot discussed *Canadiens* in a contemporary context. His exhaustive survey, arguably one of the most detailed accounts of the Ohio and Mississippi Valleys during the late eighteenth century, placed *Canadiens* at the heart of his narrative.⁴³ Beginning in Pittsburgh, near the old French site of Fort Duquesne, Collot hired two *Canadiens* and three Americans to journey down the Ohio River to the Mississippi and Missouri Rivers, and then south along the Mississippi to New Orleans. Following the introduction to the journal, he never mentions his American workers again. And yet his *canadien* guides are cited frequently throughout the ensuing five hundred pages.⁴⁴

Described as accomplished navigators—adept at handling birchbark canoes, flat-bottom boats, and pirogues—*Canadiens* are depicted by Collot as rich repositories of Indigenous knowledge, with the innate ability to read the natural landscape and survive the perils of the wilderness.⁴⁵ In typically romanticized style, he recalled his guides predicting a storm, which gave the expedition time to moor its boats, saving vessels and crew.⁴⁶ Collot reasoned that this intimate knowledge of the natural world went hand-in-hand with superior skills as navigators and boatmen, and the *Canadiens* became the standard by which all others were judged. For example, the Mississippi River could be perilous for those unfamiliar with its winding labyrinth of hidden tree roots, small enclaves, and shifting riverbanks. "From these circumstances," the Frenchman deduced, "... the navigation of this river is reckoned dangerous, although it is very seldom that any such accidents happen to boats manned by Canadians."⁴⁷

Collot clearly considered *Canadiens* uniquely qualified to help mitigate the risks associated with travel through the heart of North America. Their knowledge of the natural world made them indispensable guides, and the Frenchman routinely expounded on their awareness of local flora and fauna, and their mastery at hunting deer and bear.⁴⁸ Collot even recounted with a certain fascination an occasion whereupon his guides found turtle eggs from rubbings in the sand.⁴⁹ *Canadien* familiarity with a vast continental "waterscape" and their knowledge of places that failed to appear on Collot's maps corresponded with the Frenchman's impression of Native cognizance.⁵⁰ Thus, Collot construed *Canadiens* as new Indians, a familiar, useful, and loyal colonial other.

Collot drew both on depictions of provincials in France and the literary trope of the noble savage to construct a particular *canadien* archetype.⁵¹ In much the same manner that reference to peasants as *sauvages* in France contributed to a discourse of revolutionary regeneration and the creation of new citizens, Collot made his *Canadiens* into ideal imperial agents.⁵² The concept of the noble savage was no less influential. Gordon Sayre notes that "although the Noble Savage sometimes served to refigure Europeans' vision of their primitive past, it often served instead to justify a vision of the future in colonial America."[53] Indeed, Collot's assessment of his guides evinced greater imperial designs. Charged with surveying the interior of the continent to determine the feasibility of imperial revival, he saw the potential of harnessing *Canadiens* to serve French interests. In contrast to Indigenous peoples as independent warriors with uncertain loyalties, *Canadiens* were "perfect Natives" in that they "knew" the natural landscape, but spoke French and purportedly had loyalties to their historic homeland across the sea. In particular, he propounded that loyal *Canadiens* would abandon the British and help to wrest control of the fur trade from France's imperial rival.

> The English companies employ Englishmen neither as agents, traders, nor soldiers; but Canadians only, whose decided attachment for their nation is so well known, that it is become proverbial to say, that, under the government and rule of the English, they never cease to call themselves Frenchmen. They never see a Frenchman without emotion; and if the French or merchants of Louisiana engaged in the fur trade, they would easily draw off the Canadians from the English Companies. Although the English merchants are now in possession of Louisiana, the French merchants may still reap considerable advantages from this honorable attachment of the Canadians.[54]

Such imperial imagining perceptively identified *Canadiens* as the labor force behind the British fur trade out of Montréal, with hundreds of voyageurs fanning out across the continent each year in search of peltries.[55] In proposing to harness *Canadiens* to serve imperial interests, however, Collot fashioned them as a loyal monolith of singular concern. This, of course, was a far cry from the complex reality of late eighteenth-century French North America. War, revolution, and regime change combined with transcolonial commercial networks, *métissage*, and kinship; in this shifting geopolitical landscape loyalties were far from certain.[56]

Collot's assessment of *Canadiens* as unflinchingly loyal stemmed, in part, from his own personal experiences and interactions in the American backcountry. Reaching the Mississippi River, his guides advised him not to travel north because seasonal conditions would force him to winter at Michilimackinac or Detroit, where the authorities would easily capture him.[57] Later, he recalled encountering two *Canadiens* in Illinois Country, recently arrived from Québec with news of an impending British assault on Upper Louisiana.[58] From Collot's vantage point, *Canadiens* were already looking out for *his* French interests.

The fact that *Canadiens* appeared to cross colonial borders with relative impunity—a useful skill when dealing with imperial rivals—was undoubtedly part of their appeal. Though Collot never directly addressed where the *Canadiens* came from, his narrative rendered them figurative river rats—a mobile people at home throughout the interior of the continent.[59] He hired *canadien* guides in Pittsburgh and took on two more in Illinois Country. Planning to send his American workers back to Philadelphia or New York, Collot specified that all of the *Canadiens* would be sent to Illinois Country at the end of the voyage. Without mentioning specific individuals, Collot provided a generalized account of a people seemingly at home in Canada, the Ohio Valley, Illinois Country, and the Mississippi and Missouri river valleys; he regarded *Canadiens* as purveyors of a particular culture of mobility, one which tied disparate regions of the old French Empire in America together. *Canadien* mobility was associated with domination of the fur trade, and both equated with imperial control. Suffice it to say that *Canadiens* were the key to Collot's vision for French imperial renewal in America.

French Creole Work and Mobility

Although Collot periodically alluded to *canadien* families in select towns, such as Peoria, he more often than not simply referred to nondescript French-speaking villagers—French creoles.[60] French debates and discussions regarding illicit fur traders (*coureurs de bois*) during the seventeenth century differentiated between useful imperial servants and transient vagrants.[61] Collot built upon these tropes and in eerily similar fashion established his own dichotomy for francophones in Illinois Country; strong, helpful, and industrious *Canadiens* became holders of useful Indigenous knowledge, while ignorant, superstitious, and obstinate creoles adopted only negative traits from the Natives.[62]

Collot was not alone in his harsh views of nondescript French-speaking villagers. Indeed, a discourse of backward creoles permeates French accounts of the American backcountry written during the eighteenth and early nineteenth century, and it emanates from debates regarding the impact of work, leisure, and mobility on society. Authors asserted that the region's natural abundance, along with a certain creole proclivity for long river voyages had resulted in a lazy and self-satisfied population that saw no reason to improve that which nature had given.[63] Recalling his travels in America, Sergeant-Major Roux of the commune of Compiègne in France gave a scathing account of French creoles in 1790, bemoaning their love of leisure and contempt for luxury.[64] Complacency, he argued, meant that they only grew enough for subsistence, were consumed by their love of *tafia* (rum), and were resigned to live in decrepit conditions barely fit for livestock.[65] Thirteen years later, Nicolas de Finiels remarked that "all of the time not spent employed [on river vessels] is given over to inactivity and rest."[66]

French chroniclers linked indolent behavior to a lack of sedentary agriculture or use of outdated farming techniques, and they asserted that this ultimately detracted from colonial development.[67] Collot characterized Ouiatenon on the Wabash River as a small rundown town of ten or twelve creole families that hunted and traded but engaged in little farming.[68] His sketch of St. Charles was similar in argument, if harsher in tone, and he painted the village on the banks of Missouri River as a colonial backwater.[69]

> [The village] contains about an hundred or an hundred and twenty ill-constructed houses: the inhabitants do not till the ground, though it be extremely fertile; their ordinary occupations are hunting and trading with the Indians; a few hire themselves out as rowers; and it would be difficult to find a collection of individuals more ignorant, stupid, ugly, and miserable. Such are the sad effects of extreme poverty, with its train of cares and evils, that it destroys not only the beauty of the person but even the intellectual powers, and blunts all those feelings of delicacy and sensibility which belong to a state of ease, and the advantages of a good education.[70]

Notwithstanding the fact that Collot deemed *canadien* mobility and control of the fur trade essential for imperial revival, he nonetheless contended that when French creoles at St. Charles exhibited these same characteristics, it undermined an imperial ideal of sedentary agriculture—*la vocation agricole*.

Nicolas de Finiels gave similar assessment of creoles at Carondelet, a village located south of St. Louis on the Des Pères River.

> They have a preferred penchant for being idle, necessity alone calls them to the fields, the old folks cultivate the fields, the young people make voyages to New

Orleans, the Missouri, Michilimackinac and sometimes to the Ohio River up to Pittsburgh. They find it easier to suffer three consecutive months of hard work and to then spend eight or nine in idleness, rather than eagerly embrace jobs that would more assuredly lead to fortune, but which repeats each day and leaves little idle time to doze in indolence and sloth.[71]

Tapping into a well-worn colonial debate, Collot and de Finiels both posited that river voyages and work as boatmen pulled French creoles away from their farms. The fur trade had been a major point of contention during the colonial development of New France, and officials had frequently lamented that *habitants* abandoned their farms, even if temporarily, to seek adventure and fortune by trading in the *pays d'en haut* and *pays des Illinois*.[72] As Atlantic-centered imperial policies gave way to strategic westward expansion throughout the early to mid-eighteenth century, tensions over competing visions of empire persisted.[73] The fur trade facilitated Franco-Indigenous alliances in the West and addressed an imperative of French colonial defense, and yet it was deemed incompatible with the development and creation of a viable agricultural colony in Canada.[74] Those who partook in fur trade activities, moreover, were frequently characterized as backward and lazy, and at times, even dishonorable.[75] Of course, such distinctions created a false dichotomy that bore little resemblance to reality on the ground; colonial farming and fur trading were frequently linked, a regular part of family strategies and labor considerations throughout the eighteenth century.[76] Still, these colonial and literary debates informed French expatriates' understandings of French creoles in Illinois Country.[77] Under the old imperial axiom of *terra nullius*, perceived improper use of the land—that is, the fur trade—was interpreted as nonpossession.[78]

By contending that mobility would somehow frustrate new French imperial ambitions, French chroniclers of Illinois Country acknowledged a distinct creole culture.[79] Nicolas de Finiels's account of Upper Louisiana, for instance, elucidated a culture where honor, prestige, and respect in creole society—not French society— were tied to river voyages: "They prefer to gain their livelihoods hunting, which flatters their pride with its independence, or in rowing as *engagés* [hired laborers], on trading or commercial *bateaux*, harder work, tougher than all known occupations, but to which first preconceptions attached a point of honor, which elevated it in the eyes of the youth and enticed even children of the most well-off families to prefer it to all others."[80] The Frenchman went on to explain how understandings of masculinity were tied to specific travels, noting that "to be respected, one must have acquired a reputation for being a good boatman; to be a man, one must have made three trips paddle in hand; one to New Orleans, one to Michilimackinac; one other on the Missouri or the Ohio."[81]

As Leslie Choquette argues, a long-standing culture of labor mobility in France, the Tour de France, found new forms of articulation in North America, including fur trade mobility, which Gilles Havard refers to as *circulations pelletières*.[82] The culture of mobility that de Finiels characterized bore striking resemblance to the rites of passage, social hierarchies, and homosocial expressions of masculinity exhibited in the northwest fur trade out of Montréal.[83] In fact, Victor Collot and Nicolas de Finiels's narratives reveal a broader shared cultural ethos of mobility that made up a French river world, from Québec City and Montréal to Pittsburgh, Michilimackinac, Detroit, St. Louis, and New Orleans—what historian Jay Gitlin calls the French "creole corridor."[84] Distinctions between *canadien* and creole mobility in these French narratives were, therefore, illusory, and they emanated from efforts to chart a new imperial course for France. Collot fashioned his *canadien* guides as mobile-useful-noble Indians that offered the promise of imperial renewal, while both he and de Finiels projected an image of French creoles as mobile-contemptible-uncivilized Indians that represented a serious challenge to imperial claims and aspirations.[85]

Métissage, *Race, and Degeneration*

French chroniclers of the Illinois Country accounted for the perceived lack of creole industry by linking idle behavior to *métissage*. Authors argued that intermarriage and cultural hybridity had caused degeneration, the consequence of which being diminished work ethic and productivity.[86] François Furstenberg notes that "traveling into the backcountry, the émigrés had a sense of moving not just through space but also through time."[87] Travel narratives of Illinois Country reflected this sense of chronological displacement by depicting disinclination toward agriculture and languid comportment as a part of a literal slide backward to a state of Native simplicity.[88] French authors employed colonial conventions of negation and substitution to effectuate "willful anachronism," and they contended that creoles had divested themselves of civilization.[89] In the same vein as the trope of the noble savage, French discourses of degeneration emerged from an imperial forecast grounded in authors' understandings of empire and homeland.[90]

Victor Collot's narrative explicitly noted that which he felt creoles had forsaken, including agricultural techniques, notions of time, and standardization of language.

> In domestic life, their characters and dispositions are similar to those of the Indians with whom they live; indolent, careless, and addicted to drunkenness, they cultivate little or no ground, speak a French jargon, and have forgotten the division of time and months. If they are asked at what time such an event took place, they answer, "in the time of the great waters, of the strawberries, of the maïze, of potatoes"; if they are advised to change any practice which is evidently wrong, or if observations are made to them respecting the amelioration of agriculture, or the augmentation of any branch of commerce, the only answer they give is this: "It is the custom; our fathers did so: I have done well; my children will do the same."[91]

For Collot, this creole slippage from "modernity" to "backwardness," from "Frenchness" to "Indianness," was not just a question of agricultural work, but of *métissage* leading to a particular *mentalité*—a way of thinking and being that encapsulated a worldview.

Comte de Volney similarly employed notions of *métissage* and *mentalité* to elucidate his imperial vision.[92] Comparing creoles at Vincennes on the Wabash River to French émigrés at Gallipolis, he purported that creoles had a *mentalité* reminiscent of the monarchies of Louis XIV and XV—rooted in Old World feudalism and marked by a perceived lack of industry.[93] He contended, moreover, that imperial revival depended on French émigrés and republicanism; it was only with the help of "modern" French émigrés that "backward" creoles would be able to compete against a growing wave of American settlers.[94]

Notwithstanding the derelict state of Gallipolis in the 1790s, which was on the verge of collapse, Scioto Land Company settlers appear in Volney's writing as children of the French Revolution and propagators of liberty and peace.[95] He lamented the difficulties that émigrés had experienced at Gallipolis and contended that had they only been sent to old creole settlements on the Wabash and Mississippi Rivers, those places would have been renewed and remolded as modern French villages.[96] Volney posited that French émigrés would have pulled creoles from their Old World *mentalité* and would have ushered them unto children of the Revolution. In essence, then, he turned failed French émigré newcomers to the American backcountry into potential heroic saviors of a resurgent French Empire.

As previously noted, the comte de Volney had traveled extensively and published *récits de voyage* for the salons of Europe. A well-established politician and author prior to the French Revolution, he was imprisoned during the Reign of Terror, released in 1794, and departed for America a year later.[97] And yet he differed from many French émigrés in that he was not a political exile, "seeking refuge from the guillotine."[98] Nor had he been commissioned to survey or report on the American backcountry.[99] Despite these points of distinction, however, Volney's narrative echoed many of the same themes as evinced by those tasked with reporting on the interior of North America.

Like Collot and de Finiels, Volney viewed agriculture as a bedrock upon which imperial power and influence rested. He alleged, moreover, that to abscond this colonial responsibility was proof of backwardness and a threat to French imperial ambition. Volney reasoned that "these [creole] colonists are driven by the nature of things to prefer a life in turn restless and dissolute, indolent and trivial, like that of the *sauvages*, to the active and patient sedentary life of Anglo-American plowmen."[100] While Americans tilled the land, he argued, French creoles were preoccupied with marrying Native women and creating alliances with Indigenous peoples.[101] In much the same manner as other French authors, Volney drew on the literary tradition of *mœurs étrangères* to employ dichotomous categories of "civilized" sedentary agriculture and "backward" mobility, thereby casting creoles as Indianized, degenerate Frenchmen when they failed to "properly" occupy the land.

Making creoles into degenerate Europeans was a way to make the challenges facing France in America intelligible, and French authors regularly framed elements of creole degeneration—industry and *mentalité*—in racial terms. Indeed, racialization of creoles was a means by which conspicuous exhibition of *métissage* could be measured. Comte de Volney was struck by the physical disparity between new American settlers and the creoles he encountered at Vincennes.

> The day after my arrival, there was a meeting with the county judges: I went to make my observations on the physical appearance and character of the inhabitants who had assembled: since my arrival, I was struck to see the audience divided into two totally different races of men in both expression and physical appearance; one had blonde or chestnut hair, a rosy complexion, a full face and a portly body that signaled health and ease; the other had a very lean face, gaunt and weathered skin, and the entire body as if exhausted from hunger, not to mention clothes that indicated poverty. I soon recognized that the latter were

French colonists who had been established in this place for about sixty years, while the former were American colonists who, for only four to six years, had bought lands which they cultivated.[102]

For Volney, these creoles represented the empirically verifiable physical manifestation of *métissage*, not as cultural hybridity, but as Indianization. He argued, moreover, that English, Irish, and German immigrants were "races" that possessed superior aptitude for farming compared with Indianized French creoles.[103] Nicolas de Finiels likewise referred to the physical signs of *métissage*, with specific attention to sartorial expressions. Beyond the very tangible historical influence of Indigenous peoples on the culture and dress of colonial settlers, donning furs and skins in the winter for warmth and replacing European shoes with moccasins became for de Finiels the racial physical manifestation of a larger process of becoming Indian.[104] Like Volney, de Finiels used a comparative approach, not only transforming residents of St. Charles on the Missouri River into Indians, but also likening them to peoples in Asia.

> More hunters than farmers its *habitants* show no effects whatsoever of the civilization that one notices in St. Louis. They are nearly *sauvages* and several of them hardly understand French. Too indolent for the work that could pull them from this state, they nevertheless endure the most difficult hardships in pursuit of game, which often leads them into the mountains. They overcome the difficulties of the Missouri & Mississippi with a courage and ardor that is astonishing, considering we had seen them spend entire days in idleness that one could call indulgence were it surrounded by any of the trappings of luxury. Their slow and sedate pace in their village reminds one of that which asiatics owe to the warmth of their climate, we believe them weak and they are capable of the greatest efforts when required, if they were less white, if they were less kind, one could take them for *sauvages*, they have all of their customs without their cruelty.[105]

Accounts of racial difference in Illinois Country reflected a long history of French colonial racial categorization. More than a century earlier, French missionaries—Jesuits in particular—had broached the subjects of racial degeneration and backwardness to make sense of Indigenous beliefs and societal structures during the early years of ecclesiastical imperialism.[106] At the end of the seventeenth century, colonial policies geared toward assimilation of Indigenous peoples (*la francisation*) had given way as imperial officials, disquieted by the prevalence of colonists "going Native," questioned the effectiveness of such practices.[107] French officials endeavored to strike new policies to prevent intermarriage and stem the transmission of "bad blood" deemed to carry particular traits, though their efforts were largely ineffectual in Illinois Country.[108] Still, authors like de Finiels clung to understandings of blood, writing, "It was the *Canadiens* who first came to mix their blood with that of the French from Louisiana," which he notes prompted a descent to creole laxity and eventual "Indianness."[109]

Theories of racial difference found new elucidation throughout the Enlightenment, and the intellectual currents of the French Revolution had produced a plurality of perspectives on *métissage*.[110] The inspiration for Nicolas de Finiels's comparison of French creole "Indians" to Asiatics is difficult to substantiate, though Carl Lennaeus's human taxonomy (*Homo Americanus, Homo Europaeus, Homo Asiaticus,* and *Homo Afer*) was certainly well known by 1803. Other influences are clearer. Framing creoles in relation to Native simplicity, de Finiels borrowed heavily from Rousseau's protoromantic writings, even if somewhat inconsistently.[111] Though he deplored *métissage* when it appeared to drag creoles into "savagery," under the right circumstances and with the proper balance, de Finiels argued that one could find virtuous Native simplicity by "going Native." He thus noted "such was the retromarch of customs and character of the inhabitants of Upper Louisiana, during the period in which they settled. They shed several vices they had brought to assume new virtues, and all in appearing to degenerate from that which they were, they made giant steps towards happiness."[112] Such utopic philosophical musing stands in stark contradiction to de Finiels's appraisal of French imperial viability, which left little room for romantic notions of happiness and depended on dedicated French farmers/settlers.

Contradictions and inconsistencies were regular markers of colonial travel literature. Figures like Collot, Volney, and de Finiels frequently expounded on pragmatic imperial issues, at times lapsing into the fantastical with notions of *canadien* or French émigré—read Gallipolian—imperial saviors, or Native simplicity and happiness. Taken altogether, however, French authors depicted Franco-Indigenous *métissage* as *the* cause of creole degeneration—the slide backward toward an "Indian" *mentalité* with commensurate retrograde physical transformation. Though each author differed somewhat in their approach on how to interpret and deal with this, all French chroniclers of Illinois Country agreed that these new creole Indians presented a serious obstacle to French imperial ambitions.

Conclusion

French chroniclers of Illinois Country quickly learned that transforming imperial imaginings into reality would prove maddeningly elusive. When Victor Collot arrived in New Orleans at the end of his long and arduous six-month journey, he was quickly taken into custody and imprisoned. Governor Carondelet had caught wind of the Frenchman's covert operations; he confiscated a copy of Collot's journal and sent the spy packing after a couple of months behind bars. Deemed too dangerous by the Adams administration to return to France with detailed knowledge of the American backcountry, Collot was forced to remain in Philadelphia until 1800.[113] There is little evidence that Collot's journal had much impact on French imperial policy.

Ironically, the comte de Volney, despite never having been commissioned to report on the American backcountry or Louisiana, proved far more influential regarding French imperial renewal in America. He had already been back in France for several years by the time Collot departed Philadelphia and had maneuvered himself conspicuously close to the levers of power. Volney's friend Talleyrand, himself a former émigré in America, had been instrumental in effectuating the coup that established Napoleon as first consul. Acting as foreign minister, Talleyrand then spearheaded negotiations for the retrocession of Louisiana to France under the Treaty of San Ildefonso in 1800.[114] As if his friendship to Talleyrand was not enough to secure position and influence, Volney's previous writings on Syria and Egypt were well received by Napoleon, who sought to exploit them for his own imperial campaigns.[115]

Despite Volney's undeniable influence over French policy, imperial renewal in America ultimately proved impracticable as the geopolitical landscape of the French Atlantic shifted. A disastrous French military campaign to recapture the colony of Saint-Domingue precluded effective repossession of Louisiana. Volney's observations and musings may have informed policy, but he himself lacked the power to effectuate imperial grand designs; that authority rested with Napoleon and Talleyrand. As they weighed the prospect of imperial expansion, imaginings gave way to the harsh realities of changing developments on the ground. Ultimately, yellow fever and Haitian revolutionary forces did more to determine the future of France in America than any *récit de voyage* possibly could.

Unbeknownst to Nicolas de Finiels, Napoleon had already abandoned plans for a renewed American empire and had sold Louisiana to the United States by the time the French engineer penned his report on Upper Louisiana in June of 1803.[116] Beginning his narrative with a discussion of a French plot to wrest Louisiana from Spain in the early to mid-1790s, de Finiels prophetically asserted, "This project soon vanished like all those born of a vivid imagination, but the reports lived on."[117] De Finiels, Collot, and Volney had all evocatively dared to conceive of a new French Empire in America, which for but an instant evaporated into thin air.

Encountering francophones as colonial remnants of a defunct empire in the American backcountry, French chroniclers employed discourses of useful *Canadiens* and backward creoles to rationalize opportunities and assess obstacles to France's return to America. Whether it was *la vocation agricole*, historical and Enlightenment debates over race, or understandings of modern French republican ideals, French chroniclers of Illinois Country found a multitude of "French" characteristics from which to fashion creoles as new Indians. It was an act of profound imperial imagining and intense cultural mobility, in which France, the Atlantic World, and the American backcountry were brought into conversation with each other. *Récits de voyage* thus became places where authors and their readers could experience and reconceptualize what it meant to be French in a period of dramatic imperial dislocation.

NOTES

1. My sincerest thanks to Gilles Havard, Jean-François Lozier, and Andrew Wegmann for their feedback on this essay, and to the John Carter Brown Library for a short-term fellowship. Translations of sources are my own. Victor Collot's journal was published in translation under the guidance of the author. I have read both versions and have decided to go with the English translation for quotations. I have used my own translations of de Finiels, keeping largely in line with Carl Ekberg's excellent published translation of the text.

2. Laurent Dubois, *A Colony of Citizens: Revolution and Slave Emancipation in the French Caribbean, 1787–1804* (Chapel Hill: University of North Carolina Press, 2004); John D. Garrigus, *Before Haiti: Race and Citizenship in French Saint-Domingue*, The Americas in the Early Modern Atlantic World (New York: Palgrave Macmillan, 2006); Jeremy D. Popkin, *You Are All Free: The Haitian Revolution and the Abolition of Slavery* (New York: Cambridge University Press, 2010); Paul Friedland, "Every Island Is Not Haiti: The French Revolution in the Windward Islands," In *Rethinking the Age of Revolutions: France and the Birth of the Modern World*, ed. David A. Bell and Yair Mintzker (Oxford: Oxford University Press, 2018), 41–79; Manuel Covo, "Race, Slavery, and Colonies in the French Revolution," in *The Oxford Handbook of the French Revolution*, ed. David Andress (Oxford: Oxford University Press, 2015), 290–307; William S. Cormack, *Patriots, Royalists, and Terrorists in the West Indies: The French Revolution in Martinique and Guadeloupe, 1789–1802* (Toronto: University of Toronto Press, 2019).

3. Jean-Baptiste Donatien de Vimeur, comte de Rochambeau, was the commander of the French Armée du Nord during the American Revolution. The British occupied Guadeloupe briefly in 1794. For Collot's time as governor of Guadeloupe, see Anne Pérotin-Dumon, *Etre patriote sous les tropiques* (Basse-Terre, Guadeloupe, 1985), 179–82; Dubois, *A Colony of Citizens*, 24–26, 136–40, 143–49.

4. Dubois, *A Colony of Citizens*, 26.

5. Bibliothèque nationale de France, Paris, France, département Philosophie, histoire, sciences de l'homme, 8-LK12–73, Victor Collot (1750–1850), *Compte rendu par le général Victor Collot, ex-gouverneur de la Guadeloupe, au ministre de la Marine* [Texte imprimé, n.d.].

6. Kenneth J. Banks, "Communications and 'Imperial Overstretch': Lessons from the Eighteenth-Century Atlantic," *French Colonial History* 6 (2005): 20.

7. George W. Kyte, "A Spy on the Western Waters: The Military Intelligence Mission of General Collot in 1796," *Mississippi Valley Historical Review* 34, no. 3 (1947): 430–31.

8. Christian Ayne Crouch, *Nobility Lost: French & Canadian Martial Cultures, Indians and the End of New France* (Ithaca, NY: Cornell University Press, 2014), 153.

9. Allan Potofsky lists the number at 40,000 émigrés, but I have chosen to go with the more conservative estimate. Allan Potofsky, "La révolution transatlantique des émigrés: Des réseaux aux institutions," *Dix-Huitième Siècle* 33 (2001): 247; Catherine T. C. Spaeth, "America in the French Imagination: The French Settlers of Asylum, Pennsylvania, and Their Perceptions of 1790s America," *Canadian Review of American Studies* 38, no. 2 (2008): 248. For additional works on French émigrés in America, see Hélène Fouré-Selter, *Souvenirs français en Amérique* (Boston: Ginn & Company, 1940); Durand Echeverria, *Mirage in the West: A History of the French Image of American Society to 1815* (Princeton, NJ: Princeton University Press, 1957); Jean Vidalenc, *Les émigrés français, 1789–1825* (Caen: Association des publications de la Faculté des lettres et sciences humaines de l'Université de Caen, 1963); Arnold Whitridge, "French Émigrés in Philadelphia," *Virginia Quarterly Review* 44, no. 2 (1968): 285–301; R. Darrell Meadows, "Engineering Exile: Social Networks and the French Atlantic Community, 1789–1809," *French Historical Studies* 23, no. 1 (2000): 67–102; François Furstenberg, *When the United States Spoke French: Five Refugees Who Shaped a Nation* (Penguin, 2014).

10. Furstenberg, *When the United States Spoke French*, 274.

11. Furstenberg, *When the United States Spoke French*, 232. Also see Harry Liebersohn, *Aristocratic Encounters: European Travelers and North American Indians* (Cambridge: Cambridge University Press, 1998): 32–38; Allan Potofsky, "Geography as Geopolitics: Napoleonic France and the American West," in Nathalie Caron and Naomi Wulf, eds., *The Lewis and Clark Expedition* (Paris: Édition du temps): 158–74.

12. Edward Watts, *In This Remote Country: French Colonial Culture in the Anglo-American Imagination, 1780–1860* (Chapel Hill: University of North Carolina Press, 2006), 15.

13. A number of French émigrés, such as Antoine Soulard, settled in Illinois Country/Upper Louisiana and seem to have integrated into creole society reasonably well. Others, like Pierre-Charles de Hault de Lassus de Luzière, seem to have struggled more. See Kaia A. Knutson, "Soulard, Antoine Pierre (1766–1825)," in *Dictiionary of Missouri Biography*, ed. Lawrence O. Christensen et al. (Columbia: University of Missouri Press, 1999), 712; Carl J. Ekberg, *A French Aristocrat in the American West: The Shattered Dreams of De Lassus de Luzières* (Columbia: University of Missouri Press, 2010).

14. Dominique Deslandres, *Croire et faire croire: les missions françaises au XVIIe siècle (1600–1650)* (Paris: Fayard, 2003), 61; Saliha Belmessous, "Etre français en Nouvelle-France: Identité française et identité coloniale aux dix-septième et dix-huitième siècles," *French Historical Studies* 27, no. 3 (2004): 518; Cécile Vidal, ed., *Français? La nation en débat entre colonies et métropole, XVIe-XIXe siècle* (Paris: Éditions de l'École des hautes études en sciences sociales, 2014); Gilles Havard, *Histoire des coureurs de bois: Amérique du Nord, 1600–1840* (Les Indes savantes, 2016), 152.

15. *Récits de voyage* is being used very broadly here to include *relations, mœurs des sauvages, mœurs étrangères, relations de voyage,* and colonial reports as part of the same literary form. Most scholars agree that there was significant overlap between these, though not all scholars use them interchangeably. See Gordon Sayre, *Les Sauvages Américains: Representations of Native Americans in French and English Colonial Literature* (Chapel Hill: University of North Carolina Press, 1997), 114.

16. Réal Ouellet, *La relation de voyage en Amérique (XVIe-XVIIIe siècles) au carrefour des genres* (Québec: Les Presses de l'Université Laval, 2010), 1.

17. Roland Le Huenen, "Qu'est-ce qu'un récit de voyage?" in *Littérales No. 7: Les modèles du récit de voyage,* vol. 7 (Paris: Centre de recherches du Département de français de Paris X-Nanterre, 1990), 11–12.

18. Wendelin Guentner, "Aspects génériques du récit de voyage français: L'utile dulci," *Australian Journal of French Studies* 32, no. 2 (1995): 131, 146. It is worth noting that instruction and education were primary goals of *récits de voyage,* since many travel narratives were commissioned as reports for colonial authorities, religious orders, etc. See Ouellet, *La relation de voyage en Amérique,* 9–16. Guentner, however, is only referring to popular consumption of *récits de voyage.*

19. Réal Ouellet, "Pour une poétique de la relation de voyage," in *Écrire des récits de voyage (XVe-XVIIIe siècles),* ed. Marie-Christine Pioffet (Québec: Presses de l'Université Laval, 2008), 38.

20. Brian Brazeau, *Writing a New France, 1604–1632: Empire and Early Modern French Identity* (Burlington, VT: Ashgate, 2009), 7.

21. Ouellet, *La relation de voyage en Amérique,* 17.

22. Douglas R. Parks, "Introduction," in *A Fur Trader on the Upper Missouri: The Journal and Description of Jean-Baptiste Truteau, 1794–1796* (Lincoln: University of Nebraska Press, 2017), 27, 62–63; Robert Vézina, "Appendix 1: The Language of Truteau," in *A Fur Trader on the Upper Missouri: The Journal and Description of Jean-Baptiste Truteau, 1794–1796,* ed. Raymond J. DeMallie, Douglas R. Parks, and Robert Vézina, trans. Mildred Mott Wedel, Raymond J. DeMallie, and Robert Vézina (Lincoln and London: University of Nebraska Press, 2017), 418–25; Paul L. Stevens, "'One of the Most Beautiful Regions of the World': Paul Des Ruisseaux's Mémoire of the Wabash-Illinois Country in 1777," *Indiana Magazine of History* 83, no. 4 (1987): 360–79. Truteau was not a French émigré. He was born in Montréal in 1748 and arrived in St. Louis in 1774. Another transplanted *canadien,* Paul des Ruisseaux, wrote a short memoir concerning Illinois Country in 1777. For more on French chroniclers, see Martin Galvin, "French Travelers in the Ohio Valley, 1778–92," *Western Pennsylvania Historical Magazine* 59, no. 4 (1976): 463–72.

23. Parks, "Introduction," 58–61; W. Raymond Wood, *Prologue to Lewis and Clark: The Mackay and Evans Expedition* (Norman: University of Oklahoma Press, 2003), 82; Fernand Grenier, "Un plagiaire illustre: François Perrin du Lac," *Revue d'histoire de l'Amérique française* 7, no. 2 (1953): 207–23.

24. Similarly, French émigrés wrote narratives about the United States at the end of the eighteenth and start of the nineteenth centuries that were highly contradictory and combined ideas of progress and

retrogression, economic success and moral and intellectual failure. For an overview of how French views of the United States changed throughout the eighteenth and early nineteenth centuries, see François Furet, "De l'homme sauvage à l'homme historique: L'expérience américaine dans la culture française," *Économies, Sociétés, Civilisations* 33, no. 4 (1978): 729–39; Tangi Villerbu, *La conquête de l'Ouest: Le récit français de la nation américaine au xixe siècle* (Rennes: Presses universitaires de Rennes, 2015).

25. Echeverria, *Mirage in the West*, 192.

26. The literature on *métissage* is voluminous. For a sample of the work on Franco-Indigenous *métissage* with more specific focus on Canada, the *pays d'en haut*, and *pays des Illlinois*, see Tanis C. Thorne, *The Many Hands of My Relations: French and Indians on the Lower Missouri* (Columbia: University of Missouri Press, 1996); Susan Sleeper-Smith, "Women, Kin, and Catholicism: New Perspectives on the Fur Trade," *Ethnohistory* 47, no. 2 (2000): 423–52; Susan Sleeper-Smith, *Indian Women and French Men: Rethinking Cultural Encounter in the Western Great Lakes* (Amherst: University of Massachusetts Press, 2001); Gilles Havard, *Empire et métissages: Indiens et Français dans le Pays d'en Haut 1660–1715* (Sillery, QC: Septentrion, 2003; 2nd ed. 2017); Arnaud Balvay, *L'épée et la plume: Amérindiens et soldats des troupes de la marine en Louisiane et au Pays d'en haut (1683–1763)* (Québec: Presses Université Laval, 2006), 202–3; Kathleen DuVal, "Indian Intermarriage and Métissage in Colonial Louisiana," *William and Mary Quarterly* 65, no. 2 (2008): 267–304; Robert Michael Morrissey, "Kaskaskia Social Network: Kinship and Assimilation in the French-Illinois Borderlands, 1695–1735," *William and Mary Quarterly* 70, no. 1 (2013): 103–46; Alain Beaulieu and Stéphanie Chaffray, eds., *Représentation, métissage et pouvoir: La dynamique coloniale des échanges entre Autochtones, Européens et Canadiens (XVIe-XXe siècle)* (Québec: Presses de l'Université Laval, 2012); Sophie White, *Wild Frenchmen and Frenchified Indians: Material Culture and Race in Colonial Louisiana* (Philadelphia: University of Pennsylvania Press, 2013); Lucy Eldersveld Murphy, *Great Lakes Creoles: A French-Indian Community on the Northern Borderlands, Prairie Du Chien, 1750–1860* (New York: Cambridge University Press, 2014); Jacqueline Peterson, "Red River Redux: Métis Ethnogenesis and the Great Lakes Region," in *Contours of a People: Metis Family, Mobility, and History*, ed. Nicole St-Onge, Carolyn Podruchny, and Brenda Macdougall (Norman: University of Oklahoma Press, 2012), 22–58; Robert Englebert, "Colonial Encounters and the Changing Contours of Ethnicity: Pierre-Louis de Lorimier and Métissage at the Edges of Empire," *Ohio Valley History* 18, no. 1 (2018): 45–69.

27. Carl J. Ekberg, *French Roots in the Illinois Country: The Mississippi Frontier in Colonial Times* (Urbana: University of Illinois Press, 1998); Margaret Kimball Brown, *History as They Lived It: A Social History of Prairie Du Rocher, Ill.* (Tucson, AZ: The Patrice Press, 2005); Rénald Lessard, Jacques Mathieu, and Lina Gouger, "Peuplement colonisateur au Pays des Illinois," in *Proceedings of the Annual Meeting of the French Colonial Historical Society, Ste. Genevieve 1986*, ed. Philip Boucher and Serge Courville (Lanham, MD: University Press of America, 1988), 57–68; Cécile Vidal, "Le Pays des Illinois: Six villages français au cœur de l'Amérique du Nord, 1699–1765," in *De Québec à l'Amérique française, histoire et mémoire: Textes choisis du deuxième colloque de La Commission Franco-Québécoise sur les lieux de mémoire communs*, ed. Thomas Wien, Cécile Vidal, and Yves Frenette (Québec: Les Presses de l'Université Laval, 2006), 125–38.

28. Cécile Vidal, "Africains et Européens au Pays des Illinois durant la période française (1699–1765)," *French Colonial History* 3 (2003): 51–68; Carl J. Ekberg, *Stealing Indian Women: Native Slavery in the Illinois Country* (Urbana: University of Illinois Press, 2007); Brett Rushforth, *Bonds of Alliance:*

Indigenous and Atlantic Slaveries in New France (Chapel Hill: University of North Carolina Press, 2012); M. Scott Heerman, "Beyond Plantations: Indian and African Slavery in the Illinois Country, 1720–1780," *Slavery and Abolition: A Journal of Slave and Post-Slave Studies* (March 10, 2017): 1–22.

29. Lovejoy Library, Southern Illinois University, Edwardsville, Nicolas de Finiels, "Notice sur la Louisiane supérieure" (1803): 143.

30. Nicolas de Finiels described the population of St. Louis as, "a mix of *Canadiens*, creoles, Americans, and some French" and also described the black population of Upper Louisiana. See De Finiels, "Notice sur la Louisiane supérieure," 54, 143–46. For the Americanization of the region, see John Reda, *From Furs to Farms: The Transformation of the Mississippi Valley, 1762–1825* (DeKalb: Northern Illinois University Press, 2016). Depictions of a heterogeneous population in the late eighteenth and early nineteenth centuries were consistent with the long Indigenous history of ethnic and linguistic diversity in the region. See Susan M. Alt, *Cahokia's Complexities: Ceremonies and Politics of the First Mississippian Farmers* (Tuscaloosa: University of Alabama Press, 2018), 16–17; Robert Michael Morrissey, *Empire by Collaboration: Indians, Colonists, and Governments in Colonial Illinois Country* (Philadelphia: University of Pennsylvania Press, 2015), 14–38; Stephen Warren, *The Worlds the Shawnees Made: Migration and Violence in Early America* (Chapel Hill: University of North Carolina Press, 2014), 41–54, 78–79.

31. The John Carter Brown Library, Brown University, Providence, RI, C.-F. Volney, *Tableau du climat et du sol des Etats–Unis d'Amérique, suivi d'éclaircissemens sur la Floride, sur la colonie française au Scioto, sur quelques colonies canadiennes et sur les sauvages* (Paris: Courcier, 1803), 1: 448. Historians also regularly discuss ideas of colonial freedom, whether it is to negotiate from a position of strength, a form of rogue colonialism, or imperial officials referring to vagabonds on the fringes of empire. See Morrissey, *Empire by Collaboration*; Shannon Lee Dawdy, *Building the Devil's Empire: French Colonial New Orleans* (Chicago: University of Chicago Press, 2008). Also see Havard, *Histoire des coureurs de bois*, 326–27. For a detailed explanation of how the term French creole is being used in this essay, see Jay Gitlin, "From Private Stories to Public Memory: The Chouteau Descendants of St. Louis and the Production of History," in *Auguste Chouteau's Journal: Memory, Mythmaking & History in the Heritage of New France*, ed. Gregory P. Ames (St. Louis: Mercantile Library, University of Missouri St. Louis, 2010), 3–16; Tangi Villerbu, "Introduction," in *Une Amérique française: 1760–1860: Dynamiques du corridor créole*, ed. Guillaume Teasdale and Tangi Villerbu (Paris: Les Indes savantes, 2015), 7–16. For brevity, French creoles are also simply referred to as creoles throughout the essay, but I consistently use a lower case "c" to differentiate French creoles from mixed-race Creoles (*créoles de couleur*) in Louisiana and the Caribbean.

32. John Carter Brown Library, Brown University, Providence RI, Louis Dubroca, *L'itinéraire des français dans la Louisiane* (Paris: Fuchs, 1802), 78.

33. Dubroca, *L'itinéraire des français dans la Louisiane*, 78–83.

34. Kathleen DuVal has argued that there were limits to French-Arkansas *métissage*, while Robert Michael Morrissey has questioned the extent to which the Illinois required assistance in fighting the Iroquois. DuVal, "Indian Intermarriage and Métissage in Colonial Louisiana"; Morrissey, *Empire by Collaboration*, 31–38.

35. I examined more than twenty travel narratives that discussed Illinois Country during the latter half of the eighteenth century and early nineteenth century. Most provide a history of French colonialism with varying degrees of detail and accuracy.

36. John Carter Brown Library, Brown University, Providence RI, Berquin Duvallon, *Vue de la colonie espagnole du Mississippi, ou des provinces de Louisiane et Floride occidentale en l'année 1802* (Paris: l'Imprimerie Expéditive, 1803), 61.

37. De Finiels, "Notice sur la Louisiane supérieure," 54, 143.

38. De Finiels, "Notice sur la Louisiane supérieure," 146.

39. De Finiels, "Notice sur la Louisiane supérieure," 159.

40. De Finiels, "Notice sur la Louisiane supérieure," 163.

41. Havard, *Histoire des coureurs de bois*, 561–62. Vézina, "Appendix 1: The Language of Truteau," 415–418.

42. De Finiels, "Notice sur la Louisiane supérieure," 146–48, 157.

43. Furstenberg, *When the United States Spoke French*, 360; Parks, "Introduction," 58. Collot used Thomas Hutchins's maps from a voyage to Illinois Country between 1764 and 1775. Hutchins's journal barely mentions the francophone inhabitants, except for very short descriptions when discussing Vincennes, Ouiatenon, and St. Louis, and even then, with few details.

44. Edward Watts argues that many British and early Anglo-American travel narratives incorrectly labelled métis as *canadien*. In most cases there is no way to accurately ascertain whether all of Collot's *canadiens* were directly or a generation or two removed from the St. Lawrence Valley, or whether they were French creole (born in the country) and/or *métis* (mixed race). However, there appears to be a solid understanding on the part of Collot and other Frenchmen that *canadien* meant some type of connection with the St. Lawrence Valley. Watts, *In This Remote Country*, 136.

45. Havard, *Histoire des coureurs de bois*, 409.

46. John Carter Brown Library, Brown University, Providence RI, Victor Collot, *A Journey in North America, Containing a Survey of the Countries Watered by the Mississippi, Ohio, Missouri, and Other Affluing Rivers; with Exact Observations on the Course and Soundings of These Rivers; and on the Towns, Villages, Hamlets, and Farms of That Part of the New World; Followed by Philosophical, Political, Military and Commercial Remarks, and by a Projected Line of Frontiers and General Limits*, trans., an unknown Englishman under the supervision of the author (Paris: Arthus Bertrand, 1826), 1:165.

47. Collot, *A Journey in North America*, 2:137–38.

48. Collot, *A Journey in North America*, 1:185, 193.

49. Collot, *A Journey in North America*, 2:54–55.

50. Collot, *A Journey in North America*, 1:161–62, 214, 269. For waterscape reference, see Sayre, *Les Sauvages Américains*, 113–14.

51. Amy S. Wyngaard, *From Savage to Citizen: The Invention of the Peasant in the French Enlightenment* (Newark: University of Delaware Press, 2004), 13–16; Olive Patricia Dickason, *The Myth of the Savage: And the Beginnings of French Colonialism in the Americas* (Edmonton: University of Alberta Press, 1984), 80–84; Ter Ellingson, *The Myth of the Noble Savage* (Berkeley: University of California Press, 2001), 45–95; Havard, *Histoire des coureurs de bois*, 188–91.

52. William Max Nelson, "Colonizing France: Revolutionary Regeneration and the First French Empire," in Suzanne Desan, Lynn Hunt, and William Max Nelson, eds., *The French Revolution in Global Perspective* (Ithaca, NY: Cornell University Press, 2013), 74.

53. Sayre, *Les Sauvages Américains*, 126.

54. Collot, *A Journey in North America*, 2:194.

55. James Pritchard, *In Search of Empire: The French in the Americas, 1670–1730* (Cambridge: Cambridge University Press, 2004), 104; Robert Englebert and Nicole St.-Onge, "Paddling into History: French-Canadian Voyageurs and the Creation of a Fur Trade World, 1730–1804," in *De Pierre-Esprit Radisson à Louis Riel: Voyageurs et métis*, ed. Denis Combet, Gilles Lesage, and Luc Côté (Winnipeg: Presses universitaires de Saint-Boniface, 2014), 71–103; Havard, *Histoire des coureurs de bois*, 252–53.

56. Donald Chaput, "Treason or Loyalty? Frontier French in the American Revolution," *Illinois State Historical Society* 71, no. 4 (1978): 242–51; F. Murray Greenwood, *Legacies of Fear: Law and Politics in Quebec in the Era of the French Revolution* (Toronto: Osgoode Society, 1993), chap. 3; Jay Gitlin, *The Bourgeois Frontier: French Towns, French Traders and American Expansion* (New Haven, CT: Yale University Press, 2010), 51–59; Patricia Cleary, *The World, the Flesh, and the Devil: A History of Colonial St. Louis* (Columbia: University of Missouri Press, 2011), 285–93; Murphy, *Great Lakes Creoles*, 43–49; Catherine Cangany, *Frontier Seaport: Detroit's Transformation into an Atlantic Entrepôt* (Chicago: University of Chicago Press, 2014), 179. For more on loyalties in emerging northern borderlands in the era of American expansion, see Bethel Saler, *The Settlers' Empire: Colonialism and State Formation in America's Old Northwest* (Philadelphia: University of Pennsylvania Press, 2015); Lawrence B. A. Hatter, *Citizens of Convenience: The Imperial Origins of American Nationhood on the U.S.-Canadian Border* (Charlottesville: University of Virginia Press, 2016).

57. Collot, *A Journey in North America*, 2:2.

58. Collot, *A Journey in North America*, 2:12.

59. Peter C. Newman, *Caesars of the Wilderness: Company of Adventurers Vol. II* (Markham, ON: Viking, 1987), 23. Newman referred specifically to fur trade voyageurs as "magnificent river rats."

60. Collot, *A Journey in North America*, 1:269. Collot described Peoria as being inhabited by fifteen *canadien* families.

61. Havard, *Histoire des coureurs de bois*, 171–75.

62. Collot, *A Journey in North America*, 1:232–33.

63. Collot, *A Journey in North America*, 2:162; De Finiels, "Notice sur la Louisiane supérieure," 31–32.

64. J. G. Rosengarten, *French Colonists and Exiles in the United States* (Genealogical Publishing Com, 2009), 113. Roux traveled through America in 1784. The publication in 1790 was a propaganda piece designed to dissuade his fellow citizens back in France from moving to the failed settlement of the Scioto Land Company.

65. John Carter Brown Library, Brown University, Providence RI, Sergeant–Major Roux, *Le nouveau Mississippi, ou les dangers d'habiter les bords du Scioto, par un patriote voyageur* (Paris: Jacob–Sion, 1790), 18.

66. De Finiels, "Notice sur la Louisiane supérieure," 144.

67. The debate over *canadien* agricultural backwardness gained renewed traction in Québec in historical interpretations regarding the French-Canadian agrarian economy during the nineteenth century. See Fernand Ouellet, *Economic and Social History of Quebec, 1760–1850: Structures and Conjonctures*, trans. Institute of Canadian Studies (Ottawa: Gage Publishing, 1980); Gilles Paquet and Jean-Pierre Wallot, *Le Bas-Canada au tournant du 19e siècle: Restructuration et modernisation*, vol. 45, La Société Historique du Canada Brochure Historique (Ottawa: Canadian Historical Association, 1985).

68. Collot, *A Journey in North America*, 1:180.

69. It is worth noting that this was not exclusive to visitors to Illinois Country. A number of colonial elites also tended to describe small villages and common people and workers in this manner.

70. Collot, *A Journey in North America*, 1:277.

71. De Finiels, "Notice sur la Louisiane supérieure," 41. Nicolas de Finiels at times extolls the virtues of *Canadiens* like Collot, but he also lumps them together with creoles, such as in his description of Carondelet.

72. For examples of metropolitan ministers and colonial officials fearing unproductive agricultural and the depopulation of the St Lawrence valley because of the illicit fur trade, see ANOM, COL C11A 33/fo1.3–8v, Lettre de Vaudreuil et Bégon au ministre, Québec, 12 novembre 1712; ANOM, C11A, 125/fo1.393, Mémoire pour servir d'instruction au marquis de Beauharnois, Versailles, 7 mai 1726; ANOM, COL C11A 91/fo1.121v-122, Lettre de La Galissonière au ministre concernant le pays des Illinois, Québec, 01 septembre 1748. For an ecclesiastical response to *coureurs de bois*, see Pierre François-Xavier de Charlevoix, *Histoire et description générale de la nouvelle France* (Paris: Chez Rollin Fils, Libraire, 1744), 454, 532.

73. W. J. Eccles, "The Fur Trade and Eighteenth-Century Imperialism," *William and Mary Quarterly* 40, no. 3 (1983): 341–62; Dale Miquelon, "Envisioning the French Empire: Utrecht, 1711–1713," *French Historical Studies* 24, no. 4 (2001): 653–77; Christopher M. Parsons, *A Not-So-New World: Empire and Environment in French Colonial North America* (Philadelphia: University of Pennsylvania Press, 2018), 97–124.

74. W. J. Eccles, *Canada under Louis XIV, 1663–1701* (Toronto: McClelland & Stewart, 1964), chap. 5, "Colbert's Compact Colony Policy," 59–76. See also W. J. Eccles, *The French in North America, 1500–1783* (Markham, ON: Fitzhenry & Whiteside, 1998), 93–95, and *Frontenac: The Courtier Governor* (Toronto: McClelland & Stewart, 1959), 77–79, 97. For more on Jean-Baptiste Colbert's vision for empire and a compact colony in the St. Lawrence Valley, see James Pritchard, *In Search of Empire: The French in the Americas, 1670–1730* (Cambridge: Cambridge University Press, 2004), 197–204, 209–14, 234–37; Gilles Havard et Cécile Vidal, *Histoire de l'Amérique Française* (Paris: Flammarion, 2006), 66–67, 271; Jacob Soll, *The Information Master: Jean-Baptiste Colbert's Secret State Intelligence System* (Ann Arbor: University of Michigan Press, 2009), 51–53, 113–19; Kenneth J. Banks, *Chasing Empire across the Sea: Communications and the State in the French Atlantic, 1713–1763* (Montréal: McGill-Queen's University Press, 2002), 22–27.

75. Crouch, *Nobility Lost*, 71–72; Havard, *Histoire des coureurs de bois*, 152–54.

76. Thomas Wien, "Familles paysannes et marché de l'engagement pour le commerce des fourrures au Canada au XVIIIe siècle," in *Famille et marché XVIe-XXe siècles*, ed. Christian Dessureault, John A. Dickinson, and Joseph Goy (Sillery: Septentrion, 2003), 167–80.

77. Notions of backward French creoles pop up periodically in scholarly work, most notably in Lippincott's work, but most recently in that of Royot. See I. Lippincott, "Industry among the French in the Illinois Country," *Journal of Political Economy* 18, no. 2 (1910): 114–28; Daniel Royot, *Divided Loyalties in a Doomed Empire: The French in the West from New France to the Lewis and Clark Expedition* (Newark: University of Delaware Press, 2007).

78. A colonial culture based on notions of terra nullius was regularly employed by early modern empires, even if the term itself was rarely used. The term gained more general usage in the nineteenth century and policies were linked directly with the term itself. Andrew Fitzmaurice, *Sovereignty, Property and Empire, 1500–2000* (Cambridge: Cambridge University Press, 2014), 302–5; Robert J. Miller, "The Doctrine of Discovery, Manifest Destiny, and American Indians," in *Why You Can't Teach United States*

History without American Indians, ed. Susan Sleeper-Smith et al. (Chapel Hill: University of North Carolina Press, 2015), 88, 98; Cornelius J. Jaenen, "French Sovereignty and Native Nationhood during the French Régime," in *Sweet Promises: A Reader on Indian-White Relations in Canada,* ed. J. R. Miller (Toronto: University of Toronto Press, 1991), 19–42.

79. Havard, *Histoire des coureurs de bois,* 258–62, 409–12.

80. De Finiels, "Notice sur la Louisiane supérieure," 144.

81. De Finiels, "Notice sur la Louisiane supérieure," 155.

82. See Choquette's essay in this collection; Havard, *Histoire des coureurs de bois,* 39–60.

83. Carolyn Podruchny, "Baptizing Novices: Ritual Moments among French Canadian Voyageurs in the Montreal Fur Trade, 1780–1821," *Canadian Historical Review* 83, no. 2 (2002): 165–95; Carolyn Podruchny, *Making the Voyageur World: Travelers and Traders in the North American Fur Trade* (Toronto: University of Toronto Press, 2006), 144–45.

84. Robert Englebert, "Merchant Representatives and the French River World, 1763–1803," *Michigan Historical Review* 34, no. 1 (2008): 66; Gitlin, *The Bourgeois Frontier,* 27; Teasdale and Villerbu, eds., *Une Amérique française: 1760–1860: Dynamiques du corridor créole;* Havard, *Histoire des coureurs de bois,* 8. Gilles Havard's notion of *circulations pelletières* captures this cultural ethos of mobility, at least as it pertained to the fur trade.

85. The reality on the ground in New France had been far more complex of course. See Allan Greer, *Property and Dispossession: Natives, Empire and Land in Early Modern North America* (Cambridge: Cambridge University Press, 2018), 145–88.

86. Havard, *Histoire des coureurs de bois,* 409.

87. Furstenberg, *When the United States Spoke French,* 274.

88. Andreas Motsch, "La réception des moeurs de Joseph-François Lafitau en France et en Allemagne au XVIIIe siècle ou comment faire de Lafitau un éclaireur allemand," in *Représentation, métissage et pouvoir: La dynamique coloniale des échanges entre Autochtones, Européens et Canadiens (XVIe-XXe siècle),* ed. Alain Beaulieu and Stéphanie Chaffray (Québec: Presses de l'Université Laval, 2012), 175.

89. Sayre, *Les Sauvages Américains,* 129, 139. Sayre also indicates that "The power to take away and replace the elements of 'savagery' and of 'civilization' is fundamental to colonialism."

90. Réal Ouellet and Mylene Tremblay, "From the Good Savage to the Degenerate Indian: The Amerindian in the Accounts of Travel to American," in *Decentring the Renaissance: Canada and Europe in Multidisciplinary Perspective 1500–1700,* ed. Germaine Warkentin and Carolyn Podruchny (Toronto: University of Toronto Press, 2001), 163.

91. Collot, *A Journey in North America,* 1:232–33.

92. The words *métissage* and *mentalité* not specifically used, but rather frequently alluded to.

93. Volney, *Tableau du climat,* 1:420.

94. Volney, *Tableau du climat,* 1:420.

95. Echeverria, *Mirage in the West,* 192; Whitridge, "French Émigrés in Philadelphia," 294–95.

96. Volney, *Tableau du climat,* 1:420.

97. Furstenberg, *When the United States Spoke French,* 11.

98. Whitridge, "French Émigrés in Philadelphia," 293.

99. Ekberg notes that it is unclear if de Finiels had in fact been commissioned to write his report or if he did so with the hope of securing compensation from the governor. Nicolas de Finiels, *An Ac-*

count of Upper Louisiana, ed. Carl J. Ekberg and William E. Foley (Columbia: University of Missouri Press, 1989), 9.

100. Volney, *Tableau du climat*, 1:404.

101. Volney, *Tableau du climat*, 1:398.

102. Volney, *Tableau du climat*, 1:396.

103. Volney, *Tableau du climat*, 1:392.

104. De Finiels, "Notice sur la Louisiane supérieure," 152–54. For a few works on French colonial treatment of Indigenous sartorial expression and *métissage*, see Timothy J. Shannon, "Dressing for Success on the Mohawk Frontier: Hendrick, William Johnson, and the Indian Fashion," *William and Mary Quarterly* 53, no. 1 (1996): 13–42; Stéphanie Chaffray, "Corps, territoire et paysage à les images et les textes viatiques en Nouvelle-France (1701–1756)," *Revue d'histoire de L'Amérique française* 59 (2005): 7–52; Celine Carayon, "Beyond Words: Nonverbal Communication, Performance, and Acculturation in the Early French-Indian Atlantic (1500–1701)" (Ph.D. diss., College of William and Mary, 2010); Catherine Cangany, "Detroit, the Manufacturing Frontier, and the Empire of Consumption, 1701–1835," *William and Mary Quarterly* 69, no. 2 (April 2012): 265–304; White, *Wild Frenchmen and Frenchified Indians*.

105. De Finiels, "Notice sur la Louisiane supérieure," 66.

106. Petter A. Goddard, "The Devil in New France: Jesuit Demonology, 1611–1650," *Canadian Historical Review* 78, no. 1 (1997): 43; Tracy Neal Leavelle, "'Bad Things' and 'Good Hearts': Meditation, Meaning, and the Language of Illinois Christianity," *Church History* 76, no. 2 (2007): 377.

107. Saliha Belmessous, *Assimilation and Empire: Uniformity in French and British Colonies, 1541–1954* (Oxford: Oxford University Press, 2013), 15, 27–56; Mairi Cowan, "Education, Francisation, and Shifting Colonial Priorities at the Ursuline Convent in Seventeenth-Century Québec," *Canadian Historical Review* 99, no. 1 (2018): 7, 23–24, 28; Gilles Havard, "'Protection' and 'Unequal Alliance': The French Conception of Sovereignty over Indians in New France," in *French and Indians in the Heart of North America, 1630–1815*, ed. Robert Englebert and Guillaume Teasdale (East Lansing: Michigan State University Press, 2013), 113–17, 127–28.

108. Guillaume Aubert, "'The Blood of France': Race and Purity of Blood in the French Atlantic World," *William and Mary Quarterly* 61, no. 3 (2004): 469–72; Carl J. Ekberg, "Marie Rouensa-8cate8a and the Foundations of French Illinois," *Illinois Historical Journal* 84, no. 3 (1991): 153; Tracy Neal Leavelle, *The Catholic Calumet: Colonial Conversions in French and Indian North America* (Philadelphia: University of Pennsylvania Press, 2011); Morrissey, "Kaskaskia Social Network," 105–8; White, *Wild Frenchmen and Frenchified Indians*.

109. De Finiels, "Notice sur la Louisiane supérieure," 143, 151–52.

110. Aubert, "'The Blood of France': Race and Purity If Blood in the French Atlantic World," 476–77; Belmessous, *Assimilation & Empire: Uniformity in French & British Colonies, 1541–1954*, 51, 57–58; William Max Nelson, "Colonizing France: Revolutionary Regeneration and the First French Empire," in Suzanne Desan, Lynn Hunt, and William Max Nelson, eds. *The French Revolution in Global Perspective* (Ithaca, NY: Cornell University Press, 2013), 81–82. Also see: William Max Nelson, "Making Men: Enlightenment Ideas of Racial Engineering," *American Historical Review* 115, no. 5 (December 2010): 1364–94.

111. De Finiels, *An Account of Upper Louisiana*, 13–14.

112. De Finiels, "Notice sur la Louisiane supérieure," 149–50.

113. Furstenberg, *When the United States Spoke French*, 365–75.

114. Francis D. Cogliano, *Revolutionary America, 1763–1815: A Political History* (New York: Routledge, 2000), 178.

115. Furstenberg, *When the United States Spoke French*, 375–79.

116. De Finiels, *An Account of Upper Louisiana*, 9; Cogliano, *Revolutionary America, 1763–1815*, 178. Most *récits de voyage* discussed in this essay were published in the late eighteenth and early nineteenth centuries. Nicolas de Finiels's *An Account of Upper Louisiana* is a rare exception and was first translated/edited/published for public consumption by Carl Ekberg and William Foley in 1989.

117. De Finiels, "Notice sur la Louisiane supérieure," 1.

Chasing *La Chasse-Galerie*
Honoré Beaugrand and the Life of a Journalistic Voyageur

JAY GITLIN AND RYAN ANDRÉ BRASSEAUX

Honoré Beaugrand could not bear the intensity of Québec's winter. "During the winter days when I could not put my nose outdoors," he holed up by the hearth, finding comfort in French-Canadian folktales still circulating in the province. He immersed himself in a world of werewolves, goblins, First Nations peoples, and romantic tales about French Canada's past. "[I] amused myself by collecting these stories and compiling a personal volume of tales, which was never meant to be sold."[1] Beaugrand fixed his imagination on one legend in particular, *la chasse-galerie*—a yarn about lumbermen who make a deal with the Devil for the chance at a New Year's kiss from their sweethearts hundreds of miles away.

On New Year's Eve 1858, the deep Canadian winter enveloped the Ross timber camp situated at the head of the Gatineau River. Timber workers huddled inside of the shanty encampment, packing their pipes with strong tobacco and filling their goblets with Jamaican rum. Joe, the camp cook, who had worked at the Ross camp for forty years, regaled his colleagues with a fantastic story from his *pendard* youth. He recalled another New Year's Eve about thirty-five years earlier. After a long night of drinking, the camp boss, Baptiste Durand, abruptly roused the cook with a proposition: "I am going to Lavaltrie to see my sweetheart. Will you come with me?"[2] "To Lavaltrie," Joe exclaimed, "are you crazy?"[3] Three hundred miles of Canadian wilderness separated Lavaltrie from Ross. An expedition of that magnitude would normally take more than two months to complete. Moreover, the two lumbermen were to report to work the next morning. But Durand suggested the impossible: that he could make the roundtrip journey in only six hours. Joe the cook could too, that is, if he joined the oarsmen of Durand's enchanted canoe "under the protected wing of *le diable* [the Devil] himself."[4] Joe elaborated, "Baptiste Durand proposed that I should join him and run *la chasse-galerie;* risk the salvation of my soul for the fun of going to give a New Year's kiss to my *blonde* at Lavaltrie."[5] The cook agreed.

With the canoe filled with lumbermen, the voyageurs collectively recited an incantation: "*Satan!* king of the infernal regions, we promise to sell you our souls, if within the following six hours we pronounce *le nom du bon Dieu* [the name of God] ... or if we touch a cross on the voyage."[6] With the final utterance of the spell, the canoe rose over five hundred feet in the night air, then furiously accelerated toward Lavaltrie at 150 miles per hour with the first stroke of the paddle. The canoe's bow whistled through the winter sky under the light of a full moon. "On we went like *tous les diables,* passing over forests, rivers, towns, villages, and leaving behind us a trail of sparks," the cook explained.[7] When the oarsmen arrived at their destination, they landed on the banks of the St. Lawrence and made their way toward a New Year's house party. Baptiste Durand reminded his companions not to evoke the name of the Lord, to avoid anything shaped like a cross, and to avoid alcohol at all costs.

The party's host, Batissette Augé, welcomed the oarsmen, who gladly joined the fête. The lumbermen danced for two hours while Joe the cook enjoyed the company of Liza Guimbette. Dancing together "made me forget that I had risked the salvation of my soul to have the pleasure of pressing her soft white hand in mine."[8] Revelry continued deep into the night. But when the hour struck four o'clock, the crew quietly slipped out of the dance and headed toward their canoe for the return trip to Ross. All of the oarsmen had minded Baptiste's warning, except Durand himself, whose drunken antics caused the canoe to crash into a snow bank in Montréal. The oarsmen tackled their inebriated leader, bound him with ropes, then gagged him to prevent any utterance "that might give us up to perdition."[9] They threw Durand into the bottom of the canoe and resumed the journey. But just as the bewitched travelers reached the Ross camp, the canoe struck the top of a towering pine, forcing all of the oarsmen to fall from the sky.

"About eight o'clock the next morning," Joe recounted, concluding his story, "I awoke in my bunk, in the cabin, whither some of our *camarades [sic]* had conveyed us after having found us to our necks in a neighboring snowbank, at the foot of a monster pine-tree." Joe recalled how grateful he and his fellow travelers were for not suffering serious injury. He ended his fable with a cautionary moral. "All I can say, my friends, is that it is not so amusing as some people might think, to travel in mid-air, in the dead of winter, under the guidance of Beelzebub, running *la chasse-galerie*," especially when a drunkard is steering the boat. "Take my advice, and don't listen to anyone who would try to rope you in for such a trip," he continued, "for it is better to run all the rapids of the Ottawa and the St. Lawrence on a raft, than to travel in partnership with *le diable* himself."[10]

La chasse-galerie depicted the romance of French-Canadian history—replete with religious imagery and allure of the supernatural—in ways that resonated with Honoré Beaugrand's life experiences as a journeyman. When Beaugrand finally decided to publish the folktale in 1891 in *La Patrie*, the Montréal newspaper he owned and edited, the author deployed first-person narration to project himself into the cook character. To be sure, Beaugrand recognized his own wanderlust in Joe. The cook flirted with temptation and adventure in Catholicism's forbidden recesses. Like the oarsmen of the *chasse-galerie*, the author became a kind of legendary voyageur across his own lifetime.

Honoré Beaugrand was born on March 24, 1848, in Saint-Joseph-de-Lanoraie (Lower Canada). He began his teenage years as a prospective member of the religious order Clerics of St. Viateur, but opted instead for the secular world of ideas and adventure. He became a soldier of fortune, author and newspaper man, entrepreneur, politician, and eventually travel writer and folklorist. Beaugrand spent a lifetime crossing borders. He traveled extensively across North America, Europe, French North Africa, and Asia.[11] En route, Beaugrand exponentially expanded both his worldview and his conceptualization of francophone culture's place in North America.

Beaugrand's secular perspective, and indeed continental influence, represented an anomaly in contrast to his French-Canadian peers. Across the nineteenth century, Catholic clergy structured, and in some ways dominated, life in French Canada. The religious controlled francophone education. Bishops and priests influenced politics. In effect, Catholicism circumscribed French-Canadian conceptualizations of modernity, nationalism, and cultural identity.[12] Beaugrand realized that the only way to gain perspective, like the oarsmen of the *chasse-galerie*, was to make a deal with the Devil. He became a born-again apostate. Beaugrand married a Protestant woman (in a Protestant service no less) and refused to baptize his children in the Catholic Church. When his severe asthma accelerated his death in 1906, he eschewed his last rites while demanding to be cremated in direct opposition to church doctrine.[13]

Honoré Beaugrand found his own flying canoe in secular thought, cross-continental travel, liberalism, and Canadian folklore. Indeed, Canada looked different from a vantage point five to six hundred feet above the doldrums of daily life. This restless voyageur constantly pushed toward the horizon at the speed of modernity, redefining boundaries and parameters of French-Canadian culture along the way. Neither Québec nor Canada could fully contain Beaugrand's understanding of *canadien*. Rather, Beaugrand harnessed his own mobility to redefine from a continental, even hemispheric perspective what it meant to be from the province of Québec. The former soldier deployed print culture as a means of redefining space and place for French Canadians within a transnational context defined here as francophone North America. Beaugrand rewrote the script for francophone culture within the United States, from New Orleans to New England, while working as a roving journalist. He wrote against mainstream opinion in Canada and offered critiques of French-Canadian culture, religion, and nationalism. Perhaps most controversially, Beaugrand came out in support of the millions of French-Canadian emigrants who left their failing farms looking for work in New England's mill towns during the second half of the nineteenth century. Beaugrand took aim at those acerbic American and French-Canadian commentators who vilified these transnational communities. His campaign culminated in 1878 with a sympathetic novel highlighting those disenfranchised migrants titled *Jeanne la fileuse*.[14] A decade later, while he was visiting Paris, Beaugrand's vision reached a hemispheric scope as he contemplated the place of Canada and French-Canadian art in the world.

"Chasing *la chasse-galerie*" considers Honoré Beaugrand's cultural imprint on North America and beyond. Beaugrand celebrated French-Canadian mobility—rather than an attachment to the land, place, and parish—while reanimating an imagined voyageur identity that transcended parochial boundaries. The journalist, journeyman, and Montréal mayor believed that new technologies and republican ideas about individualism could help make francophone North America visible on the world stage. Beaugrand's secularism complicated his attachment to traditional French-Canadian nationalism. He rejected the nineteenth-century convention that effectively twined Catholicism, political identity, and the enduring idea of cultural survival. Instead, Beaugrand used his journalistic voice to amplify the call for a modern francophone North America that could withstand, even thrive against, the rapid currents of change reshaping the continent.

Marching to Mexico, Translating New England

The speed of Beaugrand's metaphorical flying canoe was only matched by its modern counterpart—the railroad. As the editor of the 1980 Fides edition of *Jeanne la fileuse*, Roger Le Moine, observed of Beaugrand: "He shows great enthusiasm for the innovation of his century. How many pages did he not dedicate to the railroad."[15] With almost magical mobility, this iron canoe delivered Beaugrand and hundreds of thousands of other French-Canadian *coureurs de facterie* to New England, providing new opportunities and perspectives.

Beaugrand left Québec for Mexico at the age of seventeen in 1865 to fight for the French emperor Maximilien. Perhaps, as with other young French Canadians, he did so to support the fading dream of a French empire in North America. Beaugrand would not reside again in his native land for thirteen years.[16] After the demise of Maximilien, and after having spent time in France with friends, Beaugrand worked briefly for New Orleans's French-language daily, *L'Abeille*.[17] Then in 1871, Beaugrand showed up in Fall River, Massachusetts, laboring as a building painter.[18]

Across the 1870s, Beaugrand became intent on finding a home, a community, and domestic life *à la façon du siècle*. In 1873, he joined the Freemasons (bringing him into closer contact with aspiring young men outside of the French community), and later he married Eliza Walker in St. Paul's Methodist Church of Fall River.[19] That same year Beaugrand founded the first of many newspapers he would create across his lifetime, *L'Echo du Canada*.[20] He also worked toward the social advancement of French-Canadian expatriates by founding a labor union for Fall River's French-Canadian laborers and, in 1874, the Association Montcalm de Fall River, a society primarily for aspiring young French Canadians who wished to discuss the issues of the day and have a reading room like those enjoyed by "the English, the Germans, and the Irish." It was to be a place having "an exclusively national character" which would also celebrate "the history of our country" and "the memory of the great deeds of our ancestors."[21]

Beaugrand helped curate a new francophone space in Fall River amidst waves of French-Canadian emigration from Québec to New England from 1865 to 1873. There were 37,420 French Canadians in New England in 1860. By 1900, the region's French-speaking population numbered 573,000.[22] In Fall River, the French-Canadian population numbered only 10 in 1860 but steadily increased to 9,000 in 1880 and 33,000 by 1900.[23] Eventually, French Canadians would comprise almost a third of the population of this small industrial city. But the "Little Canada" community was just emerging when Beaugrand arrived, which allowed him to build bridges across the broader community as he sought to thrive in his new environment. At the same time, he kept his French-Canadian voice and created a public context for others to speak, read, and think *en français*. *L'Echo du Canada* was at the center of this project. The newspaper was the first journalistic seed Honoré Beaugrand would plant in the transnational French North American community.[24] Straddling the transnational divide, Beaugrand clearly aimed to embrace an expanded notion of his people and his country, vowing in his newspaper's founding statement to support "the interest of Fall River's French-Canadian population."[25] He adopted a somewhat progressive and anticlerical position as he aligned his new Association Montcalm with the Institut canadien de Montréal.[26] Beaugrand, on his way to an increasingly progressive political stance, still maintained the *devise* or slogan of his ancestors on the masthead of his newspaper: "God, Honor, and Country."[27]

Bridging positions and borders, Beaugrand refused to cling to the orthodoxy of conservative politicians back in Québec or abandon his French-Canadian people on the move to New England. The increase in emigration that had occurred after 1865 prompted anguished cries from many leaders in Québec. Journalist and liberal politician Laurent-Olivier David wrote what a "triste bilan" (a sad state of affairs) in 1871. Others lamented the "damage" being done to Québec, now hemorrhaging population.[28] Many of the clergy and their conservative "blue" political allies blamed the emigrants themselves for seeking luxury and an easier life in the States. Jules-Paul Tardivel, the author of an ultramontanist and nationalist novel, *Pour la Patrie*, likened the United States in 1873 to "a vast Sodom."[29] Tardivel's novel represented a nearly opposite position from Beaugrand's *Jeanne la fileuse*.[30] Conservative politician Georges-Étienne Cartier is reputed to have said, "Let them go. It is only the rabble that go. We, the good ones, stay, and the country will be better for it."[31]

On February 23, 1875, the Québec assembly passed a Repatriement Act to encourage the return of expatriates. Such an act offered incentives for Franco-New Englanders to return to the unsettled Canadian lands owned by the British Crown. Beaugrand attacked the act in his newspaper, advocating instead for the annexation of Québec to the United States. Beaugrand argued that *repatriement* was not a viable plan given the true causes of emigration—namely, poverty and indebtedness; the inability, despite hard work, to make a living off the land; and the lack of industry in the province. Beaugrand almost came to blows with fellow journalist and *repatriement* champion Ferdinand Gagnon, editor of Worcester's newspaper *Le*

Travailleur.[32] Beaugrand had become more critical of the issue in his new newspaper, *La République*. He had sold *L'Echo du Canada* in June 1875 after the paper had become a weekly (*hebdomadaire*) journal in January of that year. Now writing in Boston, Beaugrand chided his opponent Gagnon about his weight and said when he appeared on the streets of Worcester, grandmothers clutched their rosaries and busybodies shouted: "C'est Croquemitaine Gagnon" (It's Gagnon the Bogeyman). In turn, Gagnon denounced Beaugrand as a Freemason and religious hypocrite and a *spadassin* (bully) to be avoided.[33] The exchange took place in December 1875.

Jeanne the Spinner

For several years, from 1875 to 1877, Beaugrand led a peripatetic life as a publisher and journalist, locating his newspaper, *La République,* for extended periods in Boston, St. Louis, and Fall River. Beaugrand finally moved to Ottawa, back in Canada, in February 1878. It was during this tumultuous period in Beaugrand's life that he published his novel, *Jeanne la fileuse: Épisode de l'émigration franco-canadienne aux États-Unis.*

Though it is hardly a literary masterpiece, *Jeanne la fileuse* is a record of Franco-American life in New England in the late nineteenth century. As with other works of fiction serialized in nineteenth-century newspapers, context affected content. Beaugrand's novel blended reportage, ethnography, and sentimental plot lines— some borrowed from real-life events in Fall River. Even as it partakes of a broader French-Canadian literary tradition, it is often credited with being the first Franco-American novel.[34] At the same time, it is very much a political statement by Beaugrand. In this work, he defends "the honour and good name of my compatriot emigrants" against the negative sentiments like those expressed by the Montréal newspaper *La Minerve,* which characterized Beaugrand and his compatriots in acerbic terms: "how cowardly, lowly, and despicable are these Canadians of the United States, wrapped in their nothingness, and with ridiculous self-conceit equaled only by their insignificance."[35] As Beaugrand states in the preface to the first edition, the book is a "response to the slander launched by certain political circles against the Franco-Canadian populations in the United States."[36]

Jeanne la fileuse emphasizes the power of mobility and travel to break through the limits of the status quo. The opportunity and adventure of being on the road also meant being detached from home. Liberation came at a cost, the sensation of exile. In that sense, *Jeanne la fileuse* belongs squarely in the Franco-North American literary tradition from the Jesuit *Relations* to Jack Kerouac. The scene that Beaugrand describes in chapter 3 of part 2, "*Le voyage,*" is a moving description, an ethnography, of the journey of emigration itself. Beaugrand—the reporter, novelist, and defender of his people—is inscribing, validating, and making legible a new landscape in French North America. Far from hounding Franco-Americans about *repatriation* and their obligations to *la patrie,* the author traces their movement through the new space they created in New England. The French-Canadian "nation" thus follows the train lines carrying emigrants south.

Beaugrand describes three railway lines serving "passengers and goods between the main cities of the Province of Quebec and the states of New England: the 'Passumpsic Railroad Company,' also known as the 'Montreal & Boston Air Line'; 'the Central Vermont Rail-Road'; and the Canadian company of Grand Trunk."[37] By the 1890s, the Boston and Maine (B & M) had leased and added a number of smaller local lines including the Connecticut and Passumpsic RR, the Concord Railroad, the Boston and Lowell RR, and others. When one looks at an older atlas and gazetteer, one easily finds the B & M outlined in a map of the region.[38] Then one notices that many of the major centers of French-Canadian emigration were stops along what Beaugrand describes as the Passumpsic Railroad Company: St. Alban's and St. Johnsbury in Vermont; Manchester in New Hampshire; Lowell, and, of course, Fall River in Massachusetts. A ticket, Beaugrand writes, cost only ten dollars, and that included baggage and shipping of the family's belongings. The fictional Dupuis family, along with Jeanne Girard (later, *la fileuse*), boarded the train in Montréal at four o'clock in the afternoon. They arrived in Lowell, Massachusetts, at seven o'clock in the morning, having traveled through Vermont and New Hampshire. An hour later, they found themselves at a beautiful, spacious station in Boston. "The emigrants could not help but admire this station," he wrote, "which is without a doubt one of the most beautiful buildings of its kind in the United States."[39] There, the family found fine accommodations and "waiting rooms for ladies and gentlemen."[40] They arrived in Fall River at two o'clock in the afternoon, less than twenty-four hours after their departure from Montréal.[41] Along the way, they found that "most of the employees speak and write in the two languages [French and English]."[42] This would certainly have been a concern for most of the émigrés.

Beaugrand eased the fears of those contemplating the trip and life change. Though some of his arguments could be debated, Beaugrand was working against the views of some back in Canada that the emigrants were either greedy, miserable in their new homes, disloyal, or all three. Accusing different Canadian administrations of being preoccupied with "a politics wholly of selfishness," Beaugrand insisted that the building of roads, canals, and railways had transformed America and created the conditions of prosperity.[43] In the United States, French-Canadian emigrants could find work and feed their families. Indeed, a large family was not a burden but a source of income.[44] To answer any lingering questions about their attachment to their church, their culture, and the memory of their ancestors, Beaugrand exclaims, in the voice of his emigrant: "My God! Father [priest], you know me too well to believe that I would leave here a past to which I am attached by the memory of my ancestors to go abroad to serve the others, if I could do otherwise."[45]

For Beaugrand, it was necessary for the French Canadian to move out and move on. If conditions were not going to change in Canada, then a new home outside the nation and the province must be found. The country followed the people. In the course of his journalistic novel, Beaugrand provides what one scholar, Cynthia Lees, describes as a "distorted representation of living and working conditions in Fall River."[46] It is certainly true that the American "hospitality" that Beaugrand reports was not much in evidence. Historians such as Mark Richard, Yves Roby, and others have documented the rather hostile environment that the emigrants found in the small cities of New England where the "welcome wagon" included KKK cross burnings and deplorable working conditions. Xenophobic attitudes even extended as far as the Bureau of Statistics of Labor for Massachusetts, where the organization's head, Carroll D. Wright, described French Canadians as "the Chinese of the Eastern States" who had no interest in America's social and political institutions.[47] An infamous *New York Times* editorial of June 6, 1892, quoted Dr. Egbert C. Smyth as saying that the "migration of these people is part of a priestly scheme now fervently fostered in Canada for the purpose of bringing New-England under the control of the Roman Catholic faith."[48]

Cynthia Lees later points out that Beaugrand's "pro-capitalist stance" in the second part of the novel "that champions industrialization (with its inherent exploitation of the working class)" contrasts uncomfortably with his celebration of the Patriots of 1837 and their "egalitarian ideology."[49] Yet, Beaugrand ends the novel with a tragic fire in Granite Mill, an episode based on a real fire in September of 1874. Beaugrand even incorporates accounts of the real fire from his newspaper into the novel, including a list of actual workers who died or were injured in the fire. The real hero of the novel, Michel Dupuis, the oldest son of the emigrant family, dies in the fire saving Jeanne and two children. The fire and its destructive wake certainly undercuts the notion of an uncritical embrace of industrialization by Beaugrand. More to the point, Beaugrand and other liberals, such as future Québec premier Louis-Alexandre Taschereau, felt strongly that they must counter the views of conservative French Canadians who supported "an antimaterialist dream-world" where an unchanging traditional lifestyle bound by the rural parish could flourish. As Bernard Vigod asserts, the old "industry versus agriculture" debate pitted liberals against "a familiar and odious ultramontane theme: that human progress was incompatible with Catholicism, and by implication with French-Canadian survival."[50] Beaugrand was supporting the need for a viable future in championing the actions and choices of those who emigrated from Québec to New England. Regardless of the conditions to be found in the region's small industrial cities, mobility was the key to freedom for Beaugrand and his fellow émigrés. Movement was an essential tool in the search for economic stability and had long been a staple in Beaugrand's life.

Beaugrand's embrace of mobility was not just spatial; it was also temporal—a movement away from Québec's traumatic history. To be sure, the Conquest (the British Conquest of 1763) initiated the source of cultural trauma.[51] However, the historical rift caused by the Rebellions of 1837–38, the second key theme in the novel, compounded the effects stemming from the fall of Québec.[52] (The Beaugrand novel sees 1837 as a real break, not only between Anglo power structures and an emerging French-Canadian republican, even democratic, voice, but also a split—perhaps of longer standing—between those who have felt oppressed and conquered all along and those who were *vendus* or at least made their peace with the new regime after 1763 and during the 1837–38 Rebellions.) One of the heroes in *Jeanne la fileuse*, Pierre Montépel, the son of a wealthy landowner in Lavaltrie, falls in love with Jeanne Girard, who comes from a poorer village across the river, Contrecœur. The previous history shared by their fathers complicates the first part of the novel. Jean-Baptiste Girard and many of his fellow villagers in Contrecœur became *Patriotes* in 1837. The grandfather of Jean-Louis Montépel (Pierre's father), however, aligned himself with English rule after 1763 and flourished economically. When violence erupted in 1837, Jean-Louis Montépel became a British informant and betrayed the hiding place of Girard and his fellow rebel Amable Marion. Forced into exile in Burlington, Vermont, Girard lost his property back home. Jeanne's father reveals this past history but accepts Pierre and grants him his daughter's hand in marriage. Jean-Louis Montépel, meanwhile, refuses to grant permission for the marriage: "Well! Pierre Montépel, I tell you never! Never! I will not give my consent to your marriage with Jean-Baptiste Girard's daughter."[53]

The first part of the novel ends with the death of the kindly Jean-Baptiste Girard. Jeanne is now an orphan.

The novel's epilogue, most of which centers on life in Fall River, provides a reconciliation. The elder Montépel relinquishes his estate to his son while finally accepting young Jeanne to the family. Despite this reconciliation, both fathers—and the historical rift they represent—must be transcended just as the deaths of Wolfe and Montcalm in the Battle on the Plains of Abraham prefigure the birth of a new nation for painter Benjamin West.[54] For a prosperous future to emerge, the conservatism of the past must be discarded. The alternative was less clear. Beaugrand, like his characters, carried his nation with him when he relocated to his native Québec, where he reinvented himself yet again in the Montréal mayor's office.

From Transnational to International

Upon his return, Beaugrand established another successful newspaper in 1879, *La Patrie*, before entering politics. From 1885 to 1887, this modern voyageur served two terms as the progressive liberal mayor of Montréal despite opposition from ultramontanist critics and the moderate liberal establishment. Beaugrand regarded himself a proactive progressive in favor of civil service reform, improved infrastructure, and public health. The mayor viewed the province's lack of industry and educational opportunities as root causes of French-Canadian poverty.

During the summer and fall of his first term, the mayor faced the challenges of a smallpox epidemic. Riots broke out in the Champs-de-Mars on September 28, 1885, when Board of Health officer Dr. Louis Laborge ordered mandatory vaccinations with the full support of Mayor Beaugrand. Fear of vaccination was especially strong in poorer French-Canadian districts in the eastern part of the city. One doctor, Emile Coderre, even founded a journal, *L'Anti-Vaccinateur canadien-français*. According to historian Le Moine, street urchins were singing about *"Monsieur le maire,"* referring to him as a *"ver de terre"* (worm) and a *"scélérat"* (scoundrel).[55] By the time the epidemic had passed, 3,164 inhabitants of Montréal's 150,000 citizens had died, many of them children and many of them French Canadian. The fear of both disease and vaccination, and the public demonstrations that ensued, fueled a second wave of riots along the Champs-de-Mars on November 22, 1885, over the hanging of Métis rebel Louis Riel.[56]

But Mayor Beaugrand's troubles were not over. In April 1886, ice floes lodged near the present-day location of the Jacques Cartier Bridge caused severe flooding across the island city. The worst of it occurred in the poor Irish neighborhood known as Griffintown, in the southwest downtown area. Near the old port, the freezing water flooding Notre-Dame and Saint-Jacques Streets was six feet deep. City lights failed. Food supplies were ruined. Darkness and hunger threw the city into a panic. The *Montreal Daily Witness* reported on April 18 that Beaugrand appeared at a police station. "He looked ill and haggard, and seemed wearied out with anxiety."[57] However, Beaugrand's consistent efforts to be forward-looking impressed the city's powerbrokers, including the *Montreal Gazette*:

> He has displayed in an eminent degree the qualities which become the occupant of the mayoralty of a city of the importance of Montreal: energy, intelligence, impartiality, firmness in the enforcement of the civic laws and an enlightened progression in their amendment.... He has been required to combat ignorance and prejudice ... and he has ever proved himself to be actuated by the single desire to promote the interests of the city irrespective of class, creed or race."[58]

This was high praise indeed from the city's most important English-language newspaper. While leaving behind the exhausting responsibilities of the mayor's office, Beaugrand the journalist would continue to support a more progressive political stance even as he rejuvenated himself on the road.

As mayor, Beaugrand had the honor "to give the signal for the departure of that first train" to make a transcontinental journey via the Canadian Pacific Railway, a voyage "of 3,000 miles across the Canadian continent."[59] In December 1886, Beaugrand embarked on the trip himself. Reflecting on that experience later that winter, he emphasized that "Montréal must, therefore, both as to interior and external trade, profit more than any other city of the Dominion by the construction of the Pacific."[60] After noting the advantages and commercial potential of the Canadian West and extolling the "immense progress" in railroad construction, Beaugrand exclaimed that this "should arouse in all Canadians, of whatever origin, a legitimate feeling of pride"—a pride, he ended by saying, "in our great common country which is our best bond of union and the most quickening stimulus to our prosperity as a people."[61] That pride and excitement would not extend to his next set of travels.

From October 18, 1888, to April 2, 1889, Beaugrand embarked on a six-month excursion to Europe, Turkey, and North Africa with his wife and daughter.[62] While in Paris, Beaugrand noted that preparations for the 1889 World's Fair did not include

Canada. He observed on November 9, 1888, that "all Nations will be represented on the Champ-de-Mars—I say all—except Canada ... Too bad for Canada."[63] He harbored resentment for this absence across his excursion. In the last letter from his journey—again from Paris—Beaugrand expresses his regret again on March 4, 1889, that Canada will not be represented on this francophone world stage: It is an abstention that can be described as criminal "from the points of view of national reputation and our industrial interest."[64]

Beaugrand particularly lamented that the great French-Canadian sculptor Philippe Hébert had no place to display his work for a global audience. The one thing that most annoyed and indeed humiliated the former mayor was to see the government working only "to please a few encrusted reactionaries which is to spare the *electoral susceptibilities*."[65] In effect, Beaugrand asked: Where is Canada? Where is our nation, my nation? Beaugrand was not simply blaming Canada, but the reactionaries in Québec who had forced the hand of federal officials looking to keep Conservative votes. As historian Yvan Lamonde elaborates, "The government of Canada was absent [from the World's Fair of 1889], wanting at all costs to avoid the trap of participating in an international event identified with the Third Republic, as well as 1789 and 1793."[66] The fair celebrated the centenary of the French Revolution. Therefore, it was literally anathema to the ultramontanes and tories of Québec. As Beaugrand's nemesis, Jules-Paul Tardivel, wrote in his newspaper, *La Verité*: "We love the France of yore, the powerful, great and glorious France, the eldest daughter of the Church. . . . But modern France, as the Revolution has made it, the France fallen from its ancient splendor, impious France, in a word, republican France, inspires in us only a feeling that is a mixture of horror and pity." In the end, the Conservative Party squeaked out a national victory in 1887 with a narrow margin in Québec despite the hanging of Louis Riel in 1885. The national Conservative strategy of avoiding the World's Fair in Paris and the taint of the Third Republic had probably helped in obtaining that result. Beaugrand faulted both "the governments of Ottawa and Québec."[67]

Before returning to Montréal, Beaugrand was made an *officier* of the Légion d'honneur.[68] He also attended a banquet at Paris's Hotel Continental organized by the La Marmite club. Beaugrand found himself a guest of honor alongside such distinguished invitees as Auguste Bartholdi, the sculptor of the Statue of Liberty, and Ferdinand de Lesseps, builder of the Suez Canal.[69] Indeed the brightest lights in politics, business, literature, and the arts were there, "united by the same republican sensitivity, gay and charming, Gallic and correct, patriotic and Parisian."[70] The banquet served as the prism through which Beaugrand's transnationalism became internationalism.

At home in the glittering circles of Paris, Beaugrand had become more than a border-crossing defender of his French-Canadian people. A progressive liberal, called a radical by some, he rejected the conservative ultramontanism and nationalism of writers such as Tardivel. But the transnational exile continued his own search, not only for a progressive future, but for the meaning of Canada and Québec. He delighted in the Canadian West, but like Henri Bourassa, at least on this point, felt that "French and English [should] constitute the double vocabulary of the entire Canadian people."[71] Language and mobility served as the two constants along Beaugrand's long and winding journey. He carried—and, in the end, reinvented—the idea of a French-Canadian nation during his travels. Issuing French- and English-language editions of his work reflected his expanding sense of both nation and audience.

Meanwhile, as Beaugrand's politics suggest, he also clearly hoped that the fresh winds of economic and intellectual progress might change the mindset of Québec. As scholar Brendan Shanahan observes in his essay on Beaugrand, the second edition of *Jeanne la fileuse*, published in 1888, had a different introduction in which the author makes a more explicit plea for the government of Québec to intervene and stimulate the economic development of the province.[72] True to his progressive ideas, Beaugrand argues that government exists to help people, and the people constitute the nation, wherever they are. But understanding Beaugrand means connecting progressivism to the panoramic vision he needed to rise above the insufficiencies and disappointments of Canada, Québec, and the British Empire. In the end, that vision manifests itself most clearly through the printed word. Literature in particular allowed him to cultivate and focus his farsightedness through voyageurs like Jeanne the spinner or the oarsmen of *la chasse-galerie*.

Beginning in January 1875, Beaugrand's Massachusetts-based newspaper, *L'Echo du Canada*, took a decidedly literary turn. "We will publish each week several stories, legends, or historic tales related to Canada," he explained.[73] "Here [in New England], even more than in the country [Canada], we need to hear the traditions and customs of our fathers. These are the rings that intimately connect the respect due to the memory of our valiant ancestors to the innate love of this homeland on which they sprinkled their blood. Let's get to know those who preceded us on the banks of the Saint Lawrence."[74] Beaugrand continued his exploration of French-

Canadian oral traditions even after he relocated to Montréal and founded a new paper, *La Patrie*, in 1879.

In 1891, *La Patrie* published what would become Beaugrand's most enduring literary legacy—*la chasse-galerie*. Beaugrand's flying canoe traveled swiftly across Québec as local daily newspapers reprinted the story for an eager readership.[75] In 1892, Beaugrand brought *la chasse-galerie* to America via an English-language translation published in *Century Magazine*. His motive for promoting the folktale remained simple: *"à sauver de l'oubli"* (to save it from oblivion).[76] Beaugrand's efforts culminated in a compilation published simultaneously as *La chasse-galerie, légendes canadiennes* and *La Chasse Galerie and Other Canadian Stories* in Montréal in 1900.[77]

Beaugrand sought to elevate the folktales of his youth to the echelons of Canadian literary culture through these limited-edition issues. Replete with a chamois cover and gold-leaf title, the flying oarsmen of the *chasse-galerie* reached new heights on *"papier de luxe."*[78] "I had to oversee everything," the author wrote to Canadian prime minister Wilfred Laurier. "The paper, the engravers, the layout, the binding, the leather . . . I had to import from France."[79] Beaugrand made sure to include famed illustrator Henri Julien's depiction of the flying canoe that accompanied the *Century Magazine* article in 1892. Readers took notice of his handsome volume. Unlike the underwhelming reception that met *Jeanne la fileuse*, *La chasse-galerie* became a classic.

The author's wavering health deteriorated further in the years following *La chasse-galerie*'s release. Acute asthmatic attacks, and the morphine he used to manage his fits, eroded his strength. He traveled to Colorado for intensive breathing treatments, only to return to Montréal, "in the desire to die in my home, in my bed, surrounded by my family."[80] The former Montréal mayor left explicit instructions for his wife and executors: "I desire, at the time of death, that my funerals shall be as modest and simple as possible. No bearers, no flowers, no religious ceremony of any kind. I wish my body to be cremated in the crematory at Montréal and on this point I hope my wish will not be discussed but will be followed implicitly."[81] Honoré Beaugrand succumbed to his ailments on October 7, 1906. He was fifty-eight years old.

As the masthead of his New England newspaper infers, Beaugrand thought deeply about the ways in which francophone Canadian culture echoed across the continent. Historians are only just beginning to listen to the echoes of Beaugrand's legacy beyond *La chasse-galerie*.⁸² Although more attention has been paid to his contemporaries like Honoré Mercier and Wilfred Laurier, Beaugrand's secularism, political posturing, and hemispheric vision foreshadowed the progressive inclinations of Québec's liberal wartime premier, Adélard Godbout (1939–1944) and the cultural politics of the Quiet Revolution. Godbout studied at university in Massachusetts, a space that afforded both politicians a kind of panoramic vision of Québec and Canada. Beaugrand and Godbout not only defended Franco-Americans living in the United States, they applied that sweeping vision in their respective attempts to modernize Montréal and the province of Québec.⁸³

René Lévesque, who also worked as a journalist and politician, later echoed Beaugrand's cutting rhetoric and protective stance during the 1970s. Beaugrand, like Lévesque early in his career, fought doggedly against stereotypes projected onto French Canadians, especially the million souls who immigrated to New England. "The peculiar situation occupied by the French-Canadian element in the Dominion of Canada is unknown or misunderstood by most English-speaking people on this continent," Beaugrand maintained.⁸⁴ "The French influence in the Province of Québec is generally held up as a kind of Popish and unprogressive bug-bear; and to read and hear all the nonsensical exaggerations that have been spoken and printed on the subject, is enough to make one dream of the old days when both Catholics and Protestants burned one another at the stake, in their enthusiastic and barbarous efforts to reach the golden gate of Paradise."⁸⁵ Moreover, Beaugrand's modernist construction of French-Canadian identity on the North American continent and in the world reverberated in René Lévesque's brand of politics. Lévesque's separatism was as much about breaking with tradition and achieving transcendence— projecting Québec into the world beyond Canada—as it was about locking down provincial borders. Beaugrand, Godbout, and Lévesque insisted on the significance of the French-Canadian experience in a global context.⁸⁶

During much of the twentieth century, French Canadians had largely forgotten Honoré Beaugrand's contributions and farsightedness even as they worked to further his vision of a secular and internationally involved Québec. The former Montréal mayor did not fit the conventional narrative in the struggle to control nationalist discourse in the province. But in 1976, the same year that Lévesque's separatist Parti Québécois (PQ) took power for the first time in Québec, the Société de transport de Montréal commemorated Honoré Beaugrand's legacy in the city he helped renew by inscribing his name on one of the city's most modern amenities—the metro. The Honoré Beaugrand station marked the eastern terminus of the metro's Green Line in the working class and predominately francophone Mercier-Hochelaga-Maisonneuve borough of East Montréal.[87] French Canada no longer needed to look to the heavens for Beaugrand's enchanted canoe. Instead, commuters follow downward arrow signs into the metro's underworld to ride trains that fly beneath the streets of the city at the speed of modernity.

NOTES

1. Jean-Philippe Warren, *Honoré Beaugrand: La plume et l'épée (1848–1906)* (Montréal: Les Éditions du Boréal, 2015), 420–21. All translations in this essay by the authors unless otherwise noted.

2. Honoré Beaugrand, "La chasse-galerie," *Century Magazine* (August 1892): 498. Lavaltrie is a settlement in the Lanaudière region northeast of Montréal.

3. Beaugrand, "La chasse-galerie," 498.

4. Beaugrand, "La chasse-galerie," 498.

5. Beaugrand, "La chasse-galerie," 498.

6. Beaugrand, "La chasse-galerie," 498.

7. Beaugrand, "La chasse-galerie," 498.

8. Beaugrand, "La chasse-galerie," 499.

9. Beaugrand, "La chasse-galerie," 500.

10. Beaugrand, "La chasse-galerie," 502.

11. *Lettres de voyage: France-Italie-Sicile-Malte-Tunisie-Algérie-Espagne* (Montréal, 1889); *Six mois dans les Montagnes-Rocheuses: Colorado, Utah, Nouveau-Mexique* (Montréal, 1890); and Warren, *Honoré Beaugrand: La plume et l'épée.*.

12. To be sure, the varying degrees of Catholic influence in Québec (and in some cases, the lack thereof) is more complex than we have space for here. For a more nuanced discussion of the Church, politics, and culture, see René Hardy's historiographic overview, "Regards sur la construction de la culture catholique quebécoise au XIXe siècle," *Canadian Historical Review* 88, no. 1 (2007): 7–40; Yvan Lamonde, *The Social History of Ideas in Quebec, 1760–1896* (Montréal: McGill-Queen's University Press, 2013).

13. Warren, *Honoré Beaugrand: La plume et l'épée.*

14. The novel was first printed in its entirety in March 1878. It was printed *en feuilleton* in Beaugrand's newspaper *La République* sometime between 1877 and 1878. See Brendan Shanahan, "The Several Lives of Joan the Spinner: *Honoré Beaugrand's Jeanne la fileuse: Épisode de l'émigration franco-canadienne aux États-Unis* and the Making and Remaking of a French-Canadian/Franco-American Novel," *Journal of Transnational American Studies* 3, no. 2 (2011): 1. This essay was originally published in *Je Me Souviens*, 34, no. 1 (Spring 2011): 19–32. https://escholarship.org/uc/item/8f156724

15. Roger Le Moine, "Introduction," in Honoré Beaugrand, *Jeanne la fileuse: Épisode de l'émigration Franco-Canadienne aux états-unis* (Montréal: Fides, 1980), 21.

16. See Honoré Beaugrand, *De Québec à Mexico* (Montréal: Duvernay Frères et Dansereau, 1874); A. I. Silver, *The French-Canadian Idea of Confederation, 1864–1900*, 2nd paperback ed. (Toronto: University of Toronto Press, 1997) 224. Beaugrand did visit Montréal in June of 1874 for the Saint-Jean-

Baptiste celebration when an attempt was made to bring together "les francophones du Québec et de la diaspora." Le Moine, "Introduction," in Beaugrand, *Jeanne la fileuse*, 55.

17. The paper ceased publication only in 1923. *L'Abeille* occasionally had English-language sections as the *New Orleans Bee* and Spanish-language sections briefly as *La Abeja*.

18. He was a "peinture en bâtiments." Le Moine, "Introduction," in Beaugrand, *Jeanne la fileuse*, 54.

19. Beaugrand joined the King Philip Lodge, which was granted a charter in 1866.

20. In November of the same year, he became a founder of l'Union canadienne-française de Fall River, a move denounced by the local clergy, foreshadowing later struggles such as *La Sentinelle* Affair. For the events in Beaugrand's life, see Le Moine, "Introduction," in Beaugrand, *Jeanne la fileuse*, 54. For La Sentinelle Affair, see Yves Roby, *The Franco-Americans of New-England: Dreams and Realities*, English edition (Quebec City: Septentrion, 2004), 241–269.

21. The union was called l'Union canadienne-française de Fall River. Le Moine, "Introduction," in Beaugrand, *Jeanne la fileuse*, 54–55. The quotes are taken by Le Moine from Beaugrand in the *April 11* issue of his newspaper, *L'Echo du Canada*.

22. Roby, *Franco-Americans*, 1.

23. Roby, *Franco-Americans*, 24. The statistics are taken from Ralph D. Vicero, "Immigration of French Canadians to New England, 1840–1900: A Geographical Analysis" (Ph.D. diss., University of Wisconsin, 1968), 289.

24. Benedict Anderson, *Imagined Communities* (London: Verso, 1983). Many thanks for this thought and others to Sonia Helen Pascale, "Honoré Beaugrand: An International Life with a Canadian Focus" (Paper written for History 168J, "Quebec and Canada," Yale University, May 13, 2016), 4.

25. Pascale, "Honoré Beaugrand," 4.

26. Montréal's Bishop Bourget politically attacked the Institut canadien de Montréal in 1858. Bourget's continuing insistence that the Church be allowed to determine what books might be read at such literary institutes or clubs resulted in a series of lawsuits and disturbances known as the Guibord Affair, lasting almost two decades and finally decided, more or less, by a decision of the Privy Council back in England. See Lovell C. Clark, *The Guibord Affair* (Toronto: Holt, Rinehart & Winston of Canada, 1971).

27. Le Moine, "Introduction," in Beaugrand, *Jeanne la fileuse*, 54.

28. Roby, *Franco-Americans*, 30.

29. Roby, *Franco-Americans*, 32.

30. Tardivel's novel was a utopian fantasy with aspects of science fiction. Beaugrand's book was journalism enhanced with a thin sentimental plot. The former imagined a separate French-Canadian state. The latter validates the French-Canadian experience in the United States. Ironically, Tardivel was born in Kentucky.

31. For this statement by Cartier, see Cynthia Lees, "Critical Approaches to *Jeanne la fileuse*: An Immigration Novel for Transnational Times," in *Selected Proceedings of the 2011 AATF Convention*, vol. 2 (Montréal: American Association of Teachers of French, 2011), 12. See also Roby, *Franco-Americans*, 31: "The paternity of this affirmation attributed to Cartier by Alexandre Belisle in his *Histoire de la presse franco-américaine et les Canadiens-Français aux État-Unis* (History of the Franco-American press and the French Canadians in the United States), Worcester, *Imprimerie de l'Opinion publique*, 1911, 14, and based on word of mouth, has never been clearly proven."

32. Gagnon—who believed the people should *"restons français"* and *"respectons notre clergé,"* that is, preserve French culture and the Catholic religion—not only supported the ideas behind *repatriement*, he served as an official *agent de repatriement* for the Québec government in New England. See Chaput, "Some *Repatriement* Dilemmas," *Canadian Historical Review* 49, no. 4 (December 1968): 402–3.

33. This sad but humorous incident was recorded by Alexandre Bellisle and reported by the *L'Echo de l'Ouest* (14 avril 1911), published in Minneapolis, Minnesota. The article, entitled "HISTOIRE DE DUEL: Beaugrand et Gagnon" appeared on page 2 of that issue. The Minnesota Historical Society in St. Paul has this newspaper as a digital resource and states the following on its website: "Founded on April 25, 1883, *Echo de l'Ouest* ("Echo of the West") was the representative newspaper of French Canadians in Minnesota and the surrounding Upper Midwest region. It was published as a four-page weekly in Minneapolis under the management of Editor Zéphirin Demeules, or members of his family, during its entire 45-year run." The paper folded on January 4, 1929. The paper described itself: *"L'Echo de l'Ouest* est le journal par excellence des familles de langue française de Nord-ouest." We are greatly indebted to Anne Juneau Craver for finding this in the course of her own research, bringing it to our attention, and providing a translation to boot.

34. Lees, "Critical Approaches to *Jeanne la fileuse*," 2.

35. As quoted by Shanahan, "The Several Lives of Joan the Spinner," 5.

36. Beaugrand, *Jeanne la fileuse*, 75.

37. Beaugrand, *Jeanne la fileuse*, 230.

38. See, for example, *Collier's World Atlas and Gazetteer* (New York: Collier & Son, 1955), 99.

39. Beaugrand, *Jeanne la fileuse*, 235.

40. Beaugrand, *Jeanne la fileuse*, 236.

41. Beaugrand, *Jeanne la fileuse*, 235–36.

42. Beaugrand, *Jeanne la fileuse*, 232.

43. Beaugrand, *Jeanne la fileuse*, 233.

44. Beaugrand, *Jeanne la fileuse*, 227.

45. Beaugrand, *Jeanne la fileuse*, 234. Describing the journey in sympathetic terms, Beaugrand anticipates a much later novelist, Ringuet (Dr. Philippe Panneton), whose brilliant 1938 novel, *Trente Arpents* (*Thirty Acres*), breaks the fierce grip of the *terroir* tradition, showing that traditional practices on the land might not sustain the people—indeed, that such practices led the rather sad hero, Euchariste Moisan, to be so stuck in his rural mindset that he perceived the "endless roof of a factory" to be "a well-ploughed field with parallel furrows" when he first arrived to be with the son who had moved to the United States. As Antoine Sirois wrote in the afterword to the English edition: "The rural *terroir* novel had long served as an instrument of propaganda for the agriculturist ideology that proclaimed that only fidelity to the soil held out any hope of future happiness to French Canadians." Though his prose is beautifully evocative of the Québécois landscape, Ringuet, observes Sirois, "was the first novelist to present a tragic hero and resist the temptation to polemic." Ringuet's evocative prose describes the landscape beautifully but implies that the long Canadian winter can be less than invigorating for the inhabitants: "The clumps of trees and the barn in the far background appeared only as dark smudges frozen fast in this whitish jelly that dulled the rays of a timid sun." Ringuet [Philippe Panneton], *Thirty Acres* (1940; reprint, Toronto: McClelland & Stewart, New Canadian Library, 1989). See afterword by Antoine Sirois, 301. Translation by Felix and Dorothea Walker for the 1940 edition.

For the quote from the novel, see English (Toronto) edition above, 27. Also see the original French in Ringuet, *Trente arpents* (1938; reprint, Montréal and Paris: Flammarion), 25.

46. Lees, "Critical Approaches to *Jeanne la fileuse*," 8.

47. Quoted in Damien-Claude Bélanger, "French-Canadian Emigration to the United States, 1840–1930," http://faculty.marianopolis.edu/c.belanger/quebechistory, accessed June 11, 2018.

48. Editorial in the *New York Times*, June 6, 1892 ("The French Canadians in New-England"), http://members.tripod.com/~Scott_Michaud/Franco-editorial.html, accessed June 11, 2018. The *Times* cites Smyth incorrectly as Eugene C. Smyth. His name was Egbert Coffin Smyth (1828–1904), a teacher at Phillips Academy in Andover, Massachusetts. Smyth also wrote an exposé on "The French-Canadians in New England," published in the *Proceedings of the American Antiquarian Society* 7, no. 3 (December 1892): 316–36.

49. Lees, "Critical Approaches to *Jeanne la fileuse*," 9.

50. Bernard L. Vigod, *Quebec before Duplessis: The Political Career of Louis-Alexandre Taschereau* (Montréal: McGill-Queen's University Press, 1986), 32.

51. Cultural trauma is a sociological concept that explains the narrative process of meaning-making around traumatic events (either contemporary or historic). Sociologists have deployed the theory of cultural trauma to describe how groups have made sense of past turbulent events including the Holocaust, slavery, and other traumatic experiences. We are applying the idea of cultural trauma to the French-Canadian experience, especially with regard to the memory of the conquest in 1759. Jeffrey C. Alexander, Ron Eyerman, et al., *Cultural Trauma and Collective Identity* (Berkeley: University of California Press, 2004); Ron Eyerman, *Is This America? Katrina as Cultural Trauma* (Austin: University of Texas Press, 2015); Kai T. Erikson, "Notes on Trauma and Community," in *Trauma: Explorations in Memory*, ed. Cathy Caruth (Baltimore: Johns Hopkins University Press, 1995), 184.

52. By invoking the idea of cultural trauma, we wish to suggest that the past remained problematic for French Canadians seeking to forge a progressive yet distinctively French-Canadian future. There are many schools of interpretation about the meaning of the British Conquest in the history of Québec, and we are not "jovialists" (those like Parkman who celebrated the benign impact or heroic triumph), "miserabilists" (those like the Montréal school of historians who emphasized the disastrous consequences for French Canadians), or even *bonne ententistes* (who seek to take a middle course, often emphasizing victimization, *survivance*, or cooperation). For more on this, see the wonderful essay by Nicole Neatby, "Remembering the Conquest: Mission Impossible?" in *Remembering 1759: The Conquest of Canada in Historical Memory*, ed. Phillip Buckner and John G. Reid (Toronto: University of Toronto Press, 2012), 251–78. Recent work that accomplishes the "normalization" of Québécois history has found ample evidence of French-Canadian agency and adjustment. Donald Fyson's work, for example, has shown how French Canadians adapted to British legal structures and exercised some power from below. See his essay "The *Canadiens* and British Institutions of Local Governance in Quebec from the Conquest to the Rebellions," in *Transatlantic Subjects: Ideas, Institutions, and Social Experience in Post-Revolutionary British North America*, ed. Nancy Christie (Montréal: McGill-Queen's University Press, 2008), 45–82. Hannah Weiss Muller, *Subjects and Sovereign: Bonds of Belonging in the Eighteenth-Century British Empire* (New York: Oxford University Press, 2017), uncovers the complexities of subjecthood in this period, finding multiple jurisdictions, legal dualities, and a diversity of rights and privileges within the empire. For the idea of "normalization" in recent Québécois historiography,

see Jocelyn Létourneau, "The Current Great Narrative of Québecois Identity," *South Atlantic Quarterly* 94, no. 4 (Fall 1995): 1039–1053. In our work on the French in the fur trade in places such as St. Louis or Detroit, we find ample evidence of successful capitalists and Freemasons utterly capable of surviving multiple regime changes. Moving past the Conquest to the rebellions of 1837–38, Michel Ducharme and Allan Greer have presented a very complex political landscape in Lower Canada, arguing that the 1837–38 events must be viewed in a broader context and may be seen "as the final chapter" of "the revolutions that shook the Atlantic world in the late eighteenth century." See Ducharme, *The Idea of Liberty: Canada during the Age of Atlantic Revolutions, 1776–1838* (Montréal: McGill-Queen's University Press, 2014), 7. See also Allan Greer, *The Patriots and the People* (Toronto: University of Toronto Press, 1993).

53. Beaugrand, *Jeanne la fileuse*, 179.

54. West's 1770 painting *The Death of General Wolfe* is often interpreted as a work that both celebrates the martyrdom of the English hero and Christ-like Wolfe and anticipates the dying hold of European powers on North America. West was a Pennsylvanian. See Simon Schama, *Dead Certainties (Unwarranted Speculations)* (New York: Knopf, 1991), 32.

55. Le Moine, "Introduction," in Beaugrand, *Jeanne la fileuse*, 61.

56. Judy Torrance, *Public Violence in Canada, 1867–1982* (Montréal: McGill-Queen's University Press, 1986), 39. See also Jennifer Reid, *Louis Riel and the Creation of Modern Canada: Mythic Discourse and the Postcolonial State* (Albuquerque: University of New Mexico Press, 2008), 139. For the history of Montréal, see Dany Fougères and Roderick MacLeod, eds., *Montréal: The History of a North American City*, 2 vols. (Montréal: McGill-Queen's University Press, 2017).

57. Ultimately, in 1899, a different mayor, Raymond Préfontaine, would oversee the completion of a flood wall to help avoid future disasters. Jonathan Monpetit, "A Haggard Nayor and Everyday Heroes: Tales from Montréal's 1886 Flood," CBC News, posted May 14, 2017, http://www.cbc.ca/news/canada/montreal/montreal-flood-1886-quebec-1.4112735.

58. George Maclean Rose, ed., *A Cyclopaedia of Canadian Biography: Being Chiefly Men of the Time* (Toronto: Rose Publishing Company, 1886–88), 694.

59. Honoré Beaugrand, *Across the Continent via the Canadian Pacific Railway: A Lecture Delivered under the Auspices of the Montreal District Board of Trade, 23rd March, 1887* (Montréal: s.n.), 2–3.

60. Beaugrand, *Across the Continent via the Canadian Pacific Railway*, 2–3.

61. Beaugrand, *Across the Continent via the Canadian Pacific Railway*, 8–9.

62. He traveled to Paris, then on to Venice, Florence, Rome, Naples, Constantinople, Algiers, Madrid, Bordeaux, and Paris again. Le Moine, "Introduction," in Beaugrand, *Jeanne la fileuse*, 63.

63. Honoré Beaugrand, *Lettres de voyage: France-Italie-Sicile-Malte-Tunisie-Algérie-Espagne* (Montréal: Des Presses de *La Patrie*, 1889), 32.

64. Beaugrand, *Lettres de voyage*, 350.

65. Beaugrand, *Lettres de voyage*, 343.

66. Both quotes taken from Yvan Lamonde, *The Social History of Ideas in Quebec, 1760–1896*. trans. Phyllis Aronoff and Howard Scott (2000; reprint and English edition, Montréal: McGill-Queen's University Press, 2013), 396.

67. Beaugrand, *Lettres de voyage*, 345.

68. He had been a *chevalier* since 1885. Le Moine, Introduction, Beaugrand, *Jeanne la fileuse*, 63.

69. Beaugrand, *Lettres de voyage*, 45–51.

70. Janelle Dietrick, *Alice and Eiffel: A New History of Early Cinema and the Love Story Kept Secret for a Century* (Portland, OR: BookBaby, 2016), chap. 24.

71. Quoted in Joseph Levitt, ed., *Henri Bourassa on Imperialism and Bi-culturalism, 1900–1918* (Toronto: Copp Clark, 1970), 135. The original essay by Bourassa, *La langue française et l'aveinir de notre race*, was published in Quebec in 1913.

72. Brendan Shanahan, "The Several Lives of Joan the Spinner," 7, 10.

73. As quoted in Marc Tremblay, "Le cycle de la chasse-galerie: Etude des variants significatives, de l'origine, de la diffusion et de la structure d'un conte folklorique canadien-français" (Ph.D. diss., Carleton University, 1996), 4.

74. Tremblay, "Le cycle de la chasse-galerie," 4.

75. Tremblay, "Le cycle de la chasse-galerie," 4.

76. Honoré Beaugrand, "Avant-propos," *La chasse-galerie, legends canadiennes* (Montréal, 1900).

77. The two volumes contained different folktales. The French edition included "La chasse-galerie," "Le loup-garou," "La bête à grand queue," "Macloune," and "Le père Louison." The English edition, on the other hand, included "La chasse galerie," "The Werewolves" (loup garou), and "La quête de l'Enfant Jésus."

78. Gustave Comte, "Notes d'art," *Les Débats*, 29 avril 1900, p. 2.

79. Tremblay, "Le cycle de la chasse-galerie," 4.

80. Warren, *Honoré Beaugrand: La plume et l'épée*, 502.

81. Jean-Philippe Warren reproduced these handwritten instructions in *Honoré Beaugrand*, 505.

82. The first biography of Beaugrand was published in 2015. Warren, *Honoré Beaugrand*, 502.

83. Not much work has been done on this forgotten French-Canadian premier, who is overshadowed by the notorious Maurice Duplessis. For Godbout's defense of francophones living in the United States, see Adélard Godbout, "Canada: Unity and Diversity," *Foreign Affairs* 21, no. 3 (April 1943): 452–61. The only biography of Godbout is Jean-Guy Genest, *Godbout* (Sillery: Le Septentrion, 1996). See also Jacques Godbout, dir., *Traitor or Patriot*, documentary, National Film Board of Canada (2000), 1 hour, 22 min.

84. Honoré Beaugrand, "The Attitude of the French Canadians," *Forum, Vol. VII*, ed. Loretus S. Metcalf (New York: Forum Publishing Co., 1888), 521–22.

85. Beaugrand, "The Attitude of the French Canadians," 521.

86. In 1976, just months before the Parti Québécois came to power, René Lévesque expressed his international plan for Québec most succinctly in the journal *Foreign Affairs*. He writes: "In brief, Québec's most privileged links, aside from its most essential relationship with the Canadian partner, would be first with the United States—where there is no imaginable reason to frown on such a tardy but natural and healthy development (especially during a Bicentennial year). Then Québec would look to other Francophone or 'Latin' countries as cultural respondents, and to France herself-who would certainly not be indifferent to the fact that this new nation would constitute the second most important French-speaking country in the world. In brief, such is the peaceful and, we confidently hope, fruitfully progressive state which may very well appear on the map of North America before the end of the decade." René Lévesque, "For an Independent Québec," *Foreign Affairs* 54, no. 4 (July 1976): 744. The international outreach of Québécois politicians and artists deserves more attention. In 1948, a group of Québécois writers and artists led by Paul-Emile Borduas created an international stir

with their anti-establishment manifesto, *Le refus global*. That same year and the following year (1949), French-Canadian politicians led by Prime Minister Louis St.-Laurent played an important role in the shaping of NATO (OTAN in Québec). Historian Gérard Bergeron argues that French Canadians saw NATO as a way of moving past the old reliance on the Commonwealth/British connection and pursuing relationships that would allow Québec (and Canada) to amplify its own voice on the world stage. See Bergeron, "Le Canada Français: Du provincialisme a l'Internationalisme" in Hugh L. Keenleyside et al., *The Growth of Canadian Policies in External Affairs* (Durham, NC: Duke University Press for the Duke University Commonwealth-Studies Center, 1960), 99–130.

87. The new station's namesake aligned with the PQ's cultural identity as the keepers of French-Canadian memory. The PQ changed the provincial slogan from the quaint *la belle province* (the beautiful province) to *je me souviens* (I remember) in 1978.

Epilogue

"Next Stop, Honoré Beaugrand":
Connections, Dislocations, and Redirections

BRETT RUSHFORTH

I first encountered the name Honoré Beaugrand, not as a man, but as a stop on Montréal's metro system, announced over a loudspeaker in muffled French. Because the station sits at the eastern terminus of the green line, the metro's central artery, it serves as a marker for travelers to know which train to catch, westward toward Angrignon or eastward toward Honoré-Beaugrand. Green line passengers encounter a series of stations named for French colonizers and their apologists, providing *aides-mémoire* to the city's colonial past: LaSalle, Charlevoix, Frontenac, Joliette, Cadillac, Radisson. The line also stops at three of Montréal's world-class universities—Concordia, McGill, and Université du Québec à Montréal—as well as the city's commercial and arts districts. As in life, so in death, Beaugrand serves as a guide through French-colonized spaces transformed by what came afterward. It is fitting, then, that Beaugrand also sits at the terminus of this collection of essays. As Jay Gitlin and Ryan Brasseaux show us, the politician, publisher, folklorist, and raconteur spent much of his life thinking and writing about the legacies of French colonization in the Americas, drawing linkages between francophone populations in Québec, New England, Louisiana, and beyond.

Like Beaugrand and the metro system that memorializes him, the essays here highlight connection rooted in movement: of people, ideas, cultural practices, conceptual frameworks, and of the goods and profits that made these movements possible. If historians of the French Atlantic once emphasized the disjointed nature of France's eighteenth-century empire, comparing it unfavorably to its powerful Spanish predecessor or its booming British competitor, the kind of innovative research featured in this volume is beginning to show the surprising degree of integration among the far-flung posts of greater France even at a time when the French themselves complained constantly about the fragmentation of their Atlantic enterprise. It might go too far to compare the early modern French Empire to an urban metro system, with clearly mapped and reliable circuits linking people and places with mechanical precision. No early modern empire functioned that way. But, over time, the movement of bodies and merchandise between French ports, West African entrepôts, Caribbean sugar islands, and North American settler colonies created increasingly predictable pathways that tied these places to one another in ways that historians are only now starting to appreciate. These bonds can be seen in both large-scale migrations and in the personal itineraries of mobile individuals on the make. Taken together, as Christopher Hodson notes, "the movement of people, as well as the exchange of goods and ideas, knit the early modern French Atlantic ... into an integrated whole."[1]

Collectively, this volume makes a strong argument for early modern French mobility as a force of cultural cohesion that enabled conceptual, and occasionally bureaucratic, integration. Centered on French settlements in Canada, the *pays d'en haut*, and Saint-Domingue (colonial Haiti), the chapters nod to a much more widespread phenomenon occurring in places like Louisiana, Martinique, Guadeloupe, Guiana, Senegambia, and Benin. As French people moved, resettled, adapted, reconsidered, communicated, and moved again, they drew upon familiar patterns of labor, land tenure, religiosity, and family formation, but they also innovated in all of these areas and more. Even when these innovations were particular to time and place, drawing French populations into very different cultural practices influenced by West Africans or Indigenous Americans, they tended to occur within a framework that was broadly French.

The colonial worlds established by early modern French expansion depended upon significant migrations, which occurred on a spectrum from the truly voluntary movement of opportunistic merchants and ambitious functionaries to the violent relocation of enslaved African and Amerindian people through slavery and dispossession. Most of the authors here emphasize ties created by voluntary migration, which was driven by a combination of cultural, economic, and demographic factors that made movement both possible and desirable. Leslie Choquette's laborers, for example, traveled to New France as part of a long French tradition of mobile labor, where rural dwellers moved to the cities for jobs, soldiers moved between garrisons and towns, and merchants and sailors moved from port to port.

Accustomed to annual rounds of short-term migrations within France, workers and those who would employ them translated these cultural practices into overseas movement to Canada. Migration to French-claimed North America thus reflected not only a demographic relationship between France and its colonies, but also a conceptual and social one. This provides a new way of seeing not only why French people migrated to New France, but also why many returned to France at the end of their tour and why, among those who remained, cycles of movable labor continued among the younger and less-established population.

Similarly, when Guillaume Teasdale's and Karen L. Marrero's farmers moved to Detroit in the first half of the nineteenth century, long-standing practices of land use, community formation, and even estate inheritance law in the St. Lawrence Valley both influenced their choices to move and shaped their practices once they arrived, much more so than the state actors who ostensibly controlled the area as part of the United States. Local conditions around Detroit, particularly relations with Native communities, converged with New France traditions to transform households in ways that combined movement and rootedness in innovative ways. These movements created, as Teasdale and Marrero write, "economic and cultural connections between Lower Canada and the Detroit River borderland" that lasted into the twentieth century.

Many individuals, too, struck out more or less voluntarily from France to other sites in the Atlantic. Three examples discussed in this volume—Marie de l'Incarnation, Paul Mascarene, and Brother Chrétien—followed idiosyncratic itineraries that revealed complex relationships between the ideological drive of religion and the more elemental thirst for influence and (in one form or another) power. Brother Chrétien might have been a shady self-dealer who ran a charity with funds of uncertain legitimacy, for example, but as he navigated the idiosyncratic legal and administrative landscapes of the various French colonies he deepened connections among them. His uncertain success led one prominent thinker to the breathless conclusion "that the French, whether they live in France or America, form one people and one family."[2] Like tens of thousands of others, Brother Chrétien embodied and thus constituted the French Atlantic even as he traveled the circuits established by those who went before him.

These networks meant that, at least for the French inhabitants of the colonies, old France and new had more in common than some have assumed. In Mairi Cowan's account of demonic possession and deliverance in seventeenth-century New

France, for example, we see that many aspects of the episode unfolded as they might have in provincial France, from the people considered most susceptible to the devil to the clergy whose expertise in ritual matters provided the first line of defense against evil forces. And yet the demon at the heart of Cowan's story, impervious to the efforts of priests and nuns, fled only upon the ritual intervention of a lay woman, who, according to Cowan, would almost certainly not have performed such a role in France proper. Demographic realities gave women more options in New France, and the constant fear of Native enemies created a heightened sense of urgency that demanded extraordinary measures. The actors in this drama thus performed "in the tradition of France, but the theater of New France changed the plot somewhat."

The tension between continuity and change in French cultural mobility is nowhere more visible than in William Brown's discussion of intercultural diplomacy in the *pays d'en haut*. Although migration as such is not the point of Brown's account of French administrators, diplomats, and borderlands negotiators, these men (and a few women) traveled far to bridge the geographic and conceptual divides between European and American worlds. The tradition of elaborate nonverbal communication in French political performance, and the imperative of diplomatic adaptation to local norms and expectations in provincial France, laid the groundwork for French adaptation to North American Native cultures of negotiation. If the particular forms of embodied political theater were "forged according to diplomatic protocols that were fundamentally Indigenous," deeper French traditions prepared colonial negotiators to adapt and innovate. That these relationships were often framed as military alliances against a common enemy, to say nothing of the Indigenous slaves who changed hands during these diplomatic rituals, only underscores the stakes of the cultural practices that Brown elaborates.[3]

These individuals and communities, then, also recall the role of violent displacement and forced migration in establishing the worlds they inhabited, placing the work in this volume in conversation with other bodies of scholarship on these topics.[4] The Protestant shape-shifter Mascarene, as Gregory Kennedy and Vincent Auffrey's essay shows, not only managed to navigate the complexities of inter-imperial and interfaith cultural negotiations, but he also played an underappreciated role in supporting the forced expulsion of tens of thousands of Acadian colonists, who themselves had settled on lands belonging to Mi'kmaq and Maliseet communities decades before. In her move to New France, Marie de l'Incarnation not only observed spiritual threats to vulnerable souls—the demonic forces of Cowan's essay—but she also demonized humans like the Haudenosaunee (Iroquois), whose defensive fight against French settler colonialism made her and other French colonists fear for their lives. It was this climate of demonization that led the good nun to describe anti-Haudenosaunee campaigns as "a holy war" and some of her contemporaries to call for a total Iroquois genocide. In an effort to "destroy utterly these barbarians," the French Crown invested in military expeditions targeting Haudenosaunee towns and making Canada appear safe for new waves of French migration.[5] That the ritual significance of Jean de Brébeuf's body parts derived, to a degree, from his death by Haudenosaunee hands only underscores these associations. Brother Chrétien, of course, moved through and profited from a world built on the stolen lives and labors of enslaved people. Even his acts of charity, which strengthened financial and conceptual ties between disparate parts of greater France, served to soften the face of colonial violence rather than to challenge its legitimacy.

Every region discussed here as a site of French cultural mobility was originally peopled many centuries before French arrival. Voluntary migration occurred alongside transatlantic and hemispheric slave trades, as well as reluctant resettlements spurred by the disease, warfare, and ecological change initiated by colonization. In French-controlled Canada alone as many as ten thousand Indigenous people, and several hundred African-descended people, were brought into French settlements as slaves.[6] In Louisiana, of course, there were far more. And if we look at the French Atlantic as a whole, the overwhelming majority of people settling in French colonies came against their will, with no previous migration culture that could explain their forced relocation to the slave labor camps of Saint-Domingue, Martinique, Guadeloupe, or Louisiana. This takes nothing away from the remarkable research presented here, but rather serves to remind us that the cultural networks created by human migration into French-colonized spaces came from multiple directions and drew on a variety of cultural traditions, both "French" and otherwise.

This is not an argument to ignore the very real power of French cultural connections so capably illustrated in this volume. On the contrary, it is an invitation to pause and meditate on that power, *as power*. Indeed, the kind of creative cultural mobility that strengthened ties among far-flung regions and the diverse populations within them was not only compatible with the violence of empire: it was itself an enabling tool of empire. Communication networks, diasporic family ties, shared cultural institutions, and even the very idea that French colonists all around the Atlantic were part of greater France all made it easier for knowledge and other resources drawn from one colonized space to serve French-directed ends in another. More important than noting the implicit arrogance of cultural expansion—an obvious and ultimately not very useful observation—attention to cultural practices like those highlighted here helps us recognize the ways that French colonists could serve the ends of an empire that they themselves often experienced very lightly. In a sense, readers of this volume will encounter cultural mobility and performance much as most French colonists themselves did, with the troubling reality of violence lurking just offstage. That realization can be a source of insight about how empires, early modern and otherwise, leveraged the actions of people who might or might not have been committed to the larger aims of administrators and strategists working in the metropole.[7]

A case in point is Robert D. Taber's innovative analysis of how Saint-Domingue's free people of color navigated social hierarchies rooted in racial violence. Perhaps nowhere in the French Atlantic—perhaps nowhere in the eighteenth-century world—were mobility and cultural connection more closely dependent upon violence than in Saint-Domingue, where half a million enslaved people labored on sugar and coffee plantations in the years leading up to the Haitian Revolution. For free people of color, the personal violence of that colonial world resided less in the physical brutality of slavery than in the psychic brutality of having to argue for one's full humanity. Seeking respect and upward mobility, Saint-Domingue's free people of color used a range of creative strategies to form families, buy property, and (yes) control the lives and labors of enslaved people. Each of these actions required their capitulation to the administrative state through performances rendered in paperwork. As Taber argues, "One of the most powerful tools in the arsenal of the colonial state was to make doing their paperwork appear worthwhile." Concrete protections and the very real privileges of property ownership, inheritance, and civil status were all secured through paperwork. Although enacted in a very different setting, this was another version of Brown's "administrative ethnography," which reduced non-French populations to paper in order to understand and then manage them. Over time, Saint-Domingue's free people of color found these strategies less and less effective in the face of cultural forces equating honor and status with whiteness. Their primary mechanism of relief had been the very administrative apparatus that now worked to fully exclude them.[8]

Another man displaced by the chaos of revolution in the French Atlantic was Georges-Henri-Victor Collot. After a brief and disastrous stint as governor of Guadeloupe that ended with his handing control of the island to the British, Collot turned to musing about the future of the French Empire. He did so by reimagining its past. Collot's French Atlantic, as Englebert's rich essay reveals, was integrated neither by the subtle circulation of French cultural practices nor by mundane capitulations to state paperwork, but by virtuous governors obeyed and appreciated by loyal French subjects. If one can recognize these musings as an effort to process his own professional failures, his writings "imagined a new French empire, built on the foundations of lost colonies in the heart of North America." In Collot's view, cultural isolation in the North American heartland had created a population of French speakers that was "ignorant, stupid, ugly, and miserable." Issued as an indictment of French settlers who had degenerated through cultural and sexual intimacy with Native people, Collot's vision of empire fit a broader pattern of equating European cultures with progress and uplift, thereby implicitly justifying the violence of Indigenous displacement.

Nearly a century later, Honoré Beaugrand was looking to forge similar ties among francophone populations in Canada and the United States. One way to do this, he believed, was to collect and publish the folklore of French-speaking people. In Gitlin's and Brasseaux's telling, he became obsessed with a particular folk tale: *la chasse-galerie*. In the tale a group of men risk their souls by forging a pact with the devil. He would help them collapse space, traveling an impossible distance in exchange for their souls should they violate a very specific set of rules. Led by one man especially eager to kiss his girlfriend, the other men agreed.

Like Beaugrand's protagonist, French colonizers made a deal with the devil in order to travel to distant lands in search of material pleasures. They reached their destination, but only by enslaving more than a million individuals and displacing countless Native communities through slave trades, disease, and warfare. The early modern French Empire in the Americas left behind a culturally rich legacy of French communities that, as the present studies have shown, were more closely integrated than we previously have appreciated. From the perspective of enslaved West Africans and displaced or enslaved Indigenous North Americans, however, the story of the early modern French Empire was more about dislocation, disconnection, and redirection, although in response to these forces there was cultural adaptation and innovation, too. In the echoes of their voices, largely but not entirely silenced in the French archives, we can hear a call for new questions, new perspectives.[9]

Epilogue

NOTES

1. Christopher Hodson and Brett Rushforth, "Absolutely Atlantic: Colonialism and the Early Modern French State in Recent Historiography," *History Compass* 8 (January 2010): 101–17, and *Discovering Empire: France and the Atlantic World from the Age of Discovery to the Age of Revolutions* (Oxford University Press, forthcoming).

2. Saint-Méry, as quoted in Christopher Hodson's essay in this volume.

3. Gilles Havard, *Empire et métissages: Indiens et Français dans le Pays d'en Haut, 1660–1715* (Paris: Presses de l'Université Paris-Sorbonne, 2003), 359–437; and Brett Rushforth, "'A Little Flesh We Offer You': The Origins of Indian Slavery in New France," *William and Mary Quarterly* 60 (October 2003): 777–808. For nonverbal communication and the context of diplomacy, see Céline Carayon, "'The Gesture Speech of Mankind': Old and New Entanglements in the Histories of American Indian and European Sign Languages," *American Historical Review* 121 (April 2016): 461–91.

4. For recent works that emphasize Native displacement in New France and the *pays d'en haut*, see Jean-François Lozier, *Flesh Reborn: The Saint Lawrence Valley Mission Settlements through the Seventeenth Century* (Montreal: McGill-Queens University Press, 2018); Kathryn Magee Labelle, *Dispersed, But Not Destroyed: A History of the Seventeenth Century Wendat People* (Vancouver: University of British Columbia Press, 2013); and Andrew K. Sturtevant, "'Inseparable Companions' and Irreconcilable Enemies: The Hurons and Odawas of French Détroit, 1701–38," *Ethnohistory* 60 (2): 219–43.

5. Michael McDonnell, *Masters of Empire: Great Lakes Indians and the Making of America* (New York: Hill & Wang, 2015), 33 ("holy war"); and Léopold Lamontaigne, "Prouville de Tracy, Alexandre de," *Dictionary of Canadian Biography*, vol. 1: http://www.biographi.ca/en/bio/prouville_de_tracy_alexandre_de_1E.html ("destroy utterly").

6. Marcel Trudel, *Dictionnaire des esclaves et de leurs propriétaires* (Quebec: Hurtubise HMH, 1990); Brett Rushforth, *Bonds of Alliance: Indigenous and Atlantic Slaveries* (Chapel Hill: University of North Carolina Press, 2012).

7. Although Kenneth J. Banks comes to a different conclusion than the authors in this volume, emphasizing cultural disjuncture more than connection, and highlighting the failures of communication more than the integration of knowledge, he argues that these things are crucial to the elaboration of empire. Banks, *Chasing Empire across the Sea: Communications and the State in the French Atlantic, 1713–1763* (Montreal: McGill-Queens University Press, 2002), esp. 3–13. See also Jacob Soll, *The Information Master: Jean-Baptiste's Secret State Intelligence System* (Ann Arbor: University of Michigan Press, 2011).

8. Rebecca J. Scott and Jean Hébrard, *Freedom Papers: An Atlantic Odyssey in the Age of Emancipation* (Cambridge, MA: Harvard University Press, 2012); Ann Laura Stoler, "Colonial Archives and the Arts of Governance," *Archival Science* 2 (2002): 87–109; and John Garrigus, *Before Haiti: Race and Citizenship in French Saint-Domingue* (New York: Palgrave MacMillan, 2006).

9. For archival silences, see Marisa J. Fuentes, *Dispossessed Lives: Enslaved Women, Violence, and the Archive* (Philadelphia: University of Pennsylvania Press, 2016); Laura Helton et al., "The Question of Recovery: An Introduction," *Social Text* 33, no. 4 (December, 2015): 1–18; Michel-Rolph Trouillot, *Silencing the Past: Power and the Production of History* (Boston: Beacon Press, 1995); and Brett Rushforth, "The Gauolet Uprising of 1710: Maroons, Rebels, and the Informal Exchange Economy of a Caribbean Sugar Island," *William and Mary Quarterly* 76 (January, 2019): esp. 81–82 and 109–10.

CONTRIBUTORS

Vincent Auffrey is a Ph.D. candidate at the Institute for the History and Philosophy of Science and Technology, University of Toronto. His research focuses on the history of medicine and, more specifically, eugenics in Canada.

Ryan André Brasseaux is a cultural historian with a special interest in francophone North America. Brasseaux holds a doctorate from Yale University, where he serves as dean of Davenport College and lecturer in American studies.

William Brown is a visiting assistant professor of history at Miami University in Oxford, Ohio. His research focuses on the political culture of empire in ancien régime France. Since receiving his doctorate from Johns Hopkins University in 2016, he has been preparing for publication a book entitled *Learning to Colonize: Knowledge, Governance, and the Making of the First French Empire, 1663–1715*.

Leslie Choquette is professor of history, Côté Professor of French Studies, and director of the French Institute at Assumption College in Worcester, Massachusetts. She is the author of *Frenchmen into Peasants: Modernity and Tradition in the Peopling of French Canada / De paysans à Français: Modernité et tradition dans le peuplement du Canada français*. She is currently associate editor for social sciences for *Québec Studies*, the scholarly journal of the American Council for Québec Studies.

Mairi Cowan is an associate professor in the Department of Historical Studies, University of Toronto Mississauga. She is the author of *Death, Life, and Religious Change in Scottish Towns, c. 1350–1560* and coauthor of *Writing History: A Guide for Canadian Students*. Her other publications examine late medieval and early modern

Scotland, seventeenth-century New France, and how best to teach history at the undergraduate level.

Robert Englebert is an associate professor in the Department of History at the University of Saskatchewan. He coedited *French and Indians in the Heart of North America* and has published articles and chapters on eighteenth-century transcolonial networks, French colonial legal and commercial history, and processes of *métissage*.

Jay Gitlin is senior lecturer in the Department of History and chair of the Committee on Canadian Studies, the MacMillan Center at Yale. His first book, *The Bourgeois Frontier: French Towns, French Traders, and American Expansion*, received the 2010 Alf Andrew Heggoy Prize from the French Colonial Historical Society.

Christopher Hodson is an associate professor in the Department of History at Brigham Young University. He is the author of *The Acadian Diaspora: An Eighteenth-Century History* and numerous articles on the early modern French Atlantic World. He is also coauthor, with Brett Rushforth, of the forthcoming *Discovering Empire: France and the Atlantic World from the Crusades to the Age of Revolutions*.

Gregory Kennedy is associate professor of history and the research director of the Acadian Studies Institute at the Université de Moncton, New Brunswick, Canada. His first book, *Something of a Peasant Paradise? Comparing Rural Societies in Acadie and the Loudunais, 1604–1755*, won the Canadian Historical Association CLIO Prize for the best new scholarly book on the history of Atlantic Canada. He is presently working on a new monograph dedicated to the history of militias and conscription in the early modern French Atlantic.

Karen L. Marrero is associate professor of history at Wayne State University in Detroit. A comparative and transnational historian of the United States and Canada and of the northern border, she explores interactions between seventeenth-, eighteenth-, and early nineteenth-century Indigenous peoples and Euro-Americans. Her work has appeared in journals and edited collections, and she is the author of *Detroit's Hidden Channels: The Power of French-Indigenous Families in the 18th Century*.

Contributors

Brett Rushforth is associate professor of history at the University of Oregon. He is the author of *Bonds of Alliance: Indigenous and Atlantic Slaveries in New France*, and the coauthor, with Christopher Hodson, of the forthcoming *Discovering Empire: France and the Atlantic World from the Crusades to the Age of Revolutions*.

Robert D. Taber is assistant professor of history at Fayetteville State University. He is the coeditor of *Free Communities of Color and the Revolutionary Caribbean* and is currently working on his monograph *Family, Slavery, and the Haitian Revolution*. He is an editor for the *Age of Revolutions* blog.

Guillaume Teasdale is assistant professor of history at the University of Windsor, Ontario. Author of *Fruits of Perseverance: The French Presence in the Detroit River Region, 1701–1815*, he also coedited the anthologies *French and Indians in the Heart of North America, 1630–1815* and *Une Amérique française, 1760–1860: Dynamiques du corridor créole*.

Andrew N. Wegmann is assistant professor of history at Delta State University. A historian of race and identity in the early American republic and Atlantic World, he is the author of *Skin Color and Social Practice: The Problem of Race and Class in the Atlantic South, 1718–1862*, and coauthor, with Sara K. Eskridge, of *U.S. History: A Top Hat Interactive Text*. A native of New Orleans, he lives in Cleveland, Mississippi.

INDEX

Abenaki (people), 114
abolition, 137–138
Acadia. *See* Acadie
Acadians, 2, 98–100, 104, 105–119; deportation of, 101, 116, 119, 247
Acadie, 2, 74, 97–100, 102, 109–110, 112, 116–118
Alpines. *See* migrant mountain folk (alpine); Savoy (France)
American Revolution, 135, 160, 193, 195
amis des noirs, Société des, 137, 138
ancien régime, 4, 73, 80, 84, 86, 125, 132, 140, 174, 194, 195
Annapolis Royal, 97–98, 103–105, 107–112, 114–116
Arkansas (people), 197
Armstrong, Lawrence, 105–106, 110–111, 119
Association Montcalm de Fall River, 225–226

Bartholdi, Auguste, 233
Batissette, Augé (character), 222
Battle of Bloody Creek, 107
Battle at Grand Pré, 116, 118
Battle of River Raisin, 183
Bay of Fundy, 97, 104
Beaubassin, 104, 109–110
Beaugrand, Honoré: mayor of Montréal, 231, 232, 236; metro honor, 236–237, 244; politics, 6, 227, 234; publisher, 223, 225, 226, 227, 231; secularist, 223–225; soldier, 225; traveler, 6, 225, 232, 233; writer, 6, 221–223, 225, 227–232, 234–235, 250

Beaver Wars, 46, 48, 51, 55
Belcher, Jonathan, 102–103, 106, 113, 117
Belley, Jean-Baptiste, 148
Belloc, David, 152
Bobé, Jean, 50
Bonaparte, Napoleon, 148, 197, 209
Bordeaux: migration from, 76–77, 99
borderlands, 171, 172, 175
Boston, 100, 102–103, 105–106, 112, 116, 119, 227–228
Boston and Maine Railroad, 228
Bouchette, Joseph, 171
Bourg, Alexander, 107, 109–112, 114–115, 118, 119
Bourgeoys, Marguerite, 86
Brébeuf, Jean de, 24; sacred objects of, 12, 21, 23–24, 248
Bretteville, Étienne Dubois de, 44
Briand, Abbé, 75–76, 79
British Conquest (of New France), 84, 171, 175, 184, 230
British Council of Nova Scotia, 97–99, 103, 109, 114
Brittany: migration from, 76
Brothers Charon, 127–132, 140
Brother Chrétien: as administrator, 127; charges against, 129–130, 132, 135, 139; as curiosity, 5, 125, 131–133, 139, 141, 246, 248; in France, 128; fundraising, 128–129, 135, 136; lawsuits, 128, 130; in New France, 127–128, 134; in Saint-Domingue, 128–130, 134–135, 138–140

Index

Cadieux, Michel, 177, 180–182, 184
Cadillac, Antoine Laumet de Lamothe, 54, 55
Callières, Louis-Hector de, 51, 53
Canada. *See* Lower Canada; Upper Canada
Canadian Pacific Railway, 232
Canadiens, 197–202, 208, 210. *See also* creole: French
Canso, 97, 104, 113
Cap Français, 134–136, 138–139, 154–157, 160
carpenters, 78, 82, 86–88, 129
Cartier, Georges-Étienne, 226
Cartier, Pierre-Claude, 177, 182, 184
Castelveyre, Louis Turc de. *See* Brother Chrétien
Catholicism, 12–14, 17–18, 20, 24–25, 127–129, 132, 134, 139, 171, 173, 175, 181, 223–224, 229, 230, 247
Cayenne (French Guiana), 137
Cayuga (people), 35
Champ-de-Mars, 231
Champlain, Samuel de, 45
Charon de la Barre, François, 126, 128, 131, 132
Chauvin, Jeanne, 178
Chauvin, Marie-Florence, 183
Chauvreulx, Claude-Jean-Baptiste, 110, 113
Chignecto, 104, 110, 111, 113, 115, 116
chimney sweeps, 78–79
Clerics of St. Viateur, 223
Club Massiac, 137–138
Code Noir, 152
colonization, harms of, 245, 247, 249–250
Collot, Georges-Henri-Victor, 5, 37, 193–196, 198, 200–203, 205–206, 208–210, 250
Compagnie de Saint-Domingue, 161
Condorcet, marquis de, 137
Cornwallis, Edward, 116, 119. *See also* Acadians: deportation of
Corpus Christi (procession), 138
Cosby, Alexander, 105–106, 112, 117
creole: Caribbean, 3, 150; French, 3, 5, 197–198, 201–208, 210, 250

cultural mobility: in Acadie, 109, 117, 118; France to New France, 13–14, 19, 24–25, 37, 42, 54, 57, 74, 84, 85, 89; French Atlantic, 244, 248, 249; French creole, 205; in Haiti, 147–148; historiography of, 2–6; marriage customs and, 16; New France to France, 55–56; Québec to Dominion of Canada, 224
cultural shifts: gender roles and, 13, 148–149, 162, 247; marriage and, 16, 150–151

d'Auberteuil, Michel-René Hilliard, 150–151
Dessalines, Jean-Jacques, 146–147, 163
Detroit, 5, 170, 173–174, 176, 178–180, 200, 204, 246
Detroit River borderlands, 170–176, 178, 180–184
diplomatic theater, 36, 38–40
Dubé, Catherine, 183
Dubreuil, Marie-Françoise (Cosquière), 152, 162, 164
Dubroca, Louis, 197
Duggan, Thomas, 177–178
Dupuis, Michel (character), 229
Durand, Baptiste (character), 221–222
Duvallon, Berquin, 198
Duvivier, François Du Pont, 113–115, 117

Echo du Canada, L', (newspaper), 225–227, 234
Edict of Nantes, 99
emigrants, 76, 79–80, 82, 86, 177, 224, 226, 228, 299. *See also* Cadieux, Michel; Cartier, Pierre-Claude; Rouleau, Charles
ethnography, 36, 38, 56, 146, 196, 227–228, 249
exorcism, 12–13, 20, 21, 22; and gender, 14, 20, 21, 23. *See also* Regnouard, Marie

Fall River (Massachusetts), 225, 228–229, 231
Finiels, Nicolas de, 195–196, 198, 202–203, 206–209
fishermen, 77–78, 84, 89–90
Five Nations of the Iroquois Confederacy (Haudenosaunee), 18–19, 35, 38, 47, 51–52, 54, 57, 82, 197, 248

Index

Fond des Nègres, 155, 157, 161, 163
Ford, Henry, 179
formerly enslaved people, 136, 139, 147, 148
Fort Duquesne, 199
Fort Anne, 101, 103–104
Fox (people). *See* Mesquakie (people)
Franciscans, 127
Freemasons, 225, 227
free people of color (*gens de couleur*), 1, 5, 139, 147–152, 154–156, 158–161, 163, 193, 249
freeholding system, 175
French Atlantic, 1–5, 124, 125–126, 131–132, 139–141, 194, 209, 244–246, 248–250
French-Canadian identity, 74, 84–85, 90, 223–227, 229–231, 233–236
French Revolution, 133, 148, 175, 195, 208, 233
Frères hospitaliers de la Croix et de Saint-Joseph, 126, 140
Frontenac (comte de), Louis de Buade, 36–37, 46, 47, 49–50, 52–54, 58, 86, 244
fur trade, 84, 174, 176, 178, 180–182, 184, 197–198, 200–204

Gagnon, Ferdinand, 226–227
Garneau, François-Xavier, 170
Gatineau River, 221
gender roles: Canada-US borderlands and, 173; Haiti, 148–149; France, 39; French creole, 203–204; New France, 13–14, 19–20, 46
George I, 103
Gifford, Robert, 75
Girard, Jeanne (character), 228, 230–231
Glorious Revolution, 99
Godbout, Adélard, 236
Gorham's Rangers, 115
Gouin, Archange, 181
Grand Dérangement. *See* Acadians: deportation of
grande recrue, 82
Great Peace of Montréal, 51, 56
Grey Nuns, 131, 140

Guadeloupe, 2, 193–194, 245, 248
Guimbette, Liza (character), 222

Haiti, 5, 146–148, 151–152, 155, 158
Haitian Armée Indigène (Haitian), 146
Haitian Revolution, 141, 148, 153, 195, 209, 249
Halifax (Canada), 116
Hallay, Barbe, 15–17; demonic possession of, 11–12, 13, 14; life after, 25
Haudenosaunee, Five Nations of the. *See* Five Nations of the Iroquois Confederacy (Haudenosaunee)
Hébert, Philippe, 233
Hennepin, Louis, 196
Hocquart, Gilles, 130, 132
Holy Cross Cemetery (Detroit), 179–180
Hudson's Bay Company, 180
Hughes, Langston, 146–147, 163
Huguenots, 4, 11, 17, 18, 86, 97, 99–100
Huron (people). *See* Wendat (people)
hypermobility, 80–81

Illinois Country, 5, 195, 197–198, 200–201, 203–204, 207–210
Indian deeds (land), 175–176, 178
Indigenous customs: performances of, 4, 36–38, 42, 45, 47, 49, 54, 56, 247
Institut canadien de Montréal, 226
Iowas (people), 49
Iroquois. *See* Five Nations of the Iroquois Confederacy (Haudenosaunee)

Jasmin (enslaved person), 136, 139
Jeanne la fileuse (Beaugrand), 224–228, 234–235; plot of, 228–231
Jesuits, 38–40, 45, 47, 49–50, 52, 58, 127, 129, 131, 135, 139, 207, 228
Joe the cook (character), 221–222
Joncaire, Louis-Thomas Chabert de, 50–51, 56
Jouette, Hillaire, 150
journeymen, 82–83, 86–88, 90

Index

Juchereau Brothers, 75, 85
Julien, Henri, 235

Kerouac, Jack, 84, 228
kinship, 200

La Barre, Joseph-Antoine Lefebvre de, 43
la chasse-galerie, 224, 234–236, 250; story, 221–223
la Dauversière, Jérôme Le Royer de, 82, 86
la Goudalie, Charles de, 110
La Potherie, Claude-Charles Le Roy de, 44, 49–50, 54–56
La Rochelle (France), 128–129, 132, 138
labor mobility, 73, 74–75, 81–83, 204, 245
labor union, 225
Laborge, Louis, 231
Labuissonnière, Pierre, 150
Lahontan (baron de), Louis-Armand de Lom d'Arce, 196
Lanaudière, Charles-Louis Tarieu de, 174
Laurier, Wilfred, 235, 236
Laval, François de, 86
Lavaltrie (Canada), 221–222, 230
Le Cap. *See* Cap Français
Le Jeune, Paul, 45
Le Loutre, Jean-Louis, 111
Le Mercier, Andrew, 105
Legislative Assembly of Canada East, 174
Leblanc, Joseph, 114
Légion d'honneur, 233
Léogane (Saint-Domingue), 150, 152, 154–155, 157–161, 163
Lesseps, Ferdinand de, 233
Lévesque, René, 236
l'Incarnation, Marie Guyart de, 11, 14–15, 19, 24, 37, 246–248
locksmiths, 87–88
Louis XIV, 1, 39, 99, 126–127, 131–132, 205
Louis XV, 136, 205
Louis XVI, 133, 135, 137

Louisbourg (Canada), 74, 84, 87–90, 111
Louisiana, 2–3, 6, 148, 196–197, 200–201, 203, 208, 210, 245, 248
Lower Canada, 170–174, 177, 181, 184, 223
lumbermen, 221–222

Maliseet (people). *See* Wolastoqiyik (people)
Mangeant, François, 108, 112
Maricourt, Paul Le Moine de, 51
Marie-Catherine. *See* Jasmin (enslaved person)
Marmite Club, La, 233
marriage, 82, 102, 108: in Canada-US borderlands, 173, 179, 181, 183, 225; in Haiti, 146–147, 149–151, 153, 155–163; interracial, 150, 158, 159, 161, 163; in New France, 15–17, 148. *See also* parish records; testimonials of freedom at marriage
Martinique, 137–138, 245, 248
Mascarene, Jean, 99
Mascarene, Marguerite, 99
Mascarene, Paul: as Bostonian, 100, 103, 105–106, 116; career of, 98, 101, 103, 106–109, 111, 112, 116–119, 246–247; charges against, 103, 105; childhood, 99; diplomatic career, 102, 105, 107, 109, 112; and military, 101–104, 113–114, 116–117; and religion, 4, 99–100, 102, 110, 119
masons, 78–79, 87–88
Massachusetts, 2, 100, 102–103, 105–106, 113, 117, 225, 228–229, 234, 236
Maufils, Louis, 108, 110
Maximilien I, 225
McKee, Alexander, 177
Mercier, Honoré, 236
Mesquakie (people), 38, 49
Métis (people), 231
métissage, 37, 197, 200, 204–208
Mexico, 6, 225
Miami (people), 181
Michigan, 171, 177–178, 180–182
Michilimackinac, 200, 203–204
Mississippi River, 195, 200–201, 205, 207

260

Index

Mississippi Valley, 198–199, 201
Mi'gma'ki. *See* Acadie
Mi'kmaq (people), 97–98, 100, 104–105, 107, 110, 112–114, 116–117, 247
migrant labor: carpenters, 78, 82, 87; chimney sweeps, 79; fishermen, 77, 78, 84; joiners, 87; locksmiths, 87, 88; masons, 78, 79, 83, 87; peddlers, 79; plasterers, 87; roofers, 87; soldiers, 80, 83, 85, 89; stonecutters, 78, 87, 88
migrant mountain folk (alpine), 77, 78, 79
migration, 4, 73–75, 77, 80, 84, 90, 134, 198, 245–247
Minas (Canada), 104, 107, 109, 111–116
Miniac, Jean-Pierre de, 110
Mirabeau (comte de), 137
Mission Iroquois, 35, 36, 50
Mississauga (people), 55
Missouri River, 196, 199, 201–204, 207
Missouri Valley, 201
mobility. *See* cultural mobility; emigrants; hypermobility; labor mobility; migration; professional mobility
Mohawk (people), 35, 45
Montépel, Pierre (character), 230
Montmagny, Charles Huault de, 45
Montréal (Canada), 6, 17, 35, 49, 51, 56, 82, 86–87, 125–128, 131–132, 134–135, 140, 170, 176, 180, 200, 204, 222–224, 227, 233, 235, 244
Morillonnet *dit* Berry, Claude, 130

Nantes: migration from, 76
Napoleon. *See* Bonaparte, Napoleon
New Brunswick, 98
New England, 4, 17, 18, 35, 116, 224–230, 234–236, 244
New France: Indigenous-settler conflict, 18–19; Indigenous-settler diplomacy, 36, 37, 38, 41, 42, 52; marriage customs, 15, 16, 17; religion, 17, 18, 127, 132, 140; theater in diplomacy, 41, 42, 44, 247
New Hampshire, 228

New Orleans, 2, 3, 6, 131, 199, 203–204, 209, 224–225
New York, 201
Newfoundland, 103, 117
Nicholson, Francis, 103, 105, 117
Nippissing (people), 35, 36
North West Company, 180
Nova Scotia. *See* Acadie

Odawa (people), 35, 48, 54–55, 175
Ohio River, 199, 203–204
Ohio Valley, 197–198, 201
Ojibwe (people), 175
Olier, Jean-Jacques, 86
Oneida (people), 35
Onondaga (people), 35, 43, 48, 51
Onontio, 35, 45–47, 50, 52, 54–56, 58
Ottawa (Canada), 223, 227, 233
Ouanaminthe (Saint-Domingue), 150, 155, 157, 159, 163
Ouiatenon (Indiana), 202
Outreouti, 43

Paris, 127–128, 130, 133, 136–137, 232–234
parish records, 149–163, 173
patriarchy, 35, 46, 48, 51, 53, 152, 162
Patrie, La (newspaper), 223, 231, 235
Penobscot (Maine), 103
Perche (France): migration from, 75
Perrin du Lac, François-Marie, 196
Perrot, Nicolas, 43–44, 49–50, 54–56, 58
Perry, Elizabeth, 102
persona (concept), 35, 36, 37, 38, 40, 42, 43, 45, 47, 48, 49, 52, 54, 57. *See also* Onontio
Petit, Emilien, 149, 151
Philadelphia, 194–195, 201, 209
Phillips, Richard, 103, 105, 108, 117
Pittsburgh, 199, 201, 203, 204
Port Royal (Canada), 97, 101–102, 105, 109, 117
Port-au-Prince, 136, 152, 158
Potawatomi (people), 55, 175, 178

Index

Prince Edward Island, 104
professional mobility, 5, 98–99, 115
Protestants, 17–18, 99, 102, 105, 117, 119, 223, 247
Providence Almshouse, 135–136, 138

Québec, 4, 11, 13–17, 22, 24–25, 40–41, 49, 75, 78–79, 84, 86–88, 97, 110–111, 126, 128–131, 170–171, 173, 177, 200–221, 224–226, 228, 230, 233–234, 236
Queen Anne, 103
Quiet Revolution, 236

racism, systemic. *See* systemic racism
Raimond, Julien, 150–151, 163
Raudot, Antoine-Denis, 44, 56
Razond, Jean-Charles, 154
récits de voyage, 5, 195–196, 206, 209–210
Regnouard, Marie, 11, 21–23; and exorcism, 12–13, 20, 22; testimony of, 12
Reign of Terror, 206
Repatriement Act, 226
République, La (newspaper), 227
rhetoric, 53–54, 56, 236
Riel, Louis, 231
Rivière, Marie Louise, 154–155
Rivière, Marie Rose, 152–155, 162, 164
Rivière, Romain, 152–153, 155
Rochambeau (comte de), Jean-Baptiste Donatien de Vimeur, 193
Ross timber camp, 221–222
Rouleau, Charles, 177–180, 182, 184
Rousseau, Jean-Jacques, 208
Royal Society of Arts and Sciences of Cap-Français, 133

sacerdotal records. *See* parish records
Saint-Augustin, Catherine de, 11, 21
Saint-Domingue, 2, 128–134, 136–138, 209, 245, 248–249. *See also* Haiti
Saint-François (Canada), 182
Saint Ignace, Françoise Marie de, 22
Saint-Joseph-de-Lanoraie (Canada), 223

Saint-Laurent (Canada), 177–178
Saint-Louis (Saint-Domingue), 155
Saint-Louis-de-Terrebonne (Canada), 180–181
Saint-Louis-du-Sud (Saint-Domingue), 161, 163
Saint-Marc (Saint-Domingue), 150, 155, 158–159, 161
Saint-Méry, Médéric-Louis-Élie Moreau de: as biographer of Brother Chrétien, 133–136, 138, 140–141; on race, 133, 137, 139–141
Saint-Pierre (Martinique), 138
Saint-Poncy, Claude de, 110
Santo Domingo, 159
Savoy (France), 79
Scioto Land Company, 205
seigneur, 75, 126, 174–176, 181
seigneuralism, 174, 184
seigneurie directe, 174–175
seigneuries, 171–172, 174, 178, 180, 182–183
Seneca (people), 35, 50, 51, 56
Seven Years' War, 136
Shirley, William, 113, 115–116, 119
Siéyès (abbé), 137
slave revolt, 137, 139, 193
slavery/enslavement: of Africans, 1, 2, 125, 128, 134–136, 138–141, 147, 149, 151–153, 155, 157–161, 164, 193, 197, 245, 248–250; of Natives, 48, 197, 245, 247, 250. *See also* formerly enslaved people
St. Anne's Parish, 171, 178–179, 181, 183
St. Lawrence River, 222, 223–234
St. Lawrence Valley, 5, 74, 87, 90, 171–178, 182–184, 197, 246
St. Louis (Missouri), 202, 204, 207
stonecutters, 78, 88–89
strike (labor), 87
Sulpicians, 110, 127
systemic racism, 148, 152, 154, 155, 156, 157, 162, 163, 249

Tailer, William, 102–103
Tailhan, Jean, 58
Talleyrand, Charles-Maurice de, 209

Index

Taouestaouis. *See* Maricourt, Paul Le Moine de
Tardivel, Jules-Paul, 226, 234
Taschereau, Louis-Alexander, 230
testimonials of freedom at marriage, 75–77, 80, 83
Third Republic (France), 233
torture, 48
Tour de France (journeymen), 73–74, 80–83, 87, 204
Treaty of Peace and Friendship, 105, 112
Treaty of San Ildefonso, 209
Treaty of Utrecht (1713), 97, 106–107, 112
Trois-Rivières, 182
Truteau, Jean-Baptiste, 196

Upper Canada, 171–172, 183
Ursuline nuns: in Canada, 18–19, 127, 131

Vaudreuil, Philippe de Rigaud de, 53, 56
Vaudreuil de Cavagnial, Pierre de Rigaud de, 85
Verrier, Louis-Guillaume, 130, 132
Versailles, 54, 56, 125, 127–130, 140

Vetch, Samuel, 100, 101–103, 117
Villerme, Nicolas de, 130
Volney (comte de), Constantin-François de Chasseboeuf, 5, 195, 197, 205–210
Voyageur Contract Database, 176–178
voyageurs, 170, 172–174, 176–178, 180, 182, 200, 222–224
Vuil, Daniel: execution of, 16; as Huguenot, 17; and witchcraft, 11, 14, 15, 17

Wabanaki (people), 35, 104, 108
Wabash River, 205
Walker, Eliza, 225
War of the Austrian Succession, 99, 101, 106, 118
War of the Spanish Succession, 97
Wendat (people), 35–36, 47, 54–55
William III, 99
witchcraft, 11, 14, 15, 17; in folklore, 222
Wolastoqiyik (people), 98, 105, 247
Women's Providence Almshouse, 136, 139
World's Fair (1889), 232–233

www.ingramcontent.com/pod-product-compliance
Lightning Source LLC
Chambersburg PA
CBHW030614230426
43661CB00053B/1980